To Tiffany & Shaun
May you have many happy times
Cooking together. With lots of Love.
Grandpa & Grandma
Prince

Cooking
a commonsense guide

A Happy Home Receipe

4 cups Love
2 cups loyalty
3 cups forgiveness
1 cup friendship

5 spoons of hope
2 spoons of tenderness
4 quarts of faith
1 barrel of Laughter

Take love and loyalty, mix
thoughly with faith. Blend it
with Tenderness, kindness and
understanding. Add friendship
and hope, sprinkle abundantly
with laughter.

Bake with sunshine, Serve
daily with generous helpings.

P.S. I see that many recipes calls for caster sugar
you can use ordinary sugar

Cooking
a commonsense guide

WHITECAP
BOOKS

CONTENTS

COOKERY RATINGS

A simple and, generally, quick recipe. Perfect for beginners.	A dish that requires a little more care and time.	A special dish that requires a greater investment of time, care and patience.

COMMONSENSE

Cooking is not difficult. To be a great chef you need flair and imagination. But to produce delicious foolproof everyday meals all you need is a little commonsense.

Good cooking begins with sensible shopping, correct storage of ingredients, handling food safely and enthusiasm for the task at hand.

The first decision you will make is 'what to cook?'. To a certain extent this question should be answered by what is in season. Make friends with your greengrocer, butcher and fishmonger and don't be afraid to ask 'what's good today?' Ideally, shop for fresh fruit and vegetables regularly, if not daily. This prevents waste and ensures that you are using the freshest possible produce. Of course this is not always possible, so if you need to shop less frequently, try to plan your meals to make the best use of your fresh ingredients. Produce which is in season is better value and quality. Don't try to make asparagus hollandaise for eight dinner guests if there are no good-quality fresh asparagus available. Choose another recipe.

The golden commonsense rule of cooking is *always read the recipe before you start*. Don't rush in at step 1 and work your way through blind, only to discover in step 4 that you need a food processor which you don't have. Even more serious, don't start working through a recipe for a dinner party that starts in 2 hours, only to get to the end and discover your fabulous centrepiece needs to be chilled overnight.

Read through the recipe and get together all the ingredients and equipment required. Preheat the oven and prepare the cooking dish. Prepare as much as you can beforehand, so you are not caught out during cooking. If you are making a stew, or a slow-cooking dish, you can probably get away with leaving some ingredients to cook by themselves while you prepare others as you go along. However, don't try this if you are making a stir-fry! There is nothing more panic-inducing than having a sizzling wok, burning onions and a pile of ingredients that need chopping. So, always

anticipate what you are going to have to do next.

If the recipe states to use a large bowl, do so, even if at first you're only mixing two ingredients. Later on you might need to add a large quantity of other ingredients.

We employ some basic commonsense rules in our recipes... If the recipe doesn't state to 'cover' the pan or dish, then it is to be cooked uncovered. We assume basic preparation

of ingredients, such as washing and trimming, and peeling of vegetables such as potatoes and onions—the recipe will, however, state if these are to be left unpeeled. With well-known vegetables such as leeks, we assume that the reader knows to use the white part of the leek only. But with less familiar ingredients such as lemon grass, we will state 'white part only' where necessary.

KITCHEN MANAGEMENT

A good cook keeps a good kitchen. This means efficient shopping, and knowing what you have (and should have) in your storecupboard and fridge. You may be shopping every few days for fresh produce, but there are certain ingredients that should have a permanent home in your kitchen.

SHOPPING

Like most other aspects of preparing food, shopping is not difficult—in fact, many of us do it fairly successfully every day. However, there is a such a thing as efficient shopping, and much of it relies on commonsense.

Check what needs topping up in your storecupboard (see opposite) and put those into your trolley first. Avoid cans that have dents in them. Meats, dairy products and other refrigerated items should be kept well chilled, so choose them last, just before you head to the checkout. A handy tip is to choose items which are stored towards the back of the refrigerator cabinet or underneath the top layer (these are sometimes close to lights and not cold enough). Don't choose refrigerator items which have swollen packaging. Vacuum packaging should not be loose. Read use-by dates (this applies to everything, not just refrigerated goods) and buy products as far from the date as possible (you might find these have been stacked at the back of the cabinet).

Frozen food should be obviously frozen, with no large ice crystals and without the food being frozen into clumps (this shows that the food has partially thawed and been refrozen). In hot weather, carry an insulated container in the car to transport shopping home.

YOUR STORECUPBOARD

Although it is best to shop regularly for meat, seafood and seasonal vegetables, there are certain products that you will want to keep permanently in your storecupboard, to provide the backbone of your daily cooking. As a general rule, you should try to have in your pantry:

Baking powder
Beans, canned and dried
Breadcrumbs, dry
Capers
Cocoa powder
Coconut milk
Cornflour
Couscous
Dried fruits, such as raisins, currants, apricots
Flour (plain and self-raising)

Gelatine
Honey
Mustards
Noodles
Nuts
Oils (olive, sesame, vegetable)
Olives
Pasta
Polenta
Rice, long-grain, short-grain
    and arborio
Soy sauce
Stocks
Sugars
Tabasco
Tomatoes, canned
Tomato paste
Vinegars, white wine, red wine,
    brown and balsamic
Worcestershire sauce
Yeast

These are best stored in a cool, dark dry pantry. Most will keep for at least 3, if not 6, months.

It is best to buy whole spices and grind them yourself, as needed—they stay fresher than the jars. Make sure bottles of oil are kept out of direct light, as they can become rancid; however, if you keep them in the fridge the oil will thicken and appear cloudy—it will return to normal once it has reached room temperature again. Most bottles of sauces and condiments should be refrigerated once opened: check the label.

Keep potatoes and onions in a cool, dark place—though not without adequate ventilation. Tomatoes, like most fruit, are best kept at room temperature, unless the weather is very hot or they are very ripe.

YOUR FRIDGE

Your fridge is somewhere where important hygiene rules come into play. When you get home with your shopping, unwrap meat or chicken and place on a plate large enough to prevent drips falling on to other food. Cover loosely with foil or plastic wrap.

Bacteria in food is killed by cooking, but take care not to put cooked food back into the fridge touching raw food, which could contaminate it. For example, never let raw meat drip onto cooked dishes. The same goes for when you are preparing food: if you chop raw meat, don't then use the same, unwashed chopping board and knife to prepare salad, or slice the cooked meat.

Store vegetables unwashed (unless they are dried thoroughly, the moisture contributes to deterioration) in the crisper compartment of the fridge.

Many recipes will instruct you to cook something, then 'cool and refrigerate'. When you are doing this, cool the food as quickly as possible before refrigerating. Transfer it from the cooking pan to a wide bowl and stir frequently to release the heat. It is not necessary for the food to be completely cold before it is refrigerated, just cooled. Don't put hot food in the fridge or freezer or it will raise the temperature inside, putting other foods at risk of deterioration.

The remaining contents of half-used cans should be transferred to a bowl or plastic container and refrigerated. Use within 2–3 days or discard.

Thaw frozen food in the fridge, not at room temperature and never in a sink full of water. If you haven't removed food from the freezer in enough time, thaw in the microwave, or have something else.

Never refreeze thawed food. (Of course, you can thaw something, cook it and then freeze again—for instance frozen chicken that you might casserole and then freeze.)

Clean out your fridge, freezer and storecupboard regularly and remember—if you ever have any doubts about the freshness of a product, throw it out.

COOKERY TERMS

This is a commonsense cookbook, so you will find every step fully explained in the recipe. But if there are any terms which aren't familiar you should find them here.

AL DENTE Italian phrase meaning 'to the tooth'. Refers to pasta and sometimes vegetables. Means slightly underdone, so still with some 'bite'.

BAIN-MARIE Also called a 'water bath'. Usually a baking dish half-filled with water so delicate food is protected from direct heat. Often used for custards.

BAKE BLIND To bake an empty pastry case before the filling is added. Ensures the pastry is cooked through and not soggy. Usually lined with baking paper and baking beads or rice or beans so it keeps its shape.

BASTE To spoon or brush cooking juices or other fat over food during cooking.

BOIL To cook liquid, or food in liquid, at 100°C. Large bubbles will break on the surface.

BOUQUET GARNI A small bunch of herbs used to flavour stocks, soups and stews. Removed before serving.

BROWN To fry food (usually meat) quickly so the outside is cooked and has changed colour.

CREAM To beat butter or butter and sugar together until light and creamy.

CUBE To chop food into even cubes. Usually bite-sized and for use in soups or stews so the size is not overly important.

DICE To chop food into very small even cubes.

DRAIN To remove liquid from food (usually with a colander or sieve). The food is kept and the liquid discarded unless specified.

EN CROUTE Cooked entirely encased in pastry. Usually refers to meat.

ESCALOPE Very thin slice of meat, such as veal or chicken.

FILLET To cut meat from the bones.

FLAMBE To pour liqueur over food (usually in the pan, over heat) and set fire to it.

FOLD To mix one ingredient into another very gently (usually flour or egg whites) with a metal spoon or plastic spatula. The idea is to combine the mixture without losing the air. To fold properly, cut through the centre of the mixture, then run the edge of the spoon or spatula around the outer edge of the bowl, turning the bowl as you go.

GLAZE A substance (often warmed jam or beaten egg) brushed over food to give it shine and colour.

GREASE To lightly coat a tin or dish with oil or melted butter to prevent food sticking.

INFUSE To flavour a liquid by heating it with aromatic ingredients (often spices) and leaving to let the flavour develop.

JULIENNE To cut into uniform thin matchsticks for quick cooking. Often used for stir-fries or in French cuisine.

KNEAD To stretch and fold dough to make it firm and smooth. This stretches the gluten in the flour and gives elasticity. Used for bread making but not for pastry making (over-handling will make pastry tough).

MARINATE To tenderize and flavour food (usually meat) by leaving it in an acidulated seasoned liquid (a marinade).

PARBOIL To partially cook in boiling water before some other form of cooking. Most commonly used for roast potatoes which are parboiled before being added to the roasting meat.

PINCH A small amount of something—as much as can be held between your thumb and forefinger.

POACH To cook food immersed in a gently simmering liquid.

PUNCH DOWN THE DOUGH A term used in bread making. A yeast dough which is left to rise is then punched with one firm blow of the fist, to remove the air from it.

PUREE Food blended or processed to a pulp.

REDUCE To boil or simmer liquid in an uncovered pan so that the liquid evaporates and the mixture becomes thicker and more concentrated in flavour. Most soups and stews are reduced—this should usually be done at a simmer so the flavour of the dish is not impaired by long hard boiling.

ROUX The basic mixture of many sauces—fat (usually melted butter) and flour. Used to thicken. Liquid is added to make a sauce.

RUB IN To mix together flour and butter with your fingertips, usually for pastry. It will resemble fine breadcrumbs.

SCORE To ensure even cooking. Make incisions with a knife (usually into fish or meat) that do not cut all the way through.

SIFT To shake dry ingredients (usually flour) through a sieve to aerate and remove lumps.

SIMMER To cook liquid, or food in liquid, over low heat, below boiling point. The surface of the liquid will be moving with a few small bubbles.

SKIM To remove fat or scum that comes to the surface of a liquid.

SOFT PEAKS A term used when egg whites are whipped. The peak will fold over on itself when the beater is lifted.

STIFF PEAKS A term used when egg whites are whipped. The peak will hold its shape when the beater is lifted.

STIR-FRY To quickly fry (usually in a wok) over high heat while stirring.

STRAIN To remove solids from a liquid by pouring through a sieve. The solids are discarded, unless specified.

WHISK To beat rapidly with a wire whisk, to incorporate air and add volume.

ZEST The coloured skin of citrus fruits. Avoid the bitter white pith below.

11

BASIC KITCHEN EQUIPMENT

A good cook needs good tools. Buy the best you can afford and look after them—they'll last you for years.

KNIVES Quality knives are expensive but it is worth saving up for stainless steel or carbon steel knives. To keep your knives sharp, use a steel and stone and make sure you cut on a chopping board.

WHISK A wire whisk is essential for beating egg whites—nothing else can incorporate as much air.

LARGE METAL SPOON Ideal for folding mixtures together without losing volume, and skimming froth from stocks.

WOODEN SPOON Perfect for long stirring jobs, since their handles don't get hot. Best for use with non-stick pans.

SPATULA Flexible rubber spatulas are ideal for folding in, and for getting every bit of cake mix out of the bowl.

TONGS Use tongs to turn frying food or pick vegetables out of boiling water.

PEELER Peels vegetable skins and the tip removes 'eyes'. Shaves Parmesan.

LADLE For safely spooning hot soups and stews from a pan.

ROLLING PIN Rolls pastry and pizza dough; beats veal, chicken or steak to flatten fillets; and crushes biscuits.

SAUCEPANS Stainless steel is the best material, even better if it has a heavy copper base. Most recipes state a 'heavy-based pan' as this distributes heat more evenly. A very large saucepan or stock pot is needed to cook pasta and stock.

FRYING PAN A non-stick deep frying pan will reduce the amount of oil needed and can be used for stir-frying if you don't have a wok. An ovenproof pan with a metal handle can go straight from stove top to oven or grill for browning. Otherwise, cover the handle with foil.

BAKING DISH You'll need a baking dish for roasting meat and vegetables. Buy one with a rack so the fat can drip down into the pan. Make sure it's heavy enough to put on top of the stove without warping. When stirring gravy, use a plastic or a wooden spoon to prevent scratching.

MIXING BOWLS The best all-purpose mixing bowls also double as pudding basins. Use them to make cakes, beat cream, and a hundred other kitchen tasks. As long as they have no metal trim, china or ceramic mixing bowls are ideal for cooking or heating food in a microwave.

CASSEROLE DISH Make sure your casserole dish has a tight-fitting lid and is a generous size. You can use ceramic dishes for oven only, but a good flameproof dish, as shown, can go straight from oven to stove top if you need to reduce a sauce over heat. Pyrex casserole dishes are also available.

COLANDER Ideal for draining pasta, vegtables or anything else cooked in liquid (except small items, such as rice, which may need a strainer). Also ideal for washing salad leaves or placing on top of a saucepan to steam vegetables.

13

MEAT SENSE

From a great Sunday roast to a quick steak sandwich, meat is versatile and easy to prepare. While not such a staple of our daily menu these days, meat still plays an important role in providing essential proteins and iron in the diet.

BUYING AND STORING

Correct handling and preparation of meat is crucial, both for safety reasons and for good eating. When buying, look for meat that has a clear, fresh appearance: meat with a greyish tinge has been poorly handled and stored and must be avoided. An unpleasant odour and slimy surface are other indicators that the product is unacceptable. Offal such as kidneys and liver that have a strong smell of ammonia should be rejected.

Meat should be kept refrigerated, so buy it last on your shopping trip and bring it straight home. Unwrap the meat and put it on a plate, then loosely wrap it with foil or greaseproof paper and place in the refrigerator. Be sure to use within a couple of days.

Meat also freezes very successfully if you need to store it for longer. Remove the original wrapping and seal the meat in a freezer bag, first expelling as much air as possible. Double bag the meat if there is any danger of the bag tearing, as meat exposed to air will suffer from freezer burn. Clearly label the bag, including the date. Most cuts of meat can be frozen for up to 6 months.

There is a huge variety of meat available. The main types are beef, veal, lamb and pork. Within these types there are myriad cuts, and each cut has its most suitable cooking method. See page 18 for our chart of cuts and their suggested cooking methods. Buy the appropriate cut for the cooking process you will be using. Each cut has distinctive qualities that can be used to advantage in a specific instance. Don't buy a cut that is more expensive than you need—a cheaper one may well give a better result in your particular recipe. Different types of meat and cooking methods require different preparation. A general first step in meat preparation is to remove the meat from the refrigerator a little while before cooking, to allow it to cool to room temperature. This ensures the meat will cook evenly and quickly, which is particularly important when using a quick cooking method such as pan-frying a steak. Sometimes the recipe will instruct you to cut away any visible fat and sinew, particularly when stewing. However, sometimes some fat present on the meat can be desirable, for instance when you are cooking a roast: the fat will melt and baste the meat as it cooks, contributing to the tenderness and flavour.

PAN-FRYS, GRILLS AND BARBECUES

Steaks and chops are the most suitable cuts for these cooking methods. Preparation is minimal, just trim away fat as required and perhaps marinate, depending on the recipe.

Marinating before cooking will tenderize the meat as well as add flavour. Always marinate meat in a glass or ceramic dish, covered and refrigerated until needed—a metallic dish will react with any acid in the marinade and give a metallic flavour.

Some recipes may say to flatten steaks before cooking, which makes the meat more tender. To do this, place the meat between two layers of plastic wrap and pound evenly with a meat mallet or rolling pin. Thin steaks, such as veal escalopes, should be nicked along the edges to prevent them curling during cooking. Cooking times will depend on the thickness of the meat and your taste.

Pan-frying: To fry steak (not thin escalopes), heat a little oil or butter in a heavy-based frying pan over high heat, add the meat and cook for 2–3 minutes on each side. If you like your meat rare, you would remove it from the pan now. Otherwise,

reduce the heat to medium and continue cooking for up to 10 minutes each side for well-done meat.

Test for doneness by pressing the centre of the meat with blunt tongs, rather than piercing (this will let the juices escape). Turn meat once only during cooking and leave the pan uncovered. Too low a heat, turning too often, or covering the pan will make the meat tough. Always drain marinated meat thoroughly before pan-frying or it will create steam and not fry efficiently.

Grilling: Drain marinated meat thoroughly before grilling to reduce steam and ensure a tender result. If your grill pan is lined with foil, puncture a few holes to allow fat to drain away. Ideally, put meat on a cold, lightly-oiled grill and cook under high heat to seal, turning once. Then lower the grill tray and continue cooking if you prefer your meat more well done.

Barbecuing: Give the barbecue plenty of time to heat up so the meat is cooking over glowing coals, not over flames. When you are barbecuing kebabs, oiled metal skewers are ideal because it is easier to remove the cooked meat from them. If threading meat onto

RARE OR WELL-DONE?

Rare: Soft to touch, red centre with a thin cooked edge.

Medium rare: Springy to touch, moist, pale-red centre.

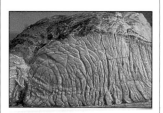

Medium: Firm to touch, pink centre and brown edge.

Well done: Very firm to touch, brown and evenly cooked.

bamboo skewers, first soak the skewers in water for 30 minutes to prevent the ends burning during cooking. Marinades add flavour and tenderness to barbecued meat.

STEWS AND SOUPS

Less expensive cuts of meat come into their own when you are stewing, as the long slow cooking time allows the connective tissue in the meat to break down and become tender. Cooking the same type of meat quickly by pan-frying or grilling would render it tough and inedible, but, by the same token, if you casserole best fillet steak it will dry out and become tough. Meat for stewing is usually cut into cubes (though not always—for Irish stew the lamb neck chops are left whole and on the bone). Cut the meat into even pieces, usually bite-sized or as instructed in the recipe, so that they all cook at the same rate

Next, the recipe may say to toss the meat in seasoned flour. This helps to thicken the pan juices, creating a sauce in the

Put the meat and flour in a bag and toss well.

finished dish. The cleanest and easiest way to do this is to put plain flour in a plastic bag, season it well with salt and pepper and then add the meat. Hold the bag tightly closed and gently toss the meat. Remove the meat from the bag, shaking off the excess flour.

The meat will usually now be browned in batches. Make sure that you follow the instruction 'in batches', even though it will take a little longer. If you put all the meat in the pan at once, it will be overcrowed, the heat will be reduced and the meat will stew in its own juices rather than brown.

Brown the meat in small batches so it doesn't stew in its own juices.

The recipe will now probably instruct you to add the other ingredients, usually including stock or other liquid, and then leave the pan either on the stove top or in the oven to cook. If you are cooking on the stove top you will be instructed to 'simmer'. Long-cooking dishes such as stews and soups are always cooked at a lazy simmer—long boiling of the ingredients would impair their flavour. If the recipe instructs you to

cover the pan, don't forget to do so. If you don't cover the pan, the liquid will evaporate into steam as it cooks and your dish will become much thicker and 'reduced'. There are times when you will want to deliberately reduce a stew, casserole or soup, by removing the lid at the end of cooking time, increasing the heat slightly and letting some of the liquid boil off so the sauce becomes thicker and the flavours stronger. Stews and soups are often best cooked a day in advance and left in the fridge overnight to let the flavours develop, before being gently reheated to serve. An added bonus is that any excess fat will come to the surface and solidify, so that you can just spoon it off the top. Most stews and soups also freeze successfully (although there are some ingredients, such as cream, which are best added when you are reheating). Spoon into a plastic bag, seal and label. Most will keep for 6 months.

Spoon the stew or soup into a bag to freeze.

MINCE

Beef, lamb, chicken, pork and veal (the last two usually as a combination) are all available minced. Mince, (known as ground meat in the USA), is suitable for all manner of fillings, or to be shaped into meatloaves, burgers, meatballs or kebabs.

Beef mince now comes in different grades such as lean, extra lean, premium or hamburger—choose the fat content and price that suits you.

If you are very concerned

Chop lean meat into mince with a sharp knife.

about fat on your meat, the best way to guarantee virtually fat-free mince is to buy lean meat and then mince it yourself at home, either with a sharp knife or in a food processor. Don't overwork the meat or it will end up as mush.

If you use a processor, don't overwork the mince.

ROASTS

Roasted meat, such as a leg of lamb or rolled roast, is usually a large piece, so to help keep the shape neat, you may want to tie it with kitchen string before cooking.

Tie meat with string so it keeps a neat shape.

Depending on the recipe, the meat is sometimes browned on top of the stove first, then transferred to the oven. Obviously, you will need a large pan to do this.

Sometimes meat is browned before roasting in the oven.

Cooking times will vary considerably depending on the cut and size of the meat, whether or not it is boned or stuffed, and your own personal taste. The most important thing is to weigh your meat properly before cooking. The following is a rough guide to cooking times in a

moderate 180°C (350°F/Gas 4) oven. For rare meat: 15–20 minutes per 500 g (1 lb); for medium: 20–25 minutes per 500 g (1 lb); for well done: 25–30 minutes per 500 g (1 lb). Large joints of pork might need an extra 30 minutes if very thick. The pinch test is a simple way to test your meat. When you think it is ready, pinch the meat in a lean section. If it springs back easily, it's rare; it it's less resilient, it's medium; and if it's firm, the meat is well done.

When the meat is cooked, set it on a board or large plate and leave it to rest for about 10 minutes before carving. This lets the juices be reabsorbed and ensures moist, tender meat. If you need to cover it, do so very loosely with foil so the steam can escape.

Carve the meat evenly across the grain using a knife with a straight, rather than serrated, edge. Use the full length of the blade, rather than a sawing motion.

Carve roast meat across the grain to minimize chewiness.

BEEF CUTS

There are many different cuts of beef and often their names can vary from country to country. For quick pan-frying, choose the best lean fillets you can afford. For casseroles, the more economical cuts will produce a tender flavoursome meal.

1. WHOLE RUMP
Oven roast.

2. FILLET
Oven roast or barbecue.

3. FILLET STEAK
Pan-fry, stir-fry, grill or barbecue.

4. SILVERSIDE STEAK
Oven roast, pot roast or casserole.

5. RUMP STEAK
Pan-fry, stir-fry, grill or barbecue.

6. DICED CHUCK STEAK (STEWING STEAK)
Pot roast or casserole.

7. SHIN (GRAVY BEEF)
Casserole.

8. SILVERSIDE ROAST
Oven roast, pot roast or casserole.

9. CHUCK
Pot roast or casserole

10. OYSTER BLADE
Pan-fry, grill or barbecue.

11. SHIN (WITH BONE)
Casserole.

12. TOPSIDE STEAK
Pan-fry or stir-fry.

13. TOPSIDE
Oven roast or pot roast.

14. BLADE (WITH BONE)
Casserole or barbecue.

15. BLADE STEAK
Pan-fry, stir-fry, casserole or barbecue.

16. WHOLE BOLAR BLADE
Oven roast or pot roast.

17. T-BONE
Pan-fry, grill or barbecue.

18. SIRLOIN STEAK (PORTERHOUSE, WITH BONE)
Pan-fry, stir-fry, grill or barbecue.

19. SIRLOIN STEAK (NEW YORK CUT, WITHOUT BONE)
Pan-fry, stir-fry, grill or barbecue.

20. RIB EYE STEAK (SCOTCH FILLET)
Pan-fry, stir-fry, grill or barbecue.

21. ROLLED ROAST (OF RIBS)
Oven roast.

22. ROUND STEAK
Pan-fry or stir-fry.

23. SKIRT
Oven roast, pot roast or casserole.

24. RIB-EYE FILLET (DELMONICO)
Oven roast or barbecue.

25. RIB STEAK
Pan-fry, grill or barbecue.

26. STANDING RIB ROAST
Oven roast.

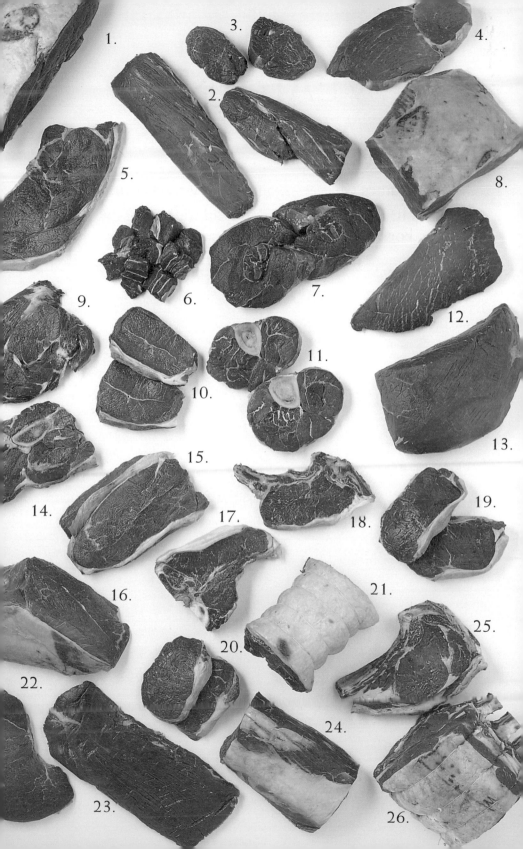

VEAL AND LAMB CUTS

Here are the most popular cuts of veal and lamb and their recommended cooking methods.

1. VEAL SCHNITZEL
Pan-fry.

2. VEAL OSSO BUCO
(KNUCKLE SLICES)
Casserole.

3. VEAL LEG STEAK
Grill or barbecue.

4. VEAL KNUTT
Oven roast.

5. VEAL RUMP ROAST
Oven roast.

6. VEAL RUMP STEAK
Pan-fry, stir-fry, grill or barbecue.

7. VEAL SHANK
Pot roast or casserole.

8. VEAL NECK (BONED AND ROLLED)
Oven roast or pot roast.

9. RACK OF VEAL
Oven roast or pot roast.

10. VEAL LOIN CUTLET
Pan-fry, grill or barbecue.

11. VEAL LOIN ROAST
(BONED AND ROLLED)
Pot roast.

12. VEAL SHOULDER
Oven roast, pot roast or casserole.

13. VEAL LOIN CHOPS
Pan-fry, grill or barbecue.

14. VEAL FOREQUARTER CHOPS
Pan-fry, grill or barbecue.

15. MID-LOIN LAMB CHOPS
Pan-fry, grill or barbecue.

16. ROLLED LAMB SHOULDER
Oven roast or pot roast.

17. LAMB FOREQUARTER CHOPS
Pan-fry, grill, barbecue or casserole.

18. LAMB SHANKS
Oven roast, pot roast or casserole.

19. LAMB LEG CHOPS
Grill or barbecue.

20. EYE OF LAMB LOIN
Pan-fry, stir-fry, grill, barbecue or oven roast.

21. LAMB LOIN (BONED AND ROLLED)
Oven roast or pot roast.

22. LAMB NECK CHOPS
Pan-fry, grill, barbecue or casserole.

23. LAMB CUTLETS
Pan-fry, grill or barbecue.

24. LAMB FILLET
Pan-fry, stir-fry, grill or barbecue.

25. LAMB CHUMP CHOPS
Pan-fry, grill, barbecue or pot roast.

26. RACK OF LAMB
Oven roast.

27. LEG OF LAMB
Oven roast or pot roast. Available with bone in or removed for easy carving.

PORK CUTS

Pork really is one of our most adaptable and easy-to-use meats, from a Sunday roast with apple sauce and crackling, to chops, steaks and even a crispy bacon sandwich. Today's cuts of pork are leaner than ever before—don't ever overcook pork or it will lose its delicious juicy texture. Here are the most popular cuts and cooking methods.

1. ROLLED LOIN
Oven roast.

2. FORELOIN NECK
Oven roast.

3. FORELOIN STEAK
Pan-fry, grill or barbecue.

4. SPARE RIBS
Grill, barbecue or oven roast.

5. LOIN STEAKS
Pan-fry, grill or barbecue.

6. FOREQUARTER CHOPS
Pan-fry, grill, barbecue or oven roast.

7. ROLLED SHOULDER (HAND OF PORK)
Oven roast.

8. AMERICAN-STYLE RIBS
Grill, barbecue or oven roast

9. LOIN MEDALLION STEAK
Pan-fry, grill, barbecue or oven roast.

10. LOIN CUTLET
Pan-fry, grill or barbecue.

11. RACK OF PORK
Oven roast.

12. PORK RUMP
Barbecue or oven roast

13. MID-LOIN BUTTERFLY STEAK
Pan-fry, grill or barbecue.

14. LOIN CHOP (TRIMMED)
Pan-fry, grill or barbecue.

15. LOIN CHOP
Pan-fry, grill or barbecue.

16. FILLET
Pan-fry, grill or oven roast.

17. RUMP STEAK
Pan-fry, grill or barbecue.

18. LEG SCHNITZELS
Pan-fry, grill or oven roast.

19. LEG STRIPS (PORK STRIPS)
Pan-fry or stir-fry.

20. LOIN ROAST
Oven roast.

21. LEG STEAK
Pan-fry, grill or barbecue.

22. SILVERSIDE
Barbecue or oven roast.

23. TOPSIDE
Barbecue or oven roast.

24. LEG
Oven roast.

CHICKEN SENSE

Chicken is a versatile and affordable food that is eaten all over the world. It is a complete protein, with minerals such as potassium and phosphorous, as well as some B vitamins and, without its skin, it is relatively low in fat.

BUYING CHICKEN

Free-range and corn-fed chickens are now widely available and have a better flavour and texture than intensively farmed chickens. Free-range chickens can be identified by a label stating that they have been reared humanely. Corn-fed chickens have a yellowy skin and flesh, but are not necessarily free-range. You will, of course, pay more for a free-range bird, but it will have better flavour. Whole chickens are sold by a number that relates to their weight, for example, a no.15 chicken will weigh 1.5 kg (3 lb) and should feed 4 people. Larger birds will feed 4–6.

Breasts can be bought on the bone or as 'fillets' (bone removed)—both are available as single or double, joined breasts. In our recipes, when we ask for '1 chicken breast' we mean one single breast. Breasts will have a small tenderloin underneath. Thighs have darker, more succulent meat than breasts, work well in curries and stews and for kebabs and satays. Thigh cutlets have both skin and a thigh bone, thigh fillets have no skin or bone, and thighs have some backbone and an 'oyster'.

STORING

Make chicken the last item to be bought and have it out of the fridge for the shortest possible time. Frozen chicken must be solid and tightly wrapped. Fresh chicken should be taken out of its packaging, covered loosely with plastic wrap and put on a plate to catch any drips. Keep it in the fridge, and not where it can drip onto other food. Cook it within 2 days. Chicken can be frozen for up to 3 months, sealed in a freezer bag with the air expelled (make sure you write the date on a label). Defrost chicken carefully as bacteria, such as salmonella, can be activated if it gets too warm. Defrost in the fridge, not at room temperature. Chicken pieces can be defrosted in the microwave (arrange the thickest portions to the outside of the plate). Don't defrost whole birds in the microwave—they defrost unevenly and some

Put the thickest part of the chicken to the outside.

parts may start to cook. Use thawed chicken within 12 hours and never refreeze. Cooked chicken can be kept in the fridge for up to 3 days.

JOINTING A CHICKEN

Cutting a whole chicken into pieces is called 'jointing'. The flavour of a dish will often be better if, rather than buying pieces, you cut up a whole bird. Large birds can be cut into four, six, eight or ten pieces. Use a pair of

Cut down the length of the backbone on either side.

kitchen scissors to cut through the length of the breastbone, then turn the chicken over and cut down either side of the backbone to remove it in one piece. Cut the bird into four pieces following the natural contours. For

Cut the chicken into pieces following the natural contours.

eight pieces, cut each breast in half, so one piece has the wing attached—you can remove the wings by bending them outwards and snipping around the joint if you want. Cut

through the leg joint to separate the drumstick from the thigh (leg pieces with the drumstick still attached to the thigh are called 'marylands').

A chicken can be cut into four, six, eight or 10 pieces.

BONING A CHICKEN

For special occasions, sometimes a chicken will be boned and then stuffed and rolled, and then usually served cold. To bone a chicken, use a small sharp knife to cut through the skin on the centre back. Separate the flesh from the bone down one side to the breast, being careful not to pierce the skin. Follow closely along the bones with the knife, gradually easing meat from the thigh, drumstick and wing. Cut through the thigh bone and cut off the wing tip. Repeat on the other side, then lift the rib cage away, leaving the flesh in one piece. Scrape all the meat from the drumsticks and wings. Turn the wing and drumstick flesh inside the chicken and lay the bird out flat, skin-side-down.

Cut through the skin on the centre back.

Separate the flesh from the bone down one side.

Repeat on the other side and lift away the rib cage.

Scrape all the meat from the drumsticks and wings.

Turn the drumstick and wing flesh inside the chicken.

GRILLING AND PAN-FRYING

Chicken breasts are the whitest and leanest portions of meat on the chicken. While thighs and drumsticks, with their darker, more succulent meat, are more suitable for stews and curries, breasts can be grilled, fried, poached and roasted. Be careful not to overcook, however, as they dry out. To grill chicken, preheat the grill and put the chicken pieces, skin-side-down, on a cold, oiled grill pan. Cook them about 10 cm (4 inches) from the heat for 15–20 minutes, then turn and cook until the juices run clear when tested with a skewer. Brush with marinade during cooking to prevent drying out. If you aren't using a marinade, brush with butter or oil.

Pan-frying is the best cooking method for small tender pieces such as breast fillets. Heat oil or butter in a heavy-based pan over high heat, pat the chicken dry with paper towels and cook for 2–3 minutes on each side to brown and seal in the juices, turning with tongs. Reduce the heat and cook until the juices run clear. Never overcrowd the pan. Always fry the chicken in a single layer and if you don't have a pan big enough, use two small pans or cook the chicken in batches.

POACHING

Poaching is an easy and healthy way to cook chicken. The chicken is gently simmered in water, stock or wine, sometimes with vegetables and herbs added for flavour. The cooking liquid must never boil or the flavour will be impaired. This method is suitable for chicken breasts, but also for cooking whole large birds. After cooking, the liquid can be strained and used to make a sauce to serve with the chicken, or it can be saved for stock. Because of the low fat content, poaching is ideal for dieters—especially if the skin is removed first.

STEWS AND CASSEROLES

The long slow cooking process is best for tougher cuts of meat, and it will make even a 'tough old bird' meltingly tender. The chicken should be gently simmered, never boiled, in the cooking liquid. Boiling will only make the flesh tough. Brown pieces or whole birds in a large pan in butter or oil, then transfer to a casserole with vegetables and cooking liquids such as stock and wine. As with other long-cooked dishes, chicken stews benefit from being left in the fridge overnight for the flavours to develop and reheated gently to serve. This also means you can scoop off any fat which solidifies on the surface.

ROASTS

To prepare a chicken for roasting, first make sure that there is nothing inside the cavity (the giblets and neck are sometimes stored in there in a plastic bag, which could lead to disaster).

Cook in one layer without overcrowding the pan.

Simmer the chicken gently, without boiling the liquid.

Trim off any excess fat with a pair of kitchen scissors.

Trim off any excess fat with a pair of kitchen scissors and then rinse and dry the skin and the cavity with a paper towel. Stuffing a whole chicken before roasting adds flavour and plumps up the bird. Do not stuff a bird more than 3 hours before cooking. If you are using warm stuffing, cook the bird immediately. A stuffed bird will take a little longer to cook. Once you have stuffed the chicken you can truss it so it keeps its shape during cooking. You can simply tuck the wings behind the body and tie the legs together with some kitchen string or you can truss the bird thoroughly. Tie the legs together, wrapping the string under the parson's nose first. After the legs, take the string towards the neck of the bird, passing it down between the legs and the body. Turn the bird over and cross the string over in the centre, underneath the wings. Wrap the string around the wings to keep them flat. Tie the string into a knot or bow to secure the chicken wings in place. Trim off the ends of the string and the chicken is ready. Cook at moderately hot 200°C (400°F/Gas 6) for 40–45 minutes per kilo. Test by inserting a skewer

into the thickest part of the thigh—if the juices run clear, it is cooked. If the juices are pink, put the bird back in the oven for 10 minutes before retesting. Chicken must always be thoroughly cooked—pink meat is unappealing and unsafe.

Tie the drumsticks together, closing the body cavity.

Pass the string between the legs and body of the bird.

Turn over and cross the string over in the centre.

Tie into a knot or bow to secure the wings in place.

CARVING

Leave the roast chicken to 'rest', loosely covered with foil for 10 minutes before carving to allow the juices to settle. Some people advise leaving the chicken upside-down while it is resting, so the juices run into the breast.

Use a two-pronged fork to hold the chicken.

Cut around the leg, separating the bone at the joint.

Cut the leg into thigh and drumstick.

Slice the breast meat parallel to the rib cage.

CHICKEN CUTS

There are many different cuts of chicken available and which one you use will depend on how you are intending to cook it. You might prefer lean chicken breast fillets (which have had the bone removed) when quickly pan-frying or stir-frying, but when you are casseroling, you would probably prefer to use a cut of chicken which still contains the bone and will cook more slowly and add more flavour to the dish. Without its skin, chicken is now well-known as a healthy 'white meat' alternative to beef and lamb. Free-range chicken has more flavour than intensively reared.

1. WHOLE CHICKEN
Oven roast, pot roast or barbecue.

2. BONED WHOLE CHICKEN
Ask your butcher to bone the chicken for you. Oven roast, pot roast, barbecue

3. BREAST ON THE BONE
Oven roast, pot roast or casserole.

4. DRUMSTICKS
Pan-fry, grill, oven roast, pot roast, casserole or barbecue.

5. CHICKEN MARYLANDS (LEG AND THIGH PIECES)
Oven roast, casserole or barbecue.

6. DOUBLE (JOINT) BREAST FILLET (TWO SKINLESS FILLETS)
Pan-fry, stir-fry, grill or barbecue.

7. CHICKEN THIGHS (WITH BONE)
Oven roast, grill, casserole or barbecue.

8. CHICKEN THIGH FILLETS (WITHOUT BONE)
Pan-fry, grill, casserole or barbecue.

9. CHICKEN TENDERLOINS (SMALL STRIPS REMOVED FROM THE UNDERSIDE OF THE BREAST)
Pan-fry, stir-fry, grill or barbecue.

10. BREAST FILLET (WITH SKIN)
Pan-fry, stir-fry, grill, oven roast or barbecue.

11. WINGS
Grill, oven roast or barbecue.

12. CHICKEN MINCE
Pan-fry.

13. CHICKEN LIVERS
Pan-fry or stir-fry.

14. BREAST FILLET (WITHOUT SKIN)
Pan-fry, stir-fry, grill, oven roast or barbecue.

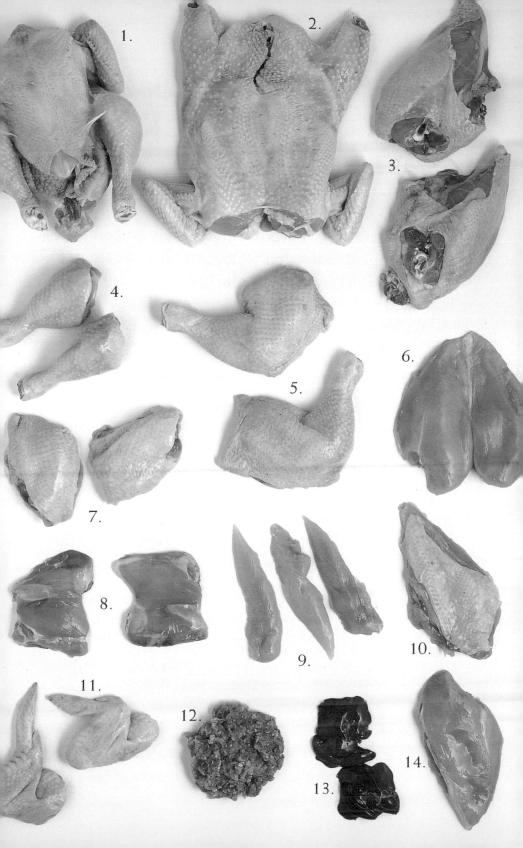

FISH AND SEAFOOD SENSE

Delicious, nutritious, generally quick cooking and easy to prepare, seafood is arguably one of nature's perfect foods. One drawback is that it is highly perishable and care must be taken when shopping for, storing and preparing seafood.

BUYING

Ideally, seafood should be the last thing you buy on your shopping trip, to ensure the shortest time possible out of refrigeration. Your fishmonger should wrap the seafood in a plastic bag to keep in the moisture and then several insulating layers of paper. While you pretty much have to take your fishmonger's word for the freshness of his wares, there are some general signs to look for. Fresh fish should have bulging and clear eyes, not sunken and cloudy. The skin should be plump and moist. Fish fillets should be plump, moist and evenly coloured. There should be no dry edges. Shellfish such as lobsters and crabs are generally best bought live, though they are also available already cooked or frozen. If you are buying them live, they should be fairly active. If you are buying them cooked, make sure the shell is intact and the there is no discoloration around the joints.

Fresh, raw prawns (also known as green prawns) should be plump and firm (not mushy), and without black spots. Cooked prawns should have a firm head and shell, and no black discoloration. Generally, all seafood should have a pleasant, characteristically fresh, fishy smell. Avoid anything that looks or smells at all unappealing.

STORING

Seafood has a very short storage life and is best used within a day of purchase. Place fish on a plate, to prevent dripping onto other foods, cover with plastic wrap or foil and store in the fridge. Seafood can actually give an undesirable smell to other foods—another reason not to store it for too long. Seafood can be frozen, if absolutely necessary. It is a great way to store fish you have caught yourself, as you can be assured of the freshness. If freezing bought fish, check with the fishmonger whether it has already been frozen and thawed—if it has been, don't ever re-freeze it (this applies to all food to be frozen, not just seafood).

Fish: Fish can be frozen whole, but must be cleaned first, and rinsed to remove any traces of blood (pat dry with paper towels). If a whole fish is going to be filleted, then do so before freezing. Put the fish into a freezer bag and extract as much air as possible. Seal firmly and clearly label with the date. To make separation easier when you come to use frozen fillets, place a sheet of freezer wrap between them. Freeze non-oily fish for up to 4 months and oily fish for up to 3 months.

Shellfish: Lobsters, crabs, prawns and other crayfish can be frozen raw or cooked, and don't need to be cleaned first. Wrap larger shellfish in plastic wrap or foil, then in a freezer bag, extracting as much air as possible. Take care that any sharp parts of the shell don't pierce the bag. Freeze for up to 2 months.

Squid and Octopus: Clean and cut into pieces for cooking. Freeze raw, in a freezer bag with as much air extracted as possible. Freeze for up to 4 months.

Molluscs: Mussels, oysters, scallops, pipis and clams should be cooked and the meat frozen, without the shell, in a freezer bag with as much air extracted as possible. Freeze for up to 3 months.

THAWING

There is no need to thaw small or thin fillets of fish, just cook a little longer than the given time. If the fillet is to have further preparation, such as coating with crumbs or batter, just thaw enough to make it easy to handle. Alternatively, fish can be crumbed before freezing—the coating sticks better this way and there is no need to defrost. Other seafood should be thawed in the fridge, never at room temperature, and never in a sink full of water. Cook any seafood as soon as it has thawed.

PREPARING

Fish: While any good fishmonger will scale and clean your fish on request, it is worth knowing how to do this yourself. Soak the fish in cold water for a few minutes to make it easier to scale. Then scale the fish by holding it firmly by the tail, and using a fish scaler or knife to scrape the the scales from the skin, working from the tail towards the head against the 'lie' of the scales. This is a messy job, so work outdoors if

Scrape against the direction of the scales with a fish scaler.

possible, or on the draining board. It is also a smelly job so be careful not to leave any stray scales lying around when you have finished. Rinse the fish regularly under running water to remove the loosened scales.

To gut a fish, slit the belly from the gills back towards the tail, but not as far as the tail (roughly two-thirds of the way along). Take care not to cut too far into the fish. Pull out the insides and rinse the fish under running water, inside and out. The other method of

Remove the gut and rinse the fish under cold water.

gutting is through the gills; this is done when you want to preserve the shape of the fish (when poaching whole, for instance). To do this, hook your fingers through the gills and remove them. Reach in and pull the guts out through the opening. Once the fish has been gutted, it can be filleted, if required. To fillet a fish, make a cut across the body, just behind the gills. Only cut halfway through

31

the fish. Using this cut as a starting point, slice horizontally along the body, as close to the backbone as possible, and down to the tail,

Cut across the body, just behind the gills.

Slice horizontally along the body. Keep close to the bone.

separating the flesh from the bone. The fillet should lift off. Repeat with the other side and lift away the fillet. If you want to skin the fillet, hold it by the tail end, skin-side-down. Dip your fingers in salt to help you grip. Cut away from you, between the flesh and the skin. Push down as you go, to stay close to the skin.

If the fish is to be cooked whole, it is a good idea to bone it first. After gutting through the stomach, extend the cut as far as the tail, on one side of the backbone. Open the fish out and run the knife

between the flesh and the bones (which will be fairly close to the cut surface), from the head to the tail. Repeat with the other side. Using scissors, snip the backbone at the tail and the head, then pull the whole bone structure out with your fingers. When cooking a whole large fish, it is advisable to score the flesh to ensure even cooking. Make three or four diagonal slashes in the fattest part of the fish, on either side.

There are many different ways to cook fish, as many as there are to cook meat or poultry. The one common factor is that fish should be cooked until it is just done, because overcooking causes the flesh to dry out and become very unappetising. The flesh of fish is naturally tender, and therefore does not require the long cooking time that some cuts of meat do. The fact that fish cooks quickly is both a blessing and a headache to the cook, as it can cause some anxiety as to the correct cooking time. Always follow the time given in the recipe, however, remember that size and thickness, particularly of fillets, can vary and will determine the cooking time. If you are unsure, check the fish a little

before the given time. This does take practice and an eye for the required result, but the most common way to check is to 'flake' the flesh gently with a fork or point of a knife. It should be opaque, separate into characteristic flakes and come away from the bone,

Gently 'flake' the flesh with a fork to see if the fish is cooked.

where appropriate. While it is best to check the thickest part of the flesh, try to be gentle, so that you do not spoil the appearance of the piece. Careful cooking also applies to other seafood, not just fish. Overcooking of shellfish, such as clams and mussels, can render them rubbery and inedible.

While seafood is a major ingredient in many grand, glamorous and complicated dishes, simple treatment is usually the best. A squeeze of lemon, a dab of butter, or a sprinkling of herbs. Just remember to always try to enhance the flavour, rather than mask it, to truly appreciate seafood.

Lobster: As lobsters are best bought live, it is necessary to kill them before preparing. The most humane way to do this is to put the lobster in the freezer for an hour first—this will stun it. Then with a large, heavy knife, cut through the

Cut through the centre of the back of the head with a knife.

Cut the lobster in half, cutting lengthways along the body.

Grasp the body and tail and twist to separate.

Remove the meat from the shell for easy serving.

centre of the back of the head. Plunge the knife right through to the cutting board, then through the rest of the head. To cut the lobster in half, cut lengthways along the body and tail, using firm pressure.

Cut a cooked lobster in half the same way, or it may be a little easier to turn it over and cut lengthways along the underside. To extract cooked meat from the legs and claws, first remove by twisting them, close to the body. Break the legs in half and insert a skewer into the cavity to push out the meat. Claws can be cracked with a hammer, or a special cracker.

To extract the cooked tail meat to cut into medallions, grasp the body and tail firmly in each hand and twist to separate. Cut through the underside of the tail with scissors, and pull away the soft undershell. Ease the meat from the tail, in one piece. Cut the meat into slices about 1 cm (^{1}/2 inch) thick.

Crabs: Like lobsters, crabs are best bought live. They should also be put in the freezer for an hour before cooking.

To extract the meat from a cooked crab, take the body and lift the tail flap (apron) from the

underside. The body of the crab is in two sections: the central part, where the legs are attached, and the shell. Tuck your thumb in under the tail flap, where the central section and the shell meet, and ease open to separate the two halves. Scoop the meat from the

Remove the tail flap, or apron, from the underside of the crab.

Ease the central section away from the shell.

Remove the gills from the central section of the crab.

Remove the claws and legs and pull out the meat.

33

shell. Take the central section and remove the gills. Then remove the legs and claws by twisting them away from the body.

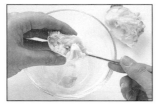

A skewer may be needed to remove the meat in the body.

Crackers, or the back of a knife, crack open the claws.

Cut the body section in half, and then, using a pick or skewer, extract all the meat you can find (this is a fiddly job). Crack the claws open and break the legs apart with your fingers. Pull out the meat with a skewer.

Prawns: To peel prawns, whether raw or cooked, grasp the head and the body close to the joint,

Twist the head off before removing the shell and legs.

and twist in opposite directions. The head can either be thrown away or used to make delicious stocks or soups. Remove the legs from the underside of the prawn and then use your thumbs to prise the shell from the flesh. If the recipe says to leave the tail intact, only work down as far as the last section before the tail, otherwise, also remove the tail. Pull away the shell and legs and discard. To devein the prawn, cut a shallow slit along the

Cut a slit along the 'back' and pull out the intestinal tract.

'back' and pull out the intestinal tract. Both raw and cooked prawns can be deveined.

Mussels: To prepare black mussels for cooking, discard those without tightly closed shells (or shells that do not close when tapped on the work surface)—this means they are already dead and could lead to food poisoning. Scrub the shells with a stiff brush, and tear away the beards (small hairy strands) from the shell. Discard any mussels that

Scrub the mussel shell and tear away the beard.

do not open during the cooking process, as this also indicates that something may be awry. However, green-lipped mussels (which are larger than the black variety) will be open when you buy them and don't close when tapped.

Octopus: To prepare the octopus, first cut into sections: the head and the tentacles. Clean the head by turning it inside out to push out the insides. The 'beak' is found at the centre of the tentacles and is removed by squeezing

Turn the head of the octopus inside out to clean it.

Squeeze the 'beak' out of the centre of the tentacles.

on either side while pushing from behind. If the octopus is very small and you want to serve it whole, clean the head by cutting a slit in the back of it and pulling out the insides. Remove the beak as before.

Oysters: Fresh, opened oysters need to be consumed within a day. To keep fresh oysters for longer than this, buy closed ones and open them yourself when you are ready to serve them. However, be careful: oyster shells can have very sharp edges. First, scrub the outside of the oyster shell under cold runnning water. Then wrap the oyster, rounded-side-down, in a thick cloth and hold it in the palm of your hand. Insert an oyster knife into the pointed end of the oyster at the hinge, to about 3 cm, and work the knife into the shell, twisting the knife to separate the shells. Slide the knife between the oyster and the top shell, cutting through the hinge muscle and removing the top shell. Similarly, cut between the oyster and the bottom shell to release the oyster. Rinse the shells and wipe the oyster clean with a damp cloth to remove any grit or sand before returning the oyster to the shell.

Squid (calamari):
To prepare squid, grasp the body pouch in one hand and, with the other, reach in and pull out the whole lower section, which includes the head and tentacles. Feel the pouch to find the transparent quill and pull

Wrap oyster shells in a thick cloth when handling them.

Hold the oyster in a cloth and work the knife into the shell.

Slide the knife between the oyster and the shell.

Release the oyster from the shell and remove any grit.

it out. Throw this away. Loosen the skin by sliding a finger between it and the flesh, then pull firmly away. Trim the flaps and skin them also. If you wish to use the tentacles, cut them from the head and remove the beak as you would for octopus.

Remove the whole of the lower section of the squid.

Pull the transparent quill out of the body pouch.

Loosen the skin by sliding a finger between it and the flesh.

Remove the skin from the squid before cooking.

FISH AND SEAFOOD

Fish and seafood can throw many people into confusion. Here are the most common types of fish and seafood, with a quick guide to the most successful ways to cook them.

1. SNAPPER
Pan-fry, grill, barbecue, oven roast, poach or steam.

2. RAINBOW TROUT
Pan-fry, grill, barbecue or oven roast.

3. JOHN DORY
Pan-fry, grill, barbecue, oven roast, poach or steam.

4. FLOUNDER
Pan-fry, grill, barbecue, oven roast, poach or steam.

5. SMOKED TROUT
Already cooked. Use in salads and dips.

6. BREAM
Pan-fry, grill, barbecue, oven roast, poach or steam.

7. SARDINES
Pan-fry, grill or barbecue.

8. SQUID
Pan-fry, stir-fry, grill, barbecue or casserole.

9. WHITEBAIT
Pan-fry, deep-fry or bake.

10. FIRM WHITE FISH FILLET (LING FILLETS AND SWORDFISH STEAK)
Pan-fry, stir-fry, grill, barbecue, oven roast, poach or steam.

11. SALMON CUTLET
Pan-fry, grill, barbecue, oven roast, casserole, steam or poach.

12. TUNA STEAK
Pan-fry, stir-fry, grill, barbecue, oven roast, casserole or steam.

13. CALAMARI (WHOLE, TUBE AND RINGS)
Pan-fry, stir-fry, barbecue or deep-fry.

14. SKATE
Pan-fry or grill.

15. OCTOPUS
Pan-fry, stir-fry, grill or barbecue.

16. SCALLOPS
Pan-fry, stir-fry, grill, barbecue, oven roast or steam.

17. RAW PRAWNS
Pan-fry, stir-fry, grill, barbecue or casserole.

18. COOKED PRAWNS
Already cooked. Use in salads, cold dishes, or add to dishes at the end of the cooking time.

19. LOBSTER
Pan-fry, stir-fry, grill, barbecue or oven roast.

20. BLUE SWIMMER CRABS (COOKED AND UNCOOKED)
Stir-fry, barbecue, oven roast, pot roast or casserole.

21. OYSTERS
Grill or barbecue.

22. CLAMS (VONGOLE)
Pan-fry, grill or casserole.

23. MUSSELS (BLACK AND NEW ZEALAND GREEN-LIPPED)
Pan-fry, grill, barbecue, oven roast, casserole or poach.

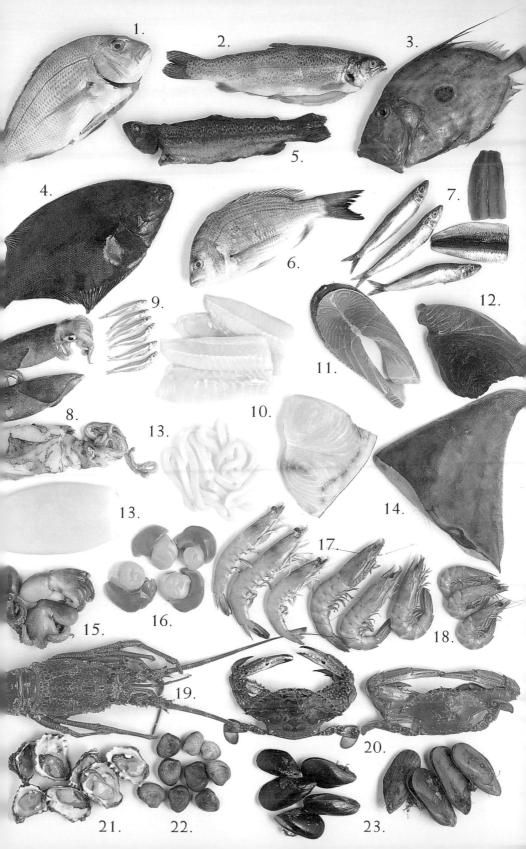

VEGETABLE SENSE

The variety of fresh vegetables available to us today is quite wonderful. Quick and easy to cook, packed with vitamins and fibre, we can revel in the colour, crunch and flavour of fresh vegetables and treat them with the respect they deserve.

ASPARAGUS

To remove the sometimes tough and woody end of the asparagus, bend the stem end of each spear. It will snap where it begins to get tough. Blanch to use in salads or, if very tender, use raw. Blanching makes vegetables such as asparagus and snow peas tender without cooking them, and preserves the bright colour. To do this, place the vegetables in a pan and cover with boiling water (it's easier to tie asparagus together into a bunch). Leave for 30–60 seconds, depending on the size. Drain, then plunge into iced water. Drain again and pat dry.

The iced water prevents the vegetables cooking further.

BEANS

Trim both ends of the bean ('top and tail') and remove the fibrous string that runs down each side, if necessary. Steam, boil or microwave until tender.

BEETROOT

Raw beetroot will stain, so take care. Trim the stalks to 2 cm (1 inch) above the bulb, leaving the skin intact. Boil whole until tender, then cool and slip off the skins. Also good raw, peeled and grated.

BROCCOLI

Cut into florets (make them fairly small if stir-frying) and steam, boil or microwave until tender.

BRUSSELS SPROUTS

Remove any tough or yellow outer leaves and score a cross in the base so the sprout cooks all the way through. Steam, boil or microwave until tender.

CABBAGE

Remove any tough outer leaves and chop or shred the inner leaves. Serve raw and shredded in coleslaw, or steam, microwave or stir-fry very briefly.

CAPSICUM

Cut into quarters and remove the seeds and white membrane. Serve raw or stir-fry, or leave whole and stuff. Removing the skin from capsicums by grilling or roasting makes the flavour of the flesh even sweeter. Cut the capsicums into large,

Grill the capsicum until the skin is black and blistered.

Cool in a plastic bag to make the skin peel away easily.

flattish pieces, removing the seeds and membrane. Place, skin-side-up, under a hot grill until the skin is black and blistered. Put in a plastic bag or under a tea towel to cool—this steams and loosens the skin, which can be peeled away.

CARROTS

Scrub the skin or peel if you like. Serve raw or steam, boil, microwave, roast or stir-fry.

CAULIFLOWER

Cut into florets. Steam, boil, microwave or stir-fry.

CELERY

Trim the stalks, removing the leaves and thick root end. Good raw, stir-fried or in soups or stews.

CORN

Remove the outside husk and silk. Boil or microwave, but take care not to overcook or the corn will become tough. Also good roasted, either in foil, or in the husk: peel back the husk and remove the silk, then pull the husk back into place to cover the kernels and roast.

EGGPLANT

The flesh from large eggplants can contain bitter juices—this is why the recipe will tell you to chop the flesh, put in a colander and sprinkle generously with salt to draw out the juice. Leave for 20 minutes, then rinse and pat dry. Fry, stir-fry or cook in curries or stews.

MUSHROOMS

Don't wash mushrooms before cooking or they will become soggy. Wipe clean with paper towels or peel, if necessary.

PARSNIPS

Peel and cut off the stalk end. Steam, microwave, roast or boil, as for potatoes.

PEAS

Remove from the pod and boil or steam until tender.

POTATOES

Peel or scrub the skin, removing any 'eyes'. Use floury or waxy variety if stated in the recipe.

PUMPKIN

Peel and remove the seeds and membrane, then steam, boil or microwave. If you are roasting pumpkin, you don't need to peel it first—the peel is easier to remove after.

SNOW PEAS

Top and tail, then stir-fry or serve raw or blanched.

SWEET POTATO

Peel and then steam, microwave, boil or roast. Mash just like potatoes. Also good roasted in the skin, after which the soft flesh can be scooped out.

TOMATO

Serve raw in salads, or fry, grill, or roast. Recipes will occasionally ask for tomatoes to be peeled, particularly in sauces where the peel can add an unpleasant texture. To do this, score a cross in the base of each tomato. Put in a heatproof bowl and cover with boiling water. Leave for about 1 minute (the ripeness of the tomato will determine how easily the skin comes

Score a cross in the base of the tomato with a knife.

The skin will easily peel away from the cross.

Cut the tomato in half and scoop out the seeds.

away), then transfer to a bowl of cold water. Peel the skin away from the cross. To remove the seeds, cut in half horizontally and scoop them out with a teaspoon.

ZUCCHINI

Trim the ends and chop. Steam, stir-fry or cook in curries or stews.

VEGETABLES

There is now a huge range of fresh vegetables available all year round. Names may vary from country to country so, if you are unsure, check the photograph opposite.

1. LETTUCE

2. BOK CHOY (PAK CHOY/CHINESE CABBAGE)

3. CHINESE BROCCOLI (GAI LARN)

4. CHILLIS

5. CAPSICUMS (PEPPERS)

6. GLOBE ARTICHOKE

7. BUTTON MUSHROOMS

8. WHITE, BROWN AND RED ONIONS

9. SUGAR SNAP PEAS

10. PEAS IN THE POD

11. SNOW PEAS (MANGE-TOUT)

12. CAULIFLOWER

13. TOMATO

14. CHERRY TOMATO

15. GARLIC

16. BULB SPRING ONION

17. SPRING ONION (GREEN ONION)

18. SHALLOT

19. EGGPLANT (AUBERGINE)

20. BROCCOLI

21. FENNEL

22. GREEN BEANS (STRING BEANS)

23. LEEK

24. ZUCCHINI (COURGETTE)

25. BRUSSELS SPROUTS

26. SQUASH

27. AVOCADO

28. BELGIAN ENDIVE (WITLOF)

29. PARSNIP

30. TURNIP

31. LEBANESE CUCUMBER

32. CELERY

33. CUCUMBER (RIDGED CUCUMBER)

34. CARROT

35. ASPARAGUS

36. GINGER

37. JERUSALEM ARTICHOKE

38. SWEET POTATO

39. BEETROOT

40. ENGLISH SPINACH

41. SILVERBEET (CHARD)

42. CORN

43. PUMPKIN

44. SWEDE (RUTABAGA)

45. POTATO

46. CABBAGE

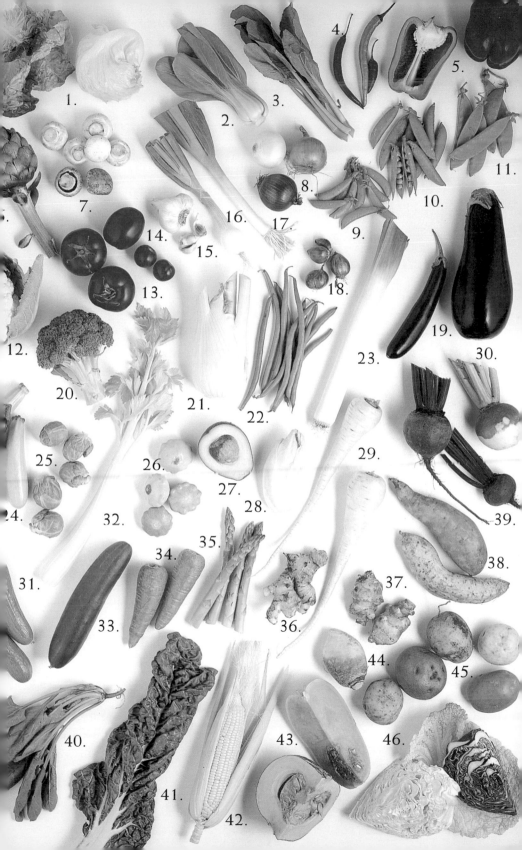

1.

2.

3.

4.

5.

7.

8.

9.

10.

11.

12.

13.

14.

15.

16.

17.

18.

19.

20.

21.

22.

23.

24.

25.

26.

27.

28.

29.

30.

31.

32.

33.

34.

35.

36.

37.

38.

39.

40.

41.

42.

43.

44.

45.

46.

HERBS

Fresh herbs give delicate flavour and colour to dishes.
They all have their favourite partners in the food world and
listed below are some of the most popular pairings.

1. CURLY LEAF PARSLEY
Pasta, mornays, egg dishes
and salads.

2. FLAT-LEAF PARSLEY
(CONTINENTAL PARSLEY)
Mediterranean cooking—
tabbouleh, fish, chicken
and vegetables.

3. ROSEMARY
Meat (especially lamb),
potatoes, breads and
tomato-based sauces.

4. TARRAGON
French cooking—fish,
poultry and sauces such as
hollandaise and bearnaise.

5. SORREL
Soups, marinades and
omelettes.

6. BAY LEAF
Used in bouquet garni
for stews, soups, chicken
dishes, sweet syrups and
poaching liquids.

7. LEMON THYME
Best with fish and chicken
dishes.

8. THYME
Soups, stews, tomato-
based sauces, veal, lamb
and roast poultry.

9. GARLIC CHIVES
Asian cuisine—rice paper
rolls, noodles and soups.

10. CHIVES
Used with eggs, potatoes
and creamy soups.

11. DILL
Best with salmon, potatoes
and pickled cucumbers.

12. CHERVIL
French cuisine—salads,
omelettes, butter sauces,
poached chicken and fish.

13. PEPPERMINT
Used in tea, sweet dishes,
cordials and liqueurs.

14. SPEARMINT
Mint jelly, African and
Middle Eastern food.

15. HOLY BASIL (KAPROW)
Asian curries, stir-fries and
soups.

16. CORIANDER
Roots, stems and leaves all
used in Asian cooking,
salads, curries and salsas.

17. MARJORAM
Used in omelettes,
stuffings, soups and stews.

18. OREGANO
Used in Mediterranean
cooking—tomato-based
sauces, cheese and beans.

19. LEMON GRASS
Asian soups, curries and
salads.

20. ROCKET
Salads, pasta, soups, pesto.

21. PURPLE BASIL
Use as basil.

22. BASIL
Tomatoes, pesto, fish,
chicken and rice.

23. LEMON BASIL
Asian salads, soup, curries.

24. SAGE
Pumpkin, game, pork.

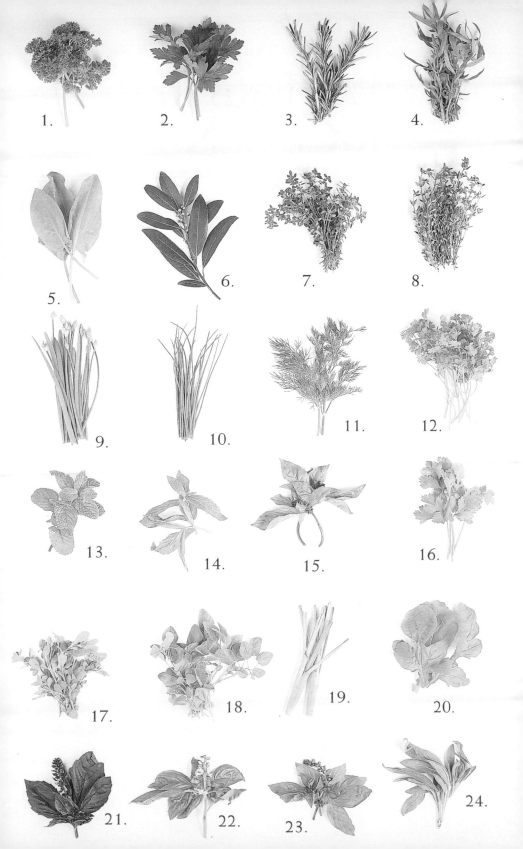

1.

2.

3.

4.

5.

6.

7.

8.

9.

10.

11.

12.

13.

14.

15.

16.

17.

18.

19.

20.

21.

22.

23.

24.

PASTA AND RICE SENSE

For two such simple foods, it is amazing how many varied opinions there are on how to cook pasta and rice. Here are our commonsense thoughts on the subject.

PASTA VARIETIES

There are a huge number of pasta varieties and shapes and each is traditionally partnered with a specific type of sauce. Smooth pastas are typically served with smooth oily sauces, while ridged or shaped pastas are perfect for holding chunky sauces (see the identification chart overleaf). You can buy pasta dried or fresh and dried pasta made in Italy is considered to be the best. It is made from semolina flour (which is made from durum wheat), a hard flour that is high in gluten. Always check that your pasta packet says 'made with durum wheat'.

COOKING PASTA

To cook perfect pasta, you will need a very large pan. Allow at least 2 litres of water for every 250 g (8 oz) pasta—this allows the pasta plenty of room to move and expand and prevents it clumping together. Bring the water to a rapid boil (cover the pan to make it come to the boil faster), then add the pasta and leave the pan uncovered.

Some people like to add a little oil to the water to prevent the pasta sticking together, but if the pan is big enough the pasta won't stick. Add salt if you like, but topped with a flavoursome sauce the pasta shouldn't need extra seasoning. Give the pasta a quick stir, then bring it back to the boil. Once it is boiling you can start timing. Use the time given on the packet as a guide, but the only way to really know if pasta is ready is to taste it. Lift a small piece from the pan, cool it slightly, then bite. The pasta should be just tender, with no raw taste, but certainly not soft and gluggy. This is known as 'al dente' and is the correct way to serve pasta. Fresh pasta cooks much more quickly than dried—in some cases it takes only a couple of minutes. Ravioli, tortellini and gnocchi will float as soon as they are cooked: test a piece, then drain immediately.

Once drained, return to the hot pan and toss with sauce. If the pasta has to sit for a couple of minutes, some people toss it with a little olive oil to prevent it clumping: this is fine depending on what sort of sauce you are then using, as the oil will prevent the sauce coating the pasta thoroughly. It is best just to make sure that your sauce is ready (it can be cooked and then reheated) when the pasta is cooked.

RICE VARIETIES

There are many different types of rice. Some are named for their origins but most are distinguished by the size of their grains: long, medium or short. Longer grains contain less starch and remain separate during cooking. Short grains contain more starch and become gluey when cooked so that they stick together. Glutinous rice has very high amounts of starch. Brown rice still has the husks which have been removed from white rice (this is what makes it higher in fibre and a healthy alternative to white rice). Wild rice is technically not a rice at all, but the grain of a water grass. It was originally grown by the Native Americans and harvested by hand. Although it is now also farmed by machine, it is expensive in comparison to other rices. It is now available mixed with brown rice and sold as a wild rice blend which is more economical. Brown rice takes much longer to cook than white because it takes time for the the water to break through the bran layer. In some recipes, such as risottos, rice is fried in oil or butter before adding any liquid. The oil then impregnates the outer layer of the rice and keeps the grains separate. The rice used for risotto is arborio rice, which swells when liquid is added and produces a creamy sauce. Even after cooking, arborio should retain a slight 'bite' in the centre. Always use the type specified in the recipe—don't try risotto with long-grain rice, or a pudding with arborio rice.

HOW MUCH WATER?

Rice absorbs water when cooking and almost trebles in bulk as a result. Many new cooks will have experienced welding a portion of rice to the base of a pan by letting it boil dry. We would love to have a fail-safe rule for preventing this but unfortunately there can be no strict water to rice ratio: the greater the quantity of rice, the less water is needed proportionately. As a very general rule, long-grain rice will absorb about three times its bulk in water, while short-grain will take far more.

COOKING RICE

With over half the population of the world eating rice two or three times a day, it is not surprising that there are many arguments over how it should be cooked. Some say you must never lift the lid, while others cook their rice uncovered. One widely accepted hint is to always use a big pan. This allows the rice to expand and lie as shallow as possible, stopping the lower levels being crushed, cooking faster and becoming soggy. A rice cooker will produce perfect rice every time. If you don't have one, try the following methods:

Absorption: Put the rice in a large pan. For every 200 g (6½ oz) rice add 315 ml (10 fl oz) water. Bring to the boil, cover tightly with a lid and reduce the heat to very low. Cook for 10 minutes. Remove from the heat and leave, covered, for

When it is fully cooked, the rice will be dotted with holes.

10 minutes. When you take off the lid the surface of the rice should be dotted with steam holes. Fluff up with a fork.

Fast boiling: Bring a pan of water to a fast boil. Add the rice and cook uncovered for 12 minutes. Stir occasionally (brown rice will take 40 minutes).

PASTA AND RICE

Certain pastas are best used for smooth or chunky sauces depending on their own smoothness and shape. Rice varieties, too, are suited to certain dishes, as shown below.

1. SPAGHETTI
Smooth long strands. Serve with pesto, creamy, tomato and meat sauces.

2. FETTUCINE (FRESH AND DRIED)
Smooth, long flat strands. Serve with pesto, creamy and tomato-based sauces.

3. LASAGNE
Smooth, flat sheets. Layer with meat, seafood or vegetable sauce and bake.

4. CANNELONI
Smooth or ridged tubes. Stuff with meat, seafood or vegetable sauce; bake.

5. FARFALLE
Smooth 'bows'. Good with all sauces and in salads.

6. PENNE
Smooth or ridged quills (rigate). Good with chunky sauces or in salads.

7. FUSILLI
Smooth spirals. Good with all sauces or in salads.

8. MACARONI
Smooth, short tubes. Good with creamy sauces, in soups, salads and bakes.

9. RISONI
Small, smooth grains like rice. Used in soups.

10. FRESH GNOCCHI
Ridged potato dumplings. Good with creamy, cheese or tomato-based sauces.

11. FRESH TORTELLINI
Smooth stuffed crescents. Serve with a sauce to match filling, or in soups.

12. FRESH RAVIOLI
Smooth stuffed 'pillows'. Serve with a sauce to match the filling.

13. WHITE SHORT-GRAIN
Sushi and paella.

14. WHITE LONG-GRAIN
Chinese cooking.

15. BASMATI
Indian cooking, biryani and pilaf.

16. JASMINE
Served with Thai dishes and curries.

17. ARBORIO
Risotto.

18. BROWN SHORT-GRAIN
Soups and patties.

19. BROWN LONG-GRAIN
Salads, vegetarian loaves and as an accompaniment

20. WILD RICE
Salads and as an accompaniment.

21. BLACK GLUTINOUS
Asian sweet dishes.

22. WHITE GLUTINOUS
Asain sweet dishes and sticky rice.

23. COUSCOUS
Used in African cooking, salads and tagines.

24. POLENTA
Used in Italian cooking, as a soft accompaniment or pressed into a cake.

1.   2.   3.   4.

5.   6.   7.   8.   9.

10.   11.   12.   13.   14.

15.   16.   17.   18.   19.

20.   21.   22.   23.   24.

FREEZING CHART

Freezing means you can prepare food in bulk, cooking larger portions when you have the time and making the most of foods that are in season. Your freezer should be at -18°C and, if you don't have a frost-free model, it should be defrosted every 6–12 months, depending on how much you use it (more frost will build up if it is opened often). If you have a large freezer, don't let it become a black hole where things disappear, only to be discovered years later and thrown away. Keep a notebook next to the freezer to record dishes and dates frozen and make sure you use them within the recommended period of time (opposite).

Once something has been frozen and thawed, never refreeze it, or you run the risk of multiplying bacteria and food poisoning. Containers suitable for freezing are plastic containers with airtight lids and aluminium foil containers with lids. Plastic clip-lock bags are also very convenient. Remove the air from the packaging before sealing—a vacuum pump is good for this. Freeze soups and stews by lining a bowl with a plastic bag, pouring the soup or stew into the bag and sealing. Freeze, then remove the bag from the bowl. Waxed or baking paper is great for separating layers or items such as crepes, fish fillets and chops, so that you can defrost one at a time, rather than the whole batch.

There are some foods that simply can't be frozen. Hard-boiled eggs will go rubbery; fried and crumbed meats will go soggy; whole egg in their shells will break the shell as they expand; vegetables with a high water content will spoil; sour cream and yoghurt separate; meringue weeps; custards, mayonnaise and dishes containing gelatine can't be frozen; herbs and spices lose their flavour after about 2 weeks.

Don't forget to label everything with a permanent marker or self-adhesive labels—it's no good knowing how long something can be stored if you don't know the date that you froze it.

Peeled fruit that discolours easily, such as apples and pears, can be dipped in a lemon juice solution (3 tablespoons lemon juice to 2 cups water) before freezing. Berries can be frozen uncovered on a tray until firm, then transferred to an airtight container for further freezing. You can also layer fruit that is to be used as pie filling with sugar (only fruit that doesn't discolour is suitable for this method of freezing).

1–2 MONTHS

Bread (sliced)
Milk
Soups
Stews
Sausages
Pancakes, pikelets and waffles
Shellfish (raw and cooked)
Scones (unbaked)
Cakes (unbaked)
Biscuits (unbaked)
Sandwiches (2 weeks to a month,
depending on the filling)

2–3 MONTHS

Cream
Cottage cheese
Cakes
Scones
Ice cream
Bread (unbaked)
Pastry (baked and unbaked)
Offal and bacon
Oily fish (sardines, trout, mullet)
Filled pies (unbaked)
Minced meats (except beef)
Poultry giblets
Leftover dishes

3–4 MONTHS

Ham
Lamb
Cheddar cheese, grated
Butter (salted)
White-fleshed fish
Fruit cake (unbaked)

4–6 MONTHS

Minced beef
Veal
Game
Pork
Butter (unsalted)

6–8 MONTHS

Bread (unsliced)
Biscuits
Pizza
Filled pies

8–12 MONTHS

Beef
Poultry
Fruit
Vegetables
Fruit cake

MEASUREMENTS

The recipes in this book were developed using a tablespoon measure of 20 ml. In some other countries the tablespoon is 15 ml. For most recipes this difference will not be noticeable but, for recipes using baking powder, gelatine, bicarbonate of soda, small amounts of flour and cornflour, we suggest that, if you are using the smaller tablespoon, you add an extra teaspoon for each tablespoon.

Weighing scales will obviously give you more accurate measurements, but many people find it very convenient to use cup measurements. You can buy special measuring cups in the supermarket or use an ordinary household cup: first you need to check it holds 250 ml (8 fl oz) by filling it with water and measuring the water (pour it into a measuring jug or even an empty yoghurt carton). This cup can then be used for both liquid and dry cup measurements.

OVEN TEMPERATURES

DESCRIPTION	°C	°F	GAS MARK
Very slow	120	250	1/2
	140	275	1
Slow	150	300	2
Warm	160	315	2–3
	170	325	3
Moderate	180	350	4
Moderately hot	190	375	5
	200	400	6
Hot	210	415	6–7
	220	425	7
Very hot	230	450	8
	240	475	9

LIQUID CUP MEASURES

1/4 cup	60 ml	2 fluid oz
1/3 cup	80 ml	2 1/2 fluid oz
1/2 cup	125 ml	4 fluid oz
3/4 cup	180 ml	6 fluid oz
1 cup	250 ml	8 fluid oz

SPOON MEASURES

1/4 teaspoon	1.25 ml
1/2 teaspoon	2.5 ml
1 teaspoon	5 ml
1 tablespoon	20 ml

WEIGHT

10 g	1/4 oz
30 g	1 oz
60 g	2 oz
90 g	3 oz
125 g	4 oz
150 g	5 oz
185 g	6 oz
220 g	7 oz
250 g	8 oz
275 g	9 oz
300 g	10 oz
330 g	11 oz
375 g	12 oz
400 g	13 oz
425 g	14 oz
475 g	15 oz
500 g	1 lb
600 g	1 1/4 lb
650 g	1 lb 5 oz
750 g	1 1/2 lb
1 kg	2 lb

LENGTH

5 mm	1/4 inch
1 cm	1/2 inch
2 cm	3/4 inch
2.5 cm	1 inch
5 cm	2 inches
6 cm	2 1/2 inches
8 cm	3 inches
10 cm	4 inches
12 cm	5 inches
15 cm	6 inches
18 cm	7 inches
20 cm	8 inches
23 cm	9 inches
25 cm	10 inches
28 cm	11 inches
30 cm	12 inches
46 cm	18 inches
50 cm	20 inches
61 cm	24 inches
77 cm	30 inches

CUP CONVERSIONS

1 cup plain/self-raising flour	125 g (4 oz)
1 cup grated Parmesan cheese	100 g (3 1/2 oz)
1 cup grated Cheddar cheese	125 g (4 oz)
1 cup breadcrumbs (fresh)	80 g (2 3/4 oz)
1 cup breadcrumbs (dry)	100 g (3 1/2 oz)
1 cup dried chickpeas	220 g (7 oz)
1 cup grated chocolate	125 g (4 oz)
1 cup choc bits	175 g (6 oz)
1 cup rice, uncooked	200 g (6 1/2 oz)
1 cup rice, cooked	185 g (6 oz)
1 cup sugar, caster/granulated	250 g (8 oz)
1 cup icing sugar	125 g (4 oz)
1 cup fresh basil/coriander/mint leaves, firmly packed	30 g (1 oz)
1 cup chopped fresh basil/coriander/ mint leaves, firmly packed	60 g (2 oz)

ALTERNATIVE INGREDIENT NAMES

bicarbonate of soda	—	baking soda
capsicum	—	red or green (bell) pepper
chickpeas	—	garbanzo beans
choc bits	—	chocolate chips
chocolate melts	—	chocolate buttons
cornflour	—	cornstarch
fresh coriander	—	cilantro
cream	—	single cream
dark chocolate	—	plain/bittersweet chocolate
eggplant	—	aubergine
fruit mince	—	mincemeat
golden syrup	—	light corn syrup
hazelnut	—	filbert
icing sugar	—	confectioners' sugar
Madeira cake	—	pound cake
plain flour	—	all-purpose flour
prawns	—	shrimp
Rice Bubbles	—	Rice Krispies
sambal oelek	—	chilli paste
snow pea	—	mange tout
spring onion	—	scallion
thick cream	—	double/heavy cream
tomato paste (US/Aus.)	—	tomato purée (UK)
zucchini	—	courgette

BREAKFAST AND BRUNCH

Breakfast is the most important meal of the day, so make it a little bit special. Instead of packet cereals and burnt toast, whip up something worthwhile in the morning. Eggs can be incredibly simple (but deliciously nutritious) and making your own muesli is as easy as it is satisfying.

SCRAMBLED EGGS

To make scrambled eggs for 2 people, beat 4 eggs and 1/4 cup (60 ml/2 fl oz) milk or cream lightly with a whisk or fork. Melt 15 g (1/2 oz) butter in a heavy-based pan over very low heat and pour in the egg. Stir constantly with a wooden spoon, lifting the mixture from the bottom of the pan so that it cooks evenly. The eggs are ready when they are just set but are still creamy—remove from the heat and serve immediately as they will continue to cook and harden. Serve on toast or English muffins. Or top with a spoonful of caviar or some strips of smoked salmon. Alternatively, stir in a couple of tablespoons of chopped fresh chives or parsley or grated cheese during cooking.

BOILED EGGS

Fill a pan three quarters full with cold water. Add the egg gently—it is less likely to crack if it is at room temperature, rather than straight from the fridge. If it does crack and the white starts to seep out, add a tablespoon of vinegar or salt to the water. Place over medium heat and slowly bring to the boil. Do not start timing until the water comes to the boil. Reduce the heat and simmer for 3 minutes for soft-boiled eggs and 10 minutes for hard-boiled. Remove the egg from the water with a slotted spoon.

FRIED EGGS

Heat 20 g (3/4 oz) butter or 1 tablespoon oil in a frying pan until sizzling, or use the hot fat from frying bacon. Gently break up to 4 eggs into the pan (break in a cup first and slide into the pan). For eggs 'sunny-side up', cook until the white has set and the yolk is still runny. If you want, turn the eggs over with a spatula when the white is set, but lift them out of the pan after a few seconds so the yolk is just sealed on the outside, not hard all the way through. If you prefer your eggs set, turn them over when the white is set, and cook until the egg is cooked through. Remove from the pan with the spatula.

EGGS are ideal breakfast food—quick and easy to prepare but packed full of nutrition.

POACHED EGGS

Fill a frying pan three-quarters full with cold water and add a couple of tablespoons of white vinegar (this stops the egg white spreading in the water). Bring to a gentle boil. Gently break an egg into the water (or into a cup and then slide into the water). Reduce the heat so that the water is barely simmering. Cook for 1–2 minutes, or until just set. Remove from the water with a slotted spoon, draining well.

NOTE: Use the freshest eggs you can find for poaching—the white will hold together better.

VARIATION: Eggs Benedict is a popular brunch dish. Serve poached eggs on toasted English muffins with a couple of slices of ham. Top with hollandaise sauce (see page 146). For Eggs Florentine, use cooked chopped spinach in place of the ham.

OMELETTE

Preparation: 5 minutes
Cooking: 2 minutes
Serves 1–2

3 eggs
30 g (1 oz) butter

1 Put the eggs in a bowl with 2 tablespoons water and some salt and pepper. Whisk together well.
2 Heat the butter in a small non-stick frying pan over high heat. When the butter is foaming, reduce the heat and add the egg mixture all at once. Swirl with a fork several times.
3 Cook until the eggs are almost set, tilting the pan and lifting the edge of the omelette occasionally to allow the uncooked egg to flow underneath.
4 Using an egg slice, fold the omelette in half in the pan. Flip it over onto a warm serving plate and serve immediately.

VARIATION: Sprinkle the omelette with shredded ham, bacon, fried mushrooms or freshly grated Gruyère cheese before folding.

HERB OMELETTE

Preparation: 10 minutes
Cooking: 5 minutes
Serves 2

4 eggs
2 tablespoons chopped fresh parsley
2 tablespoons chopped fresh chives
30 g (1 oz) butter
¹/₃ cup (40 g/1 ¹/₄ oz) grated Cheddar

1 Break the eggs into a large bowl and whisk with a fork. Add 2 tablespoons of water and the parsley and chives. Season well.
2 Heat the butter in a small non-stick frying pan over high heat. When the butter is foaming, reduce the heat and add the omelette mixture all at once. Swirl with a fork several times.
3 While the mixture is cooking, tilt the pan and lift the edge of the omelette occasionally to allow the uncooked egg to flow underneath. When the mixture is half cooked, sprinkle with the grated cheese, then leave to cook a little more (the base should be golden brown and the inside nearly set). Using an egg slice, fold the omelette in half in the pan. Flip it over onto a warm serving plate and serve immediately.

An OMELETTE with fresh herbs makes a lovely light brunch.

For a weekend brunch a PANCAKE STACK is hard to beat.

PANCAKE STACK

Preparation: 5 minutes +
20 minutes resting
Cooking: 20 minutes
Serves 4

1 1/2 cups (185 g/6 oz)
  self-raising flour
1 teaspoon baking
  powder
2 tablespoons caster
  sugar
2 eggs, lightly beaten
1 cup (250 ml/8 fl oz)
  milk
60 g (2 oz) butter,
  melted
100 g (3 1/2 oz) butter
maple syrup, to serve

1 Sift the flour, baking powder, sugar and a pinch of salt into a bowl and make a well in the centre. Mix the eggs, milk and melted butter in a jug and pour into the well all at once, whisking to form a smooth batter. Cover the bowl with plastic wrap and set the batter aside to rest for 20 minutes. You could also mix the batter in a food processor.
2 Heat a frying pan and brush lightly with melted butter or oil. Pour 1/4 cup (60 ml/2 fl oz) batter into the pan and swirl gently to make a pancake about 10 cm (4 inches) in

diameter. Cook over low heat for 1 minute, or until the underside is golden.
3 Turn the pancake over with a spatula and cook the other side very quickly, about 10 seconds. Transfer to a plate and keep warm while cooking the remaining batter. Whip the butter with a wooden spoon or electric beaters. Serve the pancakes stacked, warm or cold, with whipped butter and maple syrup.

VARIATION: For blueberry pancakes, add 1 cup (155 g/5 oz) of blueberries to the batter.

SWISS MUESLI

Preparation: 10 minutes
Cooking: Nil
Serves 2

1 apple, cored
$^{1}/_{2}$ cup (125 g/4 oz)
   thick plain yoghurt
2 tablespoons chopped
   almonds or hazelnuts
1 cup (100 g/3 $^{1}/_{2}$ oz)
   rolled oats

1 Grate the apple, including the skin. Mix well with the yoghurt, nuts and oats. Serve immediately. Delicious with fresh or canned fruit.

TOASTED MUESLI

Preparation: 20 minutes
Cooking: 50 minutes
Serves 10–12

3 cups (300 g/10 oz)
   rolled oats
$^{1}/_{3}$ cup (30 g/1 oz)
   desiccated coconut
$^{1}/_{3}$ cup (30 g/1 oz) wheat
   germ
2 tablespoons sunflower
   seeds
2 tablespoons sesame
   seeds
$^{1}/_{3}$ cup (50 g/1 $^{3}/_{4}$ oz)
   chopped almonds
50 g (1 $^{3}/_{4}$ oz) butter
2 tablespoons oil
3 tablespoons honey
$^{1}/_{3}$ cup (60 g/2 oz)
   chopped dried apricots
$^{1}/_{3}$ cup (30 g/1 oz)
   chopped dried apples
$^{1}/_{2}$ cup (60 g/2 oz)
   sultanas

1 Preheat the oven to moderate 180°C (350°F/ Gas 4). Mix the oats, coconut, wheat germ, seeds and almonds in a baking dish.
2 Put the butter, oil and honey in a pan and stir over low heat until melted and warmed through.
3 Pour into the baking dish and stir to coat the dry ingredients. Bake for 45 minutes, stirring well every 10 minutes.
4 Leave until cold, then stir in the fruit. Keep in an airtight container for up to 4 weeks.

SWISS MUESLI.

TOASTED MUESLI.

Home-made MUESLI and TOASTED GRAPEFRUIT make a wholesome and delicious breakfast.

MUESLI

Preparation: 15 minutes
Cooking: Nil
Serves 8

2 cups (200 g/6¹/₂ oz)
  rolled oats
2 tablespoons wheat
  germ
¹/₄ cup (20 g/³/₄ oz) bran
¹/₂ cup (90 g/3 oz) dried
  apricots, chopped
¹/₂ cup (35 g/1¹/₄ oz)
  dried apple, chopped
¹/₃ cup (40 g/1¹/₄ oz)
  sultanas
¹/₂ cup (60 g/2 oz)
  slivered almonds

1 Combine all the
ingredients in a bowl and
mix well. Serve with milk.
Keep in an airtight
container for up to
4 weeks. Muesli is
delicious served with fresh
fruit, thick yoghurt and a
drizzle of honey.

VARIATIONS: For a
lighter muesli, use puffed
corn or puffed rice instead
of rolled oats. Also,
experiment with your
choice of nuts: try
replacing the almonds
with brazil nuts, hazelnuts
or pecans. You can buy a
packet of dried fruit salad
and chop the fruit to use
instead of the apricot,
apple and sultanas.

TOASTED GRAPEFRUIT

Preparation: 2 minutes
Cooking: 2 minutes
Serves 2

1 grapefruit
2 tablespoons sugar

1 Cut the grapefruit in
half. Place cut-side-up on
a baking tray and sprinkle
a tablespoon of sugar over
each half. Grill under
moderate heat until the
sugar melts and bubbles.

HOME-MADE YOGHURT

Preparation: 20 minutes +
    12 hours standing/chilling
Cooking: 5 minutes
Makes about 600 ml (20 fl oz)

2 cups (500 ml/16 fl oz)
    milk
2¹/₂ tablespoons milk
    powder
2 tablespoons plain
    yoghurt

1 Combine 2 tablespoons of the milk with the milk powder to form a smooth paste. Add the remaining milk, whisking to ensure the mixture is free of lumps. Transfer to a medium pan and heat almost to boiling point.
2 Pour the mixture into a large casserole dish and cool until it is lukewarm. Blend 3 tablespoons of the lukewarm milk with the plain yoghurt, then gently stir it back into the remaining lukewarm milk. Cover with the lid of the casserole dish or foil.
3 Wrap the dish in thick towels or a blanket. Leave undisturbed in a warm place for 6–8 hours, or until thickened. Chill for at least 4 hours before using. Do not keep the yoghurt for more than 1 week—it becomes very acidic if it is stored for too long.

HINT: For a firmer consistency, wrap the yoghurt in a piece of muslin and hang over a bowl in the fridge overnight. Keep ¹/₄ cup (60 g/2 oz) of your yoghurt in a sealed jar in the refrigerator and use this as the starter for your next batch of yoghurt. Use within 3–4 days or the yoghurt will become acidic. Fruits and nuts can be added to the yoghurt just before serving.

BANANA SMOOTHIE

Preparation: 5 minutes
Cooking: Nil
Serves 2

2 bananas
¹/₄ cup (60 g/2 oz) plain
    yoghurt
1 tablespoon honey
2 tablespoons wheat
    germ
2 cups (500 ml/16 fl oz)
    milk
ground nutmeg, to taste

1 Put the bananas in a blender or food processor. Add the yoghurt, honey, wheat germ, milk and nutmeg.
2 Process or blend until smooth. Taste before serving and add more honey if you like.

VARIATION: Use other fresh fruit or drained canned fruit—berries are delicious. Fruit-flavoured yoghurt will add more flavour to your smoothie. Soy milk is a delicious, healthy alternative.

BREAKFAST SHAKE

Preparation: 10 minutes
Cooking: Nil
Serves 2

150 g (5 oz) fruit
    (mango, strawberries,
    blueberries, banana,
    passionfruit, peach)
1 cup (250 ml/8 fl oz)
    milk
2 teaspoons wheat germ
1 tablespoon honey
¹/₄ cup (60 g/2 oz)
    vanilla yoghurt
1 egg, optional
1 tablespoon malt
    powder

1 Put all the ingredients in a blender and blend for 30 seconds to 1 minute, or until well combined. Pour into chilled glasses and serve.

Clockwise from top:
BREAKFAST SHAKE,
HOME-MADE YOGHURT
and a BANANA SMOOTHIE.

:

Dip the bread in eggy milk and fry, for FRENCH TOAST.

3 Transfer the cooked French toast to a warm plate and cover with foil. Add more butter to the pan as necessary and cook the remaining bread. Serve sprinkled with cinnamon and sugar. Also good with maple syrup, or lemon juice and sugar.

FRENCH TOAST

Preparation: 10 minutes
Cooking: 10 minutes
Serves ?

2 eggs
1 cup (250 ml/8 fl oz) milk
1/2 teaspoon vanilla essence
40 g (1 1/4 oz) butter
4 thick slices of day-old bread, halved diagonally
cinnamon and sugar, to serve

1 Break the eggs into a wide, shallow dish and add the milk and vanilla essence. Whisk well.
2 Melt half the butter in a frying pan. When the butter begins to foam, quickly dip both sides of the bread into the egg mixture, letting the excess run off, then fry in the butter for 1–2 minutes, or until the underside is golden. Turn the bread

HASH BROWNS

Preparation: 10 minutes
Cooking: 20 minutes
Serves 4

2 large potatoes, halved
oil, for shallow-frying

1 Add the potato to a pan of boiling water. Return to the boil, then boil for 10 minutes, or until the potato is just tender when pierced with a knife.

Serve HASH BROWNS on their own, or with bacon and egg.

2 Drain the potatoes, and leave until cool enough to handle. Grate the potato and place in a bowl. Season with salt and pepper, and mix through.
3 Shape the grated potato roughly into patties about 10 cm (4 inches) round. The starchiness of the potato will hold the patties together.
4 Pour enough oil into a frying pan to cover the base. Heat up the oil and cook the patties over medium heat for 2–3 minutes on each side, or until golden and crispy. Drain on paper towels.

Worcestershire sauce adds tang to LAMB'S FRY AND BACON.

LAMB'S FRY AND BACON

Preparation: 20 minutes
Cooking: 15 minutes
Serves 4

500 g (1 lb) **lamb's liver ('lamb's fry')**
plain flour, to dust
30 g (1 oz) **butter**
1 tablespoon **oil**
2 **onions, sliced**
4 **rashers bacon, chopped**
1 1/2 **cups (375 ml/ 12 fl oz) chicken stock**
1 teaspoon **Worcestershire sauce**

1 Peel off and discard the outer membrane from the lamb's fry. Cut the lamb's fry into 1 cm (1/2 inch) slices. Put some of the flour in a shallow bowl and season with salt and pepper. Dust the lamb's fry with the seasoned flour and shake off the excess flour, reserving 2 tablespoons.
2 Heat the butter and oil in a frying pan and cook the onion over medium heat for 3 minutes, or until golden. Remove the onion from the pan and set aside.
3 Add the bacon to the pan and cook over medium heat until brown. Remove from the pan and set aside.
4 Add the lamb's fry to the pan and cook over high heat for 1 minute on each side, or until lightly browned. Return the onion to the pan. Blend the chicken stock, Worcestershire sauce and reserved flour in a jug. Pour into the pan and stir until the mixture boils and thickens. Reduce the heat to low and simmer for 3 minutes, or until the lamb's fry is tender. Stir in the cooked bacon. Serve immediately with toast.

NOTE: Lamb's fry should be pink in the centre when cooked. Do not be tempted to overcook it or it will become tough.

The dried fruits in the COMPOTE are simmered until plump.

CITRUS SUMMER SALAD

Preparation: 15 minutes
Cooking: 5 minutes
Serves 4–6

3 ruby grapefruits
3 large oranges
1 tablespoon caster sugar
1 cinnamon stick
3 tablespoons whole mint leaves

1 Peel and remove the pith from the grapefruit and oranges. Carefully cut out the segments and mix together in a bowl.
2 Put the sugar, cinnamon stick and mint in a small pan with 3 tablespoons water and stir over low heat until the sugar has dissolved.
3 Remove the cinnamon stick and mint, and drizzle the syrup over the fruit. If you are serving this for a special occasion, garnish with fresh mint leaves.

VARIATION: Another good combination for a citrus fruit salad is mandarines, tangelos and pomelos when they are in season.
STORAGE: This salad can be kept in the refrigerator for up to 2 days and the flavour will actually improve as it develops.

DRIED FRUIT COMPOTE

Preparation: 10 minutes
Cooking: 15 minutes
Serves 4

400 g (13 oz) dried fruit salad (dried peaches, prunes, pears, apricots, apple and nectarines)
1 3/4 cups (440 ml/ 14 fl oz) orange juice
1 tablespoon soft brown sugar
1–2 star anise
1 vanilla bean, halved lengthways
yoghurt or crème fraîche, to serve

1 Put the dried fruit salad in a pan. Add the orange juice, sugar, star anise and vanilla bean.
2 Bring slowly to the boil, then reduce the heat, cover and leave to simmer, stirring occasionally, for 15 minutes, or until the fruit is plump and juicy.
3 Discard the star anise and vanilla bean. Serve the fruit drizzled with the cooking syrup and topped with the yoghurt or crème fraîche.

VARIATION: Try flavouring with a cinnamon stick and 2 cloves instead of the star anise and vanilla bean.

Use ruby grapefruit for a colourful CITRUS SUMMER SALAD.

PORRIDGE can be served with sugar and plain yoghurt.

PORRIDGE

Preparation: 5 minutes
Cooking: 10 minutes
Serves 2

1 cup (100 g/3 ¹/₂ oz)
   rolled oats
¹/₂ cup (125 ml/4 fl oz)
   milk
soft brown sugar, plain
   yoghurt, cream or extra
   milk, to serve

1 Mix the oats with
1 ¹/₂ cups (375 ml/12 fl oz)
cold water in a small
heavy-based pan. Stir in
the milk and bring to
the boil.
2 Cook the oats for about
7 minutes, stirring
constantly until thick and
creamy. Serve
immediately with soft
brown sugar, yoghurt,
cream or extra milk.

VARIATIONS. Stir ¹/₄ cup
(30 g/1 oz) of sultanas
into the mixture for the
last 3 minutes of cooking.
Serve the porridge with
stewed apple or
dried fruit compote
(see opposite).
For a quick stove-top
porridge, replace the
rolled oats with 1-minute
oats (these have been
precooked). Cook for
1 minute, stirring
constantly until thick.

OAT AND DATE MUFFINS

Preparation: 15 minutes
Cooking: 20 minutes
Makes 12

1 cup (125 g/4 oz) self-raising flour
1 cup (150 g/5 oz) wholemeal self-raising flour
1/2 teaspoon bicarbonate of soda
1 cup (100 g/3 1/2 oz) quick rolled oats
1/4 cup (45 g/1 1/2 oz) soft brown sugar
1 cup (185 g/6 oz) chopped pitted dates
1 egg, lightly beaten
2 tablespoons vegetable oil
1/4 cup (90 g/3 oz) golden syrup
1 1/4 cups (315 ml/ 10 fl oz) milk

1 Preheat the oven to moderately hot 200°C (400°F/Gas 6). Lightly grease twelve 1/2-cup (125 ml/4 fl oz) muffin holes. Sift the flour and bicarbonate of soda into a bowl and add the husks.
2 Stir in the rolled oats, brown sugar and dates. Make a well in the centre.
3 Combine the egg, oil, golden syrup and milk in a jug. Pour the liquid all at once into the dry ingredients and stir until just combined. Do not overmix—the dough should be lumpy.
4 Fill the muffin holes three-quarters full and bake for 20 minutes, or until well risen and golden brown. Cool in the tin for 5 minutes before transferring to a wire rack.

WHOLEMEAL MUFFINS

Preparation: 20 minutes
Cooking: 20 minutes
Makes 12

2 1/2 cups (375 g/12 oz) wholemeal self-raising flour
1/3 cup (75 g/2 1/2 oz) raw sugar
2 eggs, lightly beaten
75 g (2 1/2 oz) butter, melted
1 1/4 cups (315 ml/ 10 fl oz) buttermilk

1 Preheat the oven to hot 210°C (415°F/Gas 6–7). Lightly grease twelve 1/2-cup (125 ml/4 fl oz) muffin holes. Sift the flour into a large bowl, return the husks and stir in the sugar. Make a well.
2 Stir the combined egg, butter and buttermilk into the well. Don't overmix— the dough will be lumpy.
3 Spoon into the tin and bake for 15–20 minutes, or until golden brown. Transfer to a rack to cool.

CORNMEAL BREADS

Preparation: 15 minutes
Cooking: 25 minutes
Makes 12

2 cups (250 g/8 oz) plain flour
1 teaspoon salt
3 teaspooons baking powder
1 cup (150 g/5 oz) fine cornmeal
1 cup (125 g/4 oz) grated Cheddar
2 eggs, lightly beaten
90 g (3 oz) butter, melted
1 cup (250 ml/8 fl oz) milk

1 Preheat the oven to hot 210°C (415°F/Gas 6–7). Lightly grease twelve 1/2-cup (125 ml/4 fl oz) muffin holes. Sift the flour, salt and baking powder into a large bowl. Stir in the cornmeal and cheese and make a well.
2 Pour the combined egg, butter and milk into the well. Stir to just combine. Don't overmix—the dough should be lumpy.
3 Spoon into the tin and bake for 20–25 minutes, or until golden brown. Cool on a wire rack.

From the top: CORNMEAL BREADS; WHOLEMEAL MUFFINS; OAT AND DATE MUFFINS.

SOUPS

There are few more simple or delicious ways to prepare a meal than to throw some fresh seasonal ingredients into a saucepan with a handful of herbs and a cupful or two of stock or wine, and then leave it all to simmer lazily until the aroma becomes irresistible. There are no difficult techniques for making soups so they are an enjoyable part of every cook's repertoire.

SPRING VEGETABLE SOUP

Preparation: 30 minutes + overnight soaking
Cooking: 1 1/4 hours
Serves 8

1/2 cup (100 g/3 1/2 oz) pinto beans (see Note)
2 teaspoons olive oil
2 onions, finely chopped
2 cloves garlic, finely chopped
10 cups (2.5 litres) vegetable stock
2 celery sticks, finely chopped
2 carrots
2 potatoes
150 g (5 oz) green beans
2 zucchini
100 g (3 1/2 oz) shelled peas (see Hint)
2 tablespoons chopped fresh parsley

1 Soak the pinto beans in plenty of cold water overnight, then drain.
2 Heat the oil in a large pan, add the onion and cook over low heat until soft and translucent. Add the garlic and cook for 1 minute. Add the pinto beans, stock and celery and bring to the boil. Reduce the heat to low and simmer, covered, for 45 minutes, or until the beans are almost cooked.
3 Finely chop the carrots, potatoes, green beans and zucchini and add to the pan. Simmer gently for 15 minutes, or until the vegetables are almost cooked but still a little firm. Stir in the peas and simmer for a further 10 minutes. Season well and stir through the chopped parsley.

NOTE: If you can't find pinto beans, use borlotti beans or the smaller haricot beans.
HINT: If fresh peas aren't available, use frozen peas; add them to the soup during the last 5 minutes of cooking.

Always season soups (and also stews) at the end of the cooking time. As the liquid reduces, the flavours become stronger and you won't need as much salt. If you find you have overseasoned, simmer a slice of bread in the soup for 5 minutes: you will find it soaks up the excess salt.

SPRING VEGETABLE SOUP makes a hearty main meal when served with fresh bread.

If you don't have macaroni, use any small pasta variety for MINESTRONE.

MINESTRONE

Preparation: 30 minutes +
overnight soaking
Cooking: 2³/₄ hours
Serves 6–8

1 ¹/₄ cups (250 g/8 oz)
  dried borlotti beans
2 tablespoons oil
2 onions, chopped
2 cloves garlic, crushed
¹/₂ cup (80 g/2³/₄ oz)
  chopped bacon pieces
400 g (13 oz) can peeled
  chopped Italian
  tomatoes
¹/₄ cup (15 g/¹/₂ oz)
  chopped fresh parsley
9 cups (2.25 litres) beef
  or vegetable stock
1 carrot, chopped
1 swede, diced
2 potatoes, diced

¹/₄ cup (60 g/2 oz)
  tomato paste
2 zucchini, sliced
¹/₂ cup (90 g/3 oz) peas
¹/₂ cup (90 g/3 oz) small
  macaroni
Parmesan and pesto (see
  page 180), to serve

1 Soak the borlotti beans
in water overnight and
drain. Add to a pan of
boiling water, simmer for
15 minutes, or until
tender, and drain. Heat
the oil in a large heavy-
based pan and cook the
onion, garlic and bacon
pieces, stirring, until the
onion is soft and the
bacon golden.
2 Add the tomato, parsley,
borlotti beans and stock.
Simmer, covered, over low
heat for 2 hours. Add the

carrot, swede, potato and
tomato paste, cover and
simmer for 15–20 minutes.
3 When you are nearly
ready to serve, add the
zucchini, peas and pasta.
Cover and simmer for
10–15 minutes, or until
the vegetables and
macaroni are tender.
Season to taste and serve
topped with grated
Parmesan cheese and a
little pesto.

HINT: The macaroni can
become soggy if left to sit
around in the soup before
serving. If you prefer, it
can be cooked separately
in boiling water and
added to the soup just
before serving. If you're
short on time, use canned
beans (drained well).

CHICKEN NOODLE SOUP

Preparation: 15 minutes +
1 hour refrigeration
Cooking: 1 hour 20 minutes
Serves 4–6

1.25 kg (2½ lb) chicken
  wings
2 celery sticks, chopped
1 carrot, chopped
1 onion, chopped
1 bay leaf
1 sprig fresh thyme
4 fresh parsley stalks
45 g (1½ oz) dried fine
  egg noodles, lightly
  crushed
250 g (8 oz) chicken
  breast fillets, diced
2 tablespoons chopped
  fresh parsley
chopped chives, to serve

1 To make the chicken stock, rinse the chicken wings and place in a large pan with the celery, carrot, onion, bay leaf, thyme, parsley stalks, 1 teaspoon salt and 8 cups (2 litres) of water. Bring to the boil slowly, skimming the surface as required to remove any froth. Simmer, covered, for 1 hour. Cool slightly, then strain the liquid, discarding the chicken and vegetables.

2 Leave the stock until cold, then cover and refrigerate for at least 1 hour, or until fat forms on the surface and can be spooned off.

3 Transfer the stock to a large pan and bring to the boil. Add the noodles, return to the boil and simmer for 8 minutes, or until tender. Add the chicken and parsley and simmer for a further 4–5 minutes, or until the chicken is cooked. Serve topped with the chives.

Lightly crush the noodles for CHICKEN NOODLE SOUP so they are in manageable lengths.

69

CHICKEN AND VEGETABLE SOUP

Preparation: 1 hour + cooling
Cooking: 1½ hours
Serves 6

1.5 kg (3 lb) chicken
2 carrots, roughly chopped
2 celery sticks, roughly chopped
1 onion, quartered
4 sprigs fresh parsley
2 bay leaves
2 teaspoons salt
4 black peppercorns
50 g (1¾ oz) butter
2 tablespoons plain flour
2 potatoes, chopped

250 g (8 oz) butternut pumpkin, cut into bite-sized pieces
2 carrots, extra, cut into matchsticks
1 leek, cut into matchsticks
3 celery sticks, extra, cut into matchsticks
100 g (3¼ oz) green beans, chopped
200 g (6½ oz) broccoli, cut into small florets
100 g (3¼ oz) sugar snap peas, trimmed
50 g (1¾ oz) English spinach, shredded
½ cup (125 ml/4 fl oz) cream
¼ cup (15 g/½ oz) chopped fresh parsley

1 Place the chicken in a large pan with the carrot, celery, onion, parsley, bay leaves, salt and peppercorns. Add 3 litres of water. Bring to the boil, then reduce the heat and simmer for 1 hour, skimming the surface as required. Allow to cool for at least 30 minutes. Remove the chicken and leave until cool enough to handle. Strain and reserve the liquid.
2 Remove the chicken skin and shred the chicken meat.
3 Heat the butter in a large pan over medium heat and, when foaming, add the flour. Cook,

Making chicken stock beforehand gives this CHICKEN AND VEGETABLE SOUP great flavour.

stirring, for 1 minute. Remove from the heat and gradually stir in the reserved liquid. Return to the heat and bring to the boil, stirring constantly. Add the potato, pumpkin and extra carrot, and simmer for 7 minutes. Add the leek, extra celery and beans, and simmer for 5 minutes. Finally, add the broccoli and sugar snap peas and cook for 3 minutes.

4 Just before serving, add the chicken meat, spinach, cream and parsley. Reheat gently and keep stirring until the spinach has wilted. Season with plenty of salt and freshly ground black pepper and serve immediately.

HINT: Do not overcook the vegetables—they should be tender but not soggy.

NOTE: The chicken stock (up to the end of Step 1) can be made a day in advance and kept, covered, in the refrigerator. This can, in fact, be beneficial—before reheating the stock, spoon off the fat which will have formed on the surface.

Serve FRENCH ONION SOUP with toasted cheese croûtes.

FRENCH ONION SOUP

Preparation: 15 minutes
Cooking: 1 1/2 hours
Serves 6

60 g (2 oz) butter
6 onions (about 1 kg), sliced into thin rings
1 teaspoon sugar
1/4 cup (30 g/1 oz) plain flour
9 cups (2.25 litres) beef stock
1 stick French bread, sliced
1/2 cup (65 g/2 1/4 oz) grated Gruyère cheese

1 Heat the butter in a large pan, add the onion and cook slowly over low heat for about 20 minutes, or until very tender and a deep golden brown (don't try to rush this stage).

2 Add the sugar and flour and cook, stirring, for 1–2 minutes, or until just starting to turn golden. Remove from the heat.

3 Stir in the stock gradually, return to the heat and stir until the soup boils and thickens. Reduce the heat and simmer, partially covered, over low heat for 1 hour. Season to taste.

4 Toast the bread on both sides until golden. Top with cheese and grill to melt. Serve the cheese croûtes on top of the soup.

A CHOWDER is a traditional thick soup containing potatoes.

SMOKED HADDOCK CHOWDER

Preparation: 20 minutes
Cooking: 35 minutes
Serves 4

500 g (1 lb) smoked haddock
1 potato, diced
1 celery stick, diced
1 onion, finely chopped
50 g (1 ³/₄ oz) butter
1 rasher bacon, rind removed, diced
2 tablespoons plain flour
¹/₂ teaspoon mustard powder
¹/₂ teaspoon Worcestershire sauce
1 cup (250 ml/8 fl oz) milk
¹/₂ cup (15 g/¹/₂ oz) chopped fresh parsley
¹/₄ cup (60 ml/2 fl oz) cream

1 To make the fish stock, put the fish in a frying pan, cover with water and bring to the boil. Reduce the heat and simmer for 8 minutes, or until the fish flakes easily when tested with a knife. Drain the fish, reserving the stock. Remove any bones and skin and flake the fish.
2 Put the potato, celery and onion in a pan and add enough of the fish stock to cover the vegetables (add water if necessary). Bring to the boil, reduce the heat and simmer for 8 minutes, or until the vegetables are all tender.
3 Melt the butter in a large pan, and cook the bacon, stirring, for 3 minutes. Stir in the flour, mustard and Worcestershire sauce. Cook for 1 minute, then remove from the heat and gradually pour in the milk, stirring continuously until smooth. Return to the heat and stir for 5 minutes, or until the mixture comes to the boil and thickens. Stir in the vegetables in their stock, then add the parsley and fish. Simmer the chowder over low heat for 5 minutes, or until heated through. Check the seasoning (smoked haddock can be quite salty so you may not need to add any more) and stir in the cream.

VARIATION: To make clam chowder, simply use 500 g (1 lb) fresh clams instead of the smoked haddock. Cook as for the smoked haddock chowder, but discard any clams which do not open when cooked. Alternatively, you can use 500 g (1 lb) drained canned clams.

Ask your butcher to chop the oxtails for OXTAIL SOUP.

OXTAIL SOUP

Preparation: 35 minutes +
2 hours refrigeration
Cooking: 2½ hours
Serves 4

2 oxtails, chopped (your
butcher will do this)
2 tablespoons oil
3 onions, chopped
4 cloves garlic, chopped
1 tablespoon plain flour
4 cups (1 litre) beef stock
2 bay leaves, torn in half
2 tablespoons tomato
paste
2 teaspoons
Worcestershire sauce

4 potatoes, chopped
2 parsnips, chopped
2 carrots, chopped
3 tomatoes, chopped
2 tablespoons chopped
fresh parsley

1 Cut the excess fat from
the oxtail. Heat the oil in
a heavy-based pan and
brown the oxtail in
batches. Return all the
meat to the pan. Add the
onion and garlic and cook
until just softened. Add
the flour and cook,
stirring, for 1 minute. Mix
in half the stock and bring
to the boil, stirring.
Remove from the heat and

refrigerate for 2 hours, or
until the fat can be
spooned from the surface.
2 Add the remaining
stock, 1 litre of water, the
bay leaves, tomato paste,
Worcestershire sauce and
salt and pepper. Bring to
the boil, reduce the heat
to low and simmer,
covered, for 2 hours,
stirring occasionally.
3 Add the potato, parsnip
and carrot and simmer for
10 minutes, or until
tender. Remove the bay
leaves before serving.
Serve with the chopped
tomato and parsley
as a garnish.

Fresh ripe tomatoes will give the best flavour to CREAM OF TOMATO SOUP.

CREAM OF TOMATO SOUP

Preparation: 25 minutes
Cooking: 30 minutes
Serves 4

1.25 kg (2¹/₂ lb) ripe
   tomatoes
1 tablespoon oil
1 onion, chopped
1¹/₂ cups (375 ml/
   12 fl oz) chicken stock
2 tablespoons tomato
   paste
1 teaspoon sugar
1 cup (250 ml/8 fl oz)
   cream

1 To peel the tomatoes, score a cross in the base of each tomato with a sharp knife. Put the tomatoes in a bowl, cover with boiling water and leave for 1 minute. Transfer them to a bowl of cold water and peel away the skin from the cross. Cut the tomatoes in half around their equators and scoop out the seeds with a teaspoon. Roughly chop the flesh.
2 Heat the oil in a large pan and cook the onion over moderate heat for 3 minutes, or until soft.

Add the tomato and cook, stirring occasionally, for 5 minutes, or until very soft. Stir in the stock, bring to the boil, reduce the heat and simmer for 10 minutes.
3 Cool slightly, then transfer to a food processor or blender. Process in batches until smooth, then return to the pan. Add the tomato paste and sugar and bring to the boil, stirring. Reduce the heat and stir in the cream. Season and serve with a swirl of cream and a little chopped parsley.

VARIATION: If good fresh tomatoes are not available, use tinned. Cook the onion and garlic as above, then add 3 undrained 400 g (13 oz) cans of tomatoes to the pan with 2 cups (500 ml/16 fl oz) stock, 1 tablespoon tomato paste and 2 teaspoons soft brown sugar. Partially cover the pan and simmer for 20 minutes. Purée before adding the cream.
NOTE: Shop-bought stock can be very salty—if you are using it for soups you may prefer to use half stock, half water.

PEA AND HAM SOUP

Preparation: 20 minutes +
4–8 hours soaking
Cooking: 2½ hours
Serves 4–6

2 cups (440 g/14 oz) green split peas
750 g (1½ lb) ham bones
1 celery stick, including leaves, chopped
1 carrot, chopped
1 onion, chopped
3 leeks, sliced
1 potato, chopped

1 Place the split peas in a large bowl, cover with water and leave to soak for 4–8 hours. Drain.

2 Put the ham bones, split peas, celery, carrot and onion in a large pan with 2.5 litres of water. Bring to the boil, then reduce the heat and simmer, covered, for 2 hours, or until the split peas are very soft.
3 Add the leek and potato and cook for 30 minutes, or until the vegetables are tender and the ham is falling off the bone.
4 Remove the ham bones from the soup; cut off all the meat and finely chop.
5 Transfer the soup to a bowl to cool, then push it through a large wire sieve.

Return the soup to the pan, stir in the chopped ham and reheat the soup to serve.

NOTE: For a chunkier soup, don't push the mixture through a sieve. Alternatively, mash lightly with a potato masher.
HINT: This is a great recipe for using up your ham bones at Christmas. Some ham can be quite salty—soaking the bone in cold water overnight will draw out a lot of the saltiness. Always taste at the end of cooking before adding extra salt.

Soak the split peas before making PEA AND HAM SOUP.

WON TON SOUP

Preparation: 45 minutes +
  30 minutes soaking
Cooking: 20 minutes
Serves 4

4 dried Chinese
  mushrooms
4 spring onions, very
  finely sliced, to garnish
125 g (4 oz) pork and
  veal mince
60 g (2 oz) raw prawn
  meat, finely chopped
3 teaspoons soy sauce
1 teaspoon sesame oil
1 spring onion, chopped
2 teaspoons grated fresh
  ginger
1 tablespoon finely
  chopped water
  chestnuts
24 won ton wrappers
5 cups (1.25 litres)
  chicken stock

1 Place the mushrooms in
a small bowl, cover with
boiling water and leave to
soak for 30 minutes.
Meanwhile, to prepare the
garnish, put the very fine
strips of spring onion in a
bowl of icy cold water
(this makes the strips curl
elegantly).

2 Drain the mushrooms
well, using your hands to
squeeze out the excess
liquid. Remove the stems
and chop the caps finely.
Mix together the
mushrooms, mince, prawn
meat, soy sauce, sesame
oil, chopped spring onion,
ginger, water chestnuts
and a little salt.
3 Working with one won
ton wrapper at a time
(cover the other wrappers
with a damp tea towel),
place a level teaspoon of
the filling in the centre of
each wrapper. Moisten the
edges of the wrapper with
a little water and bring the
sides up to form a pouch.
As you fill the won tons
set them aside on a plate
dusted with flour.
4 Cook the won tons in
batches in a large pan of
rapidly boiling water for
4–5 minutes, then drain.
Bring the stock to the boil
in another pan. Put the
won tons in small bowls,
garnish with the curls of
spring onion and pour in
the hot stock.

NOTE: Won ton
wrappers are available
from Asian food stores
and can be frozen very
successfully.

Garnish your WON TON SOUP with curled strips of spring onion.

For a special occasion serve PUMPKIN SOUP in a hollowed pumpkin shell.

PUMPKIN SOUP

Preparation: 25 minutes
Cooking: 40 minutes
Serves 4

1 kg (2 lb) pumpkin
60 g (2 oz) butter
1 onion, chopped
4 cups (1 litre) chicken
  stock
³/₄ cup (185 ml/6 fl oz)
  cream

1 Peel the pumpkin and chop into chunks. Heat the butter in a large pan, add the onion and cook gently for 15 minutes, or until soft.

2 Add the pumpkin and stock and simmer, covered, for 20 minutes, or until the pumpkin is tender. Allow to cool a little, then process in batches in a food processor or blender until smooth. Return the soup to the pan.

3 Stir in the cream and stir over low heat to heat through. Season with salt and pepper to taste. If you like, swirl in a little more cream to serve

HINT: If you have time, bake your pumpkin and onion, then transfer to a pan, stir in the stock and cream and heat through.

CREAM OF CHICKEN SOUP is simple but enduringly popular.

VICHYSSOISE

Preparation: 20 minutes
Cooking: 25 minutes
Serves 4

60 g (2 oz) butter
2 leeks, chopped
2 large potatoes,
  chopped
3 cups (750 ml/24 fl oz)
  chicken stock
1 cup (250 ml/8 fl oz)
  milk
**sour cream and chives,
  to serve**

1 Heat the butter in a
large pan and cook the
leek for 5 minutes, or
until soft.
2 Add the potato and
stock and simmer for
15 20 minutes, or until

CREAM OF CHICKEN SOUP

Preparation: 15 minutes
Cooking: 20 minutes
Serves 4

60 g (2 oz) butter
1/3 cup (40 g/1 1/4 oz)
  plain flour
2 cups (500 ml/16 fl oz)
  chicken stock
1 cup (250 ml/8 fl oz)
  milk
1 chicken breast fillet,
  finely chopped
1 cup (250 ml/8 fl oz)
  cream
1 celery stick, chopped
fresh parsley, to serve

1 Melt the butter in a
large pan, add the flour
and stir over low heat for
2 minutes, or until lightly
golden. Remove from the
heat and add the stock
gradually, stirring until
smooth. Return to the
heat and stir until it comes
to the boil and thickens.
2 Add the milk, chicken,
cream and celery. Simmer
for 5 minutes, or until the
chicken is tender. Season
and sprinkle with parsley.

VICHYSSOISE can be served warm or chilled.

the potato is tender. Stir in the milk and season with salt and pepper.
3 Let the soup cool a little, then blend in a food processor or blender, in batches, until smooth. Vichyssoise is traditionally served well chilled but if you prefer to serve it hot, return to the pan and reheat gently without boiling. Whether hot or chilled, spoon sour cream on top and sprinkle with chives to serve.

NOTE: Vichyssoise is a classic chilled cream soup which was created at the Ritz-Carlton, New York.

CREAM OF BROCCOLI SOUP

Preparation: 15 minutes
Cooking: 25 minutes
Serves 4

750 g (1 1/2 lb) broccoli
3 cups (750 ml/24 fl oz) chicken stock
pinch of ground nutmeg
1 cup (250 ml/8 fl oz) cream

1 Cut the broccoli stems and florets into chunks. Place in a large pan with 1 cup (250 ml/8 fl oz) of stock, cover and bring to the boil. Reduce the heat to low, cover and simmer for 10 minutes, or until

tender, stirring often.
2 Let the soup cool a little, then blend in batches in a food processor or blender. Return to the pan with the remaining stock. Add the nutmeg and cream and stir over moderate heat until heated through. Before serving, season to taste with salt and freshly ground black pepper.

HINT: If you prefer a chunkier soup, in step 2 transfer a batch of the mixture to a food

processor or blender and process until finely chopped. Add a little of the remaining stock and blend to a purée. Return to a pan. Transfer the remaining broccoli and stock to the processor in batches and process until finely chopped. Return all the soup to the pan, add the nutmeg and cream and heat through. VARIATION: Make creamy cauliflower soup in exactly the same way, simply substituting cauliflower for broccoli.

CREAM OF BROCCOLI SOUP has a fine colour and flavour.

VEGETABLE SOUP

Preparation: 25 minutes +
overnight soaking
Cooking: 1 hour
Serves 6

1 cup (220 g/7 oz) dried
soup mix
2 tablespoons oil
1 large onion, chopped
1 green capsicum,
chopped
2 zucchini, sliced
2 celery sticks, sliced
125 g (4 oz) button
mushrooms, sliced
2 carrots, sliced
1 large potato, chopped
500 g (1 lb) pumpkin,
peeled and chopped
8 cups (2 litres)
vegetable stock

1 Soak the soup mix in
water overnight, then
drain. Heat the oil in a
large heavy-based pan
and cook the onion over
medium heat for
5 minutes, or until soft.
Add the capsicum,
zucchini, celery and
mushrooms and cook for
about 5 minutes.
2 Stir in the carrot, potato
and pumpkin. Pour in the
stock and add the soup
mix. Bring to the boil,
then reduce the heat.
3 Partially cover the soup
with a loose-fitting lid and
simmer for 45 minutes, or
until the vegetables and
soup mix are very soft. If
you prefer a thinner soup
add a little water. Season
with salt and pepper
before serving.

STORING: Vegetable
soup will keep for 2 days
in the fridge or can be
frozen for 1 month.
NOTE: Soup mix is a
mixture of dried barley,
lentils and split peas and
can be bought in packets
at the supermarket.

SEAFOOD LAKSA

Preparation time: 45 minutes
Cooking: 45 minutes
Serves 6

1 kg (2 lb) raw prawns
^{1}/$_2$ cup (125 ml/4 fl oz)
oil
2–6 red chillies, seeded
1 onion, roughly
chopped
3 cloves garlic, halved
2 cm (^{3}/$_4$ inch) piece of
ginger or galangal,
quartered
1 teaspoon ground
turmeric
1 tablespoon ground
coriander
3 stalks lemon grass,
white part only,
chopped
1–2 teaspoons shrimp
paste
2^1/$_2$ cups (600 ml/
20 fl oz) coconut cream
2 teaspoons grated palm
sugar
4 kaffir lime leaves
200 g (6^1/$_2$ oz) packet
fish balls
190 g (6^1/$_2$ oz) packet
fried bean curd pieces

Use the freshest seasonal produce for VEGETABLE SOUP.

LAKSA, a coconut cream-based soup, originated in Singapore.

250 g (8 oz) fresh thin
egg noodles
250 g (8 oz) bean
sprouts
chopped fresh mint and
coriander leaves, to
serve

1 To make the prawn stock, peel and devein the prawns, keeping the shells, heads and tails. Heat 2 tablespoons of the oil in a large, heavy-based pan and add the prawn trimmings. Stir until bright orange, then add 1 litre of water. Bring to the boil, reduce the heat and simmer for 15 minutes. Strain through a fine sieve, discarding the shells. Clean the pan.
2 Put the chillies, onion, garlic, ginger (or galangal), turmeric, coriander, lemon grass and 3 tablespoons of the prawn stock in a food processor and process until finely chopped.
3 Heat the remaining oil in the clean pan and add the chilli mixture and shrimp paste. Stir over medium heat for 3 minutes, or until fragrant. Pour in the remaining stock and simmer for 10 minutes. Add the coconut cream, palm sugar, lime leaves and 2 teaspoons of salt. Simmer for 5 minutes.
4 Add the prawns and simmer for 2 minutes, or until just pink. Remove and set aside. Add the fish balls and bean curd and simmer gently until just heated through.
5 Bring a pan of water to the boil and cook the noodles for 2 minutes. Drain and divide among bowls. Top with the bean sprouts and prawns and pour the soup over the top. Sprinkle with the chopped mint and coriander leaves to serve.

VARIATIONS: For chicken laksa, replace the seafood with 1 kg (2 lb) chicken thigh fillets, thinly sliced. Use chicken stock instead of prawn stock. Laksa can also be made with fresh or dried rice noodles. Shredded cucumber can be added with the bean sprouts and, for a really fiery finish, garnish with red chilli.

HOT BEEF BORSCHT

Preparation: 30 minutes
Cooking: 2¾ hours
Serves 4

500 g (1 lb) shin of beef,
  cut into large pieces
500 g (1 lb) beetroot
1 onion, finely chopped
1 carrot, cut into short
  strips
1 parsnip, cut into short
  strips
1 cup (60 g/2 oz) finely
  shredded cabbage

1 Put the meat in a large heavy-based pan with 4 cups (1 litre) water and bring slowly to the boil. Reduce the heat, cover and simmer for 1 hour, skimming the surface as required, to remove any froth or scum.

2 Cut away the stems from the beetroot, leaving about 2 cm (1 inch) of the stem above the bulb, and place in a large heavy-based pan with 4 cups (1 litre) water. Bring slowly to the boil, reduce the heat and simmer for 40 minutes, or until tender when pierced with a skewer or sharp knife. Drain, reserving 1 cup (250 ml/8 fl oz) of the liquid. Leave the beetroot to cool, then peel and grate—wear plastic or rubber gloves to prevent staining your hands.

3 Use tongs to remove the meat from the stock. Let the meat cool, then pull from the bones and cut into small cubes. Skim any fat from the stock. Return the meat to the stock and add the onion, carrot, parsnip and grated beetroot. Add the beetroot liquid, bring to the boil, reduce the heat, cover and simmer for 45 minutes. Add more beetroot liquid if you prefer a thinner soup.

4 Add the cabbage, stir and simmer for a further 15 minutes. Add salt and pepper and serve hot. Borscht is delicious with sour cream and chives.

STORAGE TIME: Hot beef borscht can be kept covered and refrigerated for up to 4 days or frozen for up to 1 month.
NOTE: Borscht is a very hearty main meal soup, a traditional favourite in the bitter cold of the Eastern European winters. It is best served as a main meal with rye or black bread.

Serve BORSCHT topped with a dollop of sour cream.

TOM KHA GAI is a traditional Thai soup of chicken in coconut milk.

TOM KHA GAI

Preparation: 20 minutes
Cooking: 20 minutes
Serves 4

5 cm (2 inch) piece fresh
  galangal or 5 slices
  dried (see Note)
6 kaffir lime leaves
1 stem lemon grass,
  white part only,
  quartered
1–2 teaspoons finely
  chopped red chillies
2 cups (500 ml/16 fl oz)
  coconut milk
2 cups (500 ml/16 fl oz)
  chicken stock

3 chicken breast fillets,
  cut into thin strips
¹/4 cup (60 ml/2 fl oz)
  lime juice
2 tablespoons fish sauce
1 teaspoon soft brown
  sugar
¹/4 cup (15 g/¹/2 oz)
  fresh coriander leaves

1 Peel the galangal and
cut it into thin slices. Mix
the galangal, kaffir lime
leaves, lemon grass and
chilli with the coconut
milk and stock in a large
pan. Bring to the boil,
reduce the heat and
simmer for 10 minutes,
stirring occasionally.

2 Add the chicken strips
and simmer for 8 minutes.
Mix in the lime juice, fish
sauce and sugar. Serve
with the coriander leaves
and garnish with a few
coriander sprigs.

NOTE: If you can't find
fresh galangal, use 5 large
slices of dried galangal
instead. Soak in 1 cup
(250 ml/8 fl oz) of boiling
water for 10 minutes.
Drain the galangal and cut
into thin slices. Proceed
with the recipe as above.

CONSOMME is a clear light soup, of beef or chicken.

BEEF CONSOMME

Preparation: 30 minutes +
  overnight refrigeration
Cooking: 5 hours
Serves 4–6

1 kg (2 lb) gravy beef,
  cut into small pieces
500 g (1 lb) beef bones
  with marrow, cut into
  small pieces (ask your
  butcher to do this)
1 leek, finely sliced
2 onions, quartered
2 carrots, chopped
2 sticks celery, chopped
6 black peppercorns
6 whole cloves
3 sprigs fresh thyme
3 sprigs fresh parsley
3 bay leaves
1 egg shell, crumbled
1 egg white, lightly
  beaten
2 tablespoons chopped
  fresh parsley

1 Preheat the oven to
moderate 180°C (350°F/
Gas 4). Put the gravy beef
and bones in a single layer
in a baking dish. Bake
for 45 minutes, or until
just lightly browned,
turning once.

2 Put the meat, bones,
vegetables, peppercorns,
cloves, herbs, bay leaves
and 1 teaspoon of salt in a
large pan. Add 3 litres of
water and slowly bring to
the boil. Reduce the heat
to low, cover and simmer
for 4 hours. Set aside to
cool slightly. Remove the
beef bones and discard.
Ladle the liquid through a
muslin-lined sieve into a
bowl—if you don't have
any muslin, line the sieve
with a clean dry chux
cloth. Discard the
remaining meat and
vegetables.

3 Cover the liquid and
refrigerate for several
hours, or overnight. You
will then be able to spoon
off the fat from the top.
Return to a clean pan with
the egg shell and the
lightly beaten egg white.

4 Slowly heat the stock to
simmering and simmer for
10 minutes. A frothy scum
will form on the surface.
Remove from the heat and
leave for 10 minutes. Skim
the surface and ladle the
stock through a muslin-
lined sieve. Reheat, season
if needed, and serve with
the chopped parsley.

NOTE: The egg shells are
added to clarify the soup.

MULLIGATAWNY

Preparation: 20 minutes
Cooking: 1¼ hours
Serves 6

30 g (1 oz) butter
375 g (12 oz) chicken
  thighs, skin removed
1 large onion, finely
  chopped
1 green apple, peeled,
  cored and finely
  chopped
1 tablespoon curry paste
2 tablespoons plain flour
3 cups (750 ml/24 fl oz)
  chicken stock
3 tablespoons basmati
  rice

1 tablespoon chutney
1 tablespoon lemon juice
3 tablespoons cream

1 Heat the butter in a large heavy-based pan and brown the chicken for 5 minutes. Remove the chicken from the pan. Add the onion, apple and curry paste to the pan. Cook for 5 minutes, or until the onion is soft. Stir in the flour and cook for 2 minutes, then remove from the heat and stir in half the stock until smooth. Return to the heat and stir until the soup boils and thickens.
2 Return the chicken to the pan with the remaining stock. Stir until boiling, then reduce the heat, cover and simmer for 1 hour. Add the rice for the last 15 minutes of cooking (make sure it is tender by the time you finish cooking).
3 Remove the chicken with tongs, bone and dice the meat finely and return to the pan. Add the chutney, lemon juice, cream and seasoning. For a thinner soup, add up to a cup of water.

NOTE: You could use chicken thigh fillets (which have no bones).

MULLIGATAWNY is a curry-flavoured soup of Anglo-Indian origin.

CHICKEN AND CORN CHOWDER

Preparation: 15 minutes
Cooking: 30 minutes
Serves 4

20 g (³/4 oz) butter
5 spring onions, finely
chopped
2 rashers bacon, diced
1 celery stick, finely
chopped
450 g (14 oz) potatoes,
diced
2 cups (500 ml/16 fl oz)
chicken stock
2 cups (350 g/11 oz)
cooked diced chicken
meat (or from a small
barbecued chicken)
1¹/2 cups (375 ml/
12 fl oz) milk
420 g (14 oz) can
creamed corn

CHICKEN AND CORN CHOWDER.

1 Melt the butter in a large pan. Cook the spring onion, bacon and celery over medium heat for 3 minutes, or until cooked but not browned. Add the potato and cook for 2 minutes. Add the chicken stock. Cook for 20 minutes, or until the potato is tender.
2 Add the diced chicken, milk and creamed corn and heat through. Season to taste with black pepper before serving.

CREAM OF ASPARAGUS SOUP

Preparation: 20 minutes
Cooking: 55 minutes
Serves 4

1 kg (2 lb) asparagus
30 g (1 oz) butter
1 onion, finely chopped
4 cups (1 litre) chicken
stock
¹/4 cup (7 g/¹/4 oz) fresh
basil leaves, chopped
1 teaspoon celery salt
1 cup (250 ml/8 fl oz)
cream

Purée the ASPARAGUS SOUP, then add the tender tips.

1 Break off the woody ends from the asparagus by holding each end of the asparagus and bending firmly. The asparagus will snap naturally where the woodiness ends. Cut off the asparagus tips and blanch (see page 38) in boiling water for 1–2 minutes, then refresh in cold water (so they stop cooking and keep their bright colour) and set aside. Chop the remaining asparagus spears into large pieces.
2 Melt the butter in a large pan and cook the onion for 3–4 minutes over low heat, or until soft and golden. Add the asparagus spears and cook for 2 minutes, stirring continuously.
3 Add the stock, basil and celery salt. Bring to the boil, reduce the heat and simmer gently, covered, for 30 minutes.
4 Check that the asparagus is well cooked and soft. If not, simmer for a further 10 minutes. Allow to cool slightly.
5 Process in batches in a food processor or blender until smooth. Sieve into a clean pan. Return to the heat, pour in the cream and gently reheat. Season with salt and white pepper, stir in the asparagus tips and serve immediately.

Use large field mushrooms for a chunky MUSHROOM SOUP.

CREAM OF MUSHROOM SOUP

Preparation: 30 minutes
Cooking: 15 minutes
Serves 4

500 g (1 lb) large field mushrooms
50 g (1 3/4 oz) butter
4 spring onions, finely chopped
3 cloves garlic, chopped
1 teaspoon chopped fresh lemon thyme
2 teaspoons plain flour
4 cups (1 litre) chicken or vegetable stock
1 cup (250 ml/8 fl oz) cream
fresh chives and thyme, to garnish

1 Thinly slice the mushroom caps, discarding the stalks. Melt the butter in a heavy-based pan and cook the spring onion, garlic and lemon thyme, stirring, for 1 minute, or until the garlic is golden. Add the mushrooms and 1/2 teaspoon each of salt and white pepper. Cook for 3–4 minutes, or until the mushrooms start to soften. Add the flour and cook, stirring, for 1 minute.
2 Remove from the heat and add the stock, stirring continuously until smooth. Return to the heat and bring to the boil, stirring. Reduce the heat and simmer gently for 2 minutes, stirring occasionally.
3 Stir the cream into the soup, then reheat gently, stirring. Season with salt and pepper and garnish with the chives and thyme to serve.

MEAT

Many of the most well-known recipes in the world are for meat. Succulent, tender and bursting with flavour, these are dishes that should inspire enthusiasm in every cook.

ROAST BEEF AND YORKSHIRE PUDDINGS

Preparation: 15 minutes + 30 minutes standing
Cooking: 2 hours
Serves 6

2.5 kg (5 lb) roasting beef (rib eye roast, rump, or Scotch fillet)
2 cloves garlic, crushed
2 teaspoons plain flour
2 tablespoons red wine
1 1/4 cups (315 ml/ 10 fl oz) beef stock

Yorkshire puddings
2 cups (250 g/8 oz) plain flour
pinch of salt
4 eggs
400 ml (13 fl oz) milk

1 Preheat the oven to very hot 240°C (475°F/ Gas 9). Rub the outside of the roasting beef with the garlic and some freshly cracked black pepper. Place on a rack in a baking dish and roast for 15 minutes.

2 Meanwhile, to make the Yorkshire puddings, sift the flour and salt into a bowl and make a well in the centre. Add the eggs and begin to whisk them. Gradually pour in the milk as you draw in the flour, whisking to a smooth batter. Pour into a jug, cover and leave for about 30 minutes.

3 Reduce the heat to moderate 180°C (350°F/ Gas 4), and roast the meat: 1 hour for rare beef and 1 1/2 hours for well done. Cover the meat loosely with foil and leave in a warm place for 15 minutes before carving. Increase the oven to hot 220°C (425°F/Gas 7).

4 Pour off all but a tablespoon of the pan juices into a jug. Pour 1 teaspoon of pan juice into each hole of a 12-hole, deep patty pan. (If there aren't enough pan juices, use oil or melted lard.) Heat in the oven for 2–3 minutes, or until lightly smoking. Pour in the pudding batter to three-quarters fill each hole, and bake for 5 minutes. Reduce the oven to moderately hot 200°C (400°F/Gas 6) and bake for 10 minutes, or until the puddings are risen, crisp and golden. While the puddings are baking, make the gravy.

5 Put the baking dish with the 1 tablespoon of pan juices on the stove over low heat. Add the flour and stir well to scrape all the bits from the bottom of the tin. Cook over medium heat, stirring, until the flour is well browned. Combine the wine and stock, and gradually stir into the flour mixture. Cook, stirring, until the gravy boils and thickens. Simmer for 3 minutes, then season to taste and serve with the sliced beef and Yorkshire puddings.

BEEF WELLINGTON

Preparation: 25 minutes
Cooking: 1 hour 35 minutes
Serves 6

1.2 kg (2 lb 7 oz) piece
  beef fillet or rib eye
1 tablespoon oil
125 g (4 oz) pâté
60 g (2 oz) button
  mushrooms, sliced
375 g (12 oz) block puff
  pastry, thawed
1 egg, lightly beaten
1 sheet ready-rolled puff
  pastry, thawed

1 Preheat the oven to hot 210°C (415°F/Gas 6–7). Trim the meat of any excess fat and sinew. Fold the thinner part of the tail end under and tie the meat securely with kitchen string at intervals. **2** Rub the meat with freshly ground black pepper. Heat the oil in a large frying pan. Add the meat and cook over high heat, browning well all over. Remove from the heat and leave to cool. Remove the string. **3** Spread the pâté over the top and sides of the beef.

Cover with the mushrooms, pressing them onto the pâté. Roll the block pastry out on a lightly floured surface to make a rectangle large enough to completely enclose the beef. **4** Place the beef on the pastry, brush the edges with egg, and fold over to enclose the meat completely, brushing the edges of the pastry with the egg to seal and folding in the ends. **5** Put on a greased baking tray with the seam underneath. Cut leaf shapes from the sheet of pastry and use to decorate the Wellington, sticking with the egg. Brush the top of the pastry with the beaten egg. Cut a few slits in the top to allow the steam to escape. Brush the top and sides with egg and cook for 45 minutes for rare, 1 hour for medium or 1¹/₂ hours for well done. Leave in a warm place for 10 minutes before cutting into slices to serve.

NOTE: Cover the beef Wellington loosely with foil if the pastry begins to brown too much.

BEEF WELLINGTON is also known as Boeuf en croûte.

The STROGANOFF was named after a nineteenth century Russian diplomat, Count Paul Stroganoff.

BEEF STROGANOFF

Preparation: 25 minutes
Cooking: 30 minutes
Serves 6

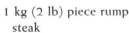

1 kg (2 lb) piece rump
  steak
1/3 cup (40 g/1 1/4 oz)
  plain flour
1/4 teaspoon black pepper
3 tablespoons oil
1 large onion, chopped
500 g (1 lb) baby
  mushrooms
1 tablespoon ground
  sweet paprika
1 tablespoon tomato
  paste
2 teaspoons French
  mustard

1/2 cup (125 ml/4 fl oz)
  dry white wine
1/4 cup (60 ml/2 fl oz)
  chicken stock
3/4 cup (185 g/6 oz) sour
  cream
1 tablespoon finely
  chopped fresh parsley

1 Trim the meat of excess
fat and sinew, and slice
across the grain evenly
into thin strips. Mix
the flour and pepper in a
plastic bag, add the meat
and shake to coat.
Shake off the excess
seasoned flour.
2 Heat 2 tablespoons of
the oil in a heavy-based
pan. Brown the meat
quickly in small batches
over medium-high heat.

Drain on paper towels.
3 Heat the remaining oil
in the pan. Add the onion
and cook over medium
heat for 3 minutes, or
until soft. Add the
mushrooms and cook
stirring, for 5 minutes.
4 Add the paprika, tomato
paste, mustard, wine,
stock and meat to the pan,
and bring to the boil.
Reduce the heat and
simmer for 5 minutes,
stirring occasionally. Add
the sour cream and stir
until just heated
through—do not boil or
the sour cream may split
and look curdled. Sprinkle
with the parsley just
before serving. Serve
with rice.

91

TRADITIONAL CORNED BEEF AND VEGETABLES

Preparation: 25 minutes +
   1 hour soaking
Cooking: 2 hours
Serves 4

1.2 kg (2 lb 7 oz) corned
   silverside (beef)
10 whole cloves
1 onion
8 black peppercorns
2 bay leaves
2 tablespoons soft brown
   sugar
4 carrots
4 potatoes
1/4 large cabbage

Parsley sauce
40 g (1 1/4 oz) butter
2 tablespoons plain flour
2 cups (500 ml/16 fl oz)
   milk
2 tablespoons chopped
   fresh parsley

CORNED BEEF AND VEGETABLES is a great family meal.

1 Soak the beef in cold water for 1 hour, changing the water 3 times. Remove the beef from the water and pat dry. Using a sharp knife, cut a diamond pattern into the white layer of fat. Press the cloves into the flesh of the onion.
2 Place the beef in a large heavy-based pan. Add enough water to just cover the beef, and add the clove-studded onion, peppercorns, bay leaves and brown sugar. Cover and bring the water to a gentle simmer. Cook for about 1 1/2 hours, spooning the cooking liquid over the top of the meat occasionally. Do not allow the water to boil or the meat will become tough. While the beef is cooking, make the parsley sauce.
3 To make the parsley sauce, melt the butter in a pan over medium heat. When the butter is foaming, stir in the flour and cook, stirring, for 1 minute. Remove from the heat and add the milk, stirring constantly until the sauce is smooth.

Return the pan to the heat and cook, stirring constantly, until the sauce boils and thickens. Boil for 1 minute further. Season well with salt and black pepper. Cover the surface of the sauce with baking paper to prevent a skin forming. Set aside.
4 When the meat is cooked and tender, remove it from the pan, wrap in foil and set aside for 15 minutes while cooking the vegetables. Halve the carrots and potatoes and add to the pan that the beef was cooked in. Simmer for 10 minutes, then add the

wedge of cabbage and cook for about 4 minutes. Test all the vegetables with a sharp knife—when they are tender, remove them from the pan and set aside. Reserve about ½ cup (125 ml/4 fl oz) of the cooking liquid to add to the sauce.

5 To serve, remove the paper from the sauce, stir in the reserved cooking liquid and parsley, and stir over low heat until the sauce is heated through. Slice the meat and arrange on a serving platter. Slice the cabbage and arrange the vegetables around the meat. Spoon a little parsley sauce over the beef and serve the remaining sauce in a jug.

BEEF BOURGUIGNON

Preparation: 10 minutes
Cooking: 2 hours
Serves 6

1 kg (2 lb) topside or round steak, cubed
plain flour, seasoned with salt and black pepper
2 tablespoons oil
3 rashers bacon, rind removed, chopped
12 pickling onions
1 cup (250 ml/8 fl oz) red wine
2 cups (500 ml/16 fl oz) beef stock
1 teaspoon dried thyme
200 g (6½ oz) button mushrooms
2 bay leaves

1 Toss the meat in the seasoned flour to coat, shaking off the excess.
2 Heat the oil in a large pan and cook the bacon over medium heat. Remove from the pan, then add the meat and brown well in batches. Remove and set aside. Add the onions to the pan and cook until golden.
3 Return the bacon and meat to the pan with the remaining ingredients. Bring to the boil, reduce the heat and simmer, covered, for 1½ hours, stirring occasionally, until the meat is very tender.

STORAGE: Can be refrigerated in an airtight container for up to 3 days.

BEEF BOURGUIGNON means 'beef in the style of Burgundy' (a region of France).

Flambé the brandy sauce for the PEPPER STEAK, then add cream.

PEPPER STEAK

Preparation: 15 minutes +
standing
Cooking: 15 minutes
Serves 4

4 pieces rib eye steak
1 clove garlic, halved
1 tablespoon oil
2 tablespoons black
   peppercorns
1 tablespoon white
   peppercorns (optional)
50 g (1 3/4 oz) butter
3 tablespoons brandy
1/2 cup (125 ml/4 fl oz)
   cream

1 Trim the meat of fat and sinew. Rub both sides of the steak with the cut edge of the garlic and then brush lightly with the oil. Coarsely crush the peppercorns and press in a thin layer all over the steaks. Leave for at least 30 minutes for the steak to absorb the flavours.

2 Heat the butter in a heavy-based frying pan and add the steaks. For rare steaks, cook the steaks for 3 minutes on each side. For medium steaks, lower the heat and cook for a further 2–3 minutes on each side. For well done, cook for a further 4–6 minutes on each side.

3 Remove the pan from the heat. Add the brandy, ignite using a long match or taper, then shake the pan until the flame subsides. Transfer the steaks to serving plates. Cover and keep warm. Add the cream to the pan, stirring to mix in the pan juices. Return to the heat and stir for 1–2 minutes to warm through. Pour over the steaks and serve.

NOTE: Use fillet or sirloin if preferred. Instead of brandy and cream, add 1 tablespoon lemon juice to the pan juices. Reheat until foaming, stirring to incorporate the pan juices. Pour over the steaks.

STEAK DIANE

Preparation: 20 minutes
Cooking: 20 minutes
Serves 4

4 fillet steaks (about
  150 g/5 oz each)
2 cloves garlic, crushed
50 g (1³/₄ oz) butter
4 spring onions, finely
  chopped
2 teaspoons Dijon
  mustard
2 tablespoons
  Worcestershire sauce
1 tablespoon brandy
¹/₃ cup (80 ml/2³/₄ fl oz)
  cream
2 tablespoons finely
  chopped fresh parsley

1 Trim the fat and sinew from the steaks. Lay each steak between 2 sheets of plastic wrap and flatten it with a meat mallet or rolling pin until it is about 1.5 cm (¹/₂ inch) thick.
2 Spread the garlic over both sides of the steak and grind some black pepper over the top.
3 Heat half the butter in a frying pan and add the steaks. For rare steaks, cook over high heat for 3 minutes on each side. For medium steaks, lower the heat and cook for a further 1 minute on each side, and for well-done steaks cook for a further 3–4 minutes on each side. Remove the meat from the pan, cover loosely with foil and keep warm.
4 Heat the remaining butter in the pan, add the spring onion and cook for 1 minute. Add the mustard, Worcestershire sauce and brandy. Stir well to mix in all the bits from the base of the pan.
5 Stir in the cream and boil for 3–4 minutes, or until the sauce has reduced and thickened slightly. Stir in the parsley. Return the steaks to the pan so that they just heat through. Serve the steaks immediately with the sauce.

HINT: Sometimes it is good to have a little fat on your steak: if you enjoy your steak well done, a marbling of fat will make it less likely to dry out and become tough during cooking. To test if your meat is cooked to your liking, press the centre of the steak with cooking tongs. Rare steak will be springy to the touch, medium a little firmer, and well-done steak very firm. Don't pierce the steak with a skewer or knife—the juices will escape and the meat may dry out.

Use lean trimmed fillet steak for STEAK DIANE.

FILET MIGNON

Preparation: 5 minutes
Cooking: 15 minutes
Serves 4

4 pieces fillet steak (each
about 4 cm/1 1/2 inches
thick)
4 small rashers bacon,
rind removed
30 g (1 oz) butter
2 teaspoons oil

1 Trim the meat of excess
fat and sinew. Put the
steaks between two sheets
of plastic wrap and flatten
with a meat mallet to
1.5 cm (1/2 inch) thick.
Wrap a rasher of bacon
around each steak and
secure with a toothpick.
2 Heat the butter and oil
in a heavy-based frying
pan and add the steaks.
For rare steaks, cook for
3 minutes on each side.
For medium steaks, reduce
the heat to medium-high
and cook for a futher
2–3 minutes each side.
Cook for a further
4–6 minutes each side for
well done. Remove the
toothpicks before serving.

STEAK SANDWICH

Preparation: 20 minutes
Cooking: 10 minutes
Serves 2

2 fillet steaks
30 g (1 oz) butter
1 small onion, cut into
rings
4 slices thick toasting
bread
2 lettuce leaves
1 small tomato, sliced
barbecue sauce

1 Trim any fat and sinew
from the steaks. Put the
steaks between two sheets
of plastic wrap and flatten
with a meat mallet or
rolling pin, until about
5 mm (1/4 inch) thick.
Nick the edges of the
steak to prevent the meat
curling as it cooks.
2 Melt the butter in a
frying pan and fry the
onion rings until soft and
lightly golden.
3 Push the onion to one
side of the pan. Add the
steaks and cook for
1–2 minutes on each side.
Keep warm.
4 Toast the bread and put
some lettuce and tomato
on two of the slices. Top
with the steak, onions and
barbecue sauce and
remaining bread.
Serve immediately.

FILET MIGNON is simple and relies on the best-quality meat.

A STEAK SANDWICH makes a quick and easy dish.

MEAT LOAF

Preparation: 20 minutes
Cooking: 1½ hours
Serves 6

1 kg (2 lb) lean minced beef
1 cup (100 g/3½ oz) dry breadcrumbs
1 onion, grated
2 teaspoons mixed dried herbs
1 egg
1 cup (250 ml/8 fl oz) tomato purée
2 tablespoons tomato sauce

1 Preheat the oven to moderate 180°C (350°F/Gas 4). Place the minced beef, breadcrumbs, onion, herbs, egg, tomato purée and some salt and pepper in a large bowl and mix together with your hands. **2** Shape the mixture into a firm loaf. Place in a greased baking dish and bake for 1 hour. **3** Carefully tip away any excess fat from the bottom of the baking dish. Spread the tomato sauce over the top of the meat loaf and bake for a further 30 minutes.

Spread the sauce over the MEAT LOAF and bake for 30 minutes.

97

BOMBAY CURRY

Preparation: 20 minutes
Cooking: 1–1¾ hours
Serves 4–6

1 tablespoon ghee or oil
1 kg (2 lb) beef or lamb,
  cubed
2 onions, chopped
2 cloves garlic, crushed
2 green chillies, chopped
1 tablespoon grated fresh
  ginger
1½ teaspoons turmeric
1 teaspoon ground cumin
1 tablespoon ground
  coriander
½–1 teaspoon chilli
  powder
1 teaspoon salt
400 g (13 oz) can
  crushed tomatoes
1 cup (250 ml/8 fl oz)
  coconut milk

1 Heat the ghee or oil in a large pan and brown the meat in small batches. Remove from the pan. Cook the onion, stirring, until it is just soft. Add the garlic, chilli, ginger, turmeric, cumin, coriander and chilli powder. Stir until just heated through.
2 Return the meat to the pan and stir until well coated with the spices.
3 Stir in the salt and tomatoes. Simmer, covered, for 1–1½ hours, or until the meat is tender.
4 Stir in the coconut milk and simmer, uncovered, for another 5 minutes, or until the sauce has thickened slightly.

NOTE: Fresh coriander leaves or raw, unsalted cashew nuts (available from health food stores and most supermarkets) make a good garnish for this dish.

BEEF IN BLACK BEAN SAUCE

Preparation: 15 minutes +
  1 hour marinating
Cooking: 10 minutes
Serves 4

750 g (1½ lb) rump
  steak
2 cloves garlic, crushed
2 teaspoons grated fresh
  ginger
2 tablespoons dry sherry
1 tablespoon soy sauce
3 tablespoons peanut oil
2 onions, cut into
  wedges
1 large green capsicum,
  cut into strips
230 g (7½ oz) can sliced
  bamboo shoots, drained
2 tablespoons canned
  black beans, rinsed,
  chopped
1 tablespoon cornflour

1 Trim the meat of any fat and sinew and slice across the grain into long, thin strips. Combine the garlic, ginger, sherry and soy sauce in a non-metallic bowl. Add the meat, stirring to coat. Cover and refrigerate for at least an hour, turning occasionally. Drain the meat, reserving the marinade.

BOMBAY CURRY.

BEEF IN BLACK BEAN SAUCE is a classic, but easy, Chinese dish. Serve with rice.

2 Heat 1 tablespoon of the oil in a wok or heavy-based frying pan, swirling gently to coat the base and side. Cook the meat quickly in small batches over high heat until browned but not cooked through. Remove from the wok and drain on paper towels. Heat the remaining oil in the wok, swirling gently to coat the base and side. Add the onion and capsicum, and stir-fry over high heat for 3 minutes, or until the onion is soft. Add the bamboo shoots and black beans; cook for 1 minute.
3 Mix the cornflour and remaining marinade with 2 tablespoons water until smooth. Add to the wok with the meat and stir-fry over high heat until the meat is cooked through and the sauce has thickened. Serve immediately with rice.

STORAGE: Store the leftover black beans in an airtight jar in the refrigerator for up to 2 weeks.

RISSOLES WITH GRAVY

Preparation: 25 minutes
Cooking: 10 minutes
Serves 4

500 g (1 lb) beef mince
1 onion, finely chopped
2 tablespoons tomato
  sauce
1 teaspoon dried mixed
  herbs
1 egg, lightly beaten
1 cup (80 g/2³/4 oz) fresh
  breadcrumbs
oil, for shallow-frying

Gravy
2 tablespoons plain flour
2 cups (500 ml/16 fl oz)
  chicken stock

1 tablespoon tomato
  paste
2 tablespoons chopped
  fresh parsley (optional)

1 Place the mince, onion, tomato sauce, herbs, egg and breadcrumbs in a bowl. Mix together well with your hands. Divide into eight portions and shape into patties.
2 Heat the oil in a large heavy-based pan and cook the rissoles four at a time. Cook over high heat for 1 minute on each side, turning once. Reduce the heat to medium and cook for 2 minutes on each side, or until cooked through. Drain on paper towels and keep warm.

3 To make the gravy, blend the flour with the chicken stock and tomato paste in a small jug until the mixture is smooth. Add to the pan juices and stir over medium heat for 3 minutes, or until the gravy boils and thickens. Strain, then stir in the chopped parsley. Serve with the rissoles.

BEEF POT ROAST

Preparation: 20 minutes
Cooking: 2¹/2 hours
Serves 6

2 kg (4 lb) piece of
  topside
1 tablespoon oil
60 g (2 oz) butter
6 baby onions
4 carrots, cut into chunks
3 parsnips, cut into
  chunks
1 cup (250 ml/8 fl oz)
  beef stock
bouquet garni
1 tablespoon plain flour

1 Remove the excess fat and sinew from the meat. Heat the oil and 40 g (1¹/4 oz) of the butter in a large heavy-based pan. Brown the meat all over, then remove from the pan.
2 Add the vegetables to the pan and cook over medium heat until golden brown, stirring

Children love RISSOLES WITH GRAVY.

The vegetables are cooked with the meat, so BEEF POT ROAST is a complete one-pot meal.

occasionally. Remove from the pan.

3 Return the meat to the pan and add the beef stock and bouquet garni. Heat until simmering, cover with a tight-fitting lid and simmer for 2–2¼ hours, turning once or twice during cooking. Be sure to simmer gently and not boil, otherwise you will find the meat shrinks and toughens. Return the vegetables to the pan for the last 30 minutes of cooking.

4 Remove and discard the bouquet garni. Transfer the meat and vegetables to a serving plate, cover and keep warm. Combine the remaining butter with the flour to form a smooth paste (this is called a *beurre manié* and is used for thickening). Stir into the pan juices. Bring to the boil, whisking until the mixture thickens slightly. Serve with the meat.

VARIATION: Silverside and bolar blade can also be used for pot roast.

101

HAMBURGER WITH THE WORKS

Preparation: 20 minutes
Cooking: 20 minutes
Serves 4

500 g (1 lb) lean beef mince
1 onion, finely chopped
1 egg, lightly beaten
1/3 cup (25 g/³/4 oz) fresh breadcrumbs
2 tablespoons tomato sauce
1 teaspoon steak seasoning
40 g (1 1/4 oz) butter
2 onions, extra, cut in thin rings
oil, for cooking

4 slices Cheddar, halved
4 eggs, extra
4 slices rindless bacon, halved
4 large hamburger buns
shredded lettuce
1 large tomato, sliced
4 large beetroot slices
4 pineapple rings
tomato sauce, to serve

1 Place the beef mince, onion, egg, breadcrumbs, tomato sauce, steak seasoning and some salt and pepper in a large bowl. Use your hands to mix well. Divide into four portions and shape into round patties—the flatter the patties, the quicker they will cook.

2 Heat 30 g (1 oz) butter in a frying pan and cook the onion rings over medium heat until brown. Remove and keep warm.

3 Heat a frying pan or barbecue grill or flatplate and brush lightly with oil. Cook the patties for 3–4 minutes each side, or until cooked through. Place a cheese slice on each patty.

4 Heat the remaining butter in another frying pan and fry the eggs and the bacon separately. Halve and toast the buns and top each one with lettuce, tomato, beetroot and pineapple. Add a meat patty and finish with the onion, egg, bacon and tomato sauce.

Pile everything on, for your HAMBURGER WITH THE WORKS.

CHILLI CON CARNE is a traditional Mexican dish, meaning 'chilli with meat'.

CHILLI CON CARNE

Preparation: 10 minutes
Cooking: 50 minutes
Serves 4

1 tablespoon olive oil
1 onion, chopped
3 cloves garlic, crushed
1 celery stick, sliced
500 g (1 lb) lean beef mince
2 teaspoons chilli powder
pinch of cayenne pepper
1 tablespoon chopped fresh oregano
400 g (13 oz) can crushed tomatoes
2 tablespoons tomato paste
1 teaspoon soft brown sugar
1 tablespoon cider vinegar or red wine vinegar
420 g (13 oz) can red kidney beans, rinsed

1 Heat the oil in a large, heavy-based pan. Add the onion, garlic and celery and stir over medium heat for 5 minutes, or until softened.

2 Add the mince and cook over high heat for 5 minutes, or until well browned. Add the chilli powder, cayenne and oregano. Stir well and cook over medium heat for 5 minutes.

3 Mix in the tomatoes, tomato paste and 1/2 cup (125 ml/4 fl oz) of water. Leave the chilli to simmer for 30 minutes, stirring occasionally.

4 Add the sugar, vinegar and beans, and season with salt and freshly ground black pepper. Heat through for 5 minutes before serving.

NOTE: Chilli is most commonly served with rice, but why not try it with corn chips and a topping of sour cream?

THAI BEEF SALAD

Preparation: 35 minutes
Cooking: 10 minutes
Serves 4

3 cloves garlic, finely
  chopped
4 coriander roots, finely
  chopped
1/2 teaspoon freshly
  ground black pepper
1/4 cup (60 ml/2 fl oz) oil
400 g (13 oz) piece
  rump or sirloin steak
1 small soft-leaved
  lettuce
200 g (6 1/2 oz) cherry
  tomatoes, halved
1 Lebanese cucumber,
  cut into chunks
4 spring onions, chopped

1/2 cup (15 g/1/2 oz) fresh
  coriander leaves

Dressing
2 tablespoons fish sauce
2 tablespoons lime juice
1 tablespoon soy sauce
2 teaspoons chopped
  fresh red chilli
2 teaspoons soft brown
  sugar

1 Combine the garlic, coriander roots, pepper and 2 tablespoons of the oil. If you have a mortar and pestle, use it to finely grind the mixture. Alternatively, blend the mixture well in a food processor or spice blender. Spread evenly over the steak.

2 Heat the remaining oil in a heavy-based frying pan or wok over high heat. Add the steak to the pan and cook for about 1 minute on each side, turning once only during the cooking time. Remove the steak from the pan and allow to cool.

3 To make the dressing, combine the fish sauce, lime juice, soy sauce, chilli and brown sugar in a small bowl, stirring until the sugar has dissolved.

4 Cut the cooled steak into thin strips across the grain. Arrange the lettuce on a plate and arrange the tomatoes on top, with the cucumber, spring onion and strips of steak. Drizzle with the dressing and scatter the coriander leaves over the top. Serve immediately.

HINT: Be careful that you don't overcook the steak—it should be pink and, therefore, succulent and tender.

NOTE: Ground herbs and spices are used extensively for flavouring in Asian cookery. Small amounts can be done with a mortar and pestle or a clean coffee grinder. For larger quantities, use a blender or food processor. To help clean the bowl after grinding spices, run some stale bread or rice through the processor.

The beef should be rare and succulent in a THAI BEEF SALAD.

BEEF NACHOS

Preparation: 30 minutes
Cooking: 25 minutes
Serves 4

oil, for cooking
400 g (13 oz) lean beef
  mince
1 onion, chopped
1–2 teaspoons chopped
  fresh chilli
1 tablespoon ground
  cumin
3 teaspoons ground
  coriander
1/4 cup (60 g/2 oz)
  tomato paste
1/2 cup (125 g/4 oz)
  bottled tomato pasta
  sauce or salsa
1/2 cup (115 g/4 oz)
  refried beans or 425 g
  (14 oz) can red kidney
  beans, drained and
  rinsed
corn chips, grated
  Cheddar cheese and
  sour cream, for serving
chilli powder, to sprinkle

Guacamole
1 ripe avocado
1 small onion, finely
  chopped
1 tomato, finely chopped
2 tablespoons chopped
  fresh coriander
2–3 tablespoons sour
  cream
3–4 teaspoons lemon
  juice
Tabasco, to taste

For a Mexican theme, serve BEEF NACHOS.

1 Heat a little oil in a frying pan and brown the beef mince in batches, stirring and breaking up any lumps with a fork or wooden spoon. Transfer to a bowl and set aside.
2 Add a little more oil to the pan and stir in the onion, chilli, cumin and coriander. Cook over medium heat for 2–3 minutes. Return the mince to the pan and stir in the tomato paste, pasta sauce and beans. Simmer for 5–10 minutes.
3 To make the guacamole, peel the avocado and mash the flesh in a bowl. Add the onion, tomato, coriander, sour cream and lemon juice. Mix well

with a fork. Add some salt, freshly ground black pepper and Tabasco.
4 Spoon the mince into a large ovenproof dish. Arrange the corn chips around the mixture and sprinkle with the cheese. Place under a preheated grill or in a moderate 180°C (350°F/Gas 4) oven for about 5–10 minutes, or until the cheese has melted. Top with the guacamole, a spoonful of sour cream and a dash of chilli powder.

NOTE: Traditionally, nachos were made using shredded cooked beef rather than mince.

LAMB SHANKS are an excellent cut for long slow cooking in a casserole.

MINTY LAMB SHANKS

Preparation: 20 minutes
Cooking: 2¼ hours
Serves 6

2 tablespoons olive oil
6 lamb shanks
1 red onion, chopped
2 cloves garlic, crushed
1 sprig fresh thyme
2 bay leaves
¾ cup (35 g/1¼ oz)
  chopped fresh mint
425 g (14 oz) can
  crushed tomatoes
2 cups (500 ml/16 fl oz)
  vegetable stock
3 tablespoons white wine

1 Preheat the oven to moderately hot 200°C (400°F/Gas 6). Heat a tablespoon of oil in a flameproof baking dish on the stove top. Brown the shanks in batches then remove from the heat and return them all to the dish in a single layer, close together. Season with salt and pepper and bake for 20 minutes. Turn over, reduce the heat to 180°C (350°F/Gas 4) and bake for a further 20 minutes.
2 Heat the remaining oil in a heavy-based frying pan. Add the onion and garlic and fry for 5–8 minutes, or until soft.

Stir in the thyme, bay leaves and ½ cup (25 g/ ¾ oz) of the mint leaves. Scatter the onion and herbs over the meat, return to the oven and bake for 15 minutes.
3 Combine the tomato, stock and wine and pour over the meat. Cover the dish tightly with foil or a lid and bake for a further 1¼ hours. Garnish with the remaining mint and serve with pasta. The flavour of the dish actually improves if it is made a day or two in advance and refrigerated.

SHEPHERD'S PIE

Preparation: 30 minutes
Cooking: 1 hour
Serves 6

750 g (1 1/2 lb) lean
 cooked roast lamb
25 g (3/4 oz) butter
2 onions, chopped
3 tablespoons plain flour
1/2 teaspoon mustard
 powder
1 1/2 cups (375 ml/
 12 fl oz) chicken stock
2 tablespoons
 Worcestershire sauce

Potato topping
1/2 cup (125 ml/4 fl oz)
 hot milk
30 g (1 oz) butter
4 large potatoes, cooked
 and mashed

1 Grease a 2 litre
casserole dish and preheat
the oven to hot 210°C
(415°F/Gas 6–7). Trim the
meat of any fat and cut it
into small cubes. Melt the
butter in a large pan. Add
the onion and cook until
golden.
2 Sprinkle the flour and
mustard into the pan and
stir for 1 minute. Remove
from the heat, gradually
add the stock and stir
until smooth. Return to
the heat, bring to the boil,
then reduce the heat and
simmer for 3 minutes.
3 Add the meat and
Worcestershire sauce to

SHEPHERD'S PIE is always made with cooked lamb.

the pan and stir. Season
with salt and pepper.
Remove from the heat and
spoon the mixture into
the casserole dish.
4 To make the potato
topping, mix the milk,
butter and salt and
pepper, to taste, into the
mashed potato. Spread
evenly over the meat and
rough up the surface with
a fork. Bake for 40–45
minutes, or until the
topping is lightly golden
and the pie is completely
heated through.

NOTE: To make a really
creamy mash, push the
potato through a sieve
with the back of a spoon,
before mixing in the milk
and butter.

Shepherd's pie is so called
because it is always made
with lamb. Cottage pie is
made with beef mince,
which is cooked with the
onion and other
vegetables to make the pie
filling. It too has a mashed
potato topping.

ROASTED RACK OF LAMB

Preparation: 15 minutes
Cooking: 45 minutes
Serves 4

2 six-cutlet racks of lamb
1 tablespoon olive oil

1 Preheat the oven to moderate 180°C (350°F/ Gas 4). Trim the meat of excess fat and sinew, brush with the oil and season with freshly ground black pepper. Wrap the ends of the bones in foil to prevent them burning.
2 Place the meat, with the bones upright and interlocking, in a baking dish. Bake for 40 minutes. When cooked, transfer to a plate, cover with foil and set aside for 5 minutes before carving. Cut the racks into portions of three cutlets to serve.

MINTED RACK OF LAMB

Preparation: 15 minutes
Cooking: 45 minutes
Serves 4

4 four-cutlet racks of lamb
1 cup (300 g/10 oz) mint jelly

2 tablespoons white wine
¼ cup (15 g/½ oz) chopped fresh chives

1 Preheat the oven to moderately hot 200°C (400°F/Gas 6). Trim any excess fat from the racks of lamb, leaving a thin layer of fat, and clean any meat or sinew from the bones with a small sharp knife. Cover the bones with foil. Place on a rack in a baking dish.
2 Mix the mint jelly and white wine together in a small pan over high heat. Cook for about 4 minutes, or until the mixture is reduced and thickened. Cool slightly, then add the chives.
3 Brush the racks of lamb with the glaze. Roast for 35 minutes for rare or 40 minutes for medium rare, brushing with the glaze every 10 minutes. Remove the foil from the lamb and leave for 5 minutes before serving.

VARIATIONS: For a mustard-crusted rack of lamb, spread the lamb with wholegrain mustard. Alternatively, mix 2 cups (160 g/5½ oz) fresh breadcrumbs with a lightly beaten egg and chopped mixed herbs, press onto the lamb and bake for 40 minutes. Cover with foil if the crumbs are overbrowning.

RACKS OF LAMB are particularly good with a mint glaze.

108

Fry CRUMBED LAMB CUTLETS a few at a time to get a good crunchy finish.

CRUMBED LAMB CUTLETS

Preparation: 30 minutes +
30 minutes chilling
Cooking: 30 minutes
Serves 4

12 lamb cutlets
¼ cup (30 g/1 oz) plain
flour
2 eggs
1½ cups (150 g/5 oz)
dry breadcrumbs
oil, for shallow-frying

1 Trim the cutlets of excess fat and sinew. Season the flour with salt and pepper on a sheet of greaseproof paper. Toss the cutlets lightly in the seasoned flour and then shake off any excess.
2 Break the eggs into a shallow bowl and beat lightly with a fork. Dip each cutlet into the egg, drain off the excess, and then quickly coat with the breadcrumbs. Using your fingers, press the crumbs lightly onto the cutlets, then shake off any excess.
3 Place the cutlets in a single layer on a paper-lined tray. Cover and refrigerate for 30 minutes. Heat the oil in a frying pan and add the cutlets a few at a time. Cook over medium heat for about 3 minutes on each side, or until golden and tender. Do not have the oil too hot or the crumbs will burn before the meat is cooked through. Drain on paper towels and serve immediately.

Serve ROAST LEG OF LAMB with roast vegetables and mint sauce.

ROAST LEG OF LAMB WITH MINT SAUCE

Preparation: 20 minutes
Cooking: 1¾ hours
Serves 6

2 kg (4 lb) leg of lamb
2 cloves garlic, cut into
  thin slivers
2 tablespoons fresh
  rosemary sprigs
2 teaspoons oil

Mint sauce
3 tablespoons caster
  sugar
½ cup (10 g/¼ oz) fresh
  mint leaves
¾ cup (185 ml/6 fl oz)
  malt vinegar

1 Preheat the oven to moderate 180°C (350°F/ Gas 4). Using a small sharp knife, cut small slits all over the lamb. Push the garlic and rosemary into the slits.

2 Brush the lamb with the oil and sprinkle with salt and black pepper. Place on a rack in a baking dish. Add ½ cup (125 ml/ 4 fl oz) water to the dish.

3 Roast for about 1½ hours for medium, or 1¾ hours for well done, basting often with the pan juices. Keep warm and leave for 10–15 minutes before serving.

4 To make the mint sauce, sprinkle 1 tablespoon of the caster sugar over the mint leaves on a chopping board. Chop the mint finely. Place in a bowl and add the remaining caster sugar. Cover with 3 tablespoons boiling water and stir until the sugar has dissolved. Stir in the vinegar. Serve with the roast lamb.

LANCASHIRE HOTPOT

Preparation: 20 minutes
Cooking: 2¼ hours
Serves 8

8 forequarter lamb
  chops, cut 2.5 cm
  (1 inch) thick
4 lamb kidneys, cut in
  quarters, cores removed
¼ cup (30 g/1 oz) plain
  flour
50 g (1¾ oz) butter
4 potatoes, thinly sliced
2 large onions, sliced
2 celery sticks, chopped
1 large carrot, chopped
1¾ cups (440 ml/
  14 fl oz) chicken or
  beef stock
200 g (6½ oz) button
  mushrooms, sliced
2 teaspoons chopped
  fresh thyme
1 tablespoon
  Worcestershire sauce

1 Preheat the oven to warm 160°C (315°F/ Gas 2–3). Brush a large casserole dish with melted butter or oil. Trim the meat of excess fat and sinew, and toss the chops and kidneys in the flour, shaking off the excess.
2 Heat the butter in a large frying pan and quickly brown the chops, in batches, on both sides. Remove the chops from the pan and brown the kidneys. Layer half the potato slices in the base of the dish and place the chops and kidneys on top of them.
3 Add the onion, celery and carrot to the pan and cook until the carrot begins to brown. Layer on top of the chops and kidneys. Sprinkle the remaining flour over the base of the pan and cook, stirring, until brown. Remove from the heat, pour in a little stock and stir until smooth. Add the rest of the stock gradually, return to the heat and stir until the mixture boils and thickens.
4 Add the mushrooms, thyme and Worcestershire sauce and season to taste with salt and black pepper. Reduce the heat and leave to simmer for 10 minutes. Pour into the casserole dish.
5 Layer the remaining potato over the top of the casserole, to cover the meat and vegetables. Bake, covered, for 1¼ hours. Uncover and cook for a further 30 minutes, or until the potatoes are brown.

Use lamb chops and kidneys in a LANCASHIRE HOTPOT.

IRISH STEW

Preparation: 20 minutes
Cooking: 2½ hours
Serves 4

1 kg (2 lb) lamb neck
    chops
3 tablespoons plain flour
4 onions, sliced
8 potatoes (about 2 kg/
    4 lb), quartered
¼ cup (15 g/½ oz)
    chopped fresh parsley

1 Preheat the oven to
warm 160°C (315°F/
Gas 2–3). Trim the lamb
chops of fat and sinew
and toss in the flour.

Shake off the excess flour.
2 Place the chops in a
2 litre ovenproof dish
with the onion and 2 cups
(500 ml/16 fl oz) water.
Bake, covered, for
1½ hours.
3 Add the potato and
bake, covered, for 1 hour,
or until the meat and
potato are tender. Stir
in the parsley just
before serving.

NOTE: Traditionally Irish
stew was made using
mutton, which is no
longer such a popular
meat. We've modernized
our version to use lamb.

ROAST PORK AND APPLE SAUCE

Preparation: 30 minutes
Cooking: 3¼ hours
Serves 6–8

4 kg (8 lb) leg of pork
oil and salt

Apple sauce
6 green apples
2 tablespoons caster
    sugar
2 cloves
1 cinnamon stick
1–2 teaspoons lemon
    juice

Gravy
1 tablespoon brandy
2 tablespoons plain flour
1½ cups (375 ml/
    12 fl oz) chicken stock
½ cup (125 ml/4 fl oz)
    unsweetened apple
    juice

1 Preheat the oven to
very hot 250°C (500°F/
Gas 10). Score the rind of
the pork with a sharp
knife at 2 cm (¾ inch)
intervals. Rub in some oil
and plenty of salt to make
crisp crackling.
2 Place the pork, rind-
side-up, on a rack in a
large baking dish. Add a
little water to the dish—
this will help prevent the
meat drying out. Roast for
30 minutes, or until the
rind turns golden and

IRISH STEW is a simple but satisfying meal.

For really crispy crackling, ROAST PORK is best served soon after cooking.

begins to crackle and bubble. Reduce the heat to moderate 180°C (350°F/Gas 4). Roast for 2 hours 40 minutes (20 minutes per 500 g/ 1 lb). The juices should run clear when the pork is pierced with a fork. Do not cover the pork or the crackling will soften. Leave in a warm place for 10 minutes.

3 To make the apple sauce, peel, core and chop the apples and place in a small pan with the sugar, cloves, cinnamon and ¹/₂ cup (125 ml/4 fl oz) water. Cover and simmer over low heat for 10 minutes, or until the apple is soft. Remove the cloves and cinnamon and mash the apples. Stir in the lemon juice, to taste.

4 To make the gravy, drain off all except 2 tablespoons of the pan juices from the baking dish. Place on top of the stove over moderate heat, add the brandy and stir quickly to scrape up the bits from the bottom of the pan. Cook for 1 minute. Remove from the heat, stir in the flour and mix well. Return the pan to the heat and cook for 2 minutes, stirring. Gradually add the stock and apple juice and cook, stirring, until the gravy boils and thickens. Season to taste with salt and pepper. Slice the pork and serve with the crackling, gravy and apple sauce.

NOTE: Any leftover pork can be kept refrigerated, covered, for up to 3 days.

Choose one of the marinades below for your ribs.

PORK RIBS

Preparation: 30 minutes + marinating
Cooking: 20 minutes
Serves 6

1 kg (2 lb) American-style ribs

Plum sauce marinade
$^1/_2$ cup (160 g/5$^1/_2$ oz) plum sauce
2 tablespoons soy sauce
2 tablespoons honey
2 teaspoons grated fresh ginger
2 cloves garlic, crushed

Barbecue marinade
1 cup (250 ml/8 fl oz) tomato sauce
$^1/_2$ teaspoon onion powder
$^1/_2$ teaspoon garlic powder
2 tablespoons vinegar
2 tablespoons soft brown sugar
2 tablespoons Worcestershire sauce

Ginger marinade
2 tablespoons grated fresh ginger
$^1/_2$ teaspoon ground pepper
1 teaspoon sesame oil
1 tablespoon lemon juice
1 small onion, grated

Chilli marinade
$^1/_2$ cup (125 ml/4 fl oz) tomato purée
2 tablespoons honey
2 tablespoons chilli sauce, or to taste
1 tablespoon hoisin sauce
2 cloves garlic, crushed

1 Cut the ribs into smaller portions and trim off any fat. Place the ribs in a single layer in a shallow glass or ceramic dish.
2 Choose one of the marinades and mix together the ingredients. Pour the marinade over the meat, turning to coat well. Cover with plastic wrap and refrigerate for at least 2 hours and no longer than 8 hours, turning occasionally.
3 Preheat a barbecue flatplate or grill and brush it lightly with oil. Drain any excess marinade from the ribs, then cook them over moderate heat for 20 minutes, or until tender, turning occasionally.

VARIATION: Pork spareribs can be used instead of American-style ribs for this recipe. Remove the rind from the ribs and trim of fat. Depending on the size, you may need to cut them in half. Marinate and cook as above.

Deep-fry the pork then finish off in the wok for SWEET AND SOUR PORK.

SWEET AND SOUR PORK

Preparation: 35 minutes +
30 minutes marinating
Cooking: 40 minutes
Serves 6

2 teaspoons sugar
1/4 cup (60 ml/2 fl oz)
soy sauce
1 tablespoon dry sherry
1 egg yolk
1 kg (2 lb) lean pork, cut
into cubes
1 cup (125 g/4 oz)
cornflour
oil, for deep-frying
1 onion, sliced
1 red capsicum, chopped
1 green capsicum,
chopped

440 g (14 oz) can
pineapple pieces,
drained, juice reserved
1/4 cup (60 ml/2 fl oz)
tomato sauce
1/4 cup (60 ml/2 fl oz)
white vinegar
1 tablespoon cornflour,
extra

1 Mix together the sugar, soy sauce, sherry and egg yolk. Pour over the pork and refrigerate, covered, for 30 minutes.

2 Drain the pork, reserving the marinade, and pat dry with paper towels. Toss the pork in the cornflour and shake off any excess. Heat the oil in a large heavy-based pan until a cube of bread browns in 15 seconds. Deep-fry the pork, in batches, until crisp and golden brown. Drain on paper towels.

3 Heat a little oil in a wok and cook the onion for 3 minutes, or until golden brown. Add the capsicum and cook for 2 minutes.

4 Mix together the pineapple juice, tomato sauce, vinegar and the reserved marinade, and add to the wok. Dissolve the extra cornflour in 1 cup (250 ml/8 fl oz) of water, add to the wok and stir until the mixture boils and thickens.

5 Add the pork and pineapple and cook until heated through.

ORANGE-GLAZED HAM is a perfect festive party meal.

ORANGE GLAZED HAM

Preparation: 45 minutes
Cooking: 3 hours 40 minutes
Serves 20

7 kg (14 lb) cooked ham
  leg
1 large orange
6 whole cloves
³/4 cup (140 g/4¹/2 oz)
  soft brown sugar
1 tablespoon French
  mustard
¹/2 cup (175 g/6 oz)
  honey
2 teaspoons soy sauce
2 tablespoons Grand
  Marnier
whole cloves, extra

Mustard cream
2 tablespoons French
  mustard
¹/2 cup (125 g/4 oz) sour
  cream
¹/2 cup (125 ml/4 fl oz)
  cream

1 Preheat the oven to moderate 180°C (350°F/Gas 4). Remove the rind from the ham by running a thumb around the edge, under the rind. Begin pulling at the widest edge. When the rind has been removed to within 6 cm (2¹/2 inches) of the shank end, cut through the rind around the shank. Using a sharp knife, remove some of the excess fat from the ham (but leave enough to give a good crispy skin).

2 Peel the orange, cut the white pith off the rind and cut the rind into long, thin strips. Squeeze about ¹/2 cup (125 ml/4 fl oz) of juice from the orange.

3 Put the ham on a rack in a deep baking dish. Add 2 cups (500 ml/16 fl oz) water to the dish with the orange rind and cloves. Cover securely with foil and cook for 2 hours.

4 Remove from the oven. Increase the heat to hot 210°C (415°F/Gas 6–7). Drain the meat and reserve 1 cup (250 ml/ 8 fl oz) of the pan juices. Using a sharp knife, score the fat with cuts into a diamond pattern.

5 Mix together the sugar, mustard, honey, soy sauce and Grand Marnier. Brush some glaze over the ham. Return to the oven and cook, uncovered, for 30 minutes, glazing every 10 minutes.

6 Remove the ham from the oven. Press one of the extra cloves into each diamond. Roast, uncovered, for 1 hour, brushing with the glaze every 10 minutes.

7 Meanwhile, to make the mustard cream, mix together the mustard, sour cream and cream. Cover and leave for 1 hour.

8 Place the reserved pan

juices and 1/2 cup
(125 ml/4 fl oz) of the
brown sugar glaze in a
small pan. Stir in the
reserved orange juice. Stir
over low heat until the
mixture boils, then boil,
without stirring, for
3 minutes. Leave the ham
for 10 minutes before
slicing. Serve hot or cold,
with the orange glaze and
mustard cream.

NOTE: The ham can be
refrigerated, covered with
a damp cloth, for about
10 days. Change the
cloth regularly.

Use cider and apples for PORK WITH NORMANDY SAUCE.

PORK WITH NORMANDY SAUCE

Preparation: 25 minutes
Cooking: 45 minutes
Serves 4

40 g (1 1/4 oz) butter
12 French shallots
2 cloves garlic, chopped
4 thick pork chops
1 1/2 cups (375 ml/
  12 fl oz) apple cider
1 tablespoon white wine
  vinegar
3 teaspoons French
  mustard
1 green apple, cored and
  cut into 8 slices
2 teaspoons soft brown
  sugar
3 tablespoons cream
2 teaspoons cornflour

1 Heat half the butter in a
large heavy-based frying
pan. Add the shallots and
garlic, and cook for
3–4 minutes, or until soft.
Remove and set aside.
Trim the chops of any
excess fat and add to the
pan. Brown over high heat
for 2–3 minutes,
turning once.
2 Reduce the heat and
return the shallots and
garlic to the pan. Pour in
the combined cider,
vinegar and mustard.
Cover and simmer for
about 20 minutes, or until
the pork chops are tender.
(The cooking time will
depend on the thickness
of the pork chops.)
3 Meanwhile, heat the

remaining butter in a
small frying pan. Add the
apple slices and brown
sugar. Cook, turning
occasionally, for
3 minutes, or until
the apple has lightly
browned and softened.
Remove and set aside.
4 Remove the pork chops
from the pan, cover with
foil and keep warm.
Combine the cream and
cornflour, then add to the
cider mixture. Whisk
quickly for 5–10 minutes,
or until the sauce has
come to the boil and
thickened slightly. Add
the apple and pork chops,
and heat through for
5 minutes. Garnish with a
few fresh thyme sprigs.

The dish is lined with thin rashers of bacon that will cover the PORK AND VEAL TERRINE.

PORK AND VEAL TERRINE

Preparation: 20 minutes +
overnight refrigeration
Cooking: 1 hour 20 minutes
Serves 6

8–10 **thin rashers bacon**
1 **tablespoon olive oil**
1 **onion, chopped**
2 **cloves garlic, crushed**
1 **kg (2 lb) pork and veal
mince**
1 **cup (80 g/2³/4 oz) fresh
breadcrumbs**
1 **egg**

3 **tablespoons brandy**
3 **teaspoons chopped
fresh thyme**
¹/4 **cup (15 g/¹/2 oz)
chopped fresh parsley**

1 Preheat the oven to
moderate 180°C (350°F/
Gas 4). Lightly grease a
1.5 litre terrine dish or tin.
Line with the rashers of
bacon, leaving them
hanging over the sides
of the dish.
2 Heat the oil in a frying
pan and fry the onion and
garlic for 2–3 minutes, or
until the onion is soft.

3 Mix together the fried
onion, mince,
breadcrumbs, egg, brandy,
thyme and parsley in a
large bowl. Use your
hands to mix it
thoroughly. Season with
salt and pepper. To taste
that there is enough
seasoning in the terrine,
fry a spoonful of the
mixture. Taste and adjust
the seasoning accordingly.
4 Spoon the mixture into
the dish, pressing it in
firmly. Fold the bacon
over the top of the terrine
to enclose the mixture,

cover with foil and place the terrine in a deep baking tray. Pour enough cold water into the baking tray to come halfway up the side of the terrine (this makes a *bain marie*).

5 Bake for 1–1¼ hours, or until the juice runs clear when pierced with a skewer. Remove from the *bain marie* and pour off the excess juice. Cover with foil and place heavy tins directly on top of the terrine to press it down. Refrigerate overnight.

WIENER SCHNITZEL

Preparation: 15 minutes +
　 30 minutes refrigeration
Cooking: 10 minutes
Serves 4

4 thin veal steaks
plain flour, for coating
1 egg, lightly beaten
1 cup (100 g/3½ oz) dry
　 breadcrumbs
¼ cup (60 ml/2 fl oz) oil
30 g (1 oz) butter
1 lemon, sliced
2 tablespoons capers
2 gherkins, sliced

1 Trim the meat of any fat and sinew. Place between sheets of plastic wrap and flatten with a meat mallet to 5 mm (¼ inch) thick. Nick the edges to prevent them from curling up

WIENER SCHNITZEL.

when the steaks are cooked. Pat dry with paper towels.

2 Season the flour with salt and pepper. Coat the veal with the seasoned flour, shaking off the excess (the least messy way to do this is to put the flour in a plastic bag, add the meat and shake well). Dip into the egg, then coat with the breadcrumbs. Place on a foil-lined tray. Cover and refrigerate for at least 30 minutes to firm up the breadcrumb coating.

3 Heat the oil and butter in a large heavy-based pan

and cook the veal over medium heat for 3–4 minutes. Turn over and cook for 2–3 minutes, or until golden. Serve at once with lemon, capers and gherkins.

NOTE: The schnitzels can be coated with breadcrumbs several hours in advance. Keep them covered and refrigerated until ready to fry.
VARIATION: Prepare chicken schnitzel in the same way. Use chicken breast fillets and flatten with a meat mallet before cooking.

VEAL PARMIGIANA

Preparation: 30 minutes +
30 minutes refrigeration
Cooking: 30 minutes
Serves 4

4 thin veal steaks
1 cup (100 g/3 1/2 oz) dry
breadcrumbs
1/2 teaspoon dried basil
3/4 cup (75 g/2 1/2 oz)
finely grated Parmesan
plain flour, for coating
1 egg, lightly beaten
1 tablespoon milk
oil, for shallow-frying
1 cup (250 g/8 oz)
tomato pasta sauce
100 g (3 1/2 oz)
mozzarella, thinly sliced

1 Trim the meat of any fat and sinew. Place between sheets of plastic wrap and flatten with a meat mallet to 5 mm (1/4 inch) thick. Nick the edges to prevent the meat curling.
2 Combine the breadcrumbs, basil and 1/4 cup (30 g/1 oz) of the Parmesan on a sheet of greaseproof paper.
3 Coat the veal in flour, shaking off the excess. Working with one at a time, dip the steaks in the combined egg and milk, then coat with the breadcrumbs. Lightly shake off the excess. Refrigerate on a paper-lined tray for 30 minutes to firm the coating.

4 Preheat the oven to moderate 180°C (350°F/ Gas 4). Heat 2 cm (1 inch) oil in a frying pan and brown the veal steaks over medium heat for 2 minutes on each side, in batches if necessary, until crisp and golden brown. Drain on paper towels.
5 Spread half the pasta sauce in a shallow ovenproof dish. Arrange the veal steaks on top in a single layer and spoon in the remaining sauce. Top with the remaining Parmesan and the mozzarella and bake for 20 minutes, or until the cheese is melted and golden brown.

PARMIGIANA can also be made with chicken and even eggplant.

OSSO BUCO WITH GREMOLATA

Preparation: 40 minutes
Cooking: 2 hours 20 minutes
Serves 4

Gremolata
1 tablespoon finely
shredded lemon rind
1–2 cloves garlic, finely
chopped
1/4 cup (15 g/1/2 oz)
finely chopped fresh
parsley

plain flour, for coating
4 veal shank pieces, each
5 cm (2 inches) thick
2 tablespoons olive oil

OSSO BUCO is a traditional Italian dish, made from veal shanks.

2 large onions, sliced
6 Roma tomatoes, finely
   chopped
2 tablespoons tomato
   paste
1 1/2 cups (375 ml/
   12 fl oz) white wine
1 tablespoon cornflour
2–3 cloves garlic,
   crushed
1 cup (60 g/2 oz) finely
   chopped fresh parsley

1 To make the gremolata, mix together the lemon rind, garlic and parsley and set aside.
2 Season the flour with salt and pepper and use to coat the veal pieces, shaking off any excess.

Heat half the oil in a heavy-based pan large enough to fit the meat in a single layer. When the oil is hot, brown the veal well on both sides. Remove and set aside.
3 Heat the remaining oil in the pan and cook the onion for 2–3 minutes, or until soft but not brown. Add the meat in a single layer so that it fits snugly in the pan. Season with salt and pepper.
4 Mix together the tomatoes, tomato paste and wine and pour the mixture over the meat. Bring to the boil, then reduce the heat, cover and

simmer for 1 1/2 hours.
5 Remove 1 cup (250 ml/ 8 fl oz) of the cooking liquid and allow to cool a little. Place the cornflour in a small bowl and whisk in the liquid, then stir in the garlic and chopped parsley and add the mixture to the dish. Simmer, uncovered, for about 30 minutes, or until the meat is very tender and the sauce has thickened. Sprinkle with the gremolata just before serving.

121

Use a boned loin of veal for VEAL WITH PEPPERCORN SAUCE.

VEAL WITH PEPPERCORN SAUCE

Preparation: 20 minutes
Cooking: 1 hour 10 minutes
Serves 6–8

1.5 kg (3 lb) loin of veal, boned
2 tablespoons Dijon mustard
1 tablespoon oil
15 g (¹/₂ oz) butter
¹/₂ cup (125 ml/4 fl oz) dry white wine
bouquet garni
1 tablespoon canned green peppercorns
2 tablespoons brandy
3 tablespoons cream

1 Place the veal, fat-side-down, on a flat surface. Spread with 1 tablespoon of the mustard and sprinkle with freshly ground black pepper.
2 Roll up the veal neatly and tie securely at regular intervals with kitchen string. Spread with the remaining mustard.
3 Preheat the oven to moderate 180°C (350°F/Gas 4). Heat the oil and butter in a large frying pan. Add the veal and cook quickly, turning to brown all sides.
4 Put the veal in a baking dish. Add the wine and bouquet garni. Cover the dish with foil and bake for 45 minutes, or until tender, basting frequently. Transfer to a serving plate, remove the string, cover and keep warm.
5 Strain the cooking liquid into a small pan, discarding the bouquet garni. Skim off any excess fat. Bring to the boil, reduce the heat and simmer for 5–10 minutes, or until reduced and slightly thickened. Crush the green peppercorns and stir in with the brandy and cream. Heat the sauce through, but do not boil. Season to taste with salt. Slice the veal thinly and serve with the peppercorn sauce.

VEAL SCALOPPINI

Preparation: 5 minutes
Cooking: 5 minutes
Serves 4

plain flour, for coating
8 thin veal steaks
¼ cup (60 ml/2 fl oz) olive oil
60 g (2 oz) butter
2 tablespoons lemon juice
2 tablespoons finely chopped fresh parsley
lemon slices, to garnish

1 Season the flour with salt and pepper and coat the veal steaks with the flour, shaking off the excess. (The least messy way to do this is to put the flour in a plastic bag, add the meat and shake well.) Heat the oil and half the butter in a large frying pan. Add the meat to the pan, in batches if necessary (if you overcrowd the pan the meat will stew rather than frying). Cook over high heat until lightly browned on one side, then turn over and brown the other side. The veal steaks should take only 1 minute on each side—cooking longer will toughen the meat. Remove from the pan.

2 Reduce the heat and add the lemon juice, parsley and remaining butter to the pan, stirring well. Add the veal steaks, turning them in the sauce.

3 Serve the veal steaks with the sauce. Garnish with lemon slices.

NOTE: If you can't buy really thin veal steaks, put your steaks between two sheets of plastic wrap and beat with a rolling pin or meat mallet until about 5mm (¼ inch) thick. Nick the edges to prevent them curling.

Add lemon juice and parsley to the buttery pan juices, for VEAL SCALOPPINI.

CHICKEN AND OTHER POULTRY

Chicken is just perfect for today's cooking—it's quick to prepare for the after-work cook, but also good value for a family. Everyone has a favourite chicken dish, whether it's a creamy curry or a crisp-skinned roast. Once reserved for special occasions, chicken is now a versatile meat to be enjoyed every day.

ROAST CHICKEN WITH BREADCRUMB STUFFING

Preparation: 40 minutes
Cooking: 1 1/2 hours
Serves 6

3 rashers bacon, rind removed, finely chopped
6 slices wholegrain bread, crusts removed
3 spring onions, chopped
2 tablespoons chopped pecans
2 teaspoons currants
1/4 cup (15 g/1/2 oz) finely chopped fresh parsley
1 egg, lightly beaten
1/4 cup (60 ml/2 fl oz) milk
1.4 kg (2 lb 13 oz) chicken
40 g (1 1/4 oz) butter, melted
1 tablespoon oil
1 1/2 cups (375 ml/12 fl oz) chicken stock
1 tablespoon plain flour

1 Preheat the oven to moderate 180°C (350°F/Gas 4). To make the stuffing, cook the bacon in a dry frying pan over high heat for 5 minutes, or until crisp. Cut the bread into 1 cm (1/2 inch) cubes and place in a large mixing bowl. Add the bacon, spring onion, pecans, currants, parsley and combined egg and milk. Season with salt and pepper and mix well.

2 Remove the giblets and any large amounts of fat from the cavity of the chicken. Rinse and pat the chicken dry, inside and out, with paper towels. Spoon the stuffing into the cavity and close with a skewer or toothpick. Tuck the wings under the chicken and tie the legs securely with string.

3 Place the chicken on a rack in a deep baking dish. Brush with the combined butter and oil. Pour any of the remaining butter and oil mixture into the baking dish with half the stock. Roast the chicken for 1–1 1/4 hours, or until brown and tender, basting occasionally with the pan juices. Transfer the chicken to a large serving dish. Cover loosely with foil and leave in a warm place for 5 minutes before carving (some people turn their chicken breast-side-down while it 'rests'—this is so

Order a free-range bird from your butcher for the best flavoured ROAST CHICKEN.

that the juices run into the breast, making the meat more moist and tender).
4 Discard all but a tablespoon of the pan juices from the baking dish. Transfer the baking dish to the stove top. Add the flour to the pan juices and blend to a smooth paste. Stir constantly over low heat for 5 minutes, or until the mixture browns. Gradually add the remaining stock and stir until the mixture boils and thickens. (Add a little extra stock or water if the gravy is too thick.) Season with salt and pepper, and strain into a jug. Serve the hot gravy with the chicken and stuffing.

VARIATION: Use white wine instead of some of the stock in the gravy.

125

Serve the ROAST TURKEY with stuffing and gravy made from the pan juices.

ROAST TURKEY WITH CASHEW STUFFING

Preparation: 45 minutes
Cooking: 2¼ hours
Serves 6–8

3 kg (6 lb) turkey
60 g (2 oz) butter
1 onion, chopped
2 cups (370 g/12 oz) cooked brown rice
1 cup (185 g/6 oz) chopped dried apricots
½ cup (90 g/3 oz) unsalted cashews
¼ cup (15 g/½ oz) chopped fresh parsley
2 tablespoons chopped fresh mint
1 tablespoon lemon juice
2 tablespoons oil
2 cups (500 ml/16 fl oz) chicken stock
2 tablespoons plain flour

1 Remove the neck and giblets from inside the turkey. Rinse the turkey well and pat dry inside and out with paper towels.
2 Preheat the oven to moderate 180°C (350°F/ Gas 4). Heat the butter in a pan, add the onion and cook, stirring, until golden. Allow to cool, then mix thoroughly with the rice, apricots, cashews, parsley, mint and lemon juice. Season with salt and pepper.
3 Spoon the stuffing loosely into the turkey cavity. Tuck the wings underneath and close the cavity with a skewer or toothpick. Tie the legs together. Place on a rack in a deep baking dish. Brush with the oil. Pour any of the remaining oil into the baking dish with ½ cup (125 ml/4 fl oz) of the stock. Roast for 2 hours, basting with the pan juices. Cover the breast and legs with foil after 1 hour if the turkey is overbrowning. Cover and leave for 15 minutes.
4 To make the gravy, drain off all but 2 tablespoons of the pan juices from the dish. Place the dish over low heat, add the flour and stir well. Stir over medium heat until well browned. Gradually add the

remaining stock, stirring until the gravy boils and thickens. Serve with the turkey and stuffing.

ROAST DUCK WITH ORANGE SAUCE

Preparation: 40 minutes
Cooking: 2 hours 20 minutes
Serves 4

2 kg (4 lb) duck
2 chicken wings
1/2 cup (125 ml/4 fl oz) white wine
1 onion, chopped
1 small carrot, sliced
1 tomato, chopped
bouquet garni
1 tablespoon orange zest
1/3 cup (80 ml/2 3/4 fl oz) orange juice
2 tablespoons Cointreau
1 teaspoon cornflour

1 To make stock, place the duck neck in a pan. Chop the chicken wings roughly and add to the pan with the wine. Simmer over medium heat for 5 minutes, or until the liquid has reduced by half. Add the onion, carrot, tomato, bouquet garni and 2 cups (500 ml/16 fl oz) water. Bring to the boil and simmer gently for 40 minutes. Strain and set aside 1 cup (250 ml/8 fl oz) of the stock.

2 Preheat the oven to moderate 180°C (350°F/Gas 4). Place the duck in a large pan, cover with boiling water, then drain. Dry with paper towels. Using a fine skewer, prick all over the outside of the duck, piercing only the skin, not the flesh. Place the duck breast-side-down in a baking dish and roast for 50 minutes.

3 Drain off the fat from the dish, turn the duck over and add the stock. Roast for 40 minutes, or until the breast is golden brown. Pour off and reserve the stock. Remove the duck from the pan and leave in a warm place.

4 Place the stock in a pan, skimming off any fat that you can see on top. Add the orange zest, orange juice and Cointreau. Bring to the boil, then reduce the heat and simmer gently for 5 minutes. Blend the cornflour into a smooth paste with 2 teaspoons water and stir into the sauce until it boils and thickens. Serve with the roast duck.

ROAST DUCK WITH ORANGE SAUCE.

127

CHICKEN SATAY

Preparation: 40 minutes +
30 minutes marinating
Cooking: 20 minutes
Serves 4

500 g (1 lb) chicken
thigh fillets
2 tablespoons honey
1/2 cup (125 ml/4 fl oz)
soy sauce
2 teaspoons sesame oil
1/4 cup (60 ml/2 fl oz) oil
1 tablespoon soft brown
sugar
cucumber slices and
chopped roasted
peanuts, to garnish

Peanut sauce
1/2 cup (125 g/4 oz)
crunchy peanut butter
1 cup (250 ml/8 fl oz)
coconut milk
1–2 tablespoons sweet
chilli sauce
1 tablespoon soy sauce
2 teaspoons lemon juice

1 Soak 20 wooden
skewers in cold water for
30 minutes. Cut the
chicken into flattish thick
strips about 6 cm
(2 inches) long and 2 cm
(1 inch) wide. Thread a
strip of chicken onto each
skewer, flattening it on
the skewer.

2 Mix together the honey,
soy sauce and sesame oil
and spread over the
chicken. Cover and
refrigerate for 30 minutes.
3 Put all the peanut sauce
ingredients in a heavy-
based pan with 1/2 cup
(125 ml/4 fl oz) water.
Stir over low heat, until
the mixture boils. Remove
from the heat. The sauce
will thicken on standing.
4 Heat a grill, char-grill
pan or barbecue flatplate
until very hot and brush
with 1 tablespoon oil.
Cook the chicken for
2–3 minutes on each side,
sprinkling with brown
sugar and the remaining
oil. Top with the peanut
sauce and garnish with
cucumber and peanuts.
Serve the remaining
peanut sauce for dipping.

You can also make beef, lamb or seafood SATAY.

TANDOORI CHICKEN

Preparation: 25 minutes +
4 1/2 hours marinating
Cooking: 45 minutes
Serves 4

6 chicken thighs
1/3 cup (80 ml/2 3/4 fl oz)
lemon juice
1/2 small onion, chopped
4 cloves garlic
1 tablespoon grated fresh
ginger
3 teaspoons ground
coriander

128

Learn to make your own spice paste and tandoori mix, for TANDOORI CHICKEN.

1 tablespoon ground
  cumin
1 teaspoon salt
1/4 teaspoon paprika
pinch of chilli powder
1 cup (250 g/8 oz)
  yoghurt
red food colouring

1 Remove the skin from the chicken thighs and brush the flesh with 3 tablespoons of the lemon juice. Cover and refrigerate for 30 minutes.
2 Put the onion, garlic, ginger, coriander, cumin, salt and the remaining lemon juice in a food processor or spice grinder and process to make a smooth paste.
3 Combine the spice paste with the paprika, chilli powder and yoghurt and mix together until smooth. Add enough food colouring to turn the mixture deep red.
4 Place the chicken pieces in a large shallow dish, and spread liberally with the tandoori mixture. Cover with plastic wrap and refrigerate for at least 4 hours (leave overnight for the best flavour).
5 Preheat the oven to moderate 180°C (350°F/ Gas 4). Place the chicken pieces on a wire rack over a large baking dish. Bake for 45 minutes, or until tender and cooked through. Serve with rice.

129

CHICKEN CORDON BLEU

Preparation: 15 minutes +
 30 minutes refrigeration
Cooking: 10 minutes
Serves 4

4 chicken breast fillets
4 thick slices Swiss
 cheese
4 slices double-smoked
 ham
plain flour, for coating
1 egg, lightly beaten
1/2 cup (50 g/1 3/4 oz) dry
 breadcrumbs
1/2 cup (125 ml/4 fl oz)
 oil

Cut into CHICKEN CORDON BLEU to reveal ham and cheese.

1 Slice through the middle of each chicken fillet without cutting right through. Open out flat and season well.
2 Place a slice of Swiss cheese and ham on one half of each fillet and fold the other half over.
3 Season the flour well and use to coat the chicken fillets, shaking off the excess. Dip into the egg, then coat with the breadcrumbs. Place on a foil-lined tray. Cover and refrigerate for 30 minutes.
4 Heat the oil in a frying pan and cook the chicken over medium heat for 5 minutes on each side, or until golden and cooked through. Serve immediately.

CHICKEN CHASSEUR

Preparation: 20 minutes
Cooking: 1 1/2 hours
Serves 4

1 kg (2 lb) chicken thigh
 fillets
2 tablespoons oil
1 clove garlic, crushed
1 large onion, sliced
100 g (3 1/2 oz) button
 mushrooms, sliced
1 teaspoon fresh thyme
400 g (13 oz) can
 chopped tomatoes
3 tablespoons chicken
 stock
3 tablespoons white wine
1 tablespoon tomato
 paste

CHICKEN CHASSEUR means 'hunter's chicken' in French.

1 Preheat the oven to moderate 180°C (350°F/ Gas 4). Trim the chicken of any fat. Heat the oil in a heavy-based frying pan and brown the chicken in batches over medium heat. Drain on paper towels, then transfer to a casserole dish.

2 Add the garlic, onion and mushrooms to the pan and cook over medium heat for 5 minutes, or until soft. Add to the chicken with the thyme and tomatoes.

3 Combine the stock, wine and tomato paste and pour over the chicken. Cover and bake for 1¼ hours, or until the chicken is tender. Serve with rice, pasta, or crusty French bread to mop up the juices.

CHICKEN KIEV

Preparation: 35 minutes +
  2 hours refrigeration
Cooking: 20 minutes
Serves 6

125 g (4 oz) butter, softened
1 clove garlic, crushed
2 tablespoons chopped fresh parsley
2 teaspoons lemon juice
2 teaspoons grated lemon rind
6 small chicken breasts, tenderloins removed
½ cup (60 g/2 oz) plain flour
4 cups (400 g/13 oz) dry breadcrumbs
2 eggs, beaten
3 tablespoons milk
oil, for frying
lemon wedges, to serve

1 Mix together the butter, garlic, parsley, lemon juice and rind. Spoon onto a sheet of foil and shape into a rectangle about 5 x 8 cm (2 x 3 inches). Roll up the foil and chill until firm.

2 Place each piece of chicken between 2 sheets of plastic wrap and use a meat mallet or rolling pin to gently flatten to about 5 mm (¼ inch) thick.

3 Cut the chilled butter into 6 pieces. Place a piece in the centre of each chicken slice, fold in the edges and roll up to completely enclose. Fasten with toothpicks and chill until firm.

4 Place the flour and breadcrumbs on separate plates or greaseproof paper. Toss the chicken in the flour, dip in the combined egg and milk, then coat with the breadcrumbs. Chill on a paper-lined tray in the fridge for 1 hour, then toss in the egg and breadcrumbs again. Half fill a heavy-based frying pan with oil and cook the chicken, in batches, for 5 minutes on each side, or until golden and cooked through. Drain on paper towels, remove the toothpicks and serve with the lemon wedges.

Roll the chicken breast around garlic butter for CHICKEN KIEV.

Serve COQ AU VIN with hunks of crusty French bread to mop up the sauce.

COQ AU VIN

Preparation: 20 minutes
Cooking: 1 hour
Serves 6

2 sprigs fresh thyme
4 sprigs fresh parsley
2 bay leaves
plain flour, for coating
2 kg (4 lb) chicken pieces
3 tablespoons oil
4 rashers bacon, sliced
12 pickling onions
2 cloves garlic, crushed
2 tablespoons brandy
1 1/2 cups (375 ml/
   12 fl oz) red wine
1 1/2 cups (375 ml/
   12 fl oz) chicken stock
1/4 cup (60 g/2 oz)
   tomato paste
250 g (8 oz) button
   mushrooms
fresh herbs, for serving

1 To make a bouquet garni, tie together the thyme, parsley and bay leaves with string, or tie them between two short lengths of celery.
2 Season the flour with salt and pepper. Toss the chicken in the flour to coat well, shaking off any excess. Heat 2 tablespoons of the oil in a heavy-based pan and brown the chicken in batches over medium heat. Remove all the chicken from the pan and drain on paper towels.
3 Heat the remaining oil in the pan. Add the bacon, onions and garlic and cook, stirring, until the onions are browned. Add the chicken, brandy, wine, stock, bouquet garni and tomato paste. Bring to the boil, then reduce the heat and simmer, covered, for 40 minutes.
4 Stir in the mushrooms and simmer, uncovered, for 10 minutes, or until the chicken is tender and the sauce has thickened. Remove the bouquet garni, sprinkle with fresh herbs and serve with crusty French bread.

Chill the CHICKEN LIVER PATE until it is firm before serving.

CHICKEN LIVER PATE

Preparation: 10 minutes +
overnight refrigeration
Cooking: 10 minutes
Serves 4

1 onion, finely chopped
100 g (3 ½ oz) butter,
  melted
1 clove garlic, crushed
1 tablespoon chopped
  fresh thyme
500 g (1 lb) chicken
  livers, cleaned
2 teaspoons green
  peppercorns in brine,
  roughly chopped
1 tablespoon brandy
6 tablespoons ghee (see
  Note)

1 Fry the onion in 2 tablespoons butter until soft. Add the garlic and thyme and cook for 1 minute. Add the livers and cook for 5 minutes, or until firm and cooked.

2 Transfer to a food processor and add the remaining butter. Blend until smooth, then season. Add the peppercorns and brandy and blend briefly.

3 Spoon into ramekins and cover the surface with plastic wrap. Refrigerate overnight to firm. Cover the pâté with ghee.

NOTE: Ghee is a form of clarified butter which cooks at high temperatures without burning. You can buy it as 'ghee' or you can clarify your own butter at home. Ghee is commonly used for cooking curries, and it is worth knowing how to make your own. To make 100 g (3 ½ oz) clarified butter, cut 180 g (6 oz) butter into cubes. Heat in a small pan set in a larger pan of hot water, over low heat. Melt the butter without stirring. Skim the foam from the top. Remove from the heat, cool slightly and pour off the clear yellow liquid, being careful to leave the milky sediment behind in the pan. Refrigerate the clarified butter in an airtight container.

THAI GREEN CHICKEN CURRY

Preparation: 25 minutes
Cooking: 35 minutes
Serves 4

2 cups (500 ml/16 fl oz) coconut milk
2 tablespoons oil
1 onion, chopped
2 tablespoons green curry paste
500 g (1 lb) chicken thigh fillets, cut into strips
4 kaffir lime leaves
100 g (3 1/2 oz) snake beans, chopped
2 tablespoons fish sauce
2 tablespoons lime juice
1 teaspoon finely grated lime rind
3 teaspoons grated palm sugar or soft brown sugar
fresh coriander leaves, to garnish

Garnish THAI GREEN CHICKEN CURRY with fresh coriander.

1 In a pan, bring the coconut milk to the boil and cook over high heat for about 10 minutes, or until small bubbles of oil begin to crack the surface of the coconut milk.
2 Heat the oil in a wok or a heavy-based pan. Add the onion and curry paste and cook over high heat for about 1 minute, or until the curry paste is fragrant. Add the chicken and stir-fry for 5 minutes, or until the chicken is almost cooked.
3 Add the coconut milk, kaffir lime leaves, snake beans and 3 tablespoons water to the wok. Bring to the boil, stirring occasionally. Reduce the heat and simmer for 10 minutes, or until the chicken is tender.
4 Stir in the fish sauce, lime juice, rind and sugar. Garnish with the coriander leaves and serve with steamed rice.

NOTE: The 'cracking' of the coconut milk is a traditional technique used in Thai cookery. It separates the oils in the coconut milk, making it more glossy.
Thai green curry paste is made using green chillies. Thai red curry paste is made from red chillies, which is why it is hotter. You can use this recipe to make a Thai red chicken curry.

SWEET CHILLI CHICKEN WINGS

Preparation: 30 minutes +
overnight marinating
Cooking: 1 hour
Serves 10

2 kg (4 lb) chicken wings
2 cloves garlic, crushed
¼ teaspoon salt
1 teaspoon ground black
pepper
1 tablespoon oil
¼ cup (60 ml/2 fl oz)
sweet chilli sauce
2 tablespoons honey
1 tablespoon white
vinegar
¼ cup (60 ml/2 fl oz)
soy sauce
2 teaspoons grated
ginger
1 tablespoon soft brown
sugar

SWEET CHILLI CHICKEN WINGS are ideal party food.

1 Trim the chicken of excess fat and sinew. Cut each wing into three sections, discarding the tips (you can freeze them and use for making stock).
2 Mix together the remaining ingredients in a large bowl. Add the chicken pieces and stir until coated. Cover and refrigerate overnight (or for several hours).
3 Preheat the oven to moderate 180°C (350°F/ Gas 4). Drain the chicken pieces and reserve the marinade. Place the chicken pieces on a roasting rack over a baking tray or in a deep baking dish. Bake for 1 hour, or until the chicken is crisp and cooked through. Brush the pieces with the reserved marinade several times during cooking. Serve hot.

STORAGE: The chicken can be cooked up to 2 days in advance and stored, covered, in the fridge. Reheat in a moderate 180°C (350°F/ Gas 4) oven for 10–15 minutes.
VARIATION: For devilled chicken wings to serve four people, mix together 1 teaspoon Dijon mustard, 1 clove crushed garlic, 2 tablespoons hoisin sauce, 1 tablespoon Worcestershire sauce, 2 tablespoons tomato sauce, 1 tablespoon lemon juice and a few drops of Tabasco in a large bowl. Season 12 chicken wings and add to the bowl. Toss and cover with plastic wrap. Refrigerate for 2 hours or overnight. Preheat the oven to moderately hot 200°C (400°F/Gas 6). Arrange the wings on a wire rack above a baking tray or in a deep baking dish and bake for 30–40 minutes, or until browned and cooked through. Eat hot or as cold picnic food.

COUNTRY RABBIT IN RED WINE

Preparation: 45 minutes
Cooking: 1½ hours
Serves 4

1.25 kg (2½ lb) rabbit
½ cup (125 ml/4 fl oz)
  olive oil
2 cloves garlic, crushed
1 sprig of fresh rosemary,
  finely chopped
1 cup (250 ml/8 fl oz)
  red wine
½ cup (125 ml/4 fl oz)
  chicken stock
4 tomatoes, peeled and
  chopped

1 Cut the forelegs from the rabbit by cutting through the connective tissue joining the body. Cut across the back of the rabbit just above the legs, then cut the legs in half. Cut the body (saddle) of the rabbit into 2 pieces, then cut the ribcage and backbone into 4 pieces, to form 8 portions.
2 Heat the oil in a heavy-based pan and brown the rabbit, in batches, over medium heat. Add the garlic and rosemary and cook for 1 minute.
3 Add the wine and stock, and season with salt and freshly ground black pepper. Cover and simmer gently for 30 minutes. Add the tomato and cook, covered, for 45 minutes over low heat, or until the rabbit is tender. Serve with crusty Italian bread.

SOUTHERN FRIED CHICKEN

Preparation: 15 minutes +
  2 hours marinating
Cooking: 30 minutes
Serves 4

1 kg (2 lb) chicken pieces
2 cups (500 ml/16 fl oz)
  buttermilk
oil, for deep-frying
1½ cups (185 g/6 oz)
  plain flour

1 Place the chicken in a bowl and pour in the buttermilk. Mix well. Cover and refrigerate for 2 hours, turning occasionally.
2 Half fill a large, deep pan with oil and heat to 180°C (350°F), or until a cube of bread browns in 15 seconds. Place the flour in a shallow dish and season with salt and pepper. Remove the chicken from the buttermilk, shake off any excess, dip it into the flour and coat well.
3 Lower the chicken into the oil, in small batches, and deep-fry for 12 minutes on each side, making sure that the oil is not too hot or the chicken will brown on the outside before it is cooked through. Drain the chicken well on paper towels before serving.

COUNTRY RABBIT IN RED WINE.

SOUTHERN FRIED CHICKEN.

CHICKEN NUGGETS WITH DIPPING SAUCE.

NOTE: For southern fried chicken, use chicken pieces that are all a similar size, or some will cook faster than others.

CHICKEN NUGGETS WITH DIPPING SAUCE

Preparation: 30 minutes +
  30 minutes refrigeration
Cooking: 30 minutes
Serves 6

4 chicken breast fillets
1/2 cup (60 g/2 oz) plain flour
1 tablespoon chicken seasoning
2 eggs
1 1/2 cups (150 g/5 oz) dry breadcrumbs
oil, for frying

Dipping sauce
1 cup (250 ml/8 fl oz) pineapple juice
1/4 cup (60 ml/2 fl oz) white wine vinegar
2 teaspoons soy sauce
2 tablespoons soft brown sugar
2 tablespoons tomato sauce
1 tablespoon cornflour

1 Cut the chicken fillets into strips about 2 cm (3/4 inch) wide. Mix the flour and seasoning in a plastic bag and add the chicken. Toss until the chicken is evenly coated with flour. Remove and shake off the excess.
2 Beat the eggs lightly in a shallow bowl, and put the breadcrumbs in a shallow bowl. Working with a few strips at a time, dip the chicken in the egg, then coat with the breadcrumbs. Refrigerate for at least 30 minutes.
3 Heat 3 cm (1 1/4 inches) of the oil in a large frying pan to moderately hot, or until a cube of bread browns in 15 seconds. Fry the nuggets in batches for 3–5 minutes, or until golden brown. Drain on paper towels.
4 To make the dipping sauce, mix the juice, vinegar, soy sauce, sugar and tomato sauce in a small pan. Stir over low heat until dissolved. Mix the cornflour to a paste with 1 tablespoon water. Add to the pan and stir until the mixture boils and thickens. Simmer for 2 minutes. Cool and serve with the chicken.

137

Serve *CHICKEN AND ALMONDS* with steamed rice.

TERIYAKI CHICKEN.

CHICKEN AND ALMONDS

Preparation: 30 minutes
Cooking: 20 minutes
Serves 4

1 tablespoon soy sauce
1 tablespoooon cornflour
300 g (10 oz) chicken
  breast fillets, sliced
  diagonally across
oil, for cooking
2 cm (³/4 inch) piece
  fresh ginger, finely
  grated
1 onion, roughly
  chopped
1 celery stick, thinly
  sliced diagonally
50 g (1³/4 oz) green
  beans, sliced in half
¹/4 cup (60 g/2 oz)
  canned bamboo shoots,
  drained
¹/4 cup (60 ml/2 fl oz)
  chicken stock
2 tablespoons Chinese
  rice wine or medium
  sherry
1 teaspoon sesame oil
2 teaspoons cornflour,
  extra
125 g (4 oz) blanched
  almonds, roasted

1 Mix together the soy
sauce and cornflour in a
small bowl. Pour over the
chicken and leave for
about 5 minutes.
2 Heat 2 tablespoons of
the oil in a wok or heavy-
based pan until it is
extremely hot. Stir-fry the

APRICOT CHICKEN is a quick and simple family dish.

add the chicken drumsticks in batches and cook over high heat until browned all over.

3 Return all the chicken to the pan, add the sauce, cover and cook for 30 minutes, or until the chicken is tender. Serve with rice.

APRICOT CHICKEN

Preparation: 30 minutes
Cooking: 55 minutes
Serves 4

6 chicken thigh cutlets, skin removed
40 g (1¼ oz) packet French onion soup mix
425 ml (14 fl oz) can apricot nectar
425 g (14 oz) can apricot halves, drained

1 Preheat the oven to moderate 180°C (350°F/ Gas 4). Place the chicken in an ovenproof dish. Mix the onion soup mix with the apricot nectar and pour over the chicken.
2 Bake, covered, for 50 minutes, add the apricot pieces and bake for a further 5 minutes. Serve with creamy mashed potato or rice to soak up the juices.

chicken over high heat for 2 minutes, then remove from the wok.
3 If there is very little oil in the wok, add an extra tablespoon, reheat the wok and stir-fry the ginger, onion and celery for 4 minutes. Add the beans and bamboo shoots, and cook for 1 minute. Add the stock, rice wine, sesame oil and 2 tablespoons of water, cover and steam for 30 seconds.
4 Mix the extra cornflour with 1 tablespoon water, stir into the sauce and stir until it comes to the boil and thickens. Return the chicken to the wok and add the almonds. Toss until heated through.

TERIYAKI CHICKEN

Preparation: 15 minutes
Cooking: 45 minutes
Serves 6

½ cup (125 ml/4 fl oz) Japanese soy sauce
2 tablespoons mirin
1 tablespoon sugar
2 tablespoons oil
12 chicken drumsticks

1 Place the soy sauce, mirin and sugar in a small pan and stir over low heat until the sugar dissolves. Bring to the boil, then reduce the heat and simmer for 2 minutes.
2 Heat the oil in a large heavy-based frying pan,

SEAFOOD

Many people find the thought of cooking seafood a little daunting. They see it as difficult and unpredictable. Few cookery myths are more undeserved than this one. Fish is really very easy to cook, and if you have a good fishmonger you won't have to do much preparation either.

FISHERMAN'S PIE

Preparation: 40 minutes
Cooking: 1 hour
Serves 4

800 g (1 lb 10 oz) firm
  white fish fillets
1 ½ cups (375 ml/
  12 fl oz) milk
1 onion, roughly
  chopped
2 cloves
50 g (1 ¾ oz) butter
2 tablespoons plain flour
pinch of ground nutmeg
2 tablespoons chopped
  fresh parsley
1 cup (155 g/5 oz) peas
750 g (1 ½ lb) potatoes,
  quartered
2 tablespoons hot milk
¼ cup (30 g/1 oz)
  grated Cheddar

1 Place the fish fillets in a frying pan and cover with the milk. Add the onion and cloves, and bring to the boil. Reduce the heat and simmer for about 5 minutes, or until the fish is cooked—the flesh should be opaque and flake easily with a fork.
2 Preheat the oven to moderate 180°C (350°F/ Gas 4). Remove the fish from the pan, reserving the milk and onion mixture. Discard the cloves. Allow the fish to cool then remove any skin and bones and flake into bite-sized pieces.
3 Heat half of the butter in a pan, stir in the flour and cook, stirring, for 1 minute. Remove from the heat, add the reserved milk mixture and stir until smooth. Return to the heat and cook, stirring, until the sauce comes to the boil and thickens. Cook for 1 minute. Remove from the heat, allow to cool slightly, then add the nutmeg, parsley and peas. Season well with salt and freshly ground black pepper, and gently fold in the fish. Spoon into a 1.25 litre ovenproof dish.
4 Cook the potatoes in boiling water until tender. Drain and add the hot milk and remaining butter. Mash until very smooth. Add the cheese. If the mash is very stiff you may need to add a little more milk—the mash should be fairly firm.
5 Spoon the mashed potato into a piping bag and pipe it over the filling; or alternatively, spoon it over the top of the filling and rough it up with a fork. Bake for about 30 minutes, or until heated through.

THAI FISH CAKES

Preparation: 30 minutes
Cooking: 10 minutes
Serves 4–6

450 g (14 oz) firm white
  boneless fish fillets
1/4 cup (45 g/1 1/2 oz) rice
  flour or cornflour
1 tablespoon fish sauce
1 egg, beaten
1/2 cup (25 g/3/4 oz)
  chopped fresh
  coriander
3 teaspoons Thai red
  curry paste
1–2 small red chillies,
  finely chopped
100 g (3 1/2 oz) green
  beans, very finely sliced
2 spring onions, chopped

1/2 cup (125 ml/4 fl oz)
  oil
sweet chilli sauce, to
  serve

1 Work the fish in a food
processor for 20 seconds,
or until smooth. Add the
rice flour, fish sauce, egg,
coriander, curry paste and
chilli. Mix for 10 seconds.
Transfer to a bowl and
mix in the beans and
spring onion. Using wet
hands, make into patties.
2 Heat the oil in a heavy-
based frying pan until a
cube of bread browns in
15 seconds. Cook four
fish cakes at a time until
golden brown on both
sides. Serve with sweet
chilli sauce.

FISH AND CHIPS

Preparation: 25 minutes
Cooking: 25 minutes
Serves 4

Beer batter
1 1/2 cups (375 ml/
  12 fl oz) beer
1 1/4 cups (155 g/5 oz)
  plain flour

4 potatoes
oil, for deep-frying
4 firm white fish fillets
cornflour, to coat
lemon wedges, to serve

1 To make the batter,
gradually whisk the beer
into the flour to make a
smooth batter.

Use red curry paste for THAI FISH CAKES.

2 Peel the potatoes and cut into chips 1 cm (3/4 inch) thick. Soak for 10 minutes in cold water. Drain and pat dry.

3 Fill a large, deep heavy-based pan two-thirds full with oil and heat until a cube of bread browns in 30 seconds. Cook the chips in batches for 4–5 minutes, or until pale golden. Remove with tongs or a slotted spoon and drain on paper towels.

4 Just before serving, reheat the oil until a cube of bread browns in 15 seconds. Re-cook the chips in batches until crisp and golden. Drain and keep hot.

5 Dry the fish on paper towels. Lightly dust with cornflour and dip into the batter. Deep-fry in batches for 5–7 minutes, or until cooked through. Drain on paper towels and serve with lemon wedges.

FISH AND CHIPS (top) with SMOKED TROUT PATE.

SMOKED TROUT PATE

Preparation: 10 minutes
Cooking: Nil
Serves 4–6

250 g (8 oz) smoked trout, skinned, boned
125 g (4 oz) butter, softened
125 g (4 oz) cream cheese, softened
1 tablespoon lemon juice
1 teaspoon horseradish cream
1/4 cup (15 g/1/2 oz) chopped fresh parsley
1/4 cup (15 g/1/2 oz) finely chopped chives
toasted brown bread, to serve

1 Place the trout, butter and cream cheese in a food processor. Process for 20 seconds, or until the mixture is smooth.

2 Add the lemon juice, horseradish, parsley and chives, and process for 10 seconds. Season with salt and freshly ground black pepper and more lemon juice, if desired.

3 Transfer to a small serving dish. Serve with the hot toasted brown bread and maybe lemon wedges on the side.

STORAGE: Best eaten on the same day, but can be kept for up to 4 days in the fridge.
VARIATION: Try smoked haddock or mackerel.

TROUT WITH ALMONDS

Preparation: 25 minutes
Cooking: 20 minutes
Serves 2

2 rainbow trout, cleaned
flour, to coat
60 g (2 oz) butter
1/4 cup (25 g/3/4 oz)
    flaked almonds
2 tablespoons lemon
    juice
1 tablespoon finely
    chopped fresh parsley

1 Wash the trout and pat dry with paper towels. Open the trout out, skin-side-up. Using a rolling pin, run along the backbone starting from the tail, pressing gently down. Turn the trout over and cut through the backbone at each end of the fish with a pair of scissors. Lever the backbone out. Check for any remaining bones, and trim the fins with scissors. **2** Coat the fish with the flour. Heat half the butter in a large frying pan and add the fish. Cook for 7 minutes on each side, or until golden brown and cooked through. Remove and place on heated plates. Cover with foil. **3** Heat the remaining butter, add the flaked almonds and stir until the almonds are light golden brown. Add the lemon juice, parsley and some salt and pepper. Stir until the sauce is heated through. Pour over the trout and serve.

NOTE: The trout can be boned several hours ahead and refrigerated.

You could ask your fishmonger to bone the TROUT for you.

BAKED SNAPPER WITH GARLIC AND TOMATOES

Preparation: 25 minutes
Cooking: 30–40 minutes
Serves 4–6

1 kg (2 lb) whole
    snapper, scaled and
    cleaned
1 lemon, sliced
1 small onion, thickly
    sliced
1 clove garlic
sprig of fresh thyme
1 tablespoon olive oil
extra thyme leaves and
    lemon slices, to garnish

Sauce
2 tablespoons olive oil
1 clove garlic, crushed
1 small onion, chopped
1 teaspoon sugar
3 anchovies, mashed
1/2 cup (125 ml/4 fl oz)
    white wine
440 g (14 oz) can
    tomatoes, chopped,
    juice reserved
1/3 cup (80 ml/2 3/4 fl oz)
    lemon juice
sprig of fresh thyme

1 Preheat the oven to moderately hot 200°C (400°F/Gas 6). Remove any loose scales from the fish, trim the tail to a V shape and remove the fins. Wipe out the gut area with damp paper towels. Place the lemon slices, onion, garlic and

BAKED SNAPPER WITH GARLIC AND TOMATOES.

thyme into the gutted cavity. Score the thickest part of the fish with two diagonal slashes. Turn the fish over and slash the other side. Rub the outside of the fish with the olive oil. Place in a baking dish.

2 To make the sauce, heat the oil in a pan, add the garlic and onion, and cook, stirring, until the onion is golden. Stir in the sugar, anchovies, wine, tomato and juice, lemon juice and fresh thyme. Simmer until the sauce has reduced by one third and has thickened slightly.

3 Pour the sauce over the fish. Bake for 20 minutes, or until the fish flakes easily. Serve on a heated platter, garnished with thyme leaves and lemon.

HINT: This dish can be served either hot or cold. Many people don't think of serving fish cold, but it is delicious. It is important to serve it at room temperature, not chilled. Cook as above, cover and set aside until it cools. To remove the bone neatly when serving, cut through the centre of the fish on one side and gently push the flesh away to either side, so the bone is exposed. Lift the tail and remove the bone.

POACHED SALMON WITH HOLLANDAISE SAUCE

Preparation: 20 minutes
Cooking: 10 minutes
Serves 4

1 cup (250 ml/8 fl oz)
white wine
2 cups (500 ml/16 fl oz)
fish stock
1 tablespoon lemon juice
1 large slice of onion
4 Atlantic salmon cutlets,
2.5 cm (1 inch) thick
fresh dill, to garnish

Hollandaise sauce
3 egg yolks
125 g (4 oz) butter,
melted and hot
$^1/_2$ teaspoon grated
lemon rind
1 tablespoon lemon juice

1 Place the wine, stock, lemon juice and onion in a shallow pan. Bring to the boil, then reduce the heat to simmer.

2 Place the salmon cutlets in a single layer in the simmering stock. Poach the fish gently for about 7 minutes, or until it is just cooked, turning once.

3 Remove the fish from the pan and drain on paper towels. Cover the fish with foil to keep it warm.

4 To make the hollandaise sauce, put the egg yolks in a food processor and process for 10 seconds. With the motor running pour the hot and bubbling butter in a slow stream onto the egg yolks. Discard the white butter residue that will be left at the bottom of the pan. Add the grated lemon rind and juice, and process for another 30 seconds, or until the sauce thickens.

5 Arrange the fish on serving dishes. Serve with the hollandaise sauce and garnish with the fresh dill.

NOTE: The hollandaise sauce is best served immediately. If necessary it can be stored in an airtight container in the fridge for up to 2 days. Reheat in a heatproof bowl over a pan of gently simmering water.

VARIATION: Ocean trout cutlets can be used instead of salmon. Or you may prefer to use a large salmon fillet or whole salmon, including the head. If using a whole salmon it is best to skin the fish after poaching. If serving whole salmon cold, leave it in the stock until it is cooled. Remove the skin when cool.

Poach the SALMON in a mixture of wine, stock and lemon juice.

Use floury potatoes that mash well for SALMON PATTIES.

SALMON PATTIES

Preparation: 1 hour
Cooking: 25 minutes
Serves 4

650 g (1 lb 5 oz) floury
  potatoes, chopped
425 g (14 oz) can red
  salmon, drained
2 spring onions, finely
  chopped
¹/₄ cup (15 g/¹/₂ oz)
  chopped fresh parsley
2 teaspoons grated lemon
  rind
1 egg
5 slices bread, crusts
  removed
40 g (1 ¹/₄ oz) butter
¹/₄ cup (60 ml/2 fl oz)
  olive oil
lemon wedges, to serve

1 Cook the potato in
boiling water until very
tender. Drain well and
mash until smooth.
2 Place the salmon in a
large bowl and break up
the flesh with a fork,
removing any bones and
skin. Add the spring
onion, parsley, lemon
rind, egg and mashed
potato. Season with salt
and pepper and stir well.
Shape into rough patties,
using about a third of a
cup for each patty.
3 Chop the bread in a
food processor until it
forms fine crumbs. Gently
roll the patties in the
breadcrumbs and neaten
the shape. Press the
breadcrumbs firmly onto
the patties with your

fingertips to coat well.
4 Heat the butter and oil
in a large frying pan.
When the butter is
foaming, add the patties
and cook each side for
3–5 minutes, or until
golden and browned.
Drain on paper towels.
Serve with lemon wedges.

VARIATION: Use canned
tuna in brine, drained,
instead of the salmon.
NOTE: Suitable floury
potatoes (those good for
mashing) are Idaho,
Sebago, King Edward and
Coliban. Or you could
even try using mashed
sweet potato.

147

TUNA MORNAY

Preparation: 40 minutes
Cooking: 35 minutes
Serves 4

1 1/2 cups (375 ml/
  12 fl oz) milk
1 bay leaf
1 slice of onion
5 whole black
  peppercorns
60 g (2 oz) butter
1 onion, finely chopped
1 celery stick, finely
  chopped
1/4 cup (30 g/1 oz) plain
  flour
425 g (14 oz) can tuna
  in brine, drained,
  flaked, brine reserved

1/4 teaspoon ground
  nutmeg
1/3 cup (80 ml/2 3/4 fl oz)
  cream
1/4 cup (15 g/1/2 oz)
  finely chopped fresh
  parsley
1 cup (125 g/4 oz)
  grated Cheddar
1/2 cup (40 g/1 1/4 oz)
  fresh breadcrumbs
paprika, to taste

1 Heat the milk, bay leaf, onion slice and peppercorns in a small pan. Bring to the boil, then remove from the heat, cover and leave to infuse for 15 minutes. Strain and reserve the milk.

2 Preheat the oven to moderate 180°C (350°F/ Gas 4). Heat the butter in a pan and add the onion and celery. Cook, stirring, for 5 minutes, or until the onion is soft. Add the flour and stir for 1 minute, or until the mixture is bubbly. Remove from the heat and gradually stir in the combined reserved milk and tuna brine. Stir until smooth. Return to the heat and stir until the mixture almost boils. Reduce the heat to low and simmer for 5 minutes, or until thickened.

3 Add the nutmeg, cream, parsley and half of the cheese. Stir for 2 minutes, or until the cheese is melted. Remove from the heat, add the flaked tuna and season with salt and freshly ground black pepper. Stir to combine.

4 Spoon the mixture into a 3-cup (750 ml/24 fl oz) greased ovenproof dish. Sprinkle the top with the combined breadcrumbs, paprika and remaining cheese. Bake for 15 minutes, then place the dish under a hot grill for 2 minutes to brown the breadcrumb topping.

NOTE: Tuna mornay can be used as a filling for pancakes or pastry cases. VARIATION: Use canned salmon instead of tuna.

Brown the topping of the TUNA MORNAY under the grill.

148

SEAFOOD CREPES

Preparation: 50 minutes +
30 minutes standing
Cooking: 30 minutes
Serves 8

1 cup (125 g/4 oz) plain
flour
1 egg, plus 1 egg yolk
1 cup (250 ml/8 fl oz)
milk
20 g (³/4 oz) butter,
melted
1 tablespoon poppy
seeds, optional

Seafood filling
1 cup (250 ml/8 fl oz)
white wine
¹/2 cup (125 ml/4 fl oz)
fish stock or water
200 g (6¹/2 oz) small
scallops
400 g (13 oz) raw
prawns, peeled,
deveined and halved
200 g (6¹/2 oz) boneless
white fish fillets
60 g (2 oz) butter
3 spring onions, chopped
2 bacon rashers, chopped
¹/4 cup (30 g/1 oz) plain
flour
³/4 cup (185 ml/6 fl oz)
cream
1 teaspoon lemon juice
¹/4 cup (15 g/¹/2 oz)
chopped fresh parsley
2 tablespoons chopped
fresh chives

We've added poppy seeds to our SEAFOOD CREPES.

1 Mix together the flour, egg, egg yolk and half the milk. Add the remaining milk, butter, and poppy seeds if you are using, and mix until smooth. Cover and leave for 30 minutes. Transfer to a jug.

2 Heat a crepe pan and brush lightly with melted butter. Add enough batter to thinly cover the base, pouring the excess back into the jug. Cook for 30 seconds, turn over and cook until lightly browned. Remove and cover while cooking the remaining crepes.

3 To make the filling, heat the wine and stock in a pan until simmering. Add the seafood and cook for 4 minutes. Drain, reserving the liquid. Flake the fish. Melt the butter in a pan, add the spring onion and bacon, and stir for 2–3 minutes, or until cooked. Add the flour, stir for 1 minute and remove from the heat. Add 1 cup (250 ml/8 fl oz) of the reserved stock mixture, return to the heat and stir for 2 minutes, or until it boils and thickens. Stir in the cream, lemon juice, parsley, chives and some pepper. Add the seafood and heat gently for 2–3 minutes, taking care not to overcook.

4 Place 2 tablespoons of the filling over a quarter of each crepe. Fold in quarters to serve.

GARLIC PRAWNS

Preparation: 20 minutes
Cooking: 5 minutes
Serves 4

1 cup (250 ml/8 fl oz) oil
60 g (2 oz) butter, cut
    into 4 cubes
8 garlic cloves
20 raw king prawns,
    peeled and deveined,
    tails left intact
2 tablespoons chopped
    fresh parsley
French bread, for serving

1 Heat the oil, butter and garlic in a pan. When bubbling, add all the prawns and cook until they turn pink.

2 Preheat the oven to hot 210°C (415°F/Gas 6–7). Heat four heatproof serving dishes in the oven until quite hot. Remove the dishes from the oven and place 5 prawns in each dish. Spoon some oil into each dish. Sprinkle with the parsley and serve with French bread.

VARIATION: Give your garlic prawns a little extra bite by adding 2 small red sliced chillies to the garlic butter, when you add the garlic in step 1. Remove the seeds from the chillies first (unless you like them extra hot).

NOTE: Garlic prawns can also be cooked on the barbecue. Divide the oil among four flameproof dishes. Add a cube of butter to each dish and heat the barbecue. Crush 2 cloves of garlic into each dish. Heat the dishes on a barbecue flatplate until the butter is very hot and bubbling. Add 5 prawns to each dish and cook for 3–4 minutes, or until the prawns are pink and cooked through. Sprinkle with the chopped parsley and serve with French bread.

Add a little extra bite to GARLIC PRAWNS with sliced red chillies.

SPAGHETTI MARINARA

Preparation: 50 minutes
Cooking: 30 minutes
Serves 4

olive oil, for cooking
1 onion, chopped
2 cloves garlic, crushed
1/2 cup (125 ml/4 fl oz)
   red wine
2 tablespoons tomato
   paste
425 g (14 oz) can
   chopped tomatoes
1 cup (250 ml/8 fl oz)
   bottled tomato pasta
   sauce
1 tablespoon chopped
   fresh basil
1 tablespoon chopped
   fresh oregano
12 mussels, scrubbed,
   beards removed
30 g (1 oz) butter
125 g (4 oz) small
   calamari tubes, sliced
125 g (4 oz) boneless
   white fish fillets, cubed
200 g (6 1/2 oz) raw
   prawns, shelled and
   deveined, leaving tails
   intact
500 g (1 lb) spaghetti

SPAGHETTI MARINARA.

1 Heat a little of the oil in a large pan and cook the onion and garlic over low heat for 2–3 minutes. Increase the heat to moderate and add the wine, tomato paste, tomato and pasta sauce. Simmer for 5–10 minutes, stirring occasionally, until the sauce reduces and thickens slightly. Stir in the herbs and season to taste with salt and pepper. Keep warm.

2 Heat 1/2 cup (125 ml/ 4 fl oz) water in a pan. Add the mussels (discarding any which are already open and don't close when tapped), cover and steam for 3–5 minutes, or until the mussels have opened (discard any mussels which haven't opened after 5 minutes). Remove and set aside. Stir the remaining liquid into the tomato sauce.

3 Heat the butter in a pan and fry the calamari, fish and prawns, in batches, for 1–2 minutes, or until cooked. Add the seafood to the warm tomato sauce and stir gently.

4 Cook the spaghetti in a large pan of rapidly boiling salted water until just tender, then drain. Toss the sauce through the spaghetti and serve.

VARIATION: Use 500 g (1 lb) marinara mix instead of the seafood.

151

OYSTERS MORNAY

Preparation: 15 minutes
Cooking: 10 minutes
Serves 4

30 g (1 oz) butter
1 tablespoon plain flour
²/₃ cup (170 ml/
  5¹/₂ fl oz) hot milk
pinch of cayenne pepper
1 tablespoon cream
24 fresh oysters in shells
rock salt
¹/₃ cup (40 g/1¹/₄ oz)
  grated Cheddar
paprika, to sprinkle

OYSTERS MORNAY.

1 Melt the butter in a small pan. Stir in the flour and cook for 2 minutes. Remove from the heat and gradually stir in the hot milk. Stir over medium heat until the mixture boils and thickens. Season with salt, pepper and the cayenne pepper.
2 Simmer the sauce very gently for 2 minutes, stirring occasionally. Stir in the cream. Remove from the heat and lay baking paper directly on the surface to prevent a skin forming.
3 Drain the juice from the oysters and add the juice to the sauce. Arrange the oysters in shells on a bed of rock salt on a baking or grill tray. Top the oysters with a teaspoon of the hot sauce and sprinkle with the cheese. Place under a hot grill for 2–3 minutes, or until lightly browned. Sprinkle with the paprika.

VARIATIONS:
For Oysters Rockefeller, arrange 24 fresh oysters in half shells on rock salt. Cover and refrigerate. Melt 60 g (2 oz) butter in a pan and cook 2 finely chopped rashers of bacon over medium heat until browned. Add 8 finely chopped English spinach leaves, 2 tablespoons each of chopped parsley and spring onion, ¹/₃ cup (30 g/1 oz) dry breadcrumbs and a drop of Tabasco. Cook for 5 minutes, or until the spinach wilts. Spoon a little over each oyster and grill for 2–3 minutes, or until lightly browned.

For Oysters Kilpatrick, Place 24 oysters in half shells on a grill tray. Heat 30 g (1 oz) butter in a small pan. Add 2 tablespoons Worcestershire sauce and simmer for 2 minutes. Spoon half a teaspoon of the sauce onto each oyster. Sprinkle with 3 finely chopped rashers of bacon and some ground black pepper. Grill for 3–4 minutes, or until the bacon is crisp. Serve immediately on a bed of rock salt.

Use scallops in their shells for COQUILLES SAINT JACQUES.

COQUILLES SAINT JACQUES

Preparation: 20 minutes
Cooking: 15 minutes
Serves 4

12 scallops on shells
1 cup (250 ml/8 fl oz)
  white wine
1 bay leaf
4 peppercorns
1 onion, chopped
30 g (1 oz) butter
1 1/2 tablespoons flour
3/4 cup (185 ml/6 fl oz)
  milk
1/2 cup (60 g/2 oz)
  grated Cheddar
2 tablespoons dry
  breadcrumbs

1 Remove the black vein from the side of each scallop with scissors.
2 Place the wine, bay leaf, peppercorns and onion in a small pan. Bring to the boil, then reduce the heat and simmer until the liquid has reduced by three quarters. Strain the liquid and set aside.
3 Melt the butter in a small pan. Add the flour and cook for 1 minute. Remove the pan from the heat and gradually stir in the milk and the strained liquid, stirring until smooth. Return to medium heat and stir until the mixture boils and thickens. Season with salt and pepper and stir in half of the cheese.
4 Spoon over the scallops in their shells. Sprinkle with the combined breadcrumbs and remaining cheese, and grill until crisp and golden brown.

153

PRAWN COCKTAIL

Preparation: 20 minutes
Cooking: Nil
Serves 4

Cocktail sauce
1 cup (250 g/8 oz) whole
  egg mayonnaise
2 tablespoons tomato
  sauce
2 tablespoons thick
  cream
dash of Tabasco sauce
1 teaspoon lemon juice
1 teaspoon
  Worcestershire sauce

24 cooked prawns,
  peeled and deveined,
  tails left intact
lettuce, lemon wedges
  and buttered brown
  bread, to serve

1 Mix together all the sauce ingredients in a large bowl.
2 Keep six or eight prawns on one side to garnish. Remove the tails from the remaining prawns and mix gently with the sauce.
3 Arrange the lettuce in serving bowls and spoon the prawns over the top.

Decorate with the reserved prawns and serve with the lemon wedges and slices of brown bread.

PRAWN CUTLETS WITH TARTARE SAUCE

Preparation: 40 minutes
Cooking: 10 minutes
Serves 4–6

24 raw king prawns,
  peeled, tails intact
4 eggs
2 tablespoons soy sauce
cornflour, to coat
dry breadcrumbs
oil, for deep-frying
lemon wedges, to serve

Tartare sauce
1 cup (250 g/8 oz)
  mayonnaise
1 tablespoon grated
  onion
1 tablespoon capers,
  chopped
1 tablespoon gherkins,
  finely chopped
1 tablespoon lemon juice
1 tablespoon finely
  chopped fresh parsley
dash of Tabasco sauce

1 Butterfly the prawns by slitting them open down the back. Devein and flatten with your hand.
2 Beat the eggs and soy sauce in a small bowl. Dip the prawns in the cornflour, then in the egg

PRAWN COCKTAIL (top) and PRAWN CUTLETS.

mixture and finally in the breadcrumbs. Refrigerate for 10 minutes to firm up.

3 Heat the oil in a deep pan until a cube of bread dropped into the oil browns in 15 seconds. Deep-fry the prawns in batches until lightly golden and then drain on paper towels.

4 To make the tartare sauce, mix together all the ingredients. Serve the prawns with the tartare sauce and lemon wedges.

MOULES MARINIERE

Mussels and wine combine in MOULES MARINIERE.

Preparation: 15 minutes
Cooking: 40 minutes
Serves 4

 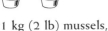

1 kg (2 lb) mussels, scrubbed, beards removed
1 onion, chopped
1 celery stick, chopped
1 cup (250 ml/8 fl oz) white wine
1¹/₂ cups (375 ml/ 12 fl oz) fish stock
4 sprigs of fresh parsley
1 sprig of fresh thyme
1 bay leaf
50 g (1³/₄ oz) butter
2 cloves garlic, crushed
2 onions, extra, chopped
1 teaspoon plain flour
fresh dill sprigs, to serve

1 Rinse the mussels several times under cold running water and discard any which are already open and don't close when tapped (it's a good idea to buy a few extra mussels in case any need to be thrown away).

2 Put the mussels, onion, celery and wine in a large pan and bring rapidly to the boil. Cover and cook, shaking the pan frequently, for 3 minutes. After 3 minutes, start removing mussels as they open. Pull apart the shells and discard the empty half. Set aside the half shells with the mussels attached, cover and keep warm. After 5 minutes discard any mussels which haven't opened.

3 Strain and reserve the remaining liquid and discard the vegetables.

4 Heat the fish stock, parsley, thyme and bay leaf in a pan. Bring to the boil, then reduce the heat, cover and simmer for 10 minutes. Strain and remove the herbs.

5 Heat the butter in a large pan. Add the garlic and extra onion, and cook gently for 5 minutes, or until the onion is soft but not browned. Stir in the flour and cook, stirring, for 1 minute. Remove from the heat and slowly stir in the reserved mussel liquid and hot fish stock. Stir until smooth, return to the heat and stir until the sauce boils and thickens. Reduce the heat and leave to simmer for 10 minutes.

6 Place the mussels in four soup bowls. Ladle the liquid over the top and garnish with dill sprigs. Serve with crusty bread.

155

MUSSELS WITH TOMATO AND WINE

Preparation: 20 minutes
Cooking: 30 minutes
Serves 6

1.5 kg (3 lb) mussels
1 1/2 cups (375 ml/
  12 fl oz) white wine
1 tablespoon olive oil
1 onion, chopped
3 cloves garlic, chopped
425 g (14 oz) canned
  tomatoes, chopped
1 tablespoon tomato
  paste
1/3 cup (10 g/1/4 oz)
  chopped fresh parsley

1 Scrub the mussels under cold running water and remove their beards. Discard any which are already open and don't close when tapped. Place the mussels and wine in a large pan. Cover and simmer over medium heat for 3–5 minutes. After 3 minutes, start removing mussels as they open. After 5 minutes discard any which haven't opened. Keep the wine.

2 Heat the oil in a frying pan and cook the onion and garlic for 3 minutes, or until the onion is soft. Stir in the tomatoes, tomato paste and reserved wine. Bring to the boil, then reduce the heat and simmer for 15–20 minutes, or until the sauce has reduced and thickened slightly. Season to taste.

3 Add the mussels and parsley to the pan. Toss through the tomato sauce.

Always buy a few extra MUSSELS in case some don't open.

LOBSTER THERMIDOR

Preparation: 25 minutes
Cooking: 15 minutes
Serves 2

1 cooked lobster
80 g (2 3/4 oz) butter
4 spring onions, finely
  chopped
2 tablespoons plain flour
1 teaspoon English
  mustard
2 tablespoons white wine
  or sherry
1 cup (250 ml/8 fl oz)
  milk
1/4 cup (60 ml/2 fl oz)
  cream
1 tablespoon chopped
  fresh parsley
1/2 cup (60 g/2 oz)
  grated Parmesan

1 Using a sharp knife, cut the lobster in half lengthways. Lift the meat from the tail and body. Crack the legs and prise the meat from them. Remove the intestinal vein and soft body matter and discard. Cut the meat into bite-sized pieces, cover and refrigerate. Wash the shell halves, drain and dry.

2 Heat 60 g (2 oz) of the butter in a frying pan and cook the spring onion for 2 minutes, or until soft. Add the flour and mustard, and cook for 1 minute. Remove from the heat and gradually stir

in the wine and milk. Return to the heat and cook, stirring, until the mixture boils and thickens. Simmer for 1 minute. Stir in the cream, parsley and lobster meat, and season with salt and freshly ground black pepper. Heat gently.

3 Spoon the mixture into the lobster shells, sprinkle with the cheese and dot with the remaining butter. Place under a preheated grill for 2 minutes, or until lightly browned.

LOBSTER MORNAY

Preparation: 25 minutes
Cooking: 15 minutes
Serves 2

1 cooked lobster
1 ¼ cups (315 ml/ 10 fl oz) milk
1 slice onion
1 bay leaf
6 black peppercorns
30 g (1 oz) butter
2 tablespoons plain flour
pinch of nutmeg
2 tablespoons cream
½ cup (60 g/2 oz) grated Cheddar

1 Using a sharp knife, cut the lobster in half lengthways. Lift the meat from the tail and body. Crack the legs and prise the meat from them.

LOBSTER THERMIDOR (top) and LOBSTER MORNAY.

Remove the intestinal vein and soft body matter and discard. Cut the meat into bite-sized pieces, cover and refrigerate. Wash the shell halves, drain and dry.

2 Heat the milk, onion, bay leaf and peppercorns in a small pan. Bring to the boil then remove from the heat, cover and leave for 15 minutes. Strain.

3 Melt the butter in a large pan, add the flour and stir for 1 minute. Remove from the heat and gradually add the infused milk. Stir until smooth. Cook, stirring over medium heat, until the mixture boils and thickens. Season with salt, white pepper and nutmeg. Stir in the cream.

4 Fold the lobster meat through the sauce. Divide the mixture between the shells and sprinkle the top with the cheese. Place under a preheated grill for 2 minutes, or until the cheese has melted.

157

Crumb and deep-fry the CALAMARI WITH CHILLI PLUM SAUCE.

CALAMARI WITH CHILLI PLUM SAUCE

Preparation: 30 minutes
Cooking: 20 minutes
Serves 4

500 g (1 lb) calamari
  tubes, rinsed
3 tablespoons plain flour
2 eggs, lightly beaten
3 cups (240 g/7½ oz)
  fresh or dry white
  breadcrumbs
oil, for deep-frying

Chilli plum sauce
1 teaspoon oil
1 clove garlic, crushed

1 cup (315 g/10 oz) dark
  plum jam
⅓ cup (80 ml/2¾ fl oz)
  white vinegar
1–2 tablespoons bottled
  chopped chilli or sweet
  chilli sauce

1 Dry the calamari with paper towels. Remove any spine and skin. Cut the calamari into rings.
2 Season the flour well and use to coat the calamari rings. Then dip in the beaten egg, drain off the excess and toss in the breadcrumbs, patting them lightly onto the rings and shaking off the excess. Refrigerate for

10 minutes. Heat the oil in a large heavy-based pan to 180°C (350°F), or until a bread cube browns in 15 seconds.
3 Fry the calamari in batches until crisp and golden; drain well. Use a slotted spoon to remove the crumbs from the oil between batches.
4 To make the sauce, heat the oil in a small pan. Add the garlic and cook until it is just starting to colour. Add the jam, vinegar and chilli. Stir over medium heat until well blended. Thin with a little warm water if necessary. Serve with the calamari rings.

Cook *CHAR-GRILLED BABY OCTOPUS under a grill or on a barbecue hotplate.*

CHAR-GRILLED BABY OCTOPUS

Preparation: 20 minutes +
  2 hours marinating
Cooking: 5 minutes
Serves 4

500 g (1 lb) baby
  octopus
1/2 cup (125 ml/4 fl oz)
  olive oil
2 tablespoons lemon
  juice
2 tablespoons finely
  chopped fresh
  coriander
2 tablespoons sweet chilli
  sauce

1 Using a sharp knife, cut the head from the octopus and remove the gut from inside. Push the beak up and out of the lower section and discard. Wash the octopus thoroughly and dry on paper towels.
2 Place the olive oil, lemon juice, coriander and sweet chilli sauce in a bowl with some salt and freshly ground black pepper, and whisk well. Add the octopus and stir well. Cover and refrigerate for 2 hours or overnight, stirring occasionally. Drain the octopus, reserving the marinade for brushing.

3 Heat the grill or a barbecue plate until very hot and brush it with oil to prevent the octopus sticking. Cook the octopus for 3 5 minutes, turning frequently until it is just tender. Brush with the marinade during cooking. Serve immediately, perhaps garnished with a few fresh coriander leaves.

STORAGE: Cover and refrigerate the cooked octopus for up to 2 days.
HINT: Octopus will toughen if overcooked.

VEGETARIAN

Today many of us live on a virtually meat-free diet without even considering ourselves vegetarian. As more and more people turn to a vegetarian lifestyle, or even just try to cut down the amount of red meat they eat, it is important to have a few delicious and reliable recipes tucked up your sleeve. Vegetarian food is usually good value and easy to cook, so if you have vegetarian friends don't just serve them up another baked potato.

NUT ROAST

Preparation: 30 minutes
Cooking: 1 hour
Serves 6

2 tablespoons olive oil
1 large onion, diced
2 cloves garlic, crushed
300 g (10 oz) field mushrooms, finely chopped
200 g (6¹/₂ oz) raw cashews
200 g (6¹/₂ oz) brazil nuts
1 cup (125 g/4 oz) grated Cheddar
¹/₄ cup (25 g/³/₄ oz) freshly grated Parmesan
1 egg, lightly beaten
2 tablespoons chopped fresh chives
1 cup (80 g/2³/₄ oz) fresh wholemeal breadcrumbs

Tomato sauce
30 ml (1 fl oz) olive oil
1 onion, finely chopped
1 clove garlic, crushed
400 g (13 oz) can tomatoes, chopped
1 tablespoon tomato paste
1 teaspoon caster sugar

1 Grease a 14 x 21 cm (5¹/₂ x 8¹/₂ inch) loaf tin and line the base with baking paper. Heat the oil in a frying pan and add the onion, garlic and mushrooms. Fry until soft, then allow to cool.
2 Process the nuts in a food processor until finely chopped, but do not overprocess. Preheat the oven to moderate 180°C (350°F/Gas 4).
3 Mix together the nuts, mushroom mixture,

cheese, egg, chives and breadcrumbs. Press firmly into the loaf tin and bake for 45 minutes, or until firm. Leave in the tin for 5 minutes, then turn out.
4 To make the sauce, heat the oil in a pan and add the onion and garlic. Fry for 5 minutes, or until soft but not brown. Add the chopped tomatoes, tomato paste, sugar and ¹/₃ cup (80 ml/2³/₄ fl oz) water. Simmer for 3–5 minutes, or until the sauce has slightly thickened. Season to taste with salt and pepper. Serve the tomato sauce with the sliced nut roast.

161

FELAFEL

Preparation: 1 hour +
4 hours soaking + resting
Cooking: 25 minutes
Serves 6

2 cups (440 g/14 oz)
chickpeas
1 small onion, chopped
2 cloves garlic, crushed
2 tablespoons chopped
fresh parsley
1 tablespoon chopped
fresh coriander
2 teaspoons ground
cumin
1/2 teaspoon baking
powder
oil, for deep-frying

Hummus
425 g (14 oz) can
chickpeas
2–3 tablespoons lemon
juice
2 tablespoons olive oil
2 cloves garlic, crushed
3 tablespoons tahini

Tomato salsa
2 tomatoes, peeled and
finely chopped
1/4 Lebanese cucumber,
finely chopped
1/2 green capsicum, finely
chopped
2 tablespoons chopped
fresh parsley
1 teaspoon sugar
2 teaspoons chilli sauce
grated rind and juice of
1 lemon

1 Soak the chickpeas in
3 cups (750 ml/24 fl oz)
water for at least 4 hours.
Drain and mix in a food
processor for 30 seconds,
or until finely ground.
2 Add the onion, garlic,
parsley, coriander, cumin,
baking powder and
1 tablespoon water, and
process for 10 seconds, or
until the mixture forms a
rough paste. Cover and
set aside for 30 minutes.
3 To make the hummus,
place the drained chick
peas, lemon juice, oil and
garlic in a food processor.
Season and process for
20–30 seconds, or until
smooth. Add the tahini
and process for a further
10 seconds.
4 To make the tomato
salsa, mix together all the
ingredients and season
with plenty of freshly
ground black pepper.
5 Shape heaped
tablespoons of the felafel
mixture into balls.
Squeeze out the excess
moisture. Heat the oil in a
deep, heavy-based pan,
until a cube of bread
browns in 15 seconds.
Lower the felafel into the
oil in batches of five.
Cook for 3–4 minutes
each batch. When well
browned, remove with a
large slotted spoon. Drain
on paper towels and serve
hot or cold with Lebanese
bread, hummus and
tomato salsa.

Serve FELAFEL with hummus and a tomato salsa.

CHILLI BEANS.

THAI VEGETABLE CURRY.

CHILLI BEANS

Preparation: 20 minutes
Cooking: 25 minutes
Serves 4

1 tablespoon oil
2 cloves garlic, crushed
2 small fresh red chillies, finely chopped
1 onion, finely chopped
1 green capsicum, diced
440 g (14 oz) can red kidney beans, rinsed
440 g (14 oz) can crushed tomatoes
1/2 cup (125 g/4 oz) tomato pasta sauce
1 teaspoon soft brown sugar

1 Heat the oil in a heavy-based pan and cook the garlic, chilli and onion for 3 minutes, or until the onion is golden.

2 Add the remaining ingredients, bring to the boil, then reduce the heat to simmer for 15 minutes, or until thickened.

THAI VEGETABLE CURRY

Preparation: 25 minutes
Cooking: 30 minutes
Serves 4

2 tablespoons Thai red curry paste
2 cups (500 ml/16 fl oz) coconut milk
4 kaffir lime leaves
1 onion, finely chopped
2 potatoes, chopped
200 g (6 1/2 oz) pumpkin, chopped
1 red capsicum, chopped
3 zucchini, chopped
90 g (3 oz) baby corn

150 g (5 oz) beans, chopped
2 tablespoons lime juice
2 tablespoons fish sauce
2 tablespoons chopped fresh coriander
1 tablespoon soft brown sugar

1 Mix the curry paste, coconut milk and 1/2 cup (125 ml/4 fl oz) water in a large pan. Bring to the boil, stirring occasionally.
2 Add the lime leaves and onion and boil for 3 minutes. Add the potato and pumpkin and cook for 15 minutes, or until tender. Add the capsicum, zucchini, corn and beans and cook for 10 minutes, or until tender.
3 Add the lime juice, fish sauce, coriander and sugar, and cook for 2 minutes. Serve with rice.

VEGETABLE LASAGNE

Preparation: 40 minutes +
  20 minutes standing
Cooking: 2¼ hours
Serves 6

2 large eggplants
½ cup (125 ml/4 fl oz)
  olive oil
2 onions, chopped
3 cloves garlic, crushed
1 carrot, diced
1 celery stick, diced
100 g (3½ oz) button
  mushrooms, sliced
1 red capsicum, chopped
810 g (1 lb 10 oz) can
  crushed tomatoes
2 tablespoons tomato
  paste

1 cup (250 ml/8 fl oz)
  red wine
1 tablespoon balsamic
  vinegar
1 tablespoon soft brown
  sugar
¼ cup (15 g/½ oz)
  chopped fresh basil
250 g (8 oz) dried
  lasagne sheets
350 g (11 oz) English
  spinach, chopped
½ cup (50 g/1¾ oz)
  grated Parmesan
½ cup (60 g/2 oz)
  grated Cheddar

Bechamel sauce
60 g (2 oz) butter
3 tablespoons plain flour
2 cups (500 ml/16 fl oz)
  milk
300 g (10 oz) ricotta

1 Slice the eggplants lengthways. Sprinkle generously with salt and leave for 20 minutes. (This draws out the bitterness. It is easiest to stand the eggplant in a colander.) Rinse well and pat dry. Brush lightly with half the olive oil. Grill under moderate heat until golden brown, then drain on paper towels.

2 Heat the remaining oil in a large heavy-based pan. Add the onion and cook over medium heat for 5 minutes, or until soft and golden. Add the garlic, carrot and celery, and cook for 3 minutes. Add the mushrooms and capsicum and cook for 3 minutes, or until the mushrooms are tender. Stir in the tomato, tomato paste, wine, vinegar and sugar. Bring to the boil, then reduce the heat and simmer for 1 hour. Add the basil.

3 To make the bechamel sauce, melt the butter in a pan and add the flour. Stir over low heat for 2 minutes, or until golden. Remove from the heat and gradually stir in the milk. Return to the heat and bring slowly to the boil, stirring, until the sauce boils and thickens. Simmer for 2 minutes, then add the ricotta and stir until smooth. Season with salt and pepper.

Leave VEGETABLE LASAGNE for 10 minutes before cutting.

4 Preheat the oven to moderate 180°C (350°F/ Gas 4). Lightly grease a 3-litre ovenproof dish. Spread a thin layer of vegetable sauce over the base of the dish and top with a layer of the lasagne sheets. Build up with a layer of vegetable sauce, spinach, eggplant and bechamel sauce. Continue layering, finishing with the bechamel sauce. Sprinkle the combined cheeses over the top and bake for 45–50 minutes, or until the lasagne is cooked and the cheese is golden brown. Leave for 10 minutes before cutting.

VEGETABLE STRUDEL is made with layers of filo pastry.

VEGETABLE STRUDEL

Preparation: 30 minutes +
   20 minutes standing
Cooking: 50 minutes
Serves 6–8

1 large eggplant
1 red capsicum
3 zucchini, sliced
   lengthways
2 tablespoons olive oil
6 sheets filo pastry
50 g (1³/₄ oz) baby
   English spinach leaves
60 g (2 oz) feta cheese,
   sliced

1 Slice the eggplant lengthways. Sprinkle generously with salt and leave for 20 minutes (this draws out the bitterness). Rinse well and pat dry.
2 Cut the capsicum into large flat pieces and place, skin-side-up, under a hot grill until the skin blackens and blisters. Put in a plastic bag, then peel the skin away. Brush the eggplant and zucchini slices with some of the olive oil and grill for 5–10 minutes, or until golden brown. Set aside to cool. Preheat the oven to moderately hot 190°C (375°F/Gas 5).
3 Brush one sheet of filo pastry at a time with olive oil, then lay them on top of each other. Place half the eggplant slices lengthways down the centre of the filo and top with layers of zucchini, capsicum, spinach and feta cheese. Repeat the layers until the vegetables and cheese are used up. Tuck in the ends of the pastry, then roll up like a parcel. Brush lightly with oil, place on a baking tray and bake for 35 minutes, or until golden brown.

NOTE: Unopened filo can be stored in the fridge for up to a month. Once opened, use within 3 days or the pastry will dry out.

165

Make CHEESE SOUFFLES in small ramekins or one large one.

CHEESE SOUFFLES

Preparation: 35 minutes
Cooking: 20 minutes
Serves 6

¹/₄ cup (25 g/³/₄ oz) dried breadcrumbs
20 g (³/₄ oz) butter
3 tablespoons plain flour
1 cup (250 ml/8 fl oz) milk
¹/₄ cup (25 g/³/₄ oz) grated Parmesan
³/₄ cup (90 g/3 oz) grated Cheddar
1 teaspoon Dijon mustard
3 eggs, separated

1 Preheat the oven to moderate 180°C (350°F/Gas 4). Grease six ¹/₂ cup (125 ml/4 fl oz) soufflé dishes with melted butter. Coat the bases and sides evenly with the breadcrumbs, shaking off the excess.
2 Heat the butter in a small pan. Add the flour and stir over low heat for 2 minutes, or until lightly golden. Remove from the heat and add the milk gradually, stirring until smooth. Return to medium heat and stir until the sauce boils and thickens. Boil for 1 minute, then remove from the heat and add the Parmesan, Cheddar and mustard. Beat in the egg yolks, then transfer the mixture to a large bowl.
3 Place the egg whites in a small, clean dry mixing bowl. Beat until soft peaks form. Using a metal spoon, gradually fold the egg whites gently through the cheese mixture, then pour immediately into the soufflé dishes.
4 Bake for 10–15 minutes, or until the soufflés are puffed and golden. Serve the soufflés immediately because they quickly lose their volume once they leave the oven.

NOTE: If you would rather make one large soufflé, this mixture can be cooked in a 14 cm (6 inch) soufflé dish for approximately 45 minutes instead. Once your soufflé is cooking, try not to open the oven door before the cooking time is up. Soufflés should wobble slightly in the centre and should be moist when cooked. Soufflés can be prepared up to Step 2 ahead of time. Gently heat the base ingredients before adding the beaten egg whites.
HINT: Always use a clean dry bowl for whisking egg whites. The slightest hint of grease or moisture in the bowl (or yolk in the egg whites) will stop the whites foaming.

VEGETABLE FRITTATA

Preparation: 25 minutes
Cooking: 25 minutes
Serves 2 (or 4 as a snack)

1 tablespoon olive oil
2 cloves garlic, crushed
1 small red onion, chopped
1 small red capsicum, chopped
500 g (1 lb) roasted, boiled or steamed potatoes, thickly sliced
1/4 cup (15 g/1/2 oz) chopped fresh parsley
6 eggs, lightly beaten
1/4 cup (25 g/3/4 oz) grated Parmesan

1 Heat the oil in a large heavy-based, non-stick frying pan. Add the garlic, onion and capsicum and stir over medium heat for 2–3 minutes. Add the potato slices and cook for 2–3 minutes more. Stir in the parsley and spread the mixture evenly in the pan.
2 Beat the eggs with 2 tablespoons water, pour into the pan and cook over medium heat for 15 minutes, without burning the base.
3 Preheat the grill to high. Sprinkle the Parmesan over the frittata and grill for a few minutes to cook the egg and lightly brown. Cut into wedges to serve.

Leftover roast potatoes are ideal for a VEGETABLE FRITTATA.

GRATED VEGETABLE FRITTATA

Preparation: 25 minutes
Cooking: 30 minutes
Serves 2 (or 4 as a snack)

3 tablespoons olive oil
1 onion, finely chopped
1 small carrot, grated
1 small zucchini, grated
1 cup (125 g/4 oz) grated pumpkin
1/3 cup (45 g/1 1/2 oz) finely diced Jarlsburg or Cheddar cheese
5 eggs, lightly beaten

1 Heat 2 tablespoons of the oil in a pan and cook the onion for 5 minutes, or until soft. Add the carrot, zucchini and pumpkin and cook over low heat, covered, for 3 minutes. Transfer to a bowl and allow to cool. Stir in the cheese and plenty of salt and pepper. Add the eggs.
2 Heat the remaining oil in a small non-stick frying pan. Add the frittata mixture and shake the pan to spread it evenly. Reduce to low and cook for 15–20 minutes, or until set almost all the way through. Tilt the pan and lift the edges occasionally to allow the uncooked egg to flow underneath. Brown the top under a preheated hot grill. Cut into wedges and serve immediately.

HOT TOFU SALAD

Preparation: 20 minutes
Cooking: 10 minutes
Serves 4

1/4 cup (60 ml/2 fl oz)
  sweet chilli sauce
1 teaspoon crushed garlic
1 teaspoon grated ginger
2 tablespoons soy sauce
500 g (1 lb) firm
  tofu, cut into 1 cm
  (1/2 inch) cubes
2 tablespoons oil
2 carrots, sliced
2 zucchini, sliced
6 spring onions, sliced
100 g (3 1/2 oz) sugar
  snap peas, topped
  and tailed

1 Mix the sweet chilli sauce, garlic, ginger and soy sauce in a bowl. Add the tofu. Cover and marinate for 10 minutes.
2 Drain the tofu, reserving the marinade. Heat half the oil in a large frying pan. Add the tofu and cook in batches over high heat for 4 minutes, or until browned all over, turning often. Set aside.
3 Heat the remaining oil. Add the vegetables and toss over high heat for 2–3 minutes. Add the tofu and reserved marinade. Bring to the boil, stirring gently to combine the mixture. Remove from the heat and serve at once.

NOTE: Tofu is made from soy beans and is low in fat, high in calcium and an excellent source of protein. Use firm tofu for this recipe—this holds its shape well when marinated and cooked, as opposed to silken tofu which is soft and can be blended and used instead of dairy products when making dips, ice creams and desserts.
VARIATION: Cut the tofu into thick slices, marinate and then cook on the barbecue. Serve on a burger bun with lettuce and tomato.
STORAGE: To store tofu, place in an airtight container, cover it with water and store in the fridge.

STUFFED FIELD MUSHROOMS

Preparation: 20 minutes
Cooking: 25 minutes
Serves 4

4 large field mushrooms
30 g (1 oz) butter
1 leek, sliced
2–4 cloves garlic,
  crushed
2 teaspoons cumin seeds
1 teaspoon ground
  coriander
1/4–1/2 teaspoon chilli
  powder
2 tomatoes, chopped

2 cups (250 g/8 oz)
  mixed frozen vegetables
1/2 cup (95 g/3 oz)
  cooked white rice
1/3 cup (40 g/1 1/4 oz)
  grated Cheddar
1/4 cup (25 g/3/4 oz)
  grated Parmesan
1/4 cup (40 g/1 1/4 oz)
  cashews, chopped

1 Preheat the oven to moderately hot 200°C (400°F/Gas 6). Wipe the mushrooms with a paper towel. Remove the stalks and chop them finely.
2 Meanwhile, melt the butter in a pan. Add the chopped mushroom stalks and leek and cook for 2–3 minutes, or until soft. Mix in the garlic, cumin seeds, ground coriander and chilli powder and cook for 1 minute, or until the mixture is fragrant.
3 Stir in the tomato and frozen vegetables. Bring to the boil, reduce the heat and simmer for 5 minutes. Stir in the rice and season well.
4 Spoon the mixture into the mushroom caps, sprinkle with the Cheddar and Parmesan and bake for 15 minutes, or until the cheese has melted. Scatter with the cashews to serve.

Use any seasonal vegetables in the HOT TOFU SALAD (top). STUFFED FIELD MUSHROOMS (below).

LENTIL BURGERS

Preparation: 30 minutes
Cooking: 25 minutes
Makes 10 burgers

1 cup (250 g/8 oz) red
  lentils
1 tablespoon oil
2 onions, sliced
1 teaspoon ground cumin
1 teaspoon ground
  coriander
1 teaspoon garam masala
425 g (14 oz) can
  chickpeas, drained
1 egg
1/4 cup (15 g/1/2 oz)
  chopped fresh parsley

2 tablespoons chopped
  fresh coriander
2 1/4 cups (180 g/6 oz)
  stale breadcrumbs
plain flour, for dusting

Coriander garlic cream
1/2 cup (125 g/4 oz) sour
  cream
1/2 cup (125 ml/4 fl oz)
  cream
1 clove garlic, crushed
2 tablespoons chopped
  fresh coriander
2 tablespoons chopped
  fresh parsley

1 Add the lentils to a
large pan of boiling water
and simmer for 8 minutes,
or until tender. Drain well.
Heat the oil in pan and
cook the onion for
3 minutes, or until soft.
Add the ground spices
and stir until fragrant.
Cool the mixture slightly.
2 Place the chickpeas,
egg, onion mixture and
half the lentils in a food
processor. Process for
20 seconds, or until
smooth. Transfer to a
bowl. Stir in the
remaining lentils, parsley,
coriander and
breadcrumbs. Mix well.
Divide into 10 portions.
3 Shape the portions into
round patties. (If the
mixture is too soft, chill
for 15 minutes, or until
firm.) Toss the patties in
flour, shaking off the
excess. Place on a lightly
greased hot barbecue grill
or flatplate. Cook for
3–4 minutes each side, or
until browned.
4 To make the coriander
garlic cream, mix together
all the ingredients.

STORAGE: The patties
can be made up to 2 days
in advance and stored,
covered, in the fridge.
The coriander garlic
cream can be kept,
covered, in the fridge, for
up to 3 days.
VARIATION: You could
also use green lentils for
this recipe, but they will
take approximately
30 minutes to cook.

Serve LENTIL BURGERS with coriander garlic cream.

SPICY VEGETABLE COUSCOUS

Preparation: 30 minutes
Cooking: 1 hour
Serves 6

2 tablespoons olive oil
2 cloves garlic, crushed
1 small red chilli, diced
1 leek, thinly sliced
2 small fennel bulbs,
  sliced
2 teaspoons ground
  cumin
1 teaspoon ground
  coriander
1 teaspoon ground
  turmeric
1 teaspoon garam masala
350 g (11 oz) sweet
  potato, chopped
2 parsnips, sliced
1 1/2 cups (375 ml/12 fl
  oz) vegetable stock
2 zucchini, thickly sliced
250 g (8 oz) broccoli,
  cut into florets
2 tomatoes, peeled and
  chopped
1 large red capsicum,
  chopped
425 g (14 oz) can
  chickpeas, drained
2 tablespoons chopped
  fresh flat-leaf parsley
2 tablespoons chopped
  fresh lemon thyme

Couscous
1 1/4 cups (230 g/7 1/2 oz)
  instant couscous
30 g (1 oz) butter
1 cup (250 ml/8 fl oz)
  hot vegetable stock

SPICY VEGETABLE COUSCOUS.

1 Heat the oil in a large pan and add the garlic, chilli, leek and fennel. Cook over medium heat for 10 minutes, or until the leek and fennel are soft and golden brown.
2 Add the cumin, coriander, turmeric, garam masala, sweet potato and parsnip. Cook for 5 minutes, stirring to coat the vegetables with spices.
3 Add the vegetable stock and simmer, covered, for 15 minutes. Stir in the zucchini, broccoli, tomato, capsicum and chickpeas. Simmer, uncovered, for 30 minutes, or until the vegetables are tender. Stir in the herbs.
4 Put the couscous and butter in a bowl. Pour in the stock and leave to absorb for 5 minutes. Fluff gently with a fork to separate the grains. Make the couscous into a 'nest' on each plate and serve the spicy vegetables in the middle.

171

POTATO GNOCCHI WITH TOMATO AND BASIL SAUCE

Preparation: 1 hour
Cooking: 45 minutes
Serves 6

Tomato sauce
1 tablespoon oil
1 onion, chopped
1 celery stick, chopped
2 carrots, chopped
2 x 400 g (13 oz) cans
   crushed tomatoes
1 teaspoon sugar
1/2 cup (30 g/1 oz) fresh
   basil, chopped

Potato gnocchi
1 kg (2 lb) old potatoes
30 g (1 oz) butter
2 cups (250 g/8 oz) plain
   flour
2 eggs, beaten
grated Parmesan, to serve

1 To make the tomato sauce, heat the oil in a large frying pan, add the onion, celery and carrot, and cook for 5 minutes, stirring regularly. Add the tomato and sugar, and season with salt and pepper. Bring to the boil, then reduce the heat to low and simmer for 30 minutes. Add the basil, and set the sauce aside.
2 To make the potato gnocchi, peel the potatoes, chop roughly and steam or boil until very tender. Drain well and mash until smooth. Using a wooden spoon, stir in the butter and flour, then beat in the eggs. Allow to cool.
3 Turn the mixture out onto a floured surface and divide it in half. Roll each piece into a long sausage shape. Cut it into short pieces and press each piece with the back of a fork to make indentations.
4 Cook the gnocchi, in batches, in a large pan of boiling salted water for about 2 minutes, or until the gnocchi rise to the surface. Using a slotted spoon, remove and drain the gnocchi, and transfer to serving bowls. Serve with the tomato sauce and Parmesan. Garnish with fresh herbs if you like

VARIATION: For a quick blue cheese sauce, put 150 g (5 oz) blue cheese and 2 cups (500 ml/ 16 fl oz) cream in a pan. Simmer for 10 minutes, or until slightly thickened.
NOTE: Potato gnocchi are traditionally made from baked rather than mashed potato. This gives a firmer, drier dough but is obviously more time-

POTATO GNOCCHI are good with both tomato- and cheese-based sauces.

Serve BEAN NACHOS topped with avocado, sour cream and sliced spring onions.

consuming. Bake 1 kg (2 lb) potatoes in the oven at 200°C (400°F/Gas 6) for 1 hour. Don't wrap in foil. Allow to cool, then peel and mash in a bowl with a masher. Add 150 g (5 oz) plain flour and work in with your hands. Knead gently on a floured surface, gradually adding another 50 g (1³/4 oz) flour until you have a light soft dough that does not stick to the work surface but is still damp to touch. Roll out the dough into a long sausage shape, cut into short lengths and then press against a fork as above.

BEAN NACHOS

Preparation: 30 minutes
Cooking: 15 minutes
Serves 4

3 tomatoes, diced
1 small red onion, diced
¹/4 cup (15 g/¹/2 oz) chopped fresh coriander
1 small red chilli, diced
2 x 400 g (13 oz) cans red kidney beans
2 x 230 g (7¹/2 oz) packets corn chips
2 cups (250 g/8 oz) grated Cheddar
1 large avocado
¹/3 cup (90 g/3 oz) sour cream
2 spring onions, sliced

1 Preheat the oven to moderate 180°C (350°F/Gas 4). Mix the tomato, onion, coriander and chilli. Put the rinsed kidney beans in a pan, cover with water and bring to the boil. Drain, return to the pan with ¹/2 cup of tomato mixture and cook for 5 minutes.
2 Place the bean mixture on a baking tray and cover with the corn chips. Sprinkle with the cheese and bake for 3–5 minutes, or until the cheese melts. Transfer to serving plates.
3 Spread the tomato mixture over the cheese. Top with lightly mashed avocado, sour cream and spring onions.

PASTA AND RICE

Pasta is one of the easiest and most versatile ingredients to use. There are very few people who don't enjoy a bowl of pasta with a tomato or creamy sauce. Rice and noodles are also quick and simple to prepare and open to a thousand different variations on a delicious theme.

CLASSIC LASAGNE

Preparation: 40 minutes
Cooking: 1 hour 40 minutes
Serves 6–8

2 tablespoons oil
30 g (1 oz) butter
1 large onion, chopped
1 carrot, finely chopped
1 celery stick, chopped
650 g (1 lb 5 oz) minced beef
1 cup (250 ml/8 fl oz) Italian tomato passata
1/2 cup (125 ml/4 fl oz) red wine
2 tablespoons chopped fresh parsley
375 g (12 oz) dried lasagne sheets

Béchamel sauce
140 g (4 1/2 oz) butter
2 tablespoons plain flour
5 cups (1.25 litres) milk
1/2 teaspoon nutmeg
75 g (2 1/2 oz) Parmesan

1 Heat the oil and butter in a large frying pan. Cook the onion, carrot and celery, stirring, over medium heat until softened. Increase the heat, add the mince and brown well, breaking up any lumps with a fork. Add the tomato passata, wine and parsley, and season with salt and pepper. Bring to the boil, then reduce the heat and simmer for 35–40 minutes.
2 To make the béchamel sauce, melt the butter over low heat until foaming, then add the flour. Cook for 2 minutes, stirring constantly. Remove the pan from the heat and gradually stir in the milk. Return to the heat and bring to the boil, stirring, until thickened. When thick, simmer for 2 minutes. Season well with salt, pepper and nutmeg. Place a piece of baking paper on the surface of the sauce to prevent a skin forming.
3 Preheat the oven to moderate 180°C (350°F/ Gas 4). Grease a 2-litre ovenproof dish. Spread a thin layer of the meat sauce over the base and top with a thin layer of béchamel. If the béchamel has cooled and become too thick, warm it gently to make spreading easier. Lay the lasagne sheets on top, gently pressing to push out any air. Continue the layers, finishing with the béchamel. Grate the Parmesan, sprinkle over the sauce and bake for 35–40 minutes, or until golden brown. Leave for 15 minutes before cutting.

NOTE: You can use 200 g (6 1/2 oz) fresh lasagne instead of the dried. Read the instructions—most do not need any precooking.

175

SPINACH AND RICOTTA CANNELLONI

Preparation: 45 minutes
Cooking: 1½ hours
Serves 4–6

2 tablespoons olive oil
1 large onion, chopped
2 cloves garlic, crushed
1 kg (2 lb) English
  spinach, finely chopped
650 g (1 lb 5 oz) ricotta
  cheese
2 eggs, lightly beaten
pinch of ground nutmeg
250 g (8 oz) dried
  cannelloni tubes
1 cup (150 g/5 oz)
  grated mozzarella
½ cup (50 g/1¾ oz)
  grated Parmesan

Tomato sauce
1 tablespoon olive oil
1 large onion, chopped
2 cloves garlic, crushed
800 g (1 lb 10 oz) can
  crushed tomatoes
½ cup (125 ml/4 fl oz)
  white wine
2 tablespoons tomato
  paste
1 teaspoon soft brown
  sugar
2 tablespoons chopped
  fresh basil

SPINACH AND RICOTTA CANNELLONI.

1 Heat the oil in a large heavy-based pan. Add the onion and cook for 3 minutes, or until golden. Stir in the garlic and cook for 1 minute. Add the spinach and cook for 2 minutes. Cover the pan and steam the spinach for 1–2 minutes, or until wilted. Allow to cool slightly. Transfer to a colander and squeeze to remove the moisture.
2 Mix the spinach with the ricotta, beaten eggs and nutmeg. Season to taste with salt and pepper. Preheat the oven to moderate 180°C (350°F/Gas 4) and grease a large ovenproof dish.
3 To make the tomato sauce, heat the oil in a large frying pan and cook the onion over low heat for 5 minutes, or until soft and golden. Add the garlic and cook for 1 minute. Add the tomato, wine, tomato paste, sugar and basil. Bring to the boil, reduce the heat and simmer for 30 minutes.
4 Spread a third of the tomato sauce in the dish. Spoon 2–3 tablespoons of the spinach mixture into each cannelloni tube and arrange neatly in the dish. Spoon the remaining tomato sauce over the top and sprinkle with the mozzarella and Parmesan. Bake for 40–45 minutes, or until the cannelloni is tender and the top is crisp and golden brown.

NOTE: This recipe can be made using fresh lasagne sheets instead of the dried cannelloni tubes. Cut the lasagne sheets into small rectangles, place the filling on the edge and roll up tightly. Place the filled tubes seam-side-down in the baking dish and cook as cannelloni tubes.

PASTA AND MEATBALLS

Preparation: 35 minutes
Cooking: 35 minutes
Serves 4

750 g (1 1/2 lb) pork and veal or beef mince
1 cup (80 g/2 3/4 oz) fresh breadcrumbs
1/4 cup (25 g/3/4 oz) grated Parmesan
1 onion, finely chopped
2 tablespoons chopped fresh parsley
1 egg, beaten
1 clove garlic, crushed
rind and juice of half a lemon
3 tablespoons plain flour
2 tablespoons olive oil
500 g (1 lb) fusilli

Sauce
425 g (14 oz) Italian tomato passata
1/2 cup (125 ml/4 fl oz) beef stock
1/2 cup (125 ml/4 fl oz) red wine
2 tablespoons chopped fresh basil
1 clove garlic, crushed

PASTA AND MEATBALLS, just like an Italian mama makes!

1 Mix together the mince, breadcrumbs, Parmesan, onion, parsley, egg, garlic, lemon rind and juice, and some salt and pepper. Roll tablespoons of the mixture into balls. Season the flour with salt and pepper and roll the meatballs in the seasoned flour.
2 Heat the oil in a large frying pan and fry the meatballs in batches until golden brown. Remove from the pan and drain on paper towels. Pour away the fat and meat juices from the pan.

3 To make the sauce, in the same pan, combine the tomato passata, stock, wine, basil, garlic and some salt and pepper. Bring to the boil. Reduce the heat, add the meatballs to the sauce and simmer for 10–15 minutes.
4 While the meatballs and sauce are cooking, add the fusilli to a large pan of rapidly boiling salted water and cook until just tender. Drain and serve with the meatballs and sauce over the top.

Add the stock, tomato, wine and sugar.

3 Bring to the boil, reduce the heat and simmer for 2 hours, stirring occasionally. Cook the pasta in boiling water until just tender. Season the sauce and serve with the spaghetti. The sauce can be kept for up to 2 days in the fridge or frozen for up to 2 months.

SPAGHETTI BOLOGNESE is an enduring family favourite.

SPAGHETTI BOLOGNESE

Preparation: 15 minutes
Cooking: 2¼ hours
Serves 6

2 tablespoons olive oil
1 large onion, chopped
1 carrot, chopped
1 celery stick, chopped
2 cloves garlic, crushed
500 g (1 lb) beef mince
1 cup (250 ml/8 fl oz) beef stock
2 x 425 g (14 oz) cans chopped tomatoes
1½ cups (375 ml/ 12 fl oz) red wine
1 teaspoon sugar
500 g (1 lb) spaghetti

1 Heat the olive oil in a large heavy-based pan and stir the onion, carrot and celery over medium heat for 5 minutes, or until softened. Add the garlic and cook for 1 minute.

2 Add the mince and cook over high heat until well browned, breaking up any lumps with a fork.

SPAGHETTI CARBONARA

Preparation: 10 minutes
Cooking: 20 minutes
Serves 4–6

8 rashers bacon
500 g (1 lb) spaghetti
4 eggs
½ cup (50 g/1¾ oz) grated Parmesan
1¼ cups (315 ml/ 10 fl oz) cream

Don't overcook CARBONARA or you will make scrambled eggs.

1 Trim away the bacon rind, then cut the bacon into thin strips. Fry over medium heat until crisp. Remove from the pan and drain on paper towels.

2 Add the spaghetti to a large pan of rapidly boiling water and cook until it is just tender. Drain in a colander, then return to the pan and keep warm.

3 Beat the eggs, cheese and cream in a bowl, then add the bacon. Pour over the hot pasta in the pan and toss gently.

4 Return the pan to very low heat and cook for $1/2$–1 minute, or until slightly thickened—don't overheat or the eggs will scramble. Season with black pepper and garnish with herb sprigs.

Serve TOMATO PASTA SAUCE over your choice of pasta.

TOMATO PASTA SAUCE

Preparation: 25 minutes
Cooking: 25 minutes
Serves 4

1.5 kg (3 lb) ripe
    tomatoes
1 tablespoon olive oil
1 onion, finely chopped
2 cloves garlic, crushed
2 tablespoons tomato
    paste
1 teaspoon dried oregano
1 teaspoon sugar

1 Score a cross in the base of each tomato, place in a bowl of boiling water for 30 seconds, then transfer to cold water and peel the skin away from the cross. Cut the tomatoes in half around their equators and scoop out the seeds with a teaspoon. Finely chop the tomato flesh.

2 Heat the oil in a pan. Add the onion and cook, stirring, over medium heat for 3 minutes, or until soft. Add the garlic and cook for 1 minute. Add the tomato, tomato paste, oregano and sugar. Bring to the boil, then reduce the heat and simmer for 20 minutes, or until the sauce has thickened slightly. Season with salt and pepper.

NOTE: Make sure you use fully ripe tomatoes for a full-flavoured sauce. If ripe tomatoes aren't available, use canned tomatoes instead.

PESTO WITH TAGLIATELLE

Preparation: 10 minutes
Cooking: 10 minutes
Serves 4

250 g (8 oz) spinach
   tagliatelle
90 g (3 oz) basil leaves
4 cloves garlic, chopped
¹/₃ cup (50 g/1³/₄ oz)
   pine nuts
1 cup (100 g/3¹/₂ oz)
   grated Parmesan
³/₄ cup (185 ml/6 fl oz)
   olive oil

1 Add the tagliatelle to a
large pan of rapidly
boiling water and cook
until tender. Drain and
return to the pan.
2 Meanwhile, put the
basil, garlic and pine nuts
in a food processor and
process until finely
ground. Add the Parmesan
and process to mix.

3 Add the olive oil slowly,
with the motor running.
Add enough sauce to the
pasta to coat when tossed.

STORAGE: Pesto can
be kept in the fridge for
2 weeks. Spoon into a jar
and cover the sauce with
a thin layer of oil.

SPAGHETTI PRIMAVERA

Preparation: 20 minutes
Cooking: 15 minutes
Serves 4

500 g (1 lb) spaghetti
1 cup (155 g/5 oz)
   frozen broad beans
200 g (6¹/₂ oz) sugar
   snap peas, trimmed
155 g (5 oz) asparagus
30 g (1 oz) butter
220 ml (7 fl oz) cream
60 g (2 oz) grated
   Parmesan

1 Cook the spaghetti in a
large pan of rapidly
boiling water until just
tender. Drain and return
to the pan to keep warm.
2 Cook the beans in
boiling water for
2 minutes. Plunge into
iced water, then drain and
remove the skins. Cook
the peas in boiling water
for 2 minutes, plunge into
iced water, then drain.
Snap the woody ends
from the asparagus and
cut the spears into short
pieces. Cook the
asparagus in boiling water
for 2 minutes, or until
bright green and tender.
Plunge into iced water,
then drain.
3 Melt the butter in a
heavy-based frying pan.
Add the vegetables, cream
and Parmesan. Simmer for
2 minutes, or until heated
through. Season with salt
and pepper. Pour over the
pasta and toss together.

PESTO WITH TAGLIATELLE.

SPAGHETTI PRIMAVERA.

FETTUCINE ALFREDO

Preparation: 10 minutes
Cooking: 15 minutes
Serves 4

500 g (1 lb) fettucine
90 g (3 oz) butter
1¹/₂ cups (150 g/5 oz)
    shredded Parmesan
1¹/₄ cups (315 ml/
    10 fl oz) cream
¹/₄ cup (15 g/¹/₂ oz)
    chopped fresh parsley

1 Add the pasta to a large pan of rapidly boiling water and cook until just tender. Drain and return to the pan to keep warm.
2 While the pasta is cooking, heat the butter in a pan over low heat. Add the Parmesan and the cream and bring to the boil, stirring. Add the parsley, season with salt and pepper, and stir well.

3 Add to the pasta and toss well.

NOTE: Fettucine Alfredo is apparently named after a restaurateur in Rome, who used a gold fork and spoon to toss each serving of the dish before sending it out to the table.

CREAMY BOSCAIOLA

Preparation: 15 minutes
Cooking: 25 minutes
Serves 4

500 g (1 lb) pasta
1 tablespoon oil
6 rashers bacon, chopped
200 g (6¹/₂ oz) button
    mushrooms, sliced
2¹/₂ cups (600 ml/
    20 fl oz) cream
2 spring onions, sliced
1 tablespoon chopped
    fresh parsley

1 Cook the pasta in boiling salted water until just tender. Drain and return to the pan to keep warm.
2 While the pasta is cooking, heat the oil in a large frying pan, add the bacon and mushrooms and cook, stirring, for 5 minutes.
3 Stir in a little of the cream and make sure there is no bacon stuck to the bottom of the pan.
4 Add the remaining cream, bring to the boil and cook over high heat for 15 minutes, or until thick enough to coat a spoon. Stir in the spring onion. Season, then pour over the pasta and toss. Serve sprinkled with the chopped parsley.

NOTE: 'Boscaiola' means woodcutter—collecting mushrooms is part of the woodcutter's heritage.

FETTUCINE ALFREDO.

CREAMY BOSCAIOLA.

Add onion and bacon to a standard MACARONI CHEESE.

MACARONI CHEESE

Preparation: 15 minutes
Cooking: 40 minutes
Serves 4

200 g (6½ oz) macaroni
60 g (2 oz) butter
1 onion, chopped
2 rashers bacon, chopped
¼ cup (30 g/1 oz) plain
  flour
2½ cups (600 ml/
  20 fl oz) milk
½ teaspoon ground
  nutmeg
1½ cups (185 g/6 oz)
  grated Cheddar

1 Preheat the oven to moderate 180°C (350°F/ Gas 4). Grease a 1.5 litre ovenproof dish. Cook the macaroni in rapidly boiling water until tender, then drain.

2 Heat the butter in a large pan and add the onion and bacon. Stir over medium heat for 4 minutes, or until soft. Add the flour and stir over low heat for 1 minute. Remove from the heat and gradually add the milk. Stir until smooth. Return to medium heat and cook, stirring, for 4 minutes, or until the mixture boils and thickens. Simmer over low heat for 1 minute. Remove from the heat and stir in the nutmeg. Season.
3 Add the pasta and two thirds of the cheese. Stir, then spoon into the dish. Sprinkle with the remaining cheese and bake for 20 minutes, or until lightly golden.

RISOTTO PARMESAN

Preparation: 20 minutes
Cooking: 40 minutes
Serves 4–6

1 litre chicken stock
60 g (2 oz) butter
2 tablespoons olive oil
1 small onion, diced
¼ teaspoon saffron
  threads or powder
250 g (8 oz) arborio rice
½ cup (50 g/1¾ oz)
  grated Parmesan
2 tablespoons finely
  chopped fresh parsley

1 Put the stock in a pan and keep at simmering point. Heat the butter and oil in a heavy-based pan. Add the onion and saffron. Cook, stirring, for 2–3 minutes. Add the rice and stir for 1–2 minutes, or until well coated.
2 Add ½ cup (125 ml/ 4 fl oz) of the stock and stir over medium heat until it is all absorbed. Continue adding ½ cup of stock at a time, stirring constantly, until the rice is tender and all the stock has been absorbed (25–30 minutes). Stir in the Parmesan and parsley.

VARIATION: For a mushroom risotto, fry 300 g (10 oz) chopped field mushrooms instead of the saffron.

VEGETABLE PILAF

Preparation: 20 minutes
Cooking: 30 minutes
Serves 6

60 g (2 oz) butter
2 onions, sliced
2 cloves garlic, crushed
1 large red capsicum,
  finely chopped
2 cups (400 g/13 oz)
  basmati rice
1.25 litres vegetable
  stock
1 fresh corn cob
1 1/2 cups (235 g/7 1/2 oz)
  peas
1/2 cup (50 g/1 3/4 oz)
  grated Parmesan
2 tablespoons chopped
  fresh chives
2 tablespoons chopped
  fresh coriander

VEGETABLE PILAF.

1 Melt the butter in a large pan. Add the onion and cook for 5 minutes over low heat, or until soft. Add the garlic and cook for 1 minute. Add the capsicum and rice and cook for 3 minutes, then stir in the stock. Bring to the boil, stirring once. Reduce the heat and simmer for 5 minutes, or until most of the stock has been absorbed.

2 Cut the corn kernels from the cob with a sharp knife (angle the knife and cut down the side of the cob). Stir the corn kernels and peas into the rice mixture. Cook, covered, over low heat for 10 minutes, or until the rice is tender.

3 Stir in the Parmesan and herbs. Season to taste with salt and pepper before serving.

Use arborio rice for a creamy RISOTTO PARMESAN.

SMOKED FISH KEDGEREE

Preparation: 20 minutes
Cooking: 35 minutes
Serves 4

600 g (1 1/4 lb) smoked
  haddock
50 g (1 3/4 oz) butter
1 onion, finely chopped
2 teaspoons curry
  powder
1 teaspoon ground cumin
1 teaspoon ground
  coriander
2 teaspoons seeded and
  finely sliced green chilli
1 cup (200 g/6 1/2 oz)
  basmati rice
3 cups (750 ml/24 fl oz)
  chicken or fish stock

1 cinnamon stick
1/3 cup (80 ml/2 3/4 fl oz)
  cream
2 hard-boiled eggs,
  chopped
2 tablespoons finely
  chopped fresh parsley
2 tablespoons finely
  chopped fresh
  coriander

1 Place the haddock in a large shallow pan, skin-side-up (the haddock must be in a single layer, so if you don't have a large enough pan you may need to poach the fish in a couple of batches). Cover with boiling water and simmer very gently for about 10 minutes. The fish is cooked when the flesh flakes easily when tested with a knife. Drain and pat dry with paper towels. Remove the skin and bones and flake into bite-sized chunks.

2 Heat the butter in a large pan and cook the onion for 5 minutes, or until soft and golden. Add the curry powder, cumin, coriander and chilli and cook, stirring, for 1 minute. Add the rice, stir well, then pour in the stock and add the cinnamon stick. Cover with a tight-fitting lid and simmer over gentle heat for about 15 minutes, or until the rice is tender.

3 Remove the cinnamon stick and gently stir in the flaked haddock. Fold in the cream, egg and herbs. Season to taste and serve immediately.

VARIATION: This dish is best made with smoked haddock, but if it is not available you could use smoked cod.

NOTE: The English adapted this recipe from the Indian 'khichiri' which was a dish of rice, spices and lentils. Kedgeree is now seen as a main meal, but it was originally a breakfast dish and is delicious for special occasion brunches.

KEDGEREE is an anglicized Indian dish.

FRIED RICE

Preparation: 15 minutes
Cooking: 10 minutes
Serves 4

2 eggs, lightly beaten
2 tablespoons peanut oil
1 onion, cut into wedges
250 g (8 oz) piece of
    ham, cut into thin strips
4 cups (740 g/1 ¹/₂ lb)
    cold, cooked rice
¹/₄ cup (40 g/1 ¹/₄ oz)
    frozen peas
2 tablespoons soy sauce
4 spring onions,
    diagonally sliced
250 g (8 oz) cooked
    small prawns, peeled

Use cold cooked rice for FRIED RICE, so the grains separate out.

1 Season the egg with salt and pepper. Heat half the oil in a wok or large frying pan and add the egg, pulling the set egg towards the centre and tilting the pan to let the uncooked egg run to the edge. When almost set, break the egg up into large pieces, so it looks like scrambled egg, and transfer to a plate.
2 Heat the remaining oil in the wok, swirling to coat the base and side. Add the onion and stir-fry over high heat until it starts to turn transparent. Add the ham and stir-fry for 1 minute. Add the rice and peas, and stir-fry for 3 minutes, or until the rice is heated through. Add the egg, soy sauce, spring onion and prawns. Heat through, then serve.

STORAGE: Cook the rice for frying a day in advance (this is an excellent recipe for using up leftovers). Cover and store in the refrigerator and the grains will separate. You will need to cook about 1¹/₂ cups of rice to produce 4 cups of cooked.
VARIATION: Use barbecued pork, lap cheong (Chinese sausage) or bacon instead of ham.

There are many different rice varieties and they are all suited to different dishes. Brown long-grain are separate long grains with husks, best used for salads, rice cakes, pilaf and patties, or serving with stir-fries or curries as a healthy alternative to white long-grain. Brown short-grain rice is used for soups and patties. It has a nutty flavour and heavy texture—a healthy alternative to white short-grain. White rice has been processed to remove the outer hull and bran, then polished until it is white and glossy.

185

PAELLA

Preparation: 30 minutes
Cooking: 55 minutes
Serves 4

12 mussels, scrubbed,
  beards removed
1/2 cup (125 ml/4 fl oz)
  white wine
1 small red onion,
  chopped
1/2 cup (125 ml/4 fl oz)
  olive oil
1 chicken breast fillet,
  cut into cubes
275 g (9 oz) raw prawns,
  shelled and deveined
100 g (3 1/2 oz) calamari,
  cut into rings
100 g (3 1/2 oz) white
  boneless fish, cubed

1/2 small red onion, extra,
  finely chopped
1 rasher bacon, diced
4 cloves garlic, crushed
1 small red capsicum,
  finely chopped
1 tomato, peeled and
  chopped
1/2 cup (80 g/2 3/4 oz)
  fresh or frozen peas
90 g (3 oz) chorizo or
  pepperoni, thinly sliced
pinch of cayenne pepper
1 cup (200 g/6 1/2 oz)
  long-grain rice
1/4 teaspoon saffron
  threads
2 cups (500 ml/16 fl oz)
  chicken stock, heated
2 tablespoons finely
  chopped fresh parsley

1 Discard any damaged mussels or any that are open and don't close when tapped on the work surface. Heat the wine and onion in a large pan. Add the mussels, cover and shake the pan for 3–5 minutes over high heat. After 3 minutes, start removing the opened mussels and set aside. At the end of 5 minutes discard any mussels that haven't opened. Reserve the cooking liquid.

2 Heat half the oil in a large frying pan. Pat the chicken dry with paper towels and fry for 5 minutes, or until golden brown. Remove from the pan. Add the prawns, calamari and fish to the pan and cook for 1 minute. Remove from the pan.

3 Heat the remaining oil in a pan and add the extra onion, bacon, garlic and capsicum. Cook for 5 minutes, or until the onion is soft. Add the tomato, peas, chorizo or pepperoni, cayenne pepper, and season with salt and pepper. Add the cooking liquid, and stir well. Add the rice and saffron and mix well.

4 Add the chicken stock and mix well. Bring slowly to the boil, then reduce the heat to low and simmer for 15 minutes, without stirring.

Add the mussels to the Spanish PAELLA just before serving.

Fry the noodles, then serve topped with chicken and vegetables for CHICKEN CHOW MEIN.

5 Place the chicken pieces, prawns, calamari and fish on top of the rice. Using a wooden spoon, gently push the pieces into the rice, then cover and continue to cook over low heat for 10–15 minutes, or until the rice is tender and the seafood cooked. If the rice is not quite cooked, add a little extra stock and cook for a few minutes more. Serve in bowls, topped with the mussels and sprinkled with the parsley.

NOTE: It's a good idea to buy a few extra mussels to allow for any that do not open. Black- and green-lip mussels are both suitable for use in this recipe.

CHICKEN CHOW MEIN

Preparation: 25 minutes
Cooking: 30 minutes
Serves 4–6

2 teaspoons cornflour
1/2 cup (125 ml/4 fl oz) chicken stock
1/2 cup (125 ml/4 fl oz) hoisin sauce
375 g (12 oz) dried fine egg noodles
3 teaspoons sesame oil
oil, for cooking
1 clove garlic, crushed
1 teaspoon grated ginger
1 onion, cut into wedges
500 g (1 lb) chicken thigh fillets, cubed
1 red capsicum, sliced
1 green capsicum, sliced
12 leaves Chinese broccoli, chopped

1 Mix the cornflour, stock and half the hoisin sauce to make a sauce. Set aside.
2 Cook the noodles in boiling water according to the packet, or until tender. Drain well, pat dry and mix in the sesame oil and remaining hoisin sauce. Heat 2 tablespoons of oil in a wok. Fry the noodles over medium heat for 10 minutes until crispy. Drain and keep warm.
3 Heat some more oil and fry the garlic, ginger and onion for 2 minutes. Add the chicken and stir-fry in batches until tender. Add the capsicum, cook for 2 minutes. Add the sauce and stir until it boils and thickens. Add the broccoli and cook until just wilted. Serve the noodles with chicken and vegetables.

SINGAPORE NOODLES.

SINGAPORE NOODLES

Preparation: 40 minutes
Cooking: 15 minutes
Serves 4–6

150 g (5 oz) dried rice
  vermicelli
oil, for cooking
250 g (8 oz) Chinese
  barbecued pork, cut
  into small pieces
250 g (8 oz) raw prawn
  meat, chopped
2 tablespoons madras
  curry powder
2 cloves garlic, crushed
1 onion, thinly sliced
100 g (3½ oz) shiitake
  mushrooms, thinly
  sliced
100 g (3½ oz) green
  beans, thinly sliced
1 tablespoon soy sauce
4 spring onions, thinly
  sliced

1 Put the vermicelli in a
large bowl, cover with
boiling water and soak for
5 minutes. Drain well and
dry on a clean tea towel.
2 Heat the wok until very
hot, add 1 tablespoon of
the oil and swirl to coat.
Stir-fry the pork and
prawns in batches over
high heat, then remove.
3 Reheat the wok, add
2 tablespoons of the oil
and stir-fry the curry
powder and garlic for
1–2 minutes, or until
fragrant. Add the onion
and mushrooms, and stir-
fry for 2–3 minutes, or
until the onion and
mushrooms are soft.
4 Return the pork and
prawns to the wok, add
the beans and 2 teaspoons
water, and toss gently.
Add the drained noodles,
soy sauce and spring
onion. Toss well.

FRIED NOODLES

Preparation: 30 minutes
Cooking: 25 minutes
Serves 4

¼ cup (40 g/1¼ oz)
  sesame seeds
2 tablespoons oil
2 teaspoons sesame oil
4 spring onions, chopped
2 cloves garlic, crushed
150 g (5 oz) raw prawn
  meat
2 teaspoons finely
  chopped red chillies
150 g (5 oz) fresh firm
  tofu, cut into small
  cubes
100 g (3½ oz) button
  mushrooms, thinly
  sliced
1 red capsicum, cut into
  thin strips
2 tablespoons soy sauce
2 teaspoons sugar
300 g (10 oz) packet
  Hokkien noodles

1 Dry-fry the sesame
seeds over low heat for
3–4 minutes, shaking the
pan gently, until the seeds
are golden. Remove, allow
to cool and then grind in
a food processor or mortar
and pestle.
2 Mix together the oils in
a small bowl. Heat half
the oil mixture in a wok
or a large heavy-based
frying pan, over medium-
high heat. Add the spring
onion, garlic and prawn
meat and stir-fry for

188

1 minute. Add the chilli, stir for another minute, then remove the mixture from the wok and set aside. Add the tofu to the wok, tossing occasionally until lightly golden, then remove from the wok and set aside. Add the remaining oil to the wok, add the mushrooms and capsicum and stir-fry for 3 minutes, or until they are just crisp.

3 Add the soy sauce, sugar, noodles and 2 teaspoons water to the wok or pan. Toss gently to separate and coat the noodles in liquid. Cover and steam for 5 minutes, then toss well. Add the prawn mixture and tofu, and toss for 3 minutes over medium heat. Sprinkle with the crushed sesame seeds and serve.

NOTE: We have specified Hokkien noodles, but you could use a variety of different types of noodle for this dish as long as you prepare them correctly beforehand. Hokkien noodles have been cooked, then tossed in oil before packaging so they require no cooking before adding them to this dish. Fresh rice noodles have been prepared in the same way and can be added straight to the dish.

Fresh egg noodles do however need to be cooked in boiling water first for 5 minutes. Dried noodles also need soaking or cooking before adding them to the dish—follow the instructions on the packet, drain well and add to the recipe as above. To drain the water thoroughly from noodles, place them in a salad spinner and spin until dry.

Leave out the prawn meat and FRIED NOODLES becomes an excellent vegetarian meal.

VEGETABLES AND SALADS

If your idea of vegetables is a packet of frozen peas, and your salad technique runs to a few limp lettuce leaves drowned in bottled dressing, it's time you became a little more creative on the 'green' front. Vegetables and salads shouldn't just be sad side dishes, they should be vibrant, crispy, crunchy stars.

STIR-FRIED VEGETABLES

Preparation: 15 minutes
Cooking: 10 minutes
Serves 4

1 tablespoon sesame seeds
2 spring onions
250 g (8 oz) broccoli
1 red capsicum
1 yellow capsicum
150 g (5 oz) button mushrooms
1 tablespoon oil
1 teaspoon sesame oil
1 clove garlic, crushed
2 teaspoons grated fresh ginger
1 tablespoon soy sauce
1 tablespoon honey
1 tablespoon sweet chilli sauce

1 Put the sesame seeds on a baking tray and toast under a hot grill until golden (or fry in a clean dry pan). Finely slice the spring onions. Cut the broccoli into small florets. Cut the capsicums into thin strips. Cut the mushrooms in half.
2 Heat the oils in a wok or large frying pan. Add the garlic, ginger and spring onion. Stir-fry over high heat for 1 minute. Add the broccoli, capsicum and mushrooms. Stir-fry for 2 minutes, or until the vegetables are just tender but still bright.
3 Mix together the soy sauce, honey and sweet chilli sauce in a jug. Pour the sauce over the cooked vegetables and toss lightly. Sprinkle with the toasted sesame seeds.

ASIAN GREENS

Preparation: 5 minutes
Cooking: 10 minutes
Serves 4

500 g (1 lb) baby bok choy
800 g (1 lb 10 oz) Chinese broccoli
1/3 cup (80 ml/2³/4 fl oz) oyster sauce
1 teaspoon sesame oil

1 Wash the bok choy and broccoli thoroughly, and shake off the excess water. Trim the ends and roughly chop into large pieces. If the bok choy stems are particularly thick, cut them in half lengthways.
2 Place the broccoli in a steamer, preferably bamboo, over a pan half full of simmering water.

A mixture of healthy ASIAN GREENS (top) and STIR-FRIED VEGETABLES.

The bottom of the steamer should not be touching the water. Cover and steam the broccoli for 5–6 minutes. Add the bok choy, cover and steam for another 2 minutes.

3 Put the vegetables in a serving bowl. Pour in the oyster sauce and toss gently to coat the vegetables. Serve drizzled with the sesame oil.

NOTE: Bok choy is a variety of Chinese cabbage with long white stalks and large deep-green leaves. The leaves are crisp with a sweet cabbage-like flavour.

191

MASHED POTATO

Preparation: 10 minutes
Cooking: 30 minutes
Serves 4

4 large potatoes
3–4 tablespoons milk
60 g (2 oz) butter

1 Chop the potatoes and cook in boiling salted water until just tender, then drain.
2 Return the potato to the pan over low heat. Add the milk and quickly mash, adding more milk, if necessary, for fluffy potatoes. Beat in the butter and season well.

HERBED MASH

Add 2 tablespoons finely chopped chives or parsley.

CREAMY PARSNIP MASH

Cook equal quantities of potato and parsnip. Mash with milk, butter and 2 tablespoons sour cream.

CHEESY POTATO

Add 2 tablespoons sour cream instead of butter. Add 2–3 tablespoons finely grated Cheddar and 1 teaspoon Dijon mustard.

COLCANNON

Fry 200 g (6½ oz) shredded green cabbage and 8 chopped spring onions until brown and add to the mash.

CHIPS

Preparation: 5 minutes
Cooking: 20 minutes
Serves 4–6

5–6 large potatoes
oil, for deep-frying

1 Cut the potatoes lengthways into 1 cm (½ inch) wide chips. Soak for 10 minutes in cold water. Drain and pat dry. Half-fill a large heavy-based pan with oil (the oil will rise as the chips give off water). Heat the oil until a cube of bread dropped into the oil browns in 30 seconds. If it browns in less than 10 seconds, the oil is far too hot, so reduce the heat. Cook the chips in batches for 4–5 minutes, or until pale golden. Remove with tongs or a slotted spoon and drain on paper towels.
2 When you're almost ready to serve, reheat the oil until a cube of bread browns in 15 seconds. Add the chips in batches and cook for 2–3 minutes, or until golden and crisp. Drain on paper towels and serve sprinkled with salt.

NOTE: The best potatoes to use for perfect chips are floury varieties such as Spunta, King Edward and Russet (Idaho).

Instead of plain mashed potato try CREAMY PARSNIP MASH.

POTATO WEDGES

Preparation: 10 minutes
Cooking: 20 minutes
Serves 4

4–5 large potatoes
1 cup (125 g/4 oz) plain
 flour
3–4 teaspoons chicken
 seasoning salt
1 teaspoon white pepper
1 teaspoon sweet paprika
2 teaspoons garlic
 powder
oil, for deep-frying

Twice-fried CHIPS (top) and POTATO WEDGES.

1 Do not peel the potatoes, but wash and scrub them, leaving them wet to help the coating stick. Cut each potato into 10 wedges.
2 Mix together the flour, chicken seasoning salt, pepper, paprika and garlic powder. Dust the wedges in the seasoned flour: put the wedges and flour in a plastic bag and shake. Reserve the remaining seasoned flour.
3 Half-fill a large heavy-based pan with oil. Heat the oil to 160°C/315°F (if you have a deep-fryer with a thermometer), or until a cube of bread dropped into the oil browns in 30 seconds. If it browns in less than 10 seconds, the oil is too hot, so reduce the heat. Deep-fry the wedges in batches for 2–3 minutes

each batch, or until pale golden. Remove with tongs or a slotted spoon. Drain on paper towels and cool a little.
4 Dust with a second coating of seasoned flour, pressing the flour onto the wedges. Return to the hot oil and cook for another 3–4 minutes, or until the wedges are dark golden and crispy. Remove and drain on paper towels. Sprinkle with a little extra chicken salt and serve hot, perhaps with sour cream and sweet chilli sauce.

NOTE: For Potato Skins, preheat the oven to moderately hot 200°C (400°F/Gas 6). Prick 1 kg (2 lb) unpeeled potatoes all over with a fork and place on a baking tray. Bake for 1–1½ hours, or until tender. Cool, then cut in half lengthways. Use a spoon to scoop out the flesh (use this to make mash, gnocchi or potato croquettes). Cut each half potato skin into three lengthways, then deep-fry in batches in hot oil (as for Potato Wedges).

BAKED JACKET POTATOES

Preparation: 5 minutes
Cooking: 1½ hours
Serves 4

4 even-sized potatoes

1 Preheat the oven to hot 220°C (425°F/Gas 7). Scrub the potatoes clean, dry and prick all over for even cooking. For crisp skins brush the potatoes with oil and sprinkle with salt. Bake directly on the oven rack for 1–1½ hours, or until tender when tested with a skewer. Alternatively, wrap the potatoes in paper towels and space evenly in the microwave. Cook on High for 8–10 minutes, or until soft. Leave to stand for about 2 minutes.
Cut a cross in the top of the cooked potato and squeeze from the base to open. Top with butter, or one of the following topping ideas:

Mix drained tuna with antipasto-style mixed beans. Add some chopped parsley and a squeeze of lemon juice and spoon into the potato with a little olive oil.

Toss a handful of peeled cooked prawns in a hot pan with a little olive oil and crushed garlic. Add some chopped fresh chives and a small amount of natural yoghurt, stir well and season to taste.

Fry some thinly sliced mushrooms in olive oil with a clove of crushed garlic and a little chopped fresh parsley. Season and top with a teaspoon of sour cream.

Finely chop a tomato and add to Greek-style yoghurt with grated cucumber, chopped mint and spring onion. Season and mix well.

Toss some small cooked cauliflower florets in a pan with chopped bacon until heated through and lightly browned. Mix a little wholegrain mustard and sour cream, spoon into the potato and top with the cauliflower.

Fill the potato with a large spoonful of herbed cream cheese and put back in the oven for 2 minutes. Meanwhile, toast a few pine nuts and scatter over the melted cream cheese.

Roughly purée some leftover cooked broccoli with a little sour cream and some cheese until you have a thick paste. Add a beaten egg and mix well.

Spoon out some of the potato, refill with the soufflé, then return to the hot oven until the soufflé is golden and risen.

Mix some butter with ½ teaspoon grated lemon rind, 1 teaspoon lemon juice and 1 tablespoon finely chopped fresh dill. Chill before spooning onto the potato.

Put a small wedge of Camembert, Brie or creamy blue cheese in the potato and return to the oven for 2–3 minutes to soften the cheese.

Mash 1 small avocado with 1 teaspoon lemon juice and a dash of Tabasco to make guacamole. Top with sour cream, or mix in chopped bacon and chives.

Make a sweet corn salsa from a small tin of sweet corn, a chopped tomato, a finely sliced spring onion, half a chopped chilli and some chopped fresh coriander. Bind with a tablespoon of olive oil and a squeeze of lemon or lime juice.

Fry 2 crushed cloves of garlic and 2 chopped spring onions in a little butter and oil. Add 150 g (5 oz) sliced mushrooms and cook for 5 minutes.

SAUTEED HERB POTATOES

Preparation: 20 minutes
Cooking: 35 minutes
Serves 4–6

750 g (1 1/2 lb) baby new
  potatoes
30 g (1 oz) butter
2 tablespoons olive oil
1/2 teaspoon cracked
  black pepper
2 cloves garlic, crushed
1 tablespoon finely
  chopped fresh rosemary
1 teaspoon rock salt

1 Wash the potatoes, pat
dry with paper towels and
cut in half. Boil or steam
until just tender. Drain.

2 Heat the butter and oil
in a large heavy-based
frying pan. When the
mixture is foaming, add
the potatoes and season
with a little black pepper.
Cook over medium heat
for 5–10 minutes, or until
golden and crisp, tossing
regularly so that the
potatoes brown evenly.

3 Stir in the garlic,
rosemary and rock salt.
Cook for 1 minute, or
until well the potatoes
are well coated. Add
more cracked black
pepper and mix well.
Serve hot or warm.

NOTE: Fresh thyme would
work nicely in this recipe,
as would fresh parsley.

HASSELBACK POTATOES

Preparation: 20 minutes
Cooking: 45 minutes
Serves 4

60 g (2 oz) butter,
  melted
4 potatoes
2 tablespoons fresh white
  breadcrumbs
3 tablespoons grated
  Parmesan
1/2 teaspoon paprika

1 Preheat the oven to
moderately hot 200°C
(400°F/Gas 6). Brush a
shallow baking tray with a
little of the melted butter.

2 Peel the potatoes and
cut in half. Put the
potatoes, cut-side-down,
on a board. Make thin
evenly-spaced cuts about
two-thirds of the way
through, then place, flat-
side-down, on the tray.
Brush liberally with
melted butter. Bake them
for 30 minutes, brushing
occasionally with butter.

3 Mix together the
breadcrumbs and
Parmesan and sprinkle
evenly over the potatoes.
Sprinkle with the paprika
and bake for another
15 minutes, or until
golden brown.

NOTE: Choose potatoes
of a similar size so they
cook evenly.

Use fresh rosemary for SAUTEED HERB POTATOES.

DUCHESS POTATOES

Preparation: 20 minutes +
40 minutes refrigeration
Cooking: 45 minutes
Serves 6

860 g (1³/₄ lb) floury
 potatoes
2 eggs, plus 1 extra yolk
3 tablespoons cream
2 tablespoons grated
 Parmesan
pinch of grated nutmeg

1 Peel the potatoes and cut into quarters, then boil or steam until just tender. Drain and return to the pan, turn the heat to very low and gently shake the pan for 1–2 minutes to dry the potato. Transfer to a bowl and mash.

2 Beat together the 2 eggs, cream, Parmesan, nutmeg and some salt and pepper. Add to the potato and mash until smooth. Cover and refrigerate for 40 minutes, or until cold. Preheat the oven to moderate 180°C (350°F/Gas 4).

3 Put the mashed potato into a piping bag with a wide star nozzle. Pipe in rosettes, not too close together as they might spread a little, onto greased oven trays. Brush lightly with the extra egg yolk, to give a golden,

DUCHESS (top) and HASSELBACK POTATOES.

crisp finish. Bake for 15–20 minutes, or until golden. Serve hot, perhaps garnished with a little paprika.

Floury potatoes, such as Russet (Idaho) and King Edward have a high starch and low moisture content and are ideal for chips, baking, mash and gnocchi. Waxy potatoes have a high moisture content and are low in starch. They hold their shape well when boiled and steamed and are good in salads and stews, grate and slice well, but do not make particularly good chips or mash. Varieties are Desiree, Bintji, Tasmanian Pink Eye, Kipfler and Bison. Some potatoes, such as Sebago, Pontiac, Spunta, Nicola, Coliban and chats are good all-purpose varieties. Most bags of potatoes now specify their uses.

197

ROSTI *can be served as an accompaniment or as a filling lunch.*

BACON AND ONION ROSTI

Preparation: 30 minutes +
 1 hour refrigeration
Cooking: 40 minutes
Serves 4

850 g (1 lb 12 oz) waxy
 potatoes, halved
60 g (2 oz) butter
6 thin bacon rashers, rind
 removed, chopped
1 small red onion,
 chopped
2 cloves garlic, crushed
2 tablespoons chopped
 fresh parsley
1 teaspoon each chopped
 fresh oregano and
 thyme

1 Boil or steam the potato
until just tender. Drain,
cover and refrigerate for
1 hour. Peel the potato

and grate into a bowl.
2 Heat half the butter in a
23 cm (9 inch) heavy-
based, non-stick frying
pan. Add the bacon,
onion and garlic and stir
for 2 minutes, or until
tender but not brown.
Add to the potato. Add
the herbs and mix well.
3 Add a little butter to the
pan, spread the potato
mixture over the base and
press with a spatula. Cook
over medium heat for
8 minutes, or until a crust
forms on the base. Shake
the pan occasionally to
stop the potato sticking.
4 Slide the rosti onto a
greased plate, add the
remaining butter to the
pan and when melted, flip
the rosti back into the pan
on its uncooked side.
Cook for 6 minutes, or
until the base is crusty.

RATATOUILLE

Preparation: 20 minutes +
 20 minutes standing
Cooking: 40 minutes
Serves 4

250 g (8 oz) eggplant,
 chopped
4 tablespoons olive oil
250 g (8 oz) zucchini,
 thickly sliced
2 onions, cut in wedges
1 red capsicum, cubed
1 green capsicum, cubed
2 cloves garlic, crushed
500 g (1 lb) ripe
 tomatoes, chopped

1 Sprinkle the eggplant
liberally with salt and
leave for 20 minutes (this
draws the bitterness from
the eggplant). Rinse and
pat dry with paper towels.
Heat 3 tablespoons oil in
a large heavy-based pan.
Lightly brown the
eggplant and zucchini in
batches. Drain well.
2 Add the remaining oil
to the pan and cook the
onion over low heat for
3 minutes, or until golden.
Add the capsicum and
cook for 5 minutes, or
until tender but not
browned. Add the garlic
and tomato and cook,
stirring, for 5 minutes.
3 Stir in the eggplant and
zucchini. Simmer for
15–20 minutes to reduce
and thicken the sauce.
Season to taste.

RATATOUILLE—a traditional French vegetable dish.

VEGETABLE FRITTERS are a great way to use up leftovers.

VEGETABLE FRITTERS

Preparation: 30 minutes
Cooking: 40 minutes
Makes 12

2 potatoes
1 carrot
2 zucchini
120 g (4 oz) sweet
  potato
1 small leek, white part
  only, thinly sliced
2 tablespoons plain flour
3 eggs, lightly beaten
oil, for shallow-frying

1 Finely grate the potatoes, carrot, zucchini and sweet potato. Put in a tea towel and squeeze out as much moisture as possible. Mix with the leek in a large bowl.

2 Sprinkle the flour over the vegetables and mix until coated. Add the eggs and mix well. Heat about 5 mm (1/4 inch) of oil in a frying pan and drop in 3 tablespoons of the mixture in a neat pile. Use a fork to gently press it into a 10 cm (4 inch) round patty. Fry two to three patties at a time over medium-high heat for 3 minutes on each side, or until golden and crispy. Drain on paper towels while cooking the remainder of the mixture.

199

ROAST VEGETABLES (top) and SCALLOPED POTATOES.

the vegetables are crisp and golden and cooked through. Turn occasionally during cooking to coat with the oil and prevent sticking. Drain on paper towels before serving.

NOTE: A variety of vegetables are suitable for roasting, such as parsnips, turnips, fennel, carrots, garlic cloves, and, of course, potatoes. For par-boiled roast potatoes, cook them in boiling water for 10 minutes and drain thoroughly before putting in the baking dish or cooking in the tin with roast meat.

ROAST VEGETABLES

Preparation: 15 minutes
Cooking: 55 minutes
Serves 6–8

500 g (1 lb) pumpkin
1 large sweet potato
8 small onions
3 tablespoons olive oil
40 g (1 ¼ oz) butter

1 Preheat the oven to moderately hot 200°C (400°F/Gas 6). Peel the pumpkin and sweet potato and cut into large pieces. Peel the onions but leave whole. Pour the oil into a large baking dish and add the butter. Put in the oven to heat the oil and butter.
2 Add the vegetables to the dish and toss to coat with the hot oil. Bake for 45–50 minutes, or until

SCALLOPED POTATOES

Preparation: 20 minutes
Cooking: 40 minutes
Serves 4–6

4 waxy potatoes (Bintji, Desiree or Kipfler)
1 onion
1 cup (125 g/4 oz) grated Cheddar
1 ½ cups (375 ml/ 12 fl oz) cream
2 teaspoons chicken stock powder

1 Preheat the oven to moderate 180°C (350°F/Gas 4). Peel the potatoes and thinly slice.

Slice the onion into rings.
2 Arrange a layer of overlapping potato slices in a baking dish and top with a layer of onion rings. Set aside half of the cheese to use as a topping. Sprinkle a little of the remaining cheese over the onion. Continue layering until all the potato and the onion have been used, finishing with a little of the grated cheese.
3 Gently whisk together the cream and stock powder, then pour over the potato and sprinkle the top with the rest of the grated cheese. Bake for 40 minutes, or until the potato is tender and the top is golden brown.

VARIATION: For boulangère potatoes, peel and thinly slice 1 kg potatoes (use all-purpose varieties). Preheat the oven to moderate 180°C (350°F/Gas 4) and grease a 1-litre casserole dish. Arrange a layer of potato in the base of the dish. Crush 2 cloves of garlic and sprinkle a little over the potato, with some salt and pepper. Continue the layers to use all the potato and garlic. Pour 400 ml (13 fl oz) chicken or vegetable stock over the potato and bake, uncovered, for 1 hour, or until the potato is tender and top is crisp.

STUFFED CAPSICUMS

Preparation: 20 minutes
Cooking: 1 hour
Serves 4

2 large red capsicums
1/2 cup (110 g/3 1/2 oz) short-grain rice
1 tablespoon olive oil
1 onion, finely chopped
2 cloves garlic, crushed
1 tomato, finely chopped
1/2 cup (60 g/2 oz) grated Cheddar
2 tablespoons finely grated Parmesan
1/4 cup (15 g/1/2 oz) chopped fresh basil
1/4 cup (15 g/1/2 oz) chopped fresh parsley

1 Preheat the oven to moderate 180°C (350°F/Gas 4). Cut the capsicums in half lengthways and remove the seeds and membrane. Cook the rice in boiling water for 12 minutes, or until tender. Drain well.
2 Heat the oil in a frying pan and cook the onion for 5–8 minutes, or until golden. Add the garlic and cook for 1 minute. Add to the rice with the tomato, cheeses, basil and parsley. Season well.
3 Spoon the filling into the capsicums and place on a baking tray. Bake for 30 minutes, or until the capsicums are soft and the filling is golden brown.

Stuff CAPSICUMS with a mixture of rice, cheese and herbs.

201

ASPARAGUS HOLLANDAISE

Preparation: 10 minutes
Cooking: 10 minutes
Serves 4–6

4 egg yolks
185 g (6 oz) butter, melted
2 tablespoons lemon juice
300 g (10 oz) asparagus

1 Put the egg yolks in a heatproof bowl over a pan of barely simmering water (don't let the base of the bowl touch the water). Add 1 tablespoon water and whisk until the eggs hold a trail. Remove from the heat and very slowly whisk in the butter (drop by drop at first). Whisk until thick and holding a trail. Stir in the lemon juice and season. (If you need to keep the sauce warm, replace the bowl over the hot water.)

2 Snap the woody ends from the asparagus and cook the spears in boiling water for 2–3 minutes, or until bright green and tender. Drain quickly and place on plates. Spoon the sauce over the top.

CREAMED SPINACH

Preparation: 5 minutes
Cooking: 10 minutes
Serves 4

30 g (1 oz) butter
1 onion, thinly sliced
500 g (1 lb) English spinach, trimmed and roughly chopped
3 tablespoon cream
pinch of ground nutmeg
¼ cup (30 g/1 oz) grated Cheddar

1 Heat the butter in a large heavy-based frying pan. Add the onion and cook over medium heat for 5 minutes, or until soft and golden. Add the spinach and cook for 3 minutes, or until wilted.

2 Stir in the cream and nutmeg and cook for 2 minutes, or until the spinach is tender and the cream heated through. Sprinkle with the cheese and serve immediately.

ASPARAGUS HOLLANDAISE (top) and CREAMED SPINACH.

HONEY-GLAZED CARROTS

Preparation: 5 minutes
Cooking: 5 minutes
Serves 4

2 carrots, sliced
30 g (1 oz) butter
2 teaspoons honey
snipped chives, to serve

1 Boil or steam the carrots until tender. Place the butter and honey in a small pan and cook over low heat until warm.
2 Pour the butter and honey over the drained carrots and toss gently. Sprinkle with the snipped chives to serve.

CAULIFLOWER CHEESE

Preparation: 10 minutes
Cooking: 15 minutes
Serves 4–6

500 g (1 lb) cauliflower
30 g (1 oz) butter
3 teaspoons plain flour
^{1}/2 cup (125 ml/4 fl oz) milk
3 tablespoons cream
^{1}/3 cup (40 g/1 ^{1}/4 oz) grated Cheddar
^{1}/4 teaspoon paprika
fresh chives, to serve

1 Cut the cauliflower into large florets and steam or

HONEY-GLAZED CARROTS (top) and CAULIFLOWER CHEESE.

boil until just tender.
2 Meanwhile, melt the butter in a pan. Stir in the flour and cook for 1 minute. Remove from the heat and gradually stir in the combined milk and cream. Return to the heat and stir until the mixture boils and thickens. Remove from the heat and stir in half the grated cheese. Season with salt and pepper to taste.

3 Put the drained cauliflower in a heatproof serving dish, spoon the cheese sauce over the top and sprinkle with the remaining grated cheese. Brown under a preheated hot grill for 3 minutes. Sprinkle with the paprika and snipped fresh chives to serve.

203

Deep-fry *POTATO CROQUETTES* in batches for a crisp finish.

evenly in the breadcrumbs and shake off the excess. Cover and refrigerate for at least 2 hours.

3 Half fill a deep heavy-based pan with oil and heat to 180°C/350°F (a cube of bread dropped in the oil will brown in 15 seconds). Cook in batches for 5 minutes, or until golden. Drain on paper towels and serve.

POTATO CROQUETTES

Preparation: 45 minutes +
  2½ hours refrigeration
Cooking: 10 minutes
Makes 12

750 g (1½ lb) floury
  potatoes, chopped
2 tablespoons cream or
  melted butter
3 eggs, lightly beaten
¼ teaspoon nutmeg
plain flour, for coating
1½ cups (150 g/5 oz)
  dry breadcrumbs
oil, for deep-frying

1 Boil the potato in salted water until tender, drain, return to the hot pan and mash. Stir in the cream or butter, a third of the beaten egg and the nutmeg. Season. Spread on a tray, cover and leave in the fridge for at least 30 minutes.

2 Divide into 12 portions and roll each portion into a long sausage shape. Roll in flour, shaking off the excess. Dip in the remaining egg, coat

STUFFED PUMPKINS

Preparation: 30 minutes
Cooking: 1 hour
Serves 4

4 nugget pumpkins
60 g (2 oz) butter
1 tablespoon oil
1 leek, sliced
1 zucchini, chopped

Stuff *PUMPKINS* with a mixture of vegetables and rice.

1 red capsicum, chopped
100 g (3¹/₂ oz) button
  mushrooms, sliced
1 tomato, chopped
¹/₂ cup (95 g/3 oz)
  cooked white rice
1 tablespoon chopped
  fresh parsley
¹/₂ cup (60 g/2 oz)
  grated Cheddar

1 Slice the top off each pumpkin and set it aside. Use a spoon to scoop out the pumpkin seeds.
2 Melt the butter and oil in a large frying pan, add the leek and cook over medium heat for 5 minutes, or until golden.
3 Add the zucchini, capsicum and mushrooms, and cook until tender. Remove from the heat and stir in the tomato, rice and parsley. Season with salt and pepper to taste.
4 Preheat the oven to moderate 180°C (350°F/ Gas 4). Spoon the filling into the pumpkin shells and place the shells into a clean ovenproof dish. Sprinkle with the grated Cheddar. Bake for 50 minutes, or until the pumpkins are tender. If you like, bake the pumpkin lids as well and replace to serve.

NOTE: To produce ¹/₂ cup (100 g/3¹/₂ oz) cooked white rice you will need ¹/₄ cup (50 g/1³/₄ oz) uncooked rice.

CHAR-GRILLED VEGETABLES with a balsamic dressing.

CHAR-GRILLED VEGETABLES

Preparation: 15 minutes
Cooking: 15 minutes
Serves 4

2 **large red capsicums**
2 **large sweet potatoes, sliced**
6 **zucchini, halved lengthways**
4 **large mushroom caps, thickly sliced**

Dressing
3 **cloves garlic, crushed**
2 **tablespoons balsamic vinegar**
2 **tablespoons chopped fresh rosemary**
4 **tablespoons olive oil**

1 Remove the seeds and membrane from the capsicums and cut the flesh into thick strips.
2 To make the dressing, whisk together the garlic, vinegar, rosemary and oil.
3 Heat a char-grill pan or barbecue plate. Brush the capsicum, sweet potato, zucchini and mushrooms with the dressing and cook for 15 minutes, or until tender. Turn occasionally and brush with the dressing.

NOTE: For a full vegetarian meal, serve with chargrilled tofu or haloumi cheese, tossed in the dressing, and a mound of creamy polenta.

CAESAR SALAD is a modern café favourite.

CAESAR SALAD

Preparation: 15 minutes
Cooking: 20 minutes
Serves 4

4 slices white bread,
  crusts removed, cubed
3 rashers bacon, chopped
1 cos lettuce
60 g (2 oz) Parmesan
  shavings, plus extra, to
  serve
2–4 anchovies, chopped
1 egg

2 tablespoons lemon
  juice
1 clove garlic, crushed
¹/₂ cup (125 ml/4 fl oz)
  olive oil

1 Preheat the oven to
moderately hot 190°C
(375°F/Gas 5). Spread the
bread cubes on a baking
tray in a single layer and
bake for 15 minutes, or
until golden.
2 Fry the bacon until
crisp, then drain on
paper towels.

3 Tear the lettuce leaves
into pieces and put in a
bowl with the bread,
bacon and Parmesan.
4 To make the dressing,
whisk together the
anchovies, egg, lemon
juice and garlic until
smooth. Start whisking in
the oil, drop by drop at
first, then in a thin stream,
until the dressing is thick
and creamy. Drizzle over
the salad, sprinkle with
extra Parmesan and serve.

WALDORF SALAD

Preparation: 20 minutes
Cooking: Nil
Serves 4–6

2 green apples
2 red apples
2 tablespoons lemon
   juice
1/4 cup (30 g/1 oz)
   walnut pieces
4 celery sticks, sliced
1 cup (250 g/8 oz)
   mayonnaise
lettuce, to serve

1 Quarter the apples, remove the seeds and cores, and cut the apples into small pieces.
2 Place the apple in a large bowl, drizzle with the lemon juice and toss to prevent the apples discolouring. Add the walnut pieces and celery and mix well.
3 Add the mayonnaise and toss well. Spoon into a lettuce-lined bowl and serve immediately.

COLESLAW

Preparation: 20 minutes
Cooking: Nil
Serves 8–10

1/2 green (Savoy) cabbage
1/4 red cabbage
3 carrots, coarsely grated
6 radishes, coarsely
   grated
1 red capsicum, chopped
4 spring onions, sliced
1/4 cup (15 g/1/2 oz)
   chopped fresh parsley
1 cup (250 g/8 oz)
   mayonnaise

1 Remove the hard cores from the cabbages and shred the leaves finely with a sharp knife. Place in a large bowl.
2 Add the carrot, radish, capsicum, spring onion and parsley. Add the mayonnaise, season with salt and freshly ground black pepper and toss the coleslaw well. Serve immediately (alternatively, cover and refrigerate the chopped vegetables for up to 3 hours, but serve immediately you have added the mayonnaise).

VARIATION: Instead of mayonnaise, dress the coleslaw with a mixture of sour cream, yoghurt, honey and mustard.

WALDORF SALAD.

COLESLAW.

GREEK SALAD

Preparation: 20 minutes
Cooking: Nil
Serves 6–8

6 ripe tomatoes, cut into
   thin wedges
1 red onion, cut into thin
   rings
2 Lebanese cucumbers,
   sliced
1 cup (185 g/6 oz)
   Kalamata olives
200 g (6¹/₂ oz) feta
   cheese
¹/₂ cup (125 ml/4 fl oz)
   extra virgin olive oil
dried oregano, to serve

1 Put the tomato, onion,
cucumber and olives in a
large bowl and season.
2 Break the feta into large
pieces and scatter over the
top of the salad. Drizzle
with olive oil and sprinkle
with a little oregano.

GREEK SALAD—very simple, yet delicious.

HOT POTATO SALAD

Preparation: 20 minutes
Cooking: 30 minutes
Serves 6–8

4 rashers bacon
1¹/₂ kg (3 lb) small
   Desiree potatoes (or
   other small, waxy, red-
   skinned potatoes)
4 spring onions, sliced
¹/₄ cup (7 g/¹/₄ oz)
   chopped fresh flat-leaf
   parsley
¹/₂ teaspoon salt

Dressing
²/₃ cup (170 ml/5¹/₂ fl
   oz) extra virgin olive oil
1 tablespoon Dijon
   mustard
¹/₃ cup (80 ml/2³/₄ fl oz)
   white wine vinegar

1 Trim the rind and fat
from the bacon and grill

Dress HOT POTATO SALAD with a Dijon vinaigrette.

until crisp. Allow to cool. Chop into small pieces.

2 Simmer the potatoes in a large pan of water until just tender, trying not to let the skins break away too much. Drain and cool.

3 To make the dressing, whisk together the oil, mustard and white wine vinegar in a jug.

4 Cut the potatoes into quarters and put in a bowl with half the bacon, the spring onion, parsley, salt and some black pepper. Pour in the dressing and toss gently. Serve, sprinkled with the remaining bacon.

COLD POTATO SALAD

Preparation: 40 minutes
Cooking: 5 minutes
Serves 4

600 g (1 ¼ lb) waxy or
  salad potatoes
1 small onion, chopped
2 celery sticks, sliced
1 small green capsicum,
  chopped
2 tablespoons finely
  chopped fresh parsley

Dressing
¾ cup (185 g/6 oz)
  mayonnaise
1–2 tablespoons vinegar
  or lemon juice
2 tablespoons sour cream

1 Wash the potatoes thoroughly, peeling them if you prefer, and cut into bite-sized pieces. Cook in boiling water for 5 minutes, or until just tender (pierce with a small sharp knife—the knife should come away easily). Drain and then leave to cool completely. Transfer to a large bowl.

2 Mix together the onion, celery, capsicum and parsley and add to the cooled potato. Mix together gently.

3 To make the dressing, mix together the mayonnaise, vinegar and sour cream, and season to taste. If you prefer a thinner dressing, add a little water. Pour over the salad and gently toss, being careful not to break up the pieces of potato.

VARIATIONS: Add chopped hard-boiled egg and crispy bacon. Instead of a mayonnaise-based dressing, whisk together yoghurt and a little sweet chilli sauce (this is a good idea for anyone watching their fat intake). For a Thai flavour, use coriander instead of parsley and top with peanuts or cashews.

Use waxy or salad potatoes for a COLD POTATO SALAD.

209

COOKING — A COMMONSENSE GUIDE

2 minutes. Rinse in cold water and drain well.
3 To make the dressing, whisk the oil, lemon juice, garlic and sugar together. Season to taste.
4 Mix the rice, peas, spring onion, capsicum, corn and mint in a bowl. Add the dressing and mix well. Cover and chill for 1 hour before serving.

TABBOULEH

Preparation: 20 minutes + 15 minutes standing
Cooking: Nil
Serves 8

^{3}/4 cup (130 g/4 ^{1}/2 oz) burghul
300 g (10 oz) fresh flat-leaf parsley
^{1}/2 cup (10 g/^{1}/4 oz) mint leaves
4 spring onions, finely chopped
4 tomatoes, finely chopped
2 cloves garlic, crushed
^{1}/3 cup (80 ml/2^3/4 fl oz) lemon juice
3 tablespoons olive oil

1 Put the burghul in a bowl with 185 ml (6 fl oz) water and leave for 15 minutes, or until all the water has been absorbed.
2 Finely chop the herbs with a large sharp knife or in a food processor—take care not to overprocess.

A RICE SALAD is perfect for barbecues or large gatherings.

RICE SALAD

Preparation: 30 minutes + 1 hour refrigeration
Cooking: 20 minutes
Serves 6–8

1^1/2 cups (300 g/10 oz) long-grain rice
^{1}/2 cup (90 g/3 oz) peas
3 spring onions, sliced
1 green capsicum, diced
1 red capsicum, diced
310 g (10 oz) can corn kernels
^{1}/4 cup (15 g/^{1}/2 oz) chopped fresh mint

Dressing
^{1}/2 cup (125 ml/4 fl oz) extra virgin olive oil
2 tablespoons lemon juice
1 clove garlic, crushed
1 teaspoon sugar

1 Bring a large pan of water to the boil and stir in the rice. Return to the boil and cook for 12–15 minutes, or until tender. Drain and cool (if possible, cook the rice a day in advance).
2 Cook the peas in boiling water for about

3 Place the burghul, herbs, spring onion, tomato, garlic, lemon juice and oil in a bowl and toss well. Refrigerate until required. Return to room temperature to serve.

PASTA SALAD

Preparation: 20 minutes
Cooking: 10 minutes
Serves 4

2¹/₂ cups (225 g/7 oz) pasta spirals
150 g (5 oz) cherry tomatoes, halved
1 red or green capsicum, cubed
3 spring onions, sliced
100 g (3¹/₂ oz) button mushrooms, sliced
¹/₂ barbecued chicken, shredded
¹/₂ cup (90 g/3 oz) cooked peas
³/₄ cup (185 g/6 oz) whole egg mayonnaise

1 Bring a large pan of salted water to the boil, add the pasta and cook for 10 minutes, or until just tender. Drain, rinse under cold water and place in a large serving bowl.
2 Add the tomato, capsicum, spring onion, mushrooms, chicken, peas and mayonnaise and toss together well.

TABBOULEH is a Middle Eastern mix of burghul and parsley.

For speed, use a barbecued chicken in your PASTA SALAD.

211

THREE-BEAN SALAD

Preparation: 30 minutes
Cooking: 5 minutes
Serves 8–10

250 g (8 oz) green beans, topped and tailed
400 g (13 oz) can chickpeas, rinsed
425 g (13½ oz) can red kidney beans, rinsed
400 g (13 oz) can cannellini beans, rinsed

270 g (9 oz) can corn kernels, rinsed
3 spring onions, sliced
1 red capsicum, chopped
3 celery sticks, chopped
4–6 gherkins, chopped
¼ cup (15 g/½ oz) chopped fresh mint
¼ cup (7 g/¼ oz) chopped fresh flat-leaf parsley

Mustard vinaigrette
½ cup (125 ml/4 fl oz) olive oil
2 tablespoons white wine vinegar
1 teaspoon sugar
1 tablespoon Dijon mustard
1 clove garlic, crushed

1 Cut the green beans into short lengths. Bring a small pan of water to the boil, add the beans and cook for 2 minutes. Drain and rinse under cold water, then leave in iced water until cold. Drain.
2 Place the green beans, chickpeas, kidney beans, cannellini beans, corn, spring onion, capsicum, celery, gherkin, mint and parsley in a large bowl. Season and mix together.
3 To make the vinaigrette, whisk together all the ingredients, drizzle over the salad and toss gently.

STORAGE: The salad can be prepared up to 3 hours in advance and refrigerated, but don't add the dressing until just before serving.
NOTE: You can make this dish using dried beans and peas. Remember to soak the beans in cold water overnight, then cook in boiling water until tender. Check the packet for cooking times—some beans take longer than others and may need to be cooked separately.

Use green, cannellini and kidney beans for THREE-BEAN SALAD.

SALAD NICOISE

Preparation: 30 minutes
Cooking: 25 minutes
Serves 4–6

4 eggs
500 g (1 lb) baby new
    potatoes
250 g (8 oz) green
    beans, topped and
    tailed
6 artichoke hearts in oil,
    drained
350 g (11 oz) salad
    leaves
4 tomatoes, cut into
    wedges
425 g (14 oz) can tuna,
    drained and flaked
1 red capsicum, cut into
    strips
1 tablespoon bottled
    capers, drained
1 tablespoon coarsely
    chopped fresh tarragon
10 Niçoise (small) olives

Dressing
1 clove garlic, crushed
3 teaspoons Dijon
    mustard
2 anchovy fillets in oil,
    drained and
    chopped
1/4 cup (60 ml/2 fl oz)
    white wine vinegar
1/2 cup (125 ml/4 fl oz)
    extra virgin olive oil

SALAD NICOISE, dressed with a garlic and anchovy vinaigrette.

1 Put the eggs in a pan of water and bring to the boil, stirring occasionally to centre the yolks. Boil for 10 minutes, drain and cool in cold water. Peel and cut into wedges.

2 Boil the potatoes until tender, drain and cool. Cut into thick slices. Cook the beans in a pan of boiling water until tender, then drain and rinse under cold water. Chill in a bowl of iced water. Halve or quarter the artichokes.

3 Arrange the salad leaves on a serving platter. Top with the potato, beans, tomato, artichoke, tuna, egg and capsicum.

Sprinkle with the capers, tarragon and olives.

4 To make the dressing, whisk the garlic, mustard, anchovies and vinegar until smooth. Gradually add the oil and blend until smooth. Season with salt and pepper, and drizzle over the salad.

NOTE: Niçoise salad gets its name from the cuisine of Nice. All dishes described as 'niçoise' contain beans, tomatoes, olives and anchovies.

213

SANDWICH FILLINGS

EGG AND MIXED CRESS

Combine 1/2 cup (125 g/ 4 oz) mayonnaise with 1 tablespoon chopped capers and 1 tablespoon wholegrain mustard. Spread half this mixture onto twelve slices of dark rye bread. Top six of the bread slices with 2 cups (60 g/2 oz) watercress, 6 thinly sliced hard-boiled eggs, 1 cup (45 g/1 1/2 oz) mustard cress or alfalfa sprouts, salt and freshly ground black pepper. Drizzle with the remaining mayonnaise mixture. Top with the other six slices. Serves 6.

COLD MEAT AND MUSTARD

Steam or boil 2 small carrots until tender. Cut into small dice and combine with 2 chopped spring onions, 1 thinly sliced celery stick including the leaves, 1 chopped gherkin and 140 g (4 1/2 oz) chopped cooked ham, corned beef or other cold meat. Mix 1 tablespoon Dijon mustard, 2 teaspoons lemon juice, 2 tablespoons mayonnaise, 2 tablespoons sour cream and 2 teaspoons chopped dill and add to the salad. Mix until combined. Season with salt and pepper. Put two thinly sliced tomatoes on lavash bread, top with the salad and roll up. Serves 4.

COTTAGE CHEESE, ASPARAGUS AND AVOCADO

Split open four bagels. Top with 2 cups (500 g/ 1 lb) cottage cheese combined with 1/2 cup (10 g/1/4 oz) chervil or parsley leaves. Blanch 155 g (5 oz) asparagus, drain well and cut into short lengths. Place 12 semi-dried tomatoes, 1 thinly sliced avocado and the asparagus on top of the cottage cheese, season to taste with salt and pepper, and replace the tops. Serves 4.

EGGPLANT AND ROCKET

Cut 400 g (13 oz) eggplant into quarters lengthways. Cut 1 red capsicum into quarters lengthways, removing the seeds and membrane. Bake the vegetables in a moderate 180°C (350°F/ Gas 4) oven for 1 hour, or until soft and tender. Cool and cut into small pieces. Combine the vegetables with 100 g (3 1/2 oz) quartered cherry tomatoes, 2 chopped spring onions, 100 g (3 1/2 oz) crumbled feta cheese, 2 tablespoons each of coarsely chopped fresh flat-leaf parsley and mint leaves, 1 tablespoon chopped capers, 1 finely chopped clove garlic, 1/4 cup (60 ml/2 fl oz) lemon juice and 2 tablespoons olive oil. Season with salt and freshly ground black pepper. Split 4 slices of Turkish bread open. Fill with 150 g (5 oz) rocket leaves and the salad. Serves 4.

TUNA SALAD

Drain a 425 g (14 oz) can of tuna in oil. Break up the tuna with a fork and mix with 2 chopped hard-boiled eggs, 3 chopped spring onions, 2 teaspoons grated lemon rind, 1 chopped celery stick, 1 tablespoon chopped fresh flat-leaf parsley, 1/2 cup (125 g/ 4 oz) mayonnaise, 1/4 cup (60 g/2 oz) sour cream, salt and freshly ground black pepper to taste. Mix lightly with a fork. Serve with mixed lettuce leaves on bread rolls. Serves 4.

Clockwise from top left: EGG AND MIXED CRESS; COLD MEAT AND MUSTARD; COTTAGE CHEESE, ASPARAGUS AND AVOCADO; TUNA SALAD; EGGPLANT AND ROCKET.

SAVOURY PASTRIES

Savoury pastries can vary from sausage rolls for entertaining, to family dinners like chicken and leek cobbler. Perfect pastry, with a light buttery touch, can make any dish special. It has a reputation for difficulty, but once you've mastered the commonsense rules you'll probably find it rather easy.

QUICHE LORRAINE

Preparation: 35 minutes + 35 minutes refrigeration
Cooking: 1 hour
Serves 4–6

1 1/2 cups (185 g/6 oz) plain flour
90 g (3 oz) cold butter, chopped
1 egg yolk

Filling
20 g (3/4 oz) butter
1 onion, chopped
4 rashers bacon, cut into thin strips
2 tablespoons chopped fresh chives
2 eggs
3/4 cup (185 ml/6 fl oz) cream
1/4 cup (60 ml/2 fl oz) milk
100 g (3 1/2 oz) Swiss cheese, grated

1 Sift the flour into a bowl. Add the butter and, using your fingertips, rub the butter into the flour until it resembles fine breadcrumbs. Add the egg and mix with a knife, until the mixture just comes together. Add a little water if needed. Turn the mixture out onto a floured surface and gather together into a ball. Cover with plastic wrap and chill for at least 15 minutes.
2 Roll the pastry out between two sheets of baking paper until it is large enough to cover the base and side of a shallow loose-based round flan tin measuring 25 cm (10 inches) across the base. Lift the pastry into the tin and use a spare wad of pastry to press it firmly into the side of the tin. Trim off any excess pastry with a sharp knife or by rolling the rolling pin across the top. Place the pastry-lined flan tin in the refrigerator for 20 minutes. Preheat the oven to moderately hot 190°C (375°F/Gas 5).
3 Cover the pastry shell with crumpled baking paper, fill evenly with baking beads or uncooked rice or beans and bake for 15 minutes. Remove the paper and beads, and bake the pastry for 10 minutes, or until lightly golden and dried out. Reduce the oven to moderate 180°C (350°F/Gas 4).
4 To make the filling, heat the butter in a heavy-based pan. Add the onion and bacon and cook for 10 minutes, stirring frequently, until the onion is soft and the bacon cooked. Stir in the chives and set aside to cool.
5 Beat the eggs, cream and milk in a jug. Season with black pepper. Spread

QUICHE LORRAINE is the basic bacon-and-egg quiche.

the onion and bacon mixture evenly over the pastry shell. Pour in the egg mixture and sprinkle with the cheese. Bake for 30 minutes, or until golden and set.

VARIATION: To make a herb quiche, simply change the filling. Whisk together 3 eggs and 1 cup (250 ml/8 fl oz) cream. Stir in ½ cup of chopped fresh herbs (chives, parsley and dill all work well in a quiche) and 100 g (3½ oz) grated cheese. Pour into the pastry case and bake for 30 minutes, or until set.

Use a can of red salmon for SALMON AND SPRING ONION QUICHE.

SALMON AND SPRING ONION QUICHE

Preparation: 20 minutes +
  20 minutes refrigeration
Cooking: 1 hour
Serves 6

2 cups (250 g/8 oz) self-
  raising flour
160 g (5 1/2 oz) butter,
  melted
1/2 cup (125 ml/4 fl oz)
  milk

Filling
415 g (13 oz) can red
  salmon, drained and
  flaked
4 spring onions, sliced
1/3 cup (20 g/3/4 oz)
  chopped fresh parsley

4 eggs, lightly beaten
1/2 cup (125 ml/4 fl oz)
  milk
1/2 cup (125 ml/4 fl oz)
  cream
1/2 cup (60 g/2 oz)
  grated Cheddar

1 Sift the flour into a
large bowl and make a
well in the centre. Pour in
the melted butter and
milk and mix until the
mixture comes together
and forms a dough.
Refrigerate for 20 minutes.
Preheat the oven to
moderately hot 200°C
(400°F/Gas 6). Roll out
the pastry between two
sheets of baking paper
until it is large enough to
cover the base and side of
a 26 cm (10 1/2 inch) round

shallow loose-based fluted
flan tin. Trim off any
excess with a sharp knife
or by rolling a rolling pin
across the top of the tin.
2 Cover the pastry with
crumpled baking paper
and fill evenly with
baking beads or uncooked
rice or beans. Bake for
15 minutes. Remove the
paper and beads and bake
for 10 minutes, or until
golden and dry. Allow to
cool. Reduce the oven
to moderate 180°C
(350°F/Gas 4).
3 Place the salmon in the
pastry base. Mix together
the spring onion, parsley,
eggs, milk, cream and
cheese and pour over the
salmon. Bake for
30 minutes, or until set.

CARAMELIZED ONION QUICHE

Preparation: 45 minutes +
20 minutes refrigeration
Cooking: 1³/₄ hours
Serves 6

1¹/₂ cups (185 g/6 oz)
plain flour
125 g (4 oz) cold butter,
chopped
1 egg yolk

Filling
75 g (2¹/₂ oz) butter
800 g (1 lb 10 oz)
onions, thinly sliced
1 tablespoon soft brown
sugar
³/₄ cup (185 g/6 oz) sour
cream
2 eggs
40 g (1¹/₄ oz) prosciutto,
cut into strips
40 g (1¹/₄ oz) grated
mature Cheddar
2 teaspoons fresh thyme
leaves

Cook the onions slowly for CARAMELIZED ONION QUICHE

1 Sift the flour into a bowl, add the butter and rub between your fingertips until the mixture resemble fine breadcrumbs. Cut in the egg yolk with a knife and add 1–2 tablespoons of water until the dough just comes together. Add extra water if needed. Turn out and gather into a ball. Cover with plastic wrap and chill for 20 minutes.
2 Melt the butter in a pan and cook the onion over low heat for 25 minutes, or until soft and browned (this will produce sweet caramelized onions so do not be tempted to rush the process). Stir in the brown sugar and cook for 15 minutes, stirring occasionally to prevent burning. Preheat the oven to moderately hot 200°C (400°F/Gas 6). Grease a loose-based 22 cm (8³/₄ inch) round flan tin.
3 Roll out the pastry large enough to fit the flan tin. Fit the pastry into the tin, trimming off any excess with a sharp knife. Cover with crumpled baking paper and fill evenly with baking beads or uncooked rice or beans. Bake for 15 minutes, then remove the paper and beads and bake for 5 minutes. Cool slightly.
4 Lightly beat the sour cream and eggs. Add the prosciutto, cheese and thyme leaves. Season with salt and pepper. Stir in the onion and pour into the pastry shell. Bake for 40 minutes, or until set. If the pastry starts to over-brown, cover with foil.

CHICKEN AND LEEK COBBLER

Preparation: 1 hour
Cooking: 1 hour
Serves 4–6

50 g (1 3/4 oz) butter
1 kg (2 lb) chicken breast
  fillets, cut into strips
1 large leek, finely sliced
1 celery stick, sliced
1 tablespoon plain flour
1 cup (250 ml/8 fl oz)
  chicken stock
1 cup (250 ml/8 fl oz)
  cream
3 teaspoons Dijon
  mustard
3 teaspoons green
  peppercorns

Topping
400 g (13 oz) potatoes,
  quartered
1 1/3 cups (165 g/5 1/2 oz)
  self-raising flour
1/2 teaspoon salt
1/4 cup (30 g/1 oz)
  grated mature Cheddar
100 g (3 1/2 oz) cold
  butter, chopped
1 egg yolk, lightly
  beaten, to glaze

1 Melt half the butter in a pan. When foaming, add the chicken in batches and cook until golden. Remove from the pan. Add the remaining butter and cook the leek and celery until soft. Return the chicken to the pan.

2 Sprinkle the flour over the chicken and stir for 1 minute. Remove from the heat and stir in the stock and cream. Mix well, making sure that there are no lumps. Return to the heat and stir until it comes to the boil and thickens. Reduce the heat and simmer for 20 minutes. Add the mustard and peppercorns and season with salt and pepper. Transfer to a 1.5 litre casserole dish and cool. Preheat the oven to moderately hot 200°C (400°F/Gas 6).

3 To make the topping, cook the potatoes in boiling water until tender. Drain and mash until smooth. Rub together the flour, salt, cheese and butter with your fingertips until it resembles fine crumbs. Add to the potato and bring together with your hands into a dough.

4 Roll out the dough on a floured surface, until 1 cm (1/2 inch) thick. Cut into rounds with a 6 cm (2 1/2 inch) pastry cutter, re-rolling and cutting to use all the dough. Arrange the rounds overlapping on top of the cooled filling.

5 Brush the topping with the egg yolk, adding a little milk if more glaze is needed. Bake for 30 minutes, or until the filling is heated through and the topping golden.

Use a potato dough for the CHICKEN AND LEEK COBBLER.

COUNTRY VEGETABLE PIE

Preparation: 50 minutes +
  30 minutes refrigeration
Cooking: 45 minutes
Serves 6

2 cups (250 g/8 oz) plain
  flour
125 g (4 oz) cold butter,
  chopped
2 egg yolks

Filling
2 new potatoes, cubed
350 g (11 oz) butternut
  pumpkin, cubed
100 g (3¹/₂ oz) broccoli,
  cut into small florets
100 g (3¹/₂ oz)
  cauliflower, cut into
  small florets
1 zucchini, grated
1 carrot, grated
3 spring onions, chopped
³/₄ cup (90 g/3 oz)
  grated Cheddar
¹/₂ cup (125 g/4 oz)
  ricotta cheese
¹/₂ cup (50 g/1³/₄ oz)
  grated Parmesan
¹/₄ cup (15 g/¹/₂ oz)
  chopped fresh parsley
1 egg, lightly beaten
1 egg yolk, lightly beaten

1 Sift the flour into a
bowl. Add the butter and,
using your fingertips, rub
in until it resembles fine
breadcrumbs. Add the
yolks and mix with a
knife, until the dough just
comes together. Add

Fold or plait the pastry top for COUNTRY VEGETABLE PIE.

3–4 tablespoons water if
needed. Turn out onto a
floured surface and gather
together. Cover with
plastic wrap and chill for
at least 15 minutes.
2 To make the filling,
steam or boil the potato
and pumpkin for
10–15 minutes, or until
tender. Drain and place in
a large bowl to cool.
Gently fold in the
broccoli, cauliflower,
zucchini, carrot, spring
onion, cheeses, parsley
and beaten egg. Season.
3 Grease a deep 18 cm
(7 inch) loose-bottomed
flan tin. Roll out two-
thirds of the dough on a
lightly floured surface to
fit the base and side of

the tin. Spoon the filling
into the pastry base.
4 To make the lattice top,
roll out the remaining
dough a little larger than
the pie. Cut the dough
into thin strips and lay
half on baking paper in
one direction and the
other half at right angles.
Interweave the strips to
make a lattice. Invert onto
the pie and press the edge
to seal. Cover and chill
for 15 minutes. Brush
with egg yolk. Place the
tin on a baking tray.
Preheat the oven to
moderately hot 190°C
(375°F/Gas 5). Bake for
25–30 minutes, or until
the pastry is cooked and
lightly golden.

DEEP-DISH CHICKEN PIE

Preparation: 45 minutes + refrigeration
Cooking: 1 hour 10 minutes
Serves 6

1 tablespoon olive oil
1 large onion, chopped
2 cloves garlic, crushed
600 g (1 1/4 lb) chicken thigh fillets, chopped
2 large carrots, chopped
2 large parsnips, chopped
1 large potato, chopped
2 bay leaves
2 celery sticks, sliced
3 tablespoons plain flour
1 1/4 cups (315 ml/ 10 fl oz) milk
1/2 cup (125 ml/4 fl oz) chicken stock
3 sheets frozen butterpuff pastry, thawed (see Note)
1 egg yolk, beaten

1 Heat the oil in a large deep frying pan and cook the onion and garlic for 3 minutes, or until the soft. Add the chicken and cook for 10 minutes, or until golden brown, turning regularly.

2 Add the chopped carrot, parsnip, potato, bay leaves and celery with 1/4 cup (60 ml/2 fl oz) water, and mix well. Cook over low heat, covered, for 10 minutes, or until the carrot, parsnip and potato are just tender.

3 Stir in the flour and cook for 2 minutes. Remove from the heat and add the milk and stock, stirring until blended and smooth. Return to the heat and stir until the sauce boils and thickens. Transfer to a large bowl, cover and refrigerate until completely cold.

4 Grease a deep 20 cm (8 inch) round springform tin. Using 1 sheet of the pastry, cut a circle to fit the base of the tin. Cut the second sheet of pastry into 3 strips and press each strip around the side of the tin, pressing the edges together gently with your fingertips. (Make sure the pastry is well sealed or the filling will leak.) Refrigerate for 20 minutes.

5 Preheat the oven to moderately hot 200°C (400°F/Gas 6). Spoon the cold filling into the pastry case and smooth with the back of the spoon. Using the last sheet of pastry, cut a circle 2 cm (3/4 inch) larger than the tin. Cut a 2 cm (3/4 inch) hole in the centre of the pastry. Gently place it over the pie and trim the edge. Pinch the edges together firmly to seal. Decorate with shapes cut from the pastry trimmings. Brush the top of the pie with the

Decorate your DEEP-DISH CHICKEN PIE with pastry trimmings.

beaten egg yolk. Bake for 35 minutes, or until crisp and golden. Leave in the tin for 10 minutes before removing and cutting.

NOTE: Butterpuff pastry will produce the best result for this pie. If you can't find butterpuff pastry, buy plain puff pastry and brush it with melted butter. The pastry sheets will take 5–10 minutes to defrost at room temperature.

Use layers of buttery filo pastry for SPINACH PIE.

SPINACH PIE

Preparation: 25 minutes
Cooking: 45 minutes
Serves 6–8

1 kg (2 lb) English
   spinach
1 tablespoon oil
6 spring onions, chopped
125 g (4 oz) feta cheese,
   crumbled
3/4 cup (90 g/3 oz)
   grated Cheddar
5 eggs, lightly beaten
16 sheets filo pastry
1/3 cup (80 ml/2 3/4 fl oz)
   olive oil
1 egg, lightly beaten
1 tablespoon poppy
   seeds

1 Preheat the oven to hot 210°C (415°F/Gas 6–7). Brush a 30 x 25 cm (12 x 10 inch) baking dish with oil. Wash the spinach thoroughly and shred finely. Place in a large pan with just the water clinging to the leaves, cover and cook over low heat for 2 minutes, or until just wilted. Cool, then wring the moisture from the spinach and spread out the strands.

2 Heat the oil in a small pan and cook the spring onion for 3 minutes, or until soft. Transfer to a large bowl and add the spinach, cheeses and eggs. Season with salt and pepper and mix well.

3 Place 1 sheet of pastry in the baking dish, letting the edges hang over. Cover the remaining pastry with a clean, damp tea towel to prevent it drying out. Brush the pastry in the dish with some of the oil. Repeat the process with another 7 layers of pastry, brushing each sheet lightly with the oil.

4 Spread the filling over the pastry and fold in the edges. Brush each remaining sheet of pastry lightly with oil and place on top of the pie. Tuck the edges of pastry down the sides, brush the top with the egg and sprinkle with the poppy seeds. Bake for 35–40 minutes, or until golden. Serve immediately.

223

Chill PORK PIE overnight, then cut into wedges to serve.

PORK PIE

Preparation: 45 minutes +
  overnight refrigeration
Cooking: 1¾ hours
Serves 6–8

3 cups (375 g/12 oz)
  plain flour
2 egg yolks
125 g (4 oz) lard
600 g (1¼ lb) boneless
  pork, cubed
4 rashers bacon, chopped
1 red onion, chopped
½ celery stick, chopped
1 tablespoon fresh thyme
1 cup (80 g/2¾ oz) fresh
  breadcrumbs
1 egg, lightly beaten
1 egg, lightly beaten, to
  glaze

Aspic
½ cup (125 ml/4 fl oz)
  apple juice or water
1 teaspoon chicken stock
  powder
2 teaspoons gelatine

1 Grease a deep 17 cm
(6¾ inch) round
springform tin. Sift the
flour into a large bowl.
Make a well in the centre
and add the egg yolks.
Cover the egg yolks with
the flour and set aside.
Place the lard and ⅔ cup
(170 ml/5½ fl oz) water
in a small pan, and stir
over medium heat until
the lard has melted. Bring
to the boil and then
quickly pour it over the
flour and eggs. Mix to a
soft dough with a wooden
spoon. Turn out onto a
lightly floured surface and
gather together into a
smooth ball. Wrap in
plastic wrap and
refrigerate for 30 minutes.
2 Work the pork, in
batches, in a processor
until roughly chopped but
not minced (or chop with
a sharp knife). Transfer to
a bowl. Add the bacon,
onion, celery, thyme,
breadcrumbs and egg. Mix
well, cover and chill.
3 Roll out two-thirds of
the pastry between
two sheets of greaseproof
paper and line the base
and side of the tin. Trim
the edge and brush with
some of the egg. Spoon
the filling into the tin and
smooth the surface. Roll
the remaining pastry out
to a 20 cm (8 inch) circle.
Cut a 2 cm (¾ inch) hole
in the centre. Fit over the
filling, trim the pastry and
press to seal the edges
together. Decorate with
the pastry scraps, then
refrigerate for 30 minutes.
4 Preheat the oven to hot

210°C (415°F/Gas 6–7). Brush the pie with the egg. Bake for 45 minutes, then reduce the heat to moderate 180°C (350°F/Gas 4) and continue to cook for 1 hour. Cover with foil if the pastry is browning too much. Cool in the tin.

5 To make the aspic, mix the apple juice with the stock powder in a small pan. Sprinkle with the gelatine and stir over low heat until dissolved. Pour the aspic, a little at a time, into the pie hole, letting it soak in each time. Cover and refrigerate overnight. Serve cold, in wedges.

butter and, using your fingertips, rub the butter and salt into the flour until it resembles fine breadcrumbs. Add 3–4 tablespoons water and mix with a knife until the dough just comes together. Turn out onto a floured surface and gather together into a ball.

2 Roll out two thirds of the pastry and line the pie plate. Cover with plastic wrap and refrigerate for 20 minutes. Preheat the oven to moderately hot 200°C (400°F/Gas 6).

3 Heat the oil in a frying pan and cook the bacon for 5 minutes, or until soft and slightly golden.

Remove from the heat and cool slightly. Arrange over the pastry base.

4 Crack the eggs into a cup, one at a time, then slide on top of the bacon at regular intervals (so, when the pie is sliced, each person will get some egg). Sprinkle with the parsley and season well. Roll out the remaining pastry and lay it over the top of the pie. Press the edges together and trim with a sharp knife. Pinch the edges in a decorative pattern, cut a steam hole in the top and decorate with pastry scraps. Brush with the egg and bake for 15–20 minutes. Serve hot.

BACON AND EGG PIE

Preparation: 40 minutes
Cooking: 30 minutes
Serves 4–6

2 cups (250 g/8 oz) plain flour
125 g (4 oz) chilled butter, chopped
pinch of salt
2 teaspoons oil
6 rashers bacon, chopped
6 eggs
1 tablespoon chopped fresh parsley
1 egg, beaten

1 Lightly grease a 20 cm (8 inch) pie plate. Sift the flour into a bowl. Add the

BACON AND EGG PIE.

225

STEAK AND KIDNEY PUDDING

Preparation: 30 minutes
Cooking: 4 hours
Serves 4–6

200 g (6½ oz) lamb
  kidneys
500 g (1 lb) round or
  rump steak, cubed
2 tablespoons plain flour
30 g (1 oz) butter
1 tablespoon oil
1 onion, sliced
1 clove garlic, crushed
125 g (4 oz) button
  mushrooms, quartered
1 bay leaf
½ cup (125 ml/4 fl oz)
  red wine
1 cup (250 ml/8 fl oz)
  beef stock
2 tablespoons chopped
  fresh parsley

Suet pastry
1½ cups (185 g/6 oz)
  self-raising flour
90 g (3 oz) suet, finely
  grated

1 Peel the skin from the kidneys, cut into quarters and trim any fat or sinew. Toss the kidneys and steak cubes in the flour.

2 Heat the butter and oil in a heavy-based pan and cook the onion and garlic, stirring until soft; remove from the pan. Add the steak and kidneys to the pan in small batches and brown over high heat. Drain on paper towels.

3 Return the onion, garlic, steak and kidneys to the pan with the mushrooms, bay leaf, wine, stock and parsley and bring to the boil. Reduce the heat and simmer, covered, for 1 hour, or until the steak is tender, stirring occasionally. Cool.

4 To make the suet pastry, sift the flour into a bowl and stir in the suet. Add about ½ cup (125 ml/ 4 fl oz) water, or enough to mix to a firm dough. Turn out onto a lightly floured surface and gather together into a smooth ball. Roll out two-thirds of the pastry to line a 2-litre pudding basin. Brush the top edge with water.

5 Spoon the filling into the pastry. Roll the remaining pastry to cover the basin, then press the edges of the pastry firmly together to seal. Lay a sheet of foil on the work surface and cover with baking paper. Make a large pleat in the middle. Grease the paper with melted butter. Place, paper-side-down, on top of the basin and tie securely with string. Place the basin in a large pan. Add enough water to

Use traditional suet pastry for STEAK AND KIDNEY PUDDING.

come halfway up the side of the basin. Bring to the boil, then reduce the heat to a simmer and cook, covered, for 3 hours, checking and replenishing the water when necessary. Serve immediately.

HINT: Suet gives the pastry a slightly crisp texture: it can be bought from your butcher. If you can't find it, use butter. VARIATION: To make steak and kidney pie, place the cooled filling in a 23 cm (9 inch) pie dish and cover with a sheet of puff pastry. Press the edge to seal and cut a hole in the top to let the steam escape. Bake in a preheated moderately hot 200°C (400°F/Gas 6) oven for 25 minutes or until the top is golden brown and the filling has thoroughly heated through.

Serve SAUSAGE ROLLS with extra tomato sauce.

SAUSAGE ROLLS

Preparation: 35 minutes
Cooking: 25 minutes
Makes 48

1 teaspoon oil
1 onion, finely chopped
500 g (1 lb) sausage
  mince
1 cup (80 g/2³/₄ oz) fresh
  breadcrumbs
2 tablespoons tomato
  sauce

1 egg, lightly beaten
3 sheets frozen ready-
  rolled puff pastry,
  thawed
egg or milk, to glaze

1 Preheat the oven to moderately hot 200°C (400°F/Gas 6). Lightly grease a baking tray. Heat the oil in a frying pan and cook the onion over low heat until soft and transparent. Transfer to a bowl and mix with the mince, breadcrumbs, tomato sauce and egg.
2 Lay the pastry sheets on a lightly floured board and cut each sheet into two strips. Divide the filling into six equal portions and spoon across the long edge of the

pastry. Roll up to make a long sausage shape. Brush lightly with a little beaten egg or milk. Cut the rolls into 4 cm (1¹/₂ inch) lengths and place on the tray, seam-side-down.
3 Bake for 20 minutes, or until the rolls are crisp and golden. Serve with tomato sauce.

NOTE: Sausage rolls can be frozen for up to 2 weeks after baking. Thaw and reheat in a preheated moderate 180°C (350°F/Gas 4) oven for 30 minutes. VARIATION: This recipe can also be made using chicken mince.

227

PIZZA BASE

Preparation: 20 minutes
Cooking: 30 minutes
Makes one thick or two thin
30 cm (12 inch) bases

7 g (¹/₄ inch) sachet dry
   yeast
¹/₂ teaspoon salt
¹/₂ teaspoon sugar
2¹/₂ cups (310 g/10 oz)
   plain flour
2 tablespoons olive oil
2 teaspoons semolina or
   polenta

1 Combine the yeast, salt,
sugar and 1 cup (250 ml/
8 fl oz) warm water in a
small bowl. Leave,
covered with plastic wrap,
in a warm place for
10 minutes, or until the
mixture is foamy.
2 Sift the flour into a
large bowl. Make a well in
the centre, add the yeast
mixture and mix to a
dough. Knead the dough
on a lightly floured
surface for 5 minutes, or
until smooth and elastic.
For thick pizza, roll the
dough out to a 35 cm
(14 inch) round. For thin
pizza, divide the dough in
half and roll out each
portion to a 35 cm
(14 inch) round.
3 Brush a 30 cm (12 inch)
pizza tray with oil and
sprinkle with semolina or
polenta. Place the dough
on the tray and tuck the
edge underneath to make
a rim. Spread with pizza
sauce and then your
choice of toppings. Bake
at hot 210°C (415°F/
Gas 6–7) for 30 minutes.

VARIATION: For
wholemeal pizza base:
Use 1¹/₂ cups (185 g/6 oz)
plain flour and 1 cup
(150 g/5 oz) plain
wholemeal flour.

PIZZA SAUCE

Preparation: 10 minutes
Cooking: 25 minutes
Makes sauce for two 30 cm
   (12 inch) pizzas

1 tablespoon olive oil
1 onion, finely chopped
2 cloves garlic, crushed
425 g (14 oz) can peeled
   tomatoes, crushed
1 teaspoon dried basil
1 teaspoon dried oregano
1 teaspoon sugar

1 Heat the oil in a pan
and cook the onion over
low heat for 5 minutes, or
until soft. Add the garlic
and cook for 1 minute.
2 Stir in the tomato, herbs
and sugar and cook over
high heat for 20 minutes,
or until reduced and
thickened. Season to taste
and cool before using.

NOTE: The sauce can be
made up to 2 days in
advance. Refrigerate in an
airtight container until
required. The sauce may
also be frozen for up to
2 months. You may like to
make a double batch and
freeze the remaining sauce
for future use.

SUPER SUPREME

Preparation: 20 minutes
Cooking: 30 minutes
Serves 4

30 cm (12 inch) pizza
   base
3 tablespoons pizza
   sauce
1 cup (150 g/5 oz)
   grated mozzarella
   cheese
1 green capsicum,
   chopped
100 g (3¹/₂ oz) small
   button mushrooms,
   sliced
45 g (1¹/₂ oz) sliced ham,
   cut into strips
45 g (1¹/₂ oz) cabanossi,
   thinly sliced
30 g (1 oz) sliced salami,
   cut into quarters
2 pineapple rings, sliced
pitted black olives, sliced

1 Preheat the oven to hot
210°C (415°F/Gas 6–7).
Lightly oil a 35 cm
(14 inch) pizza tray. Place
the pizza base on the tray
and spread evenly with
the sauce.
2 Sprinkle three-quarters
of the cheese over the

SUPER SUPREME pizza with all the toppings—or you can make up your own.

pizza base. Top with the capsicum and mushrooms. Arrange the ham, cabanossi, salami, pineapple and olives evenly over the top. Sprinkle with the remaining cheese.

3 Bake for 30 minutes, or until the base is crunchy and golden, and the cheese has melted. Cut into wedges and serve.

VARIATION: You can put pretty much anything on a pizza—try chilli, anchovies, ground beef, sun-dried tomatoes or cooked prawns.

For a simple vegetarian pizza, brush the base with a mixture of crushed garlic and olive oil, top with thin slices of potatoes and sprinkle with fresh herbs, salt and a little Parmesan. For a special occasion antipasto pizza, spread with pizza sauce and top with marinated vegetables, sliced bocconcini and pesto.

229

SPRING ROLLS

Preparation: 35 minutes
Cooking: 30 minutes
Makes about 20

4 dried Chinese
  mushrooms
1 clove garlic, crushed
3/4 teaspoon finely grated
  fresh ginger
6 spring onions,
  chopped
3 cups (135 g/4 1/2 oz)
  shredded Chinese
  cabbage
1 large carrot, grated
150 g (5 oz) can water
  chestnuts, chopped
1 tablespoon oyster
  sauce

1 packet spring roll
  wrappers
oil, for deep-frying
sweet chilli sauce, to
  serve

1 Soak the mushrooms in
boiling water for
10 minutes. Drain and
squeeze out the liquid.
Remove the stems and
chop the caps finely.
2 Heat a little oil in a wok
or frying pan and cook
the garlic, ginger, spring
onion, cabbage, carrot,
water chestnuts and
mushrooms for 5 minutes
over high heat, or until
softened. Stir in the oyster
sauce and leave to cool.
3 Work with one wrapper

at a time, keeping the rest
covered with a damp tea
towel. Place 2 tablespoons
filling on each wrapper
and fold one point over.
Fold in the two side
points and roll up towards
the last point, making a
parcel. Seal with a little
flour and water paste.
4 Half-fill the wok with
oil and heat until a cube
of bread browns in
15 seconds. Deep-fry the
rolls, four at a time, for
about 3 minutes, or until
golden. Drain the rolls on
paper towels and serve
with sweet chilli sauce.

MEAT PIE

Preparation: 30 minutes +
  overnight refrigeration
Cooking: 3 hours
Serves 4

1/3 cup (40 g/1 1/4 oz)
  plain flour, seasoned
750 g (1 1/2 lb) gravy
  beef, cut into chunks
1/3 cup (80 ml/2 3/4 fl oz)
  oil
3 onions, sliced
2 cups (500 ml/16 fl oz)
  beef stock
1 tablespoon
  Worcestershire sauce
2 tablespoons chopped
  fresh parsley
1 sheet ready-rolled
  shortcrust pastry
1 egg yolk, to glaze
1 sheet ready-rolled puff
  pastry

Serve SPRING ROLLS with sweet chilli sauce, for dipping.

Glazing the MEAT PIE with egg yolk will give it a lovely crisp and shiny crust.

1 Put the seasoned flour in a plastic bag, add the meat and shake to coat with the flour. Remove the meat and shake off the excess flour. Heat a little oil in a large heavy-based pan and fry the meat, in batches, until golden brown. Remove all the meat from the pan.

2 Add the onion to the pan and cook over medium heat until it is golden and translucent. Return the meat to the pan, add the stock and Worcestershire sauce and stir until it boils and thickens. Reduce the heat, cover and simmer for 2 hours, or until the meat is very tender, stirring every 30 minutes to prevent sticking. Stir in the parsley. Cool, then refrigerate (preferably overnight—most meat stew mixtures are better left overnight for the flavours to develop).

3 Place a baking tray in the oven and preheat the oven to hot 220°C (425°F/Gas 7). Grease a deep 20 cm (8 inch) round pie plate. Line the base and side of the dish with the shortcrust pastry. You may need to roll the square of pastry a little larger to fit into the dish. Place the cold filling into the pastry shell.

4 Mix the egg yolk with 2 teaspoons of water and brush the pastry edge. Place the puff pastry over the top, press the edge gently to seal, then trim away the extra pastry. Pinch or crimp the edges to decorate. Cut two small slits in the pastry to allow the steam to escape during cooking. Brush with the egg yolk glaze. Put on the preheated tray and bake for 20 minutes. Reduce the heat to moderate 180°C (350°F/Gas 4) and cook for 15–20 minutes. Check the pastry during cooking and cover with foil if overbrowning.

231

CORNISH PASTIES

Preparation: 30 minutes
Cooking: 30 minutes
Makes 6 pasties

Shortcrust pastry
2¹/₂ cups (310 g/10 oz)
    plain flour
¹/₂ teaspoon dry mustard
120 g (4 oz) butter,
    chopped

Filling
250 g (8 oz) round or
    blade steak, finely
    chopped
2 small floury potatoes,
    finely chopped
1 onion, finely chopped

¹/₄ cup (15 g/¹/₂ oz)
    chopped fresh parsley
¹/₄ cup (60 ml/2 fl oz)
    beef or chicken stock
¹/₄ teaspoon English
    mustard
1 teaspoon grated
    horseradish
beaten egg, to glaze

1 Preheat the oven to hot 210°C (415°F/Gas 6–7) and grease a baking tray. Put the flour, mustard and butter in a bowl and rub in the butter with your fingertips until the mixture resembles fine breadcrumbs. Add 2 tablespoons water and mix with a knife until the mixture comes together, adding more water if necessary. Gather into a ball, wrap in plastic wrap and refrigerate.

2 To make the filling, mix together the steak, potato, onion and parsley. Add the stock, mustard and horseradish, and season with salt and white pepper. Mix well.

3 Roll the pastry out to 3 mm (¹/₈ inch) thickness. Cut out six 16 cm (6¹/₂ inch) rounds, using a saucer as a guide. Spoon the filling into the centres of the six pastry rounds.

4 Glaze the edge of the pastry with egg and bring up two sides over the filling to make a half circle. Pinch the edges together to form a frill. Brush with the egg and bake on a baking tray for 10 minutes. Reduce the heat to moderate 180°C (350°F/Gas 4) and cook for a further 20 minutes. Serve hot or cold.

NOTE: Cold pasties are excellent for work or school lunches. They were originally baked for farmers who worked outside all day, and for miners. Family members would have their own preferences for fillings, and each pasty would be marked with its owner's initials. The pasty has the frill so that it can easily be held to eat.

CORNISH PASTIES can be served hot from the oven, or cold.

CHEESE AND PINE NUT FILO TRIANGLES

Preparation: 30 minutes
Cooking: 15 minutes
Makes 28 triangles

125 g (4 oz) feta cheese
125 g (4 oz) ricotta
cheese
2 tablespoons chopped
fresh basil
1/4 cup (40 g/1 1/4 oz)
pine nuts, toasted
1 egg, lightly beaten
14 sheets filo pastry
125 g (4 oz) butter,
melted

CHEESE AND PINE NUT FILO TRIANGLES.

1 Preheat the oven to moderately hot 200°C (400°F/Gas 6). Mix together the cheeses, basil, pine nuts and egg. Season well with salt and black pepper.
2 Place a sheet of pastry on a work surface and brush all over with the melted butter. Top with another sheet of pastry and brush with the butter. Cut the pastry lengthways into four strips.
3 Place 3 level teaspoons of the mixture on the end of each strip. Fold the pastry diagonally over and up to enclose the filling and make a triangle. Brush the triangles with butter and place on a baking tray. Repeat with the remaining pastry and

filling. Bake the triangles for 15 minutes, or until golden brown. Serve hot.

STORAGE: The triangles can be made several hours ahead and kept in the fridge under a damp tea towel. Bake just before serving. Cooked triangles can be frozen in a single layer on a baking tray until firm, then transferred to an airtight container in the freezer.
HINT: Handle filo pastry quickly and carefully as it becomes brittle when exposed to air. To prevent it drying out, cover the spare sheets with a damp tea towel while assembling the triangles.

VARIATION: For prawn and crab triangles, melt 30 g (1 oz) butter in a small pan and cook 3 finely chopped spring onions for 2 minutes. Stir in 1 tablespoon plain flour, then 1/2 cup (125 ml/4 fl oz) milk. Stir until thickened then remove from the heat, add 1 tablespoon each of cream and lemon juice and 3 tablespoons finely chopped parsley. Squeeze dry 170 g (5 1/2 oz) canned white crab meat and 200 g (6 1/2 oz) canned prawns and stir into the sauce. Use to fill the filo triangles as before.

BREAD AND BUNS

Baking your own bread is one of the most satisfying skills in cooking. It is a shame the 'baking day' has fallen from favour—there are few smells as wonderful as those from fresh-baked bread. We've selected recipes for everything from everyday breads to special occasion hot cross buns.

BRIOCHE

Preparation: 1 hour +
3 hours standing
Cooking: 30 minutes
Makes 6 small and 1 medium
brioche

7 g (¹/₄ oz) sachet dried
yeast
¹/₂ cup (125 ml/4 fl oz)
warm milk
1 teaspoon caster sugar
4 cups (500 g/1 lb)
unbleached plain flour
1 teaspoon salt
2 tablespoons caster
sugar, extra
4 eggs, lightly beaten
175 g (6 oz) butter,
chopped and softened
extra flour, for kneading
1 egg yolk, to glaze
1 tablespoon cream

1 Grease six small brioche moulds and a 21 x 11 cm (8¹/₂ x 4¹/₂ inch) bread or loaf tin. (If you don't have

brioche moulds you could bake the dough as two medium loaves.) Dissolve the yeast in the warm milk. Stir in the sugar, cover with plastic wrap and leave for 5 minutes, or until frothy. Sift the flour, salt and extra sugar into a bowl and make a well in the centre. Pour in the eggs and yeast mixture. Using a wooden spoon, beat well until the mixture forms a rough ball.
2 Turn the dough out onto a lightly floured surface and knead for 5 minutes, or until it is smooth and firm. Gradually incorporate small amounts of the softened butter into the dough. Pull and stretch the dough until all the butter has been incorporated: do this with your hand with the fingers slightly apart, using a slapping motion from the

wrist. It will take about 10 minutes and the dough will be very sticky.
3 Clean your working surface and hands, and sprinkle the surface, hands and dough with a small amount of the extra flour. Knead the dough lightly for 10 minutes, or until it is smooth and elastic. Place in a large buttered bowl, brush the surface of the dough with oil and cover with plastic wrap. Leave in a warm place for 1¹/₂–2 hours, or until the dough has doubled.
4 Punch down the dough (give it one good hard punch in the centre with your fist) and divide it in half. Cover one half with plastic wrap. Divide the other half into six even-sized pieces. Remove a quarter of the dough from each piece. Mould the larger pieces into rounds and place in the brioche

The BRIOCHE dough makes enough for six small rolls and a medium-sized loaf.

moulds. Brush with a glaze made of the mixed egg yolk and cream. Shape the small pieces into balls and place on top of each roll.

5 Push a floured wooden skewer through the centre of the top ball to the base of the roll, then pull the skewer out. This secures the ball to the roll. Brush again with the glaze,

cover and leave in a warm place for 45 minutes, or until well risen. Preheat the oven to hot 210°C (415°F/Gas 6–7) and bake for 10 minutes. Reduce the heat to moderate 180°C (350°F/Gas 4) and bake for 10 minutes, or until golden and cooked. Turn out immediately onto a wire rack to cool.

6 Meanwhile place the

other half of the dough in the bread tin and brush with the glaze. Cover and leave to rise for 1 hour. Bake in a hot 210°C (415°F/Gas 6–7) oven for 15 minutes. Reduce the heat to moderate 180°C (350°F/Gas 4) and bake for 15 minutes, or until golden and cooked. Turn out immediately onto a wire rack to cool.

CHELSEA BUNS

Preparation: 25 minutes +
1½ hours standing
Cooking: 25 minutes
Makes 8

7 g (¼ oz) sachet dried
yeast
1 teaspoon sugar
1 tablespoon plain flour
½ cup (125 ml/4 fl oz)
milk, warmed
2½ cups (310 g/10 oz)
plain flour, sifted, extra
125 g (4 oz) butter,
chopped
1 tablespoon sugar, extra
1 teaspoon mixed spice
1 egg, lightly beaten
2 teaspoons grated lemon
rind
60 g (2 oz) butter, extra
¼ cup (45 g/1½ oz) soft
brown sugar
1 cup (185 g/6 oz) mixed
dried fruit

Glaze
1 tablespoon milk
2 tablespoons sugar

Glacé icing
½ cup (60 g/2 oz) icing
sugar
1–2 tablespoons milk

1 Grease a large baking
tray. Combine the yeast,
sugar and flour in a small
bowl. Gradually add the
milk and blend until
smooth. Cover with
plastic wrap and leave in a
warm place for 5 minutes,

CHELSEA BUNS are glazed, then drizzled with glacé icing.

or until foamy. Place the
extra flour, butter, sugar
and half the mixed spice
in a bowl and rub in the
butter with your fingertips
until the mixture is fine
and crumbly. Add the egg,
lemon rind and yeast
mixture, and mix together
until the mixture almost
forms a dough.
2 Turn onto a lightly
floured surface and knead
for 2 minutes, or until the
dough is smooth. Shape
into a ball and place in a
large, lightly oiled bowl.
Cover with plastic wrap
and leave in a warm place
for 1 hour, or until well
risen. Punch down the
dough (give it a hard
punch in the centre with
your fist) and knead for

2 minutes, until smooth.
3 Using electric beaters,
beat the extra butter and
brown sugar in a small
bowl until light and
creamy. Roll the dough
out to 40 x 25 cm
(16 x 10 inches). Spread
the butter and sugar all
over the dough, leaving a
small border along one of
the longer sides. Spread
with the combined fruit
and remaining mixed
spice. Roll the dough
lengthways, firmly and
evenly into a log, swiss-
roll style. Cut the roll into
eight slices. Arrange the
slices, close together, on
the baking tray. Place the
seams inwards and flatten
the pieces slightly. Cover
with plastic wrap and

leave in a warm place for 30 minutes to rise. Preheat the oven to hot 210°C (415°F/Gas 6–7).

4 Bake the buns for 20 minutes, or until well browned and cooked through. To make the glaze, put the milk and sugar in a small pan. Stir over low heat until the sugar dissolves and the mixture is almost boiling. Remove from the heat, brush liberally over the buns and transfer them to a wire rack to cool.

5 To make the glacé icing, mix together the icing sugar and milk, and stir until smooth. Drizzle over the glazed and cooled buns.

DAMPER

Preparation: 20 minutes
Cooking: 25 minutes
Makes 1 damper

3 cups (375 g/12 oz)
  self-raising flour
1–2 teaspoons salt
90 g (3 oz) butter,
  melted
½ cup (125 ml/4 fl oz)
  milk plus a little extra,
  to glaze

1 Preheat the oven to hot 210°C (415°F/Gas 6–7) and grease a baking tray. Sift the flour and salt into a large mixing bowl, and make a well in the centre. Combine the butter, milk and ½ cup (125 ml/ 4 fl oz) water, and add it to the flour. Stir with a knife until just combined.

2 Turn onto a lightly floured surface and knead for 20 seconds, or until smooth. Transfer the dough to the tray and press out to a 20 cm (8 inch) round.

3 Use the tip of a knife to score the damper into eight sections, with cuts 1 cm (½ inch) deep. Brush with a little milk, to glaze, and dust with a little extra flour. Bake for 10 minutes.

4 Reduce the heat to moderate 180°C (350°F/Gas 4). Bake for 15 minutes, or until the damper is golden and sounds hollow when tapped. Serve with butter and golden syrup.

VARIATIONS: The damper can be made into individual rolls. Use wholemeal self-raising flour for a more healthy version. For a savoury damper, ideal for eating with soup, add grated cheese and chopped mixed herbs, or sliced sun-dried tomatoes and finely sliced ham to the mixture. Simply add to the bowl with the flour and salt at the beginning of the recipe.

Serve DAMPER with butter and golden syrup (cocky's joy).

237

FINGER BUNS

Preparation: 45 minutes +
1½ hours standing
Cooking: 15 minutes
Makes 12

4 cups (500 g/1 lb)
unbleached plain flour
⅓ cup (35 g/1¼ oz) full
cream milk powder
2 x 7 g (¼ oz) sachets
dried yeast
½ teaspoon salt
½ cup (125 g/4 oz)
caster sugar
½ cup (60 g/2 oz)
sultanas
60 g (2 oz) butter,
melted
1 egg, lightly beaten
1 egg yolk, extra

Glacé icing
1¼ cups (155 g/5 oz)
icing sugar
20 g (¾ oz) butter,
melted
2–3 teaspoons water
pink food colouring

1 Brush two large baking trays with melted butter or oil. Put 3 cups (375 g/ 12 oz) of the flour in a large bowl with the milk powder, yeast, salt, sugar and sultanas. Mix well and make a well in the centre. Mix together the butter, egg and 1 cup (250 ml/ 8 fl oz) warm water and then pour into the well. Stir for 2–3 minutes to combine. Add enough of the remaining flour to make a soft dough.

2 Turn out onto a lightly floured surface and knead for 10 minutes, or until smooth and elastic. Place the dough in a large, lightly oiled bowl and brush the surface with oil. Cover with plastic wrap and leave in a warm place for 1 hour, or until well risen.

3 Punch the down dough (give it one firm punch in the centre with your fist) and knead for 1 minute. Divide into twelve pieces. Shape each piece into a 15 cm (6 inch) oval and place on the trays, spaced 5 cm (2 inches) apart. Cover with plastic wrap and leave in a warm place for 20 minutes, or until well risen.

4 Preheat the oven to moderate 180°C (350°F/ Gas 4). Brush the buns well with the combined egg yolk and 1 tablespoon water. Bake for 12–15 minutes, or until cooked through. Cool on a rack.

5 To make the glacé icing, mix the icing sugar and butter with 2–3 teaspoons water. Stir until smooth. Mix in the colouring. Use a knife to spread the icing over the buns.

NOTE: Can be kept for two days in an airtight container. They can be frozen, before icing, for up to a month.

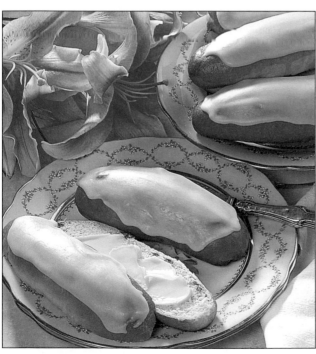

Use unbleached plain flour to make FINGER BUNS.

HOT CROSS BUNS

Preparation: 30 minutes +
1 hour standing
Cooking: 25 minutes
Makes 12

2 x 7 g (¹/₄ oz) sachets
dry yeast or 30 g (1 oz)
fresh yeast
4 cups (500 g/1 lb) plain
flour
2 tablespoons caster sugar
1 teaspoon mixed spice
1 teaspoon ground
cinnamon
40 g (1¹/₄ oz) butter
1¹/₄ cups (155 g/5 oz)
sultanas

Paste for crosses
¹/₄ cup (30 g/1 oz) plain
flour
¹/₄ teaspoon caster sugar

Glaze
1¹/₂ tablespoons caster
sugar
1 teaspoon gelatine

Pipe the crosses on the HOT CROSS BUNS, then glaze.

1 Place the yeast,
2 teaspoons of the flour,
1 teaspoon of the sugar
and ¹/₂ cup (125 ml/
4 fl oz) water in a small
bowl. Leave in a warm
place until foamy.
2 Sift the remaining flour
and spices into a large
bowl, stir in the sugar and
rub in the butter with
your fingertips. Stir in the
sultanas. Make a well in
the centre, stir in the

yeast mixture and up to
³/₄ cup (185 ml/6 fl oz)
water to make a soft
dough. Turn the dough
out onto a lightly floured
surface and knead for
5 minutes or until smooth,
adding more flour to
prevent sticking
if neccessary.
3 Put the dough in a large
floured bowl, cover
loosely with plastic and
leave in a warm place for
30–40 minutes, or until
doubled in size.
4 Preheat the oven to
200°C (400°F/Gas 6).
Turn the dough out onto a
lightly floured surface and
knead gently to deflate.
Divide into 12 portions
and roll each one into a

ball. Place the balls on a
lightly greased oven tray,
just touching each other,
in a rectangle 3 rolls wide
and 4 rolls long. Cover
loosely with a tea towel
and leave in a warm place
for 20 minutes, or until
nearly doubled in size.
5 To make the crosses,
mix the flour, sugar and
2¹/₂ tablespoons water
into a paste. Spoon into a
paper piping bag and pipe
crosses on the buns.
6 Bake for 20 minutes, or
until golden brown. Put
the sugar, gelatine and
1 tablespoon water in a
small pan and stir over the
heat until dissolved. Brush
over the hot buns and
allow to cool.

239

Make a variety of different shaped WHITE DINNER ROLLS.

WHITE DINNER ROLLS

Preparation: 15 minutes
+ 1½ hours standing
Cooking: 20 minutes
Makes 12 rolls

1 teaspoon dried yeast
½ teaspoon caster sugar
2 cups (250 g/8 oz) plain
  flour
½ teaspoon salt
1 tablespoon dried whole
  milk powder
2 teaspoons caster sugar,
  extra
1½ tablespoons oil
1 tablespoon milk

poppy seeds, sesame
seeds, caraway seeds,
sea salt flakes or plain
flour, to decorate

1 Combine the yeast,
sugar and 3 tablespoons
warm water in a bowl.
Cover and leave in a
warm place for
10 minutes until foamy.
2 Mix the flour, salt, milk
powder and extra sugar in
a bowl. Make a well in the
centre and pour in the oil,
yeast and ½ cup (125 ml/
4 fl oz) warm water. Mix
to a soft dough and knead
for 10 minutes, or until
smooth and elastic. Add a

little extra flour if needed.
3 Put in a lightly oiled
bowl, cover loosely with
greased plastic wrap and
leave in a warm place for
1 hour, or until the dough
has doubled in size.
4 Punch down the dough
(give it one firm punch
with your fist in the
centre), knead for
1 minute and divide into
twelve portions. Make a
variety of different shaped
rolls. To make spiral rolls,
roll each portion into a
30 cm (12 inch) rope, coil
tightly and tuck under the
end to seal. Alternatively,
tie the ropes to make knot
rolls. Or simply shape the
dough into ovals and
leave plain or slash
diagonally with a knife.
5 Arrange the rolls apart
on lightly greased trays
and cover loosely with a
damp tea towel. Leave to
rise for 20 minutes.
Preheat the oven to
moderate 180°C (350°F/
Gas 4). Brush the dinner
rolls with the milk and
then sprinkle with your
choice of seeds, sea salt
flakes or plain flour
topping. Bake for
15–20 minutes, or until
lightly browned.

Use a mixture of sultanas, currants, mixed peel and pecans in FRUIT AND NUT BREAD.

FRUIT AND NUT BREAD

Preparation: 30 minutes +
    1¼ hours standing
Cooking: 30 minutes
Makes 1 loaf

2¼ cups (280 g/9 oz)
    plain unbleached flour
7 g (¼ oz) sachet dried
    yeast
1 teaspoon ground mixed
    spice
2 tablespoons caster
    sugar
2 teaspoons grated
    orange rind
⅓ cup (40 g/1¼ oz)
    sultanas
¼ cup (35 g/1¼ oz)
    currants
1 tablespoon mixed peel
¼ cup (30 g/1 oz)
    chopped pecans
1 egg

⅓ cup (80 ml/2¾ fl oz)
    orange juice
30 g (1 oz) butter,
    melted
oil or melted butter, for
    brushing
1 tablespoon milk
1 tablespoon sugar

1 Sift the flour into a
large bowl. Add the yeast,
mixed spice, caster sugar,
orange rind, sultanas,
currants, mixed peel and
pecans and mix well.
Make a well in the centre.
2 Combine the egg,
orange juice, butter and
⅓ cup (80 ml/2¾ fl oz)
warm water and pour into
the well. Using a wooden
spoon, mix to a soft
dough. Turn onto a lightly
floured surface and knead
for 10 minutes, or until
the dough is smooth and
elastic, adding extra flour,

if needed. Place in a large
oiled bowl and brush with
oil. Cover and leave in
a warm place for
45 minutes, or until
well risen. Preheat the
oven to moderate 180°C
(350°F/Gas 4).
3 Punch down the dough
and knead for 1 minute.
Shape into an oblong or
round and place either in
an oiled 21 x 11 cm
(9 x 5 inch) loaf tin or on
a greased tray and pat out
to a 23 cm (9 inch) circle.
4 Brush the loaf with oil
or melted butter. Cover
and leave in a warm place
for 30 minutes. Bake for
20–30 minutes, or until
cooked through. Turn out
onto a wire rack. While
still hot, brush with the
combined milk and sugar.
Serve warm or cold.

241

SOUR CREAM POLENTA BREAD

Preparation: 15 minutes
Cooking: 50 minutes
Makes 1 loaf

1 1/2 cups (225 g/7 oz) fine polenta
1/2 cup (60 g/2 oz) plain flour
2 tablespoons soft brown sugar
1 teaspoon baking powder
1/2 teaspoon bicarbonate of soda
1/2 teaspoon salt
1 egg
1/3 cup (80 ml/2 3/4 fl oz) milk
1 1/4 cups (310 g/10 oz) sour cream
2 tablespoons vegetable oil
1/2 teaspoon poppy seeds

1 Preheat the oven to moderately hot 200°C (400°F/Gas 6) and grease an 11 x 18 cm (5 x 7 inch) loaf tin.
2 Mix together the polenta, flour, sugar, baking powder, bicarbonate of soda and salt in a large bowl.
3 Whisk together the egg, milk, sour cream and oil, and add them to the dry ingredients, mixing just long enough for them to be evenly combined. Pour the mixture into the tin and sprinkle with the poppy seeds.
4 Bake for 30 minutes, then reduce the temperature to moderate 180°C (350°F/Gas 4) and continue baking for a further 15–20 minutes, or until the loaf is golden. Delicious served warm with butter.

NOTE: There are different grades of polenta, some finer than others, and it is worth checking brands before you buy. The fine polenta is best for this recipe—it produces a less coarse and gritty bread.

Use fine-textured polenta for this SOUR CREAM POLENTA BREAD.

WHOLEMEAL BREAD

Preparation: 40 minutes +
2 hours rising
Cooking: 40 minutes
**Makes 4 small or 2 large
loaves**

15 g (¹/₂ oz) fresh yeast
or 7 g (¹/₄ oz) sachet
dried yeast
1 tablespoon caster sugar
¹/₂ cup (125 ml/4 fl oz)
warm milk
4 cups (600 g /1¹/₄ lb)
wholemeal plain flour
1 teaspoon salt
¹/₄ cup (60 ml/2 fl oz) oil
1 egg, lightly beaten

1 Lightly grease four
13 x 6.5 cm (5 x 3 inch)
loaf tins, or two
11 x 18 cm (4 x 7 inch)
loaf tins. Mix the yeast,
sugar and milk in a small
bowl. Cover and leave in
a warm place until frothy.
2 Mix the flour and salt
in a large bowl. Make a
well in the centre and
pour in the oil, frothy
yeast and 1 cup (250 ml/
8 fl oz) warm water. Mix
to a soft dough and gather
into a ball; turn out onto
a floured surface and
knead for 10 minutes.
Add a little extra flour if
the dough is too sticky.
Put in a large oiled bowl,
cover loosely with
greased plastic wrap and
leave in a warm place for

This recipe for WHOLEMEAL BREAD makes four small loaves.

1 hour, or until well risen.
3 Punch down the dough
(give it one firm punch in
the centre), turn out onto
a floured surface and
knead for 1 minute, or
until smooth: push the
dough away from you
with the palm of your
hand, roll it and turn it;
continue pushing, rolling
and turning. Divide into
four or two; knead into
shape and put in the tins.

Cover with a damp tea
towel and leave in a warm
place for 45 minutes, or
until risen. Preheat the
oven to hot 210°C
(415°F/Gas 6–7).
4 Brush the tops with the
egg. Bake for 10 minutes,
reduce the oven to 180°C
(350°F/Gas 4) and bake
for 30 minutes, or until
the base sounds hollow
when tapped. Cover with
foil if overbrowning.

CAKES AND BISCUITS

Cakes and biscuits are an excellent start for the novice cook. Beat together the ingredients and spoon them into a tin, or roll out a dough and cut out biscuits with a cookie-cutter—either way, it's not too difficult and the results are usually appreciated by all. Top with buttercream or a sticky icing and you could find yourself rather popular!

CHOCOLATE MUD CAKE

Preparation: 20 minutes
Cooking: 2¼ hours
Serves 8

1½ cups (185 g/6 oz) self-raising flour
½ cup (60 g/2 oz) plain flour
⅓ cup (40 g/1¼ oz) cocoa powder
250 g (8 oz) butter, chopped
1 tablespoon oil
200 g (6½ oz) dark chocolate, chopped
1½ cups (375 g/12 oz) caster sugar
1 tablespoon instant coffee powder
2 eggs, lightly beaten

Chocolate topping
150 g (5 oz) butter, chopped
150 g (5 oz) dark chocolate, chopped

1 Preheat the oven to warm 160°C (315°F/ Gas 2–3). Grease a deep 20 cm (8 inch) round cake tin and line with baking paper. Sift the flours and cocoa powder into a large mixing bowl and make a well in the centre.
2 Combine the butter, oil, chocolate, sugar and coffee powder with 1 cup (250 ml/8 fl oz) water in a pan. Stir over low heat until the chocolate and butter are melted and the sugar has dissolved. Pour into the well in the dry ingredients. Whisk until just combined. Add the

eggs and mix well, but do not overbeat.
3 Pour the mixture into the tin and bake for 2 hours, or until a skewer comes out clean when inserted into the centre of the cake. Leave in the tin to cool completely, then turn out onto a wire rack.
4 To make the topping, combine the butter and chocolate in a pan. Stir over low heat until melted. Remove from the heat to cool slightly.
5 Trim the top of the cake so it will sit flat, then place it upside down on a wire rack over a baking tray. Pour the topping over the cake, letting it run down the side. This cake is delicious served with cream or ice cream.

SPONGE CAKE

Preparation: 15 minutes
Cooking: 25 minutes
Serves 8

75 g (2¹/₂ oz) plain flour
150 g (5 oz) self-raising
  flour
6 eggs
220 g (7 oz) caster sugar
2 tablespoons boiling
  water
¹/₂ cup (160 g/5¹/₂ oz)
  strawberry jam
1 cup (250 ml/8 fl oz)
  cream, whipped
icing sugar, to dust

1 Preheat the oven to moderate 180°C (350°F/ Gas 4). Brush two deep 23 cm (9 inch) round cake tins with melted butter and line the bases with baking paper. Dust lightly with flour, shaking off the excess.

2 Sift the flours three times onto greaseproof paper. Beat the eggs in a small bowl with electric beaters for 7 minutes, or until thick and pale.

3 Gradually add the sugar to the eggs, beating well after each addition. Transfer to a large bowl and, using a metal spoon, fold in the sifted flour and hot water. Spread evenly into the tins and bake for 25 minutes, or until the sponge is lightly golden and shrinks slightly from the side of the tin. Leave the sponges in their tins for 5 minutes before turning out onto a wire rack to cool.

4 Spread the jam evenly over one of the sponges, top with the whipped cream and sandwich with the second sponge. Dust the top with icing sugar.

STORAGE: This sponge is best eaten on the day it is made as it only contains a very small amount of fat. Alternatively, it can be frozen, immediately after cooling, for up to 1 month.

Sandwich the two SPONGE CAKES together with a jam and cream filling.

Use orange or apricot jam in the mixture for ORANGE POPPY SEED CAKE.

ORANGE POPPY SEED CAKE

Preparation: 40 minutes
Cooking: 1 hour
Serves 8

1 1/2 cups (185 g/6 oz)
  self-raising flour
1/3 cup (60 g/2 oz)
  ground almonds
1/4 cup (40 g/1 1/4 oz)
  poppy seeds
185 g (6 oz) butter
2/3 cup (160 g/5 1/2 oz)
  caster sugar
1/4 cup (80 g/2 3/4 oz)
  orange or apricot jam
2–3 teaspoons finely
  grated orange rind
1/3 cup (80 ml/2 3/4 fl oz)
  orange juice
3 eggs

Icing
100 g (3 1/2 oz) **butter**
100 g (3 1/2 oz) **cream
  cheese**
1 cup (125 g/4 oz) **icing
  sugar, sifted**
1–2 teaspoons **lemon
  juice or vanilla essence**

1 Preheat the oven
to moderate 180°C
(350°F/Gas 4). Grease
a deep 20 cm (8 inch)
round cake tin and line
the base and side with
baking paper. Sift the
flour into a large bowl and
add the almonds and
poppy seeds. Make a well
in the centre.
2 Put the butter, sugar,
jam, orange rind and juice
in a pan. Stir over low
heat until melted and

smooth. Gradually pour
into the well in the dry
ingredients, stirring with
a whisk until smooth.
Add the eggs and whisk
until combined.
3 Pour into the tin and
bake for 50–60 minutes,
or until a skewer comes
out clean when inserted
into the centre of the
cake. Leave in the tin for
at least 15 minutes before
turning out onto a wire
rack to cool.
4 To make the icing, beat
the butter and cream
cheese until smooth. Add
the icing sugar and lemon
juice or vanilla gradually,
and beat until thick and
creamy. Spread the icing
over the cooled cake.

247

CARROT CAKE

Preparation: 30 minutes
Cooking: 45 minutes
Serves 8

3 eggs
1 cup (250 ml/8 fl oz) oil
1 1/4 cups (230 g/7 1/2 oz)
    soft brown sugar
1 1/2 cups (185 g/6 oz)
    self-raising flour
1 teaspoon bicarbonate
    of soda
pinch of salt
2 teaspoons ground
    cinnamon
3/4 cup (90 g/3 oz)
    chopped pecans
1 2/3 cups (255 g/8 oz)
    grated carrot
125 g (4 oz) cream
    cheese, softened
30 g (1 oz) butter
1 cup (125 g/1 oz) icing
    sugar
2 teaspoons orange juice

1 Preheat the oven to
moderate 180°C (350°F/
Gas 4). Grease a deep
23 cm (9 inch) square
cake tin and line the
base and sides with
baking paper.
2 Combine the eggs, oil
and brown sugar in a large
bowl. Add the sifted flour,
soda, salt and cinnamon,
and beat with electric
beaters until the mixture is
smooth. Add the nuts and
carrot and stir well.
3 Pour the mixture into
the tin and bake for

45 minutes, or until a
skewer comes out clean
when inserted into the
centre of the cake. Leave
for at least 20 minutes
before turning out onto a
wire rack to cool.
4 To make a cream cheese
topping, put the cream
cheese, butter, sugar and
orange juice in a bowl and
beat together until the
mixture is spreadable.
Spread over the cake and
perhaps sprinkle with a
few extra chopped pecans
to serve.

COCONUT CAKE

Preparation: 15 minutes
Cooking: 55 minutes
Serves 8

185 g (6 oz) butter,
    chopped and softened
1 cup (250 g/8 oz) caster
    sugar
1 cup (90 g/3 oz)
    desiccated coconut
1/2 cup (125 ml/4 fl oz)
    buttermilk or plain
    yoghurt
2 teaspoons vanilla
    essence
3 eggs, lightly beaten
1 1/2 cups (185 g/6 oz)
    self-raising flour
1/3 cup (40 g/1 1/4 oz)
    cornflour
1 tablespoon caster
    sugar, extra
2 tablespoons desiccated
    coconut, extra

1 Preheat the oven to
moderate 180°C (350°F/
Gas 4). Lightly grease a
23 x 13 x 7 cm (9 x 5 x
3 inch) loaf tin with
melted butter or oil. Line
the base and sides with
baking paper.
2 Beat the butter, sugar,
coconut, buttermilk or
yoghurt, vanilla and eggs
briefly with electric
beaters until combined.
Add the sifted flours and
beat on low speed to
combine. Beat on medium
speed for 1 minute, or
until the mixture is
smooth and creamy. Do
not overbeat.
3 Carefully spoon the
mixture into the tin and
smooth the surface with a
spatula. Sprinkle the
combined extra sugar and
coconut over the top.
Bake for 50–55 minutes,
or until a skewer comes
out clean when inserted
into the centre of the
cake. Cover the cake
loosely with foil during
the last 15 minutes of
cooking to prevent the
coconut topping from
overbrowning. Leave the
cake in the tin for
5 minutes before turning
out onto a wire rack
to cool.

*CARROT CAKE (top) with a
cream cheese icing, and
COCONUT CAKE.*

A CHRISTMAS FRUIT CAKE can be stored for up to 3 months.

CHRISTMAS FRUIT CAKE

Preparation: 30 minutes +
4 hours standing
Cooking: 3 hours
Serves 10

1 kg (2 lb) mixed dried
fruit
1 1/2 cups (280 g/9 oz)
chopped dried dates
1 cup (185 g/6 oz)
chopped dried apricots
1/2 cup (95 g/3 oz) mixed
peel
1/2 cup (60 g/2 oz)
chopped glacé fruits
3/4 cup (185 ml/6 fl oz)
brandy
1 cup (185 g/6 oz) soft
brown sugar
250 g (8 oz) butter
5 eggs
1 1/2 cups (105 g/6 oz)
plain flour
1/3 cup (40 g/1 1/4 oz)
self-raising flour
1 teaspoon ground
cinnamon
1 teaspoon mixed spice

1 Preheat the oven to
slow 150°C (300°F/
Gas 2). Grease a 23 cm
(9 inch) round cake tin
and line the base and sides
with a double thickness of
baking paper. In a bowl,
mix the mixed fruit, dates,
apricots, mixed peel, glacé
fruits and brandy, cover
with plastic wrap and
leave at room temperature
for at least 4 hours.

2 Using electric beaters,
beat the sugar and butter
in a small bowl until just
combined (overbeating
will result in a crumbly
cake). Add the eggs
gradually, beating after
each addition. Transfer
to a large bowl.
3 Stir in the fruits and
brandy. Fold in the sifted
flours and spices. Stir
gently, but don't overbeat.
4 Spoon into the tin and
smooth the surface. Bake
for 3 hours, or until firm
to the touch and golden
brown. Cool completely
in the tin. Turn out and
wrap tightly in plastic
wrap. Store for up to
3 months in an airtight
container in the fridge.

BOILED FRUIT CAKE

Preparation: 30 minutes
Cooking: 1½ hours
Serves 10

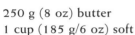

250 g (8 oz) butter
1 cup (185 g/6 oz) soft brown sugar
1 kg (2 lb) mixed dried fruit
½ cup (125 ml/4 fl oz) sweet sherry
½ teaspoon bicarbonate of soda
1½ cups (185 g/6 oz) self-raising flour
1 cup (125 g/4 oz) plain flour
1 teaspoon mixed spice
4 eggs, lightly beaten

1 Preheat the oven to moderate 180°C (350°F/ Gas 4). Lightly grease a 22 cm (9 inch) round cake tin. Line the base and side with greaseproof paper.

2 Put the butter, sugar, mixed fruit, sherry and ¾ cup (185 ml/6 fl oz) water in a pan. Stir over low heat until the butter has melted and the sugar dissolved. Bring to the boil, reduce the heat and simmer for 10 minutes. Remove from the heat, stir in the soda and cool.

3 Sift the flours and mixed spice into a large bowl and make a well in the centre. Add the eggs to the fruit mixture and mix together. Pour into the well and mix well. Pour into the tin and smooth the surface. Bake for 1–1¼ hours, or until a skewer comes out clean when inserted into the centre of the cake. Leave in the tin for at least an hour before turning out. The flavour of this cake improves if left for 3 days before eating. Can be kept for up to 2 months.

NOTE: The colour of your fruit cake will largely depend on the dried fruit you use. If you prefer a dark cake, use raisins, currants and sultanas. For a lighter coloured cake, mix in chopped glacé fruit.

The flavour of a BOILED FRUIT CAKE actually improves on keeping.

MADEIRA CAKE

Preparation: 20 minutes
Cooking: 55 minutes
Serves 8

150 g (5 oz) butter
3/4 cup (185 g/6 oz)
   caster sugar
3 eggs, lightly beaten
2 teaspoons finely grated
   orange or lemon rind
1/2 cup (95 g/3 oz)
   ground almonds
1 3/4 cups (215 g/7 oz)
   self-raising flour
icing sugar, to dust

1 Preheat the oven to
moderate 180°C (350°F/
Gas 4). Grease a 23 x 13 x
7 cm (9 x 5 x 3 inch) loaf
tin and line the base and
sides with baking paper.
Using electric beaters,
beat the butter and caster
sugar in a small mixing
bowl until light and
creamy. Add the eggs
gradually, beating
thoroughly after each
addition. Add the orange
or lemon rind and beat
until combined.
2 Transfer the mixture to
a large bowl. Using a
metal spoon, fold in the
ground almonds and
sifted flour. Stir until the
mixture is combined
and smooth.
3 Spoon into the tin and
smooth the surface. Bake
for 55 minutes, or until a
skewer comes out clean
when inserted into the
centre of the cake.
4 Leave the cake in the
tin for 10 minutes before
turning out onto a wire
rack. Lightly dust the top
with icing sugar before
serving.

STORAGE: Cake will
keep for up to four days in
an airtight container.

DATE AND NUT ROLLS

Preparation: 25 minutes
Cooking: 1 hour
Serves 8

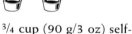

3/4 cup (90 g/3 oz) self-
   raising flour
3/4 cup (90 g/3 oz) plain
   flour
1/2 teaspoon bicarbonate
   of soda
1 teaspoon mixed spice
1 cup (125 g/4 oz)
   chopped walnuts
100 g (3 1/2 oz) butter
3/4 cup (140 g/4 1/2 oz)
   soft brown sugar
1 1/2 cups (280 g/9 oz)
   chopped dates
1 egg, lightly beaten

1 Preheat the oven to
moderate 180°C (350°F/
Gas 4). Grease two 17 x
8 cm (7 x 3 inch) tube tins
(nut roll tins) and lids.
Sift the flours, bicarbonate
of soda and mixed spice
into a large mixing bowl.
Add the walnuts, stir to
combine and make a well
in the centre.
2 Combine the butter,
sugar, 1/2 cup (125 ml/
4 fl oz) water and dates
in a pan. Stir over low
heat until the butter has
melted and the sugar has
dissolved. Remove from
the heat and leave to
cool slightly.
3 Pour the butter mixture
and the egg into the well
in the dry ingredients, and
stir until combined. Spoon
the mixture evenly into
the tins. Bake with the
tins upright for 1 hour, or
until a skewer comes out
clean when inserted into
the centre. Leave the
cakes in the tins, with the
lids on, for 10 minutes,
then turn onto a wire
rack. Serve sliced,
with butter.

STORAGE: This is a very
moist cake that will keep
fresh in an airtight
container for a week.
NOTE: If you don't have
nut roll tins, bake this
mixture in a 23 x 13 cm
(9 x 5 inch) loaf tin.
HINT: Store walnuts in
the freezer to prevent
them becoming rancid.

*MADEIRA CAKE (top) and
DATE AND NUT ROLLS.*

CHOCOLATE CAKE topped with glossy chocolate buttercream.

CHOCOLATE CAKE

Preparation: 25 minutes
Cooking: 50 minutes
Serves 8

125 g (4 oz) butter
1/2 cup (125 g/4 oz)
  caster sugar
1/3 cup (40 g/1 1/4 oz)
  icing sugar, sifted
2 eggs, lightly beaten
1 teaspoon vanilla
  essence
1/4 cup (80 g/2 3/4 oz)
  blackberry jam
1 1/4 cups (155 g/5 oz)
  self-raising flour
1/2 cup (60 g/2 oz) cocoa
  powder
1 teaspoon bicarbonate
  of soda
1 cup (250 ml/8 fl oz)
  milk

Chocolate buttercream
50 g (1 3/4 oz) dark
  chocolate, finely
  chopped
25 g (3/4 oz) butter
3 teaspoons cream
1/4 cup (30 g/1 oz) icing
  sugar, sifted

1 Preheat the oven to
moderate 180°C (350°F/
Gas 4). Grease the base
and sides of a deep
20 cm (8 inch) square
cake tin and line with
baking paper.
2 Beat the butter, caster
sugar and icing sugar with
electric beaters in a small
mixing bowl until the
mixture is light and
creamy. Add the eggs
gradually, beating
thoroughly after each
addition. Add the vanilla
essence and jam and beat
until combined.
3 Transfer the mixture to
a large bowl. Using a
metal spoon, fold in the
combined sifted flour,
cocoa and soda alternately
with the milk. Stir until
the mixture is just
combined and
almost smooth.
4 Pour into the tin and
smooth the surface. Bake
for 45 minutes, or until a
skewer comes out clean
when inserted into the
centre of the cake. Leave
in the tin for 15 minutes,
then cool on a wire rack.
5 To make the butter-
cream, combine the
chopped chocolate,
butter, cream and icing
sugar in a small pan. Stir
over low heat until the
mixture is smooth and
glossy. Spread the
chocolate buttercream
over the top of the cake
with a flat-bladed knife.

BANANA CAKE

Preparation: 20 minutes
Cooking: 1 hour
Serves 8

125 g (4 oz) butter
1/2 cup (125 g/4 oz)
  caster sugar
2 eggs, lightly beaten
1 teaspoon vanilla
  essence
1 1/2 cups (360 g/12 oz)
  mashed ripe banana
  (about 4 bananas)
1 teaspoon bicarbonate
  of soda
1/2 cup (125 ml/4 fl oz)
  milk
2 cups (250 g/8 oz) self-
  raising flour

Butter frosting
125 g (4 oz) butter
3/4 cup (90 g/3 oz) icing
  sugar
1 tablespoon lemon juice
1/4 cup (15 g/1/2 oz)
  flaked coconut

Use very ripe bananas to make a flavoursome BANANA CAKE.

1 Preheat the oven to moderate 180°C (350°F/Gas 4). Grease a 20 cm (8 inch) round cake tin and line the base with baking paper. Using electric beaters, beat the butter and sugar in a small mixing bowl until light and creamy. Add the eggs gradually, beating well after each addition. Add the vanilla essence and mashed banana, and beat until combined.

2 Transfer the mixture to a large mixing bowl. Dissolve the bicarbonate of soda in the milk. Using a metal spoon, fold in the sifted flour alternately with the milk. Stir until all the ingredients are just combined and the mixture is smooth. Spoon into the tin and smooth the surface. Bake for 1 hour, or until a skewer comes out clean when inserted into the centre of the cake. Leave the cake in the tin for 10 minutes before turning out onto a wire rack.

3 To make the frosting, beat the butter, icing sugar and lemon juice with electric beaters until smooth and creamy. Spread onto the cooled cake. Toast the coconut flakes in a moderate 180°C (350°F/Gas 4) oven for 5 minutes and sprinkle around the edge of the top of the cake.

STORAGE: The un-iced cake can be kept for one week in an airtight container. Alternatively, freeze for up to a month before icing.
HINT: Very ripe bananas are best for this recipe as they have the best developed flavour.

BLACK FOREST GATEAU

Preparation: 45 minutes
Cooking: 15 minutes
Serves 8

1/3 cup (40 g/1 1/4 oz)
  plain flour
1/3 cup (40 g/1 1/4 oz)
  self-raising flour
2 tablespoons cocoa
  powder
4 eggs, separated
1/2 cup (125 g/4 oz)
  caster sugar
1/4 cup (60 ml/2 fl oz)
  Kirsch (see Note)
3 1/2 cups (875 ml/28 fl
  oz) cream, whipped

700 g (1 lb 6 oz) jar
  morello cherries or two
  425 g (14 oz) cans
  pitted dark cherries,
  well drained (see Note)
250 g (8 oz) dark
  chocolate
maraschino cherries, to
  garnish
icing sugar, to dust

1 Preheat the oven to moderate 180°C (350°F/ Gas 4). Grease two shallow 20 cm (8 inch) round sandwich tins and line with baking paper. Sift the flours and cocoa powder onto greaseproof paper three times.
2 Beat the egg whites in a small, clean, dry mixing bowl until firm peaks form. Add the sugar gradually, beating constantly until the sugar has dissolved and the mixture is thick and glossy. Add the yolks and beat for 20 seconds. Transfer the mixture to a larger bowl.
3 Fold in the flours and cocoa quickly and lightly in 2–3 batches. Spread the mixture evenly into the tins and bake for 15 minutes, or until the cakes are springy to the touch. Leave them in the tins for 5 minutes before turning out onto wire racks to cool. Cut each cake in half horizontally.
4 Brush the top of one round of cake with some of the Kirsch. Spread with a layer of the whipped cream and top with one third of the cherries. Place another round of cake on top. Repeat brushing with the Kirsch and layering with the cream and cherries, finishing with the last round of cake. Spread the rest of the cream all over the cake, keeping a little aside for decorating the top.
5 Using a potato peeler, shave curls from the edge of the chocolate. Press some of the curls lightly onto the cream around the side of the cake. Decorate the top with

BLACK FOREST GATEAU.

rosettes of whipped cream and the maraschino cherries. Pile some more chocolate curls in the centre and dust the cake with icing sugar.

NOTES: Kirsch is a cherry-flavoured liqueur. Black Forest gateau is traditionally made with fresh morello cherries, poached in a sugar syrup and pitted. Bottled morello cherries or canned, pitted cherries are a good substitute. Drain the cherries well on paper towels to prevent their juices staining the whipped cream.

HUMMINGBIRD CAKE

Preparation: 20 minutes
Cooking: 1 hour
Serves 8

Use banana and pineapple in a HUMMINGBIRD CAKE.

1 cup (125 g/4 oz) plain flour
1/2 cup (60 g/2 oz) self-raising flour
1 teaspoon ground cinnamon
1/2 teaspoon bicarbonate of soda
3/4 cup (185 g/6 oz) caster sugar
2 eggs, lightly beaten
1/2 cup (125 ml/4 fl oz) vegetable oil
1 1/2 cups (360 g/12 oz) mashed ripe banana
3/4 cup (195 g/6 1/2 oz) undrained crushed unsweetened pineapple
100 g (3 1/2 oz) cream cheese, softened
3/4 cup (90 g/3 oz) icing sugar, sifted

1 Preheat the oven to moderate 180°C (350°F/ Gas 4). Lightly grease a 20 cm (8 inch) square cake tin. Sift the flours, cinnamon and bicarbonate of soda into a bowl. Stir in the sugar and make a well in the centre.

2 Stir together the eggs, oil, banana and pineapple and pour into the well in the dry ingredients. Stir until just combined, then spoon into the tin.
3 Bake for 1 hour or until a skewer inserted into the centre of the cake comes out clean. Leave in the tin for 10 minutes before turning out and cooling on a wire rack.
4 Beat the cream cheese and icing sugar until smooth and fluffy. Spread over the cake.

257

PINEAPPLE UPSIDE-DOWN CAKE

Preparation: 20 minutes
Cooking: 40 minutes
Serves 8

20 g (³/₄ oz) butter, melted
2 tablespoons soft brown sugar
440 g (14 oz) can pineapple slices in natural juice
90 g (3 oz) butter
¹/₂ cup (125 g/4 oz) caster sugar
2 eggs, lightly beaten
1 teaspoon vanilla essence
1 cup (125 g/4 oz) self-raising flour

1 Preheat the oven to moderate 180°C (350°F/Gas 4). Grease a 20 cm (8 inch) ring tin. Pour the melted butter into the tin and tip to coat the base evenly. Sprinkle the brown sugar over the butter. Drain the pineapple, reserving ¹/₃ cup (80 ml/2³/₄ fl oz) of the juice. Cut the pineapple pieces into halves and arrange over the brown sugar.
2 Using electric beaters, beat the butter and sugar in a small bowl until light and creamy. Add the eggs gradually, beating well after each addition. Beat in the vanilla essence.
3 Transfer the mixture to a large bowl. Using a metal spoon, fold in the flour alternately with the reserved pineapple juice.
4 Spoon the mixture evenly over the pineapple and smooth the surface. Bake for 35–40 minutes, or until a skewer comes out clean when inserted into the centre. Leave in the tin for 10 minutes, then cool on a wire rack.

JAM SWISS ROLL

Preparation: 30 minutes
Cooking: 12 minutes
Makes one roll

¹/₂ cup (60 g/2 oz) self-raising flour
¹/₄ cup (30 g/1 oz) plain flour
3 eggs
¹/₂ cup (125 g/4 oz) caster sugar
2 tablespoons caster sugar, extra
¹/₂ cup (160 g/5¹/₂ oz) strawberry jam
¹/₂ cup (125 ml/4 fl oz) cream, whipped

1 Preheat the oven to hot 210°C (415°F/Gas 6–7). Grease a 30 x 25 cm (12 x 10 inch) swiss roll tin and line the base with baking paper, leaving the paper to hang over the two long sides (this will help you lift the cake out of the tin after cooking). Sift the flours three times onto greaseproof paper.
2 Beat the eggs with electric beaters for 5 minutes, or until thick, frothy and pale. Add the sugar gradually, beating constantly until it has completely dissolved and the mixture is pale and glossy. Using a metal spoon, fold in the flour quickly and lightly.
3 Spread the mixture evenly into the tin and smooth the surface. Bake for 12 minutes, or until lightly golden and springy to the touch. Turn the cake out onto a dry, clean tea towel covered with greaseproof paper that has been sprinkled with the extra caster sugar. Leave for 1 minute, then use the tea towel as a guide to carefully roll the cake up from the short side, with the paper. Leave the cake for 5 minutes, or until it is cool.
4 Unroll the cake and remove the paper. Spread the cake with the jam and cream and re-roll. Trim the ends with a knife and cut into slices to serve.

PINEAPPLE UPSIDE-DOWN CAKE (top) and JAM SWISS ROLL.

SEMOLINA LEMON SYRUP CAKE

Preparation: 30 minutes

Cooking: 45 minutes

Serves 6

150 g (5 oz) butter

³/4 cup (185 g/6 oz) caster sugar

2 eggs, lightly beaten

2 teaspoons finely grated lemon rind

1¹/2 cups (185 g/6 oz) fine semolina

1 cup (185 g/6 oz) ground almonds

1¹/2 teaspoons baking powder

¹/4 cup (60 ml/2 fl oz) milk

icing sugar, to dust

Lemon syrup

¹/2 cup (125 ml/4 fl oz) lemon juice

rind of 1 lemon

¹/2 cup (125 g/4 oz) caster sugar

1 Preheat the oven to moderate 180°C (350°F/ Gas 4). Grease a deep 23 cm (9 inch) fluted ring tin with oil or melted butter. Using electric beaters, beat the butter and sugar in a small bowl until light and creamy. Add the eggs gradually, beating well after each addition. Add the grated lemon rind and beat until well combined.

Use finely ground semolina in your LEMON SEMOLINA CAKE.

2 Transfer the mixture to a large bowl. Using a metal spoon, fold in the combined semolina, almonds and baking powder alternately with the milk. Stir the mixture until smooth.

3 Spoon into the tin and smooth the surface. Bake for 45 minutes, or until a skewer comes out clean when inserted into the centre of the cake. Leave the cake in the tin for 5 minutes, then turn onto a serving plate.

4 To make the lemon syrup, combine the lemon juice, rind and sugar in a small pan. Stir over medium heat without boiling until the sugar has dissolved. Bring to the boil, then reduce the heat

and simmer for 5 minutes. Brush the syrup over the top and sides of the cake. Dust with sifted icing sugar to serve.

LAMINGTONS

Preparation: 1 hour

Cooking: 1 hour

Makes 25

1¹/2 cups (185 g/6 oz) self-raising flour

¹/3 cup (40 g/1¹/4 oz) cornflour

185 g (6 oz) butter, softened

1 cup (250 g/8 oz) caster sugar

2 teaspoons vanilla essence

3 eggs, lightly beaten

½ cup (125 ml/4 fl oz)
milk
¾ cup (185 ml/6 fl oz)
thick cream

Icing

4 cups (500 g/1 lb) icing
sugar
⅓ cup (40 g/1¼ oz)
cocoa powder
30 g (1 oz) butter,
melted
⅔ cup (170 ml/
5½ fl oz) milk
3 cups (270 g/9 oz)
desiccated coconut,
approximately

1 Preheat the oven to
moderate 180°C (350°F/
Gas 4). Grease a shallow
23 cm (9 inch) square
cake tin and line the base
and sides with baking
paper. Sift the flour and
cornflour into a large
bowl. Add the butter,
sugar, vanilla essence,
eggs and milk. Using
electric beaters, beat on
low speed for 1 minute,
or until the ingredients
are just lightly moistened.
Beat on high speed for
3 minutes, or until the
mixture is free of lumps
and has increased
in volume.
2 Pour the mixture into
the tin and smooth the
surface. Bake for 1 hour,
or until a skewer comes
out clean when inserted
into the centre of the
cake. Leave the cake in
the tin for 3 minutes

LAMINGTONS *are a welcome family treat.*

before turning out onto a
wire rack to cool.
3 Using a serrated knife,
trim the top of the cake
until it is flat. Trim the
crusts from the sides of
the cake. Cut the cake in
half horizontally. Using
electric beaters, beat the
cream in a small mixing
bowl until stiff peaks
form. Place the first layer
of cake on a board and
spread evenly with the
cream. Top with the other
cake layer. Cut the cake
into 25 squares.
4 To make the icing, sift
the icing sugar with the
cocoa. Combine with the

butter and milk in a
heatproof bowl. Stand
the bowl over a pan of
simmering water, stirring
until the icing is smooth
and glossy. Remove from
the heat. Place 1 cup
(90 g/3 oz) of the coconut
on a sheet of greaseproof
paper. Using two forks,
roll a piece of cake in
the icing. Hold the cake
over the bowl and allow
the excess to drain. Roll
the cake in the coconut,
then put on a wire rack.
Repeat with the remaining
cake, adding extra
coconut for rolling
as needed.

261

Sprinkle CINNAMON TEA CAKE with a mixture of sugar and ground cinnamon.

CINNAMON TEA CAKE

Preparation: 20 minutes
Cooking: 30 minutes
Serves 8

60 g (2 oz) butter
1/2 cup (125 g/4 oz)
  caster sugar
1 egg, lightly beaten
1 teaspoon vanilla
  essence
3/4 cup (90 g/3 oz) self-
  raising flour
3 tablespoons plain flour
1/2 cup (125 ml/4 fl oz)
  milk
20 g (3/4 oz) butter,
  melted
1 tablespoon caster
  sugar, extra
1 teaspoon ground
  cinnamon

1 Preheat the oven to moderate 180°C (350°F/ Gas 4). Grease a 20 cm (8 inch) round cake tin and line the base with baking paper. Beat the butter and sugar until light and creamy. Add the egg gradually, beating well after each addition. Beat in the vanilla.
2 Fold in the sifted flours alternately with the milk. Stir until smooth. Spoon into the tin and smooth the top. Bake for 30 minutes, or until a skewer comes out clean when inserted into the centre. Cool in the tin for 5 minutes, then on a wire rack. Brush with melted butter while still warm and sprinkle with the sugar and cinnamon.

ROCK CAKES

Preparation: 25 minutes
Cooking: 15–20 minutes
Makes about 20

2 cups (250 g/8 oz) self-
  raising flour, sifted
90 g (3 oz) butter, cubed
1/2 cup (125 g/4 oz)
  caster sugar
1/2 cup (95 g/3 oz) mixed
  dried fruit
1 tablespoon chopped
  mixed nuts
1/2 teaspoon ground
  ginger
1 egg
3 tablespoons milk

1 Preheat the oven to moderately hot 200°C (400°F/Gas 6). Place the flour in a large bowl and rub in the butter with your fingertips until fine and crumbly.

2 Mix in the sugar, fruit, nuts and ginger. Whisk the egg into the milk and add to the mixture. Mix to a stiff dough.

3 Spoon in small heaps onto greased baking trays. Bake for 15–20 minutes, or until golden brown. Transfer to a wire rack to cool. Serve buttered.

MERINGUES

Preparation: 10 minutes
Cooking: 25 minutes
Makes about 30

2 egg whites
¹/₂ cup (125 g/4 oz)
  caster sugar

1 Preheat the oven to slow 150°C (300°F/ Gas 2). Beat the egg whites until stiff peaks form. Gradually add the sugar, beating well after each addition. Beat until thick and glossy, and the sugar has dissolved.

2 Spoon into a piping bag and pipe into shapes on baking trays lined with baking paper. Bake for 20–25 minutes, or until the meringues are just crisp. Turn off the oven, leaving the meringues inside with the door ajar to cool.

ROCK CAKES are ideal for a cup of tea with friends.

MERINGUES can be piped into shapes, rounds or nests.

263

BUTTERCAKE

Preparation: 20 minutes
Cooking: 45 minutes
Serves 8

125 g (4 oz) butter
3/4 cup (185 g/6 oz)
  caster sugar
2 eggs, lightly beaten
1 teaspoon vanilla
  essence
2 cups (250 g/8 oz) self-
  raising flour
1/2 cup (125 ml/4 fl oz)
  milk

Buttercream
60 g (2 oz) butter
1/3 cup (40 g/1 1/4 oz)
  icing sugar
1 teaspoon vanilla
  essence

1 Preheat the oven to moderate 180°C (350°F/ Gas 4). Grease a 20 cm (8 inch) round cake tin and line the base with baking paper. Using electric beaters, beat the butter and sugar in a small mixing bowl until light and creamy. Add the eggs gradually, beating well after each addition. Add the vanilla essence and beat until combined.

2 Transfer the mixture to a large bowl. Using a metal spoon, fold in the sifted flour alternately with the milk. Stir until the mixture is just combined and almost smooth. Spoon the mixture into the tin and smooth the surface. Bake for 45 minutes, or until a skewer comes out clean when inserted into the centre of the cake. Leave in the tin for 10 minutes, then cool on a wire rack.

3 To make the buttercream, beat the butter and sifted icing sugar with electric beaters until light and creamy. Add the vanilla essence and beat for another 2 minutes, or until the mixture is quite smooth and fluffy. Spread over the top of the cake with a flat-bladed knife. Decorate with chopped almonds, or other nuts.

STORAGE: Buttercake will keep, iced, for two days in an airtight container in the fridge. It can be frozen, un-iced and wrapped tightly in plastic wrap, for up to a month.
VARIATIONS: For lemon cake, add 2 tablespoons grated lemon rind to the basic buttercake mixture. To make coffee cake,

You can add many variations to the basic BUTTERCAKE mix.

dissolve a tablespoon of instant coffee in the milk before adding to the dry ingredients. For chocolate cake, add 3 tablespoons cocoa to the dry ingredients and an extra tablespoon of milk at the end. For ginger cake, add a teaspoon of ground ginger to the dry ingredients.

CUSTARD ORANGE CAKE

Preparation: 15 minutes
Cooking: 50 minutes
Serves 6–8

2 cups (250 g/8 oz) self-raising flour
$^1/_3$ cup (40 g/1$^1/_4$ oz) custard powder
80 g (2$^3/_4$ oz) butter, chopped
1 $^1/_3$ cups (340 g/11 oz) caster sugar
3 eggs
2 teaspoons finely grated orange rind
1 cup (250 ml/8 fl oz) orange juice
125 g (4 oz) cream cheese, softened
2 tablespoons icing sugar

CUSTARD ORANGE CAKE has a tang of fresh orange.

1 Preheat the oven to moderate 180°C (350°F/ Gas 4). Grease a deep 23 cm (9 inch) round cake tin and line the base with baking paper. Sift the flour and custard powder into a bowl and add the butter and sugar. Rub in the butter with your fingertips until the mixture resembles fine crumbs.

2 Add the eggs, orange rind and juice and mix until smooth. Spoon into the tin and smooth the surface. Bake for 50 minutes, or until a skewer comes out clean when inserted into the centre of the cake.

3 Leave the cake in the tin for 5 minutes before turning out onto a wire rack to cool.

4 Mix together the cream cheese and icing sugar and spread over the top of the cake. If you like, decorate with thin strips of orange rind.

265

CAKE ICINGS

Many of our recipes have their own icings and buttercreams included. But for when you've just made a plain buttercake or muffin and want to turn it into something special, try one of the following:

CITRUS FROSTING
100 g (3 1/2 oz) cream cheese, softened
3/4 cup (90 g/3 oz) icing sugar, sifted
1–2 teaspoons finely grated lemon rind (or orange, lime or mandarin rind)
2 teaspoons milk

Beat the cream cheese and icing sugar until light and creamy. Add the rind and milk. Beat for 2 minutes, or until the frosting is smooth and fluffy. Spread over the cake.

HONEY FROSTING
100 g (3 1/2 oz) cream cheese, softened
3/4 cup (90 g/3 oz) icing sugar, sifted
1–2 teaspoons honey, warmed
2 teaspoons milk

Beat the cream cheese and icing sugar until light and creamy. Add the honey and milk and beat for 2 minutes, or until the frosting is smooth and fluffy. Spread the frosting over the cake.

PASSIONFRUIT FROSTING
100 g (3 1/2 oz) cream cheese, softened
3/4 cup (90 g/3 oz) icing sugar, sifted
1–2 tablespoons passionfruit pulp

Beat the cream cheese and icing sugar until light and creamy. Add the passion-fruit pulp and beat for 2 minutes, or until smooth and fluffy. Spread over the cake.

RICH CHOCOLATE ICING

60 g (2 oz) butter
100 g (3½ oz) dark
  chocolate, chopped
1 tablespoon cream

Put the butter, chocolate and cream in a small heatproof bowl. Bring a pan, half full of water, to the boil and remove from the heat. Place the bowl over the pan (don't let the base of the bowl sit in the water) and stir until the butter and chocolate have melted and the mixture is smooth. Leave to cool slightly until the icing is spreadable.

GINGER ICING

60 g (2 oz) butter
1 tablespoon golden
  syrup
1 tablespoon finely
  chopped glacé ginger
⅓ cup (60 g/2 oz) soft
  brown sugar
2 tablespoons milk
1½ cups (185 g/6 oz)
  icing sugar, sifted

Put the butter, golden syrup, ginger and sugar in a pan. Stir over low heat until the mixture is melted and smooth. Using a wooden spoon, beat in 1 tablespoon of the milk and enough icing sugar to make a stiff but spreadable icing. Use the extra milk if necessary to reach the right consistency.

CHOCOLATE SOUR CREAM ICING

200 g (6½ oz) milk
  chocolate, chopped
⅓ cup (90 g/3 oz) sour
  cream

Combine the chocolate and sour cream in a small pan. Whisk over low heat until the chocolate has melted and the mixture is smooth. Remove from the heat and allow to cool slightly until spreadable.

SCONES

Preparation: 25 minutes
Cooking: 20 minutes
Makes 12

2¹/₄ cups (280 g/9 oz)
    self-raising flour
pinch of salt
1 tablespoon sugar
20 g (³/₄ oz) butter,
    chopped
1 egg
³/₄ cup (185 ml/6 fl oz)
    milk
extra milk, for glazing

1 Preheat the oven to hot 220°C (425°F/Gas 7). Sift the flour, salt and sugar into a large bowl. Rub in the butter, using your fingertips, until the mixture is fine and crumbly. Make a well in the centre of the mixture. **2** Lightly beat the egg and milk in a small bowl. Pour almost all the egg mixture into the well. Mix lightly with a flat-bladed knife to form a soft dough, adding the remaining egg mixture if needed.

3 Gather the dough together and turn it out onto a lightly floured surface. Press out the dough until it is 2.5 cm (1 inch) thick. Cut out rounds with a floured 5 cm (2 inch) cutter.

4 Heat a baking tray in the oven for 5 minutes. Place the rounds on the heated tray, leaving a little room for spreading. Brush with the extra milk. Bake on the middle shelf of the oven for 15–20 minutes, or until golden brown on top. If you are serving the scones warm, straight from the oven, wrap them in a clean tea towel while still hot. Serve warm or cold, with butter or with cream and jam or strawberries.

VARIATIONS: For sultana scones, add 1 cup (125 g/4 oz) sultanas in step 1 when you sift the flour into the bowl.
For date scones, add 1 cup (185 g/6 oz) finely chopped pitted dates to the flour in step 1.
For wholemeal scones, replace one of the cups of flour with wholemeal self-raising flour.
For cheese scones, add 1 cup (125 g/4 oz) grated Cheddar cheese to the flour in step 1.

The secret to making perfect scones is to use a light touch and handle the dough as little as possible. Do not knead the dough. Merely turn it out onto a floured surface and then press out before cutting into rounds.

For a Devonshire tea, serve SCONES with jam and cream.

Butternut pumpkin is excellent for PUMPKIN SCONES as it is less watery than some.

PUMPKIN SCONES

Preparation: 20 minutes
Cooking: 15 minutes
Makes about 15

2¹/₂ cups (310 g/10 oz)
   self-raising flour
¹/₄ teaspoon dried mixed
   herbs
60 g (2 oz) butter,
   chopped
1 egg, lightly beaten
1 cup (250 g/8 oz)
   cooked, mashed
   pumpkin (350 g/11 oz
   raw pumpkin)

1–2 tablespoons milk
milk, extra, for glazing

1 Preheat the oven to hot 210°C (415°F/Gas 6–7). Grease a 28 x 18 cm (11 x 7 inch) shallow tin. Sift the flour into a large mixing bowl. Stir in the mixed herbs and add the chopped butter. Using your fingertips, rub in the butter until the mixture is fine and crumbly.
2 Combine the egg, mashed pumpkin and milk. Add to the flour mixture and stir with a knife until just combined.

3 Gather the dough together and turn it out onto a lightly floured surface. Press out gently until the dough is about 2 cm (³/₄ inch) thick. Cut out rounds with a floured 5 cm (2 inch) cutter.
4 Place the rounds in the tin and brush the tops with the extra milk. Bake for 15 minutes, or until the tops of the scones are lightly golden. Turn out onto a wire rack to cool. Serve warm or cold, with butter.

MUFFINS

Preparation: 15 minutes
Cooking: 20 minutes
Makes 12

3 cups (375 g/12 oz)
  self-raising flour
1 cup (250 g/8 oz) caster
  sugar
2 eggs, lightly beaten
1 cup (250 ml/8 fl oz)
  milk
90 g (3 oz) butter,
  melted

1 Preheat the oven to hot
210°C (415°F/Gas 6–7).
Lightly grease a 12-hole,
1/2-cup (125 ml/4 fl oz)
muffin tin. Sift the flour
into a large bowl and stir
in the sugar. Make a well
in the centre.
2 Mix together the eggs,
milk and butter and pour
into the well all at once.
Using a wooden spoon,
stir until just mixed. Do
not overbeat—the batter
should be lumpy.
3 Spoon the mixture into
the muffin holes. Bake for
15–20 minutes, or until
puffed and golden. Cool
on a wire rack.

VARIATION: For a low-
fat muffin, use skim milk
and use orange juice
instead of half the butter.

BANANA MUFFINS

Preparation: 15 minutes
Cooking: 15 minutes
Makes 12

2 cups (250 g/8 oz) self-
  raising flour
1 cup (150 g/5 oz) oat
  bran
3/4 cup (185 g/6 oz)
  caster sugar
2 eggs, lightly beaten
3/4 cup (185 ml/6 fl oz)
  milk
60 g (2 oz) butter,
  melted
2 ripe bananas, mashed

1 Preheat the oven to hot
210°C (415°F/Gas 6–7).
Lightly grease a 12-hole,
1/2-cup (125 ml/4 fl oz)
muffin tin. Sift the flour
into a large bowl and stir
in the oat bran and sugar.
Make a well in the centre.
2 Mix together the eggs,
milk, butter and mashed
banana and pour into the
well all at once. Using a
wooden spoon, stir until
just mixed. Do not
overbeat—the batter
should be lumpy.
3 Spoon the mixture into
the muffin holes. Bake for
15 minutes, or until the
muffins are puffed and
golden brown. Transfer to
a wire rack to cool.

Use very ripe bananas for the best BANANA MUFFINS.

We've decorated our CHOCOLATE MUFFINS with chocolate buttercream and icing sugar.

CHOCOLATE MUFFINS

Preparation: 15 minutes
Cooking: 15 minutes
Makes 6 large muffins

2 cups (250 g/8 oz) plain flour
2¹/₂ teaspoons baking powder
3 tablespoons cocoa powder
2 tablespoons caster sugar
1 cup (175 g/6 oz) dark choc bits

1 egg, lightly beaten
¹/₂ cup (125 g/4 oz) sour cream
³/₄ cup (185 ml/6 fl oz) milk
90 g (3 oz) butter, melted

1 Preheat the oven to hot 210°C (415°F/Gas 6–7). Lightly grease a 6-hole, 1-cup (250 ml/8 fl oz) muffin tin. Sift the flour, baking powder and cocoa powder into a large bowl and stir in the sugar and choc bits. Make a well in the centre.

2 Mix together the egg, sour cream, milk and butter and pour into the well all at once. Using a wooden spoon, stir until just mixed. Do not overbeat—the batter should be lumpy.

3 Spoon the mixture into the muffin holes. Bake for 12–15 minutes, or until the muffins are firm. Loosen from the tin with a flat-bladed knife and transfer to a wire rack to cool completely.

271

HONEY ROLL

Preparation: 40 minutes
Cooking: 12 minutes
Serves 6–8

³/4 cup (90 g/3 oz) self-raising flour
2 teaspoons mixed spice
3 eggs
²/3 cup (125 g/4 oz) soft brown sugar
¹/4 cup (25 g/³/4 oz) desiccated coconut

Honey cream
125 g (4 oz) butter
¹/3 cup (90 g/3 oz) caster sugar
2 tablespoons honey

1 Preheat the oven to hot 210°C (415°F/Gas 6–7). Grease a 30 x 25 cm (12 x 10 inch) swiss roll tin and line the base with baking paper, leaving the paper to hang over two sides. Sift the flour and spice onto greaseproof paper three times.
2 Using electric beaters, beat the eggs in a large mixing bowl for 5 minutes, or until thick, frothy and pale. Add the sugar gradually, beating constantly until it has dissolved and the mixture is pale and glossy. Use a metal spoon to fold in the flour quickly and lightly.
3 Spread the mixture evenly in the tin and smooth the surface. Bake for 12 minutes, or until the cake is lightly golden and springy to touch. Lay out a clean, dry tea towel, cover with greaseproof paper and sprinkle the paper with the coconut. Turn the cooked cake onto the coconut and leave for 1 minute.
4 Using the tea towel as a guide, carefully roll the cake, along with the paper, up from the short side. Leave for 5 minutes, or until cool. Unroll the cake and discard the paper.
5 To make the honey cream, beat the butter, sugar and honey in a small mixing bowl with electric beaters until light and creamy. Remove the bowl from the electric mixer. Cover the mixture with cold water, swirl the water around, then pour it off. Beat the mixture again with electric beaters for another 2 minutes. Repeat this process six times, or until the cream is white and fluffy, and the sugar has completely dissolved. Spread the honey cream over the cake, re-roll and trim the ends with a knife. Serve sliced.

Make HONEY ROLL like a swiss roll, with a creamy honey filling.

AFGHANS

Preparation: 20 minutes
Cooking: 20 minutes
Makes 20

150 g (5 oz) butter
1/3 cup (60 g/2 oz) soft
  brown sugar
1 egg, lightly beaten
1 teaspoon vanilla
  essence
1 cup (125 g/4 oz) plain
  flour
2 tablespoons cocoa
  powder
1/3 cup (30 g/1 oz)
  desiccated coconut
1 1/2 cups (75 g/2 1/2 oz)
  lightly crushed
  cornflakes
1/2 cup (90 g/3 oz) choc
  bits

Spread melted chocolate topping over AFGHANS.

1 Preheat the oven to moderate 180°C (350°F/ Gas 4). Grease a 32 x 28 cm (13 x 11 inch) baking tray and line with baking paper.
2 Using electric beaters, beat the butter and sugar in a small bowl until the mixture is light and creamy. Add the egg and vanilla essence a little at a time, beating thoroughly after each addition. Transfer the mixture to a large bowl and add the sifted combined flour and cocoa with the coconut and cornflakes. Using a metal spoon, fold in gently until just combined.

3 Drop level tablespoons of the mixture onto the tray. Bake for 20 minutes, or until lightly browned. Allow the biscuits to cool on the tray.
4 Put the choc bits in a heatproof bowl. Half fill a saucepan with water and bring it to the boil. Remove from the heat and place the bowl over the pan, making sure the base of it is not sitting in the water. Stir occasionally until the chocolate has melted. Remove from the heat. Spread the biscuit tops thickly with chocolate and leave for the topping to set.

VARIATIONS: Afghans can be sprinkled with toasted shredded coconut. To toast coconut, spread it on a baking tray and toast in a preheated moderate 180°C (350°F/Gas 4) oven for 5 minutes. Alternatively, top the Afghans with finely chopped walnuts or pecans. You may prefer to use dark chopped chocolate instead of choc bits.

FLORENTINES

Preparation: 25 minutes
Cooking: 20 minutes
Makes 24

1/4 cup (30 g/1 oz) plain
flour
2 tablespoons chopped
walnuts
2 tablespoons chopped
flaked almonds
2 tablespoons finely
chopped glacé cherries
2 tablespoons finely
chopped mixed peel
75 g (2 1/2 oz) butter
1/4 cup (45 g/1 1/2 oz) soft
brown sugar
180 g (6 oz) dark
compound chocolate,
chopped

1 Preheat the oven to
moderate 180°C (350°F/
Gas 4). Line a 32 x 28 cm
(13 x 11 inch) baking tray
with baking paper. Sift the
flour into a mixing bowl.
Add the walnuts, almonds,
cherries and mixed peel.
Stir and make a well in
the centre.
2 Combine the butter and
sugar in a small pan. Stir
over low heat until the
butter has melted and the
sugar has dissolved. Pour
into the well in the dry
ingredients. Using a
wooden spoon, stir until
just combined, but do not
overbeat. Drop heaped
teaspoons of the mixture
onto the tray, leaving

plenty of room between
each one. Press into neat
5 cm (2 inch) rounds.
Bake for 7 minutes. While
the florentines are still
soft, use a flat-bladed
knife to push them into
neat rounds. Cool on the
tray for 5 minutes before
transferring to a wire rack
to cool completely.
3 Put the chocolate in a
heatproof bowl. Half fill a
pan with water and bring
it to the boil. Remove
from the heat and place
the bowl of chocolate
over the pan, making sure
it is not touching the
water. Stir occasionally
until the chocolate is
melted. Using a flat-
bladed knife, carefully
spread the chocolate on
the underside of the
florentines. Place the
biscuits chocolate-side-up
on a wire rack to set. Best
eaten on the same day.

COCONUT JAM SLICE

Preparation: 30 minutes +
    10 minutes refrigeration
Cooking: 35 minutes
Makes 25 squares

1 1/2 cups (185 g/6 oz)
plain flour
150 g (5 oz) butter,
cubed
1/2 cup (60 g/2 oz) icing
sugar

Topping
1/3 cup (90 g/3 oz) caster
sugar
2 eggs
2 cups (180 g/6 oz)
desiccated coconut
1/3 cup (105 g/3 1/2 oz)
blackberry jam

1 Preheat the oven to
moderate 180°C (350°F/
Gas 4). Grease a 23 cm
(9 inch) square cake tin
and line with baking
paper, extending over
two sides.
2 Put the flour, butter and
sugar in a bowl and, with
your fingertips, rub in the
butter until crumbly. Turn
out onto a lightly floured
surface and gather
together. Press the dough
into the tin and refrigerate
for 10 minutes. Bake for
15 minutes, or until just
golden. Cool.
3 To make the topping,
whisk the sugar and eggs
until combined. Stir in the
coconut.
4 Spread the jam over the
cooled base. Spread the
topping over the jam,
pressing down with the
back of a spoon, and bake
for 20 minutes, or until
light golden. Cut into
squares when cool.

STORAGE: Store for up
to 3 days in an airtight
container.

*FLORENTINES (top) and
COCONUT JAM SLICE.*

CHOCOLATE CHIP COOKIES

Preparation: 15 minutes
Cooking: 15 minutes
Makes about 24

150 g (5 oz) unsalted
   butter
1/4 cup (45 g/1 1/2 oz) soft
   brown sugar
1/3 cup (90 g/3 oz) caster
   sugar
1 egg yolk
1 teaspoon vanilla
   essence
1 1/2 cups (185 g/6 oz)
   self-raising flour
1/2 cup (90 g/3 oz) dark
   choc bits
1/2 cup (90 g/3 oz) milk
   choc bits

1 Preheat the oven to
moderate 180°C (350°F/
Gas 4). Grease two baking
trays and line with non-
stick baking paper. Using
electric beaters, beat the
butter, sugars and egg
yolk in a small bowl until
light and creamy. Add the
vanilla and beat until
combined.
2 Transfer the mixture to
a large bowl and add the
flour and half the choc
bits. Using a metal spoon,
stir until just combined.
Use your hands to press
the mixture together to
form a soft dough.
3 Roll level tablespoons of
the mixture into balls.
Press the remaining
chocolate bits firmly onto
the tops of the balls.
Arrange the balls on the
tray, leaving room for
spreading. Bake for
15 minutes, or until crisp
and lightly browned, and
then cool on the trays.

Press chocolate bits into the CHOCOLATE CHIP COOKIES.

PEANUT BUTTER BISCUITS

Preparation: 20 minutes
Cooking: 15 minutes
Makes 36

125 g (4 oz) butter
155 g (5 oz) soft brown
   sugar
1/2 cup (125 g/4 oz)
   peanut butter
2 teaspoons vanilla
   essence
1 egg
1 3/4 cups (215 g/7 oz)
   plain flour
1 cup (160 g/5 1/2 oz)
   raw peanuts

1 Preheat the oven to
moderate 180°C (350°F/
Gas 4). Line two or three
baking trays with baking
paper. Using electric
beaters, beat the butter
and sugar until light and
creamy. Beat in the peanut
butter, vanilla essence
and egg.
2 Transfer the mixture to
a large bowl. Sift in the
flour and add the peanuts.
Stir until combined, using
a large metal spoon.
3 Place tablespoons of the
mixture on the trays,
leaving room for
spreading. Bake for
15 minutes, or until
golden. Leave the biscuits
on the trays for at least
2 minutes before
transferring them to a
wire rack to cool.

NOTE: Try adding 90 g (3 oz) chopped chocolate or choc bits to the dough. For neater biscuits, roll the mixture into balls and flatten on the tray.

JAM DROPS

Preparation: 20 minutes
Cooking: 15 minutes
Makes 32

80 g (2³/₄ oz) butter
¹/₃ cup (90 g/3 oz) caster sugar
2 tablespoons milk
¹/₂ teaspoon vanilla essence
1 cup (125 g/4 oz) self-raising flour
¹/₃ cup (40 g/1¹/₄ oz) custard powder
2 tablespoons raspberry jam

1 Preheat the oven to moderate 180°C (350°F/ Gas 4). Line two baking trays with baking paper. Beat the butter and sugar until light and creamy. Beat in the milk and vanilla. Add the sifted flour and custard powder and mix to form a soft dough.

2 Roll 2 teaspoonfuls at a time into balls and put on the trays. Press the centre of each ball with your thumb. Fill the hole with jam. Bake for 15 minutes, then cool on a wire rack.

Use raw peanuts in your PEANUT BUTTER BISCUITS.

JAM DROPS are simple for children to make, and fun too.

MONTE CREAMS

Preparation: 30 minutes
Cooking: 20 minutes
Makes 25

125 g (4 oz) butter
1/2 cup (125 g/4 oz)
  caster sugar
3 tablespoons milk
1 1/2 cups (185 g/6 oz)
  self-raising flour
1/4 cup (30 g/1 oz)
  custard powder
1/3 cup (30 g/1 oz)
  desiccated coconut

Filling
75 g (2 1/2 oz) butter
2/3 cup (85 g/3 oz) icing
  sugar
2 teaspoons milk
1/3 cup (105 g/3 1/2 oz)
  strawberry jam

1 Preheat the oven to moderate 180°C (350°F/ Gas 4). Line two baking trays with baking paper. Using electric beaters, beat the butter and sugar until light and creamy. Add the milk and beat until combined. Sift the flour and custard powder and add to the bowl with the coconut. Mix to form a soft dough.
2 Roll two teaspoons of the mixture into balls. Place on the trays and press with a fork. Dip the fork in custard powder occasionally to prevent it from sticking. Bake for 15–20 minutes, or until just golden. Transfer to a wire rack to cool completely before filling.
3 To make the filling, beat the butter and sugar with electric beaters until light and creamy. Beat in the milk. Spread one biscuit with about half a teaspoon of the filling and one with about half a teaspoon of the jam, and sandwich the halves together.

STORAGE: These will keep for up to 4 days in an airtight container.

Sandwich the MONTE CREAMS together with filling and jam.

Decorate MELTING MOMENTS with half a glacé cherry in the middle of each one.

MELTING MOMENTS

Preparation: 30 minutes
Cooking: 15 minutes
Makes 40

180 g (6 oz) butter
1/3 cup (40 g/1 1/4 oz) icing sugar
1 teaspoon vanilla essence
1/3 cup (40 g/1 1/4 oz) cornflour
1 cup (125 g/4 oz) plain flour
100 g (3 1/2 oz) glacé cherries

1 Preheat the oven to moderate 180°C (350°F/Gas 4). Grease a 32 x 28 cm (13 x 11 inch) baking tray and line with baking paper.
2 Using electric beaters, beat the butter, sugar and vanilla essence in a small bowl until light and creamy. Beat in the sifted cornflour and flour gradually, beating until the mixture is just combined and smooth.
3 Spoon into a piping bag fitted with a 1 cm (1/2 inch) fluted nozzle. Pipe the mixture in rosettes 4 cm (1 1/2 inches) in diameter onto the tray.

Top each biscuit with half a glacé cherry. Bake for 15 minutes, or until lightly golden and crisp. Cool on a wire rack.

VARIATION: Sandwich the biscuits together with jam and a creamy filling. To make the filling, beat 60 g (2 oz) butter with electric beaters until creamy. Gradually add 1/2 cup (60 g/2 oz) icing sugar alternately with 2 teaspoons milk. Beat until the mixture is light and fluffy. Sandwich the biscuits together with a little filling and jam. Dust with icing sugar to serve.

ANZAC BISCUITS

Preparation: 12 minutes
Cooking: 20 minutes
Makes 26

1 cup (125 g/4 oz) plain
  flour
2/3 cup (160 g/5 1/2 oz)
  sugar
1 cup (100 g/3 1/2 oz)
  rolled oats
1 cup (90 g/3 oz)
  desiccated coconut
125 g (4 oz) butter
1/4 cup (90 g/3 oz)
  golden syrup
1/2 teaspoon bicarbonate
  of soda

1 Preheat the oven to moderate 180°C (350°F/ Gas 4). Line two baking trays with baking paper. Sift the flour and sugar into a large mixing bowl. Add the rolled oats and coconut and make a well in the centre of the dry ingredients.
2 Put the butter and syrup in a small pan. Stir over low heat until melted and smooth. Dissolve the soda in 1 tablespoon boiling water, then add immediately to the butter mixture. It will foam up instantly. Pour into the well in the dry ingredients. Stir well with a wooden spoon.
3 Drop level tablespoons of the mixture onto the tray. Flatten gently with your fingers, leaving room for spreading. Bake for 20 minutes, or until just browned. Remove from the oven and transfer to a wire rack to cool.

STORAGE: Will keep in an airtight container for up to three days.
VARIATION: Use treacle or honey instead of syrup.
HINT: Instant or 1-minute oats are quite suitable for this recipe.

You can use instant or 1-minute oats for ANZAC BISCUITS.

GINGERBREAD PEOPLE

Preparation: 1 hour +
  15 minutes refrigeration
Cooking: 10 minutes
Makes about 16

125 g (4 oz) butter
1/3 cup (60 g/2 oz) soft
  dark brown or soft
  brown sugar
1/3 cup (115 g/4 oz)
  golden syrup
1 egg, lightly beaten
2 cups (250 g/8 oz) plain
  flour
1/3 cup (40 g/1 1/4 oz)
  self-raising flour
1 tablespoon ground
  ginger
1 teaspoon bicarbonate
  of soda

Use tinted icing to pipe faces and clothing onto GINGERBREAD PEOPLE.

Icing

1 egg white
$^1/_2$ teaspoon lemon juice
1 cup (125 g/4 oz) **pure icing sugar, sifted**
assorted food colourings

1 Preheat the oven to moderate 180°C (350°F/Gas 4). Grease two or three baking trays and line with baking paper. Using electric beaters, beat the butter, sugar and syrup until light and creamy. Add the egg gradually, beating well after each addition.
2 Sift the flours, ginger and bicarbonate of soda onto the butter mixture and use a knife to mix until just combined. Use a well-floured hand to combine the dough thoroughly, then turn onto a floured surface and knead for 1–2 minutes, or until smooth.
3 Line a large board with baking paper. Roll out the dough on the board to 5 mm ($^1/_4$ inch) thickness. (Flour the rolling pin, if necessary, to prevent the dough sticking.) Put the dough on the board in the fridge for 15 minutes, or until firm enough to cut.
4 Cut out the dough with people-shaped biscuit cutters. Press any remaining dough together, then re-roll and cut out again. Put on the trays and bake for 10 minutes, or until lightly browned. Cool the biscuits on trays, and then ice.
5 To make the icing, put the egg white in a small dry bowl and beat with electric beaters until foamy. Add the lemon juice and icing sugar gradually, and beat until thick and creamy. Divide the icing among several bowls and tint with food colourings. Spoon into small paper icing bags and pipe faces and clothing onto the biscuits.

281

COCONUT MACAROONS

Preparation: 15 minutes
Cooking: 20 minutes
Makes about 60

3 egg whites
1 1/4 cups (310 g/10 oz) caster sugar
1/2 teaspoon coconut essence
1 teaspoon grated lemon rind
2 tablespoons cornflour
3 cups (270 g/9 oz) desiccated coconut
3 tablespoons shredded coconut, to sprinkle
60 g (2 oz) dark chocolate, chopped

1 Preheat the oven to warm 160°C (315°F/Gas 2–3). Grease two baking trays and line with baking paper. Place the egg whites in a small, dry bowl. Using electric beaters, beat the egg whites until firm peaks form. Add the sugar gradually, beating constantly until the mixture is thick and glossy and all the sugar has dissolved. Add the coconut essence and lemon rind, and beat until just combined.

2 Transfer the mixture to a large bowl and add the sifted cornflour and the coconut. Using a metal spoon, stir until just combined. Drop 1 or 2 level teaspoons of the mixture onto the prepared trays about 3 cm (1 1/4 inches) apart. Sprinkle with shredded coconut and bake for 15–20 minutes, or until golden. Transfer to a wire rack to cool.

3 Put the chocolate in a heatproof bowl. Bring a pan of water to a simmer, remove from the heat and place the bowl over the pan (make sure the base of the bowl isn't sitting in the water). Stir occasionally until the chocolate has melted. Dip the cooled macaroons in the melted chocolate and return to the wire rack to set.

VARIATION: To make plain almond macaroons, beat 115 g (4 oz) ground almonds with 1 cup (250 g/8 oz) caster sugar and 2 egg whites for 5 minutes. Add 1 tablespoon plain flour and 2 teaspoons vanilla essence and beat until smooth. Add a little finely grated orange or lemon rind, if you like, and then bake as directed above. Makes 25–30.

Decorate MACAROONS with coconut and melted chocolate.

BRANDY SNAPS

Preparation: 15 minutes
Cooking: 45 minutes
Makes 25

60 g (2 oz) butter
2 tablespoons golden
  syrup
1/3 cup (60 g/2 oz) soft
  brown sugar
1/4 cup (30 g/1 oz) plain
  flour
1 1/2 teaspoons ground
  ginger
60 g (2 oz) dark
  chocolate, chopped

1 Preheat the oven to moderate 180°C (350°F/ Gas 4). Lightly grease two baking trays and line with baking paper.

2 Combine the butter, golden syrup and sugar in a small pan. Stir over low heat until the butter has melted and the sugar has dissolved, then remove from the heat. Add the sifted flour and ginger to the pan. Use a wooden spoon to stir the mixture until well combined, taking care not to overbeat.

3 Using 3 level teaspoons of the mixture for each brandy snap, drop the mixture onto the trays about 12 cm (5 inches) apart. Bake for 5–6 minutes, or until lightly browned. Leave the biscuits on the trays

Dip the ends of the BRANDY SNAPS in melted dark chocolate.

for 30 seconds then, while still hot, lift off the tray and wrap around the handle of a thin wooden spoon. Slide off the spoon and set aside to cool while you curl the remaining brandy snaps.

4 Put the chocolate in a heatproof bowl. Bring a pan of water to a simmer, remove from the heat and place the bowl over the pan (make sure the base of the bowl isn't sitting in the water). Stir occasionally until the chocolate has melted.

Dip the ends of the brandy snaps in the melted chocolate and leave on a foil-lined tray to dry.

HINT: There is a real art to working with these biscuits: work quickly, as they harden and crack when cooled. Use a large flat knife or spatula to lift them off the tray. If they cool too much, return to the oven for a few minutes to warm, then try again.

CUSTARD TARTS

Preparation: 30 minutes +
  20 minutes refrigeration
Cooking: 45 minutes
Makes 12

2 cups (250 g/8 oz) plain
  flour
1/3 cup (60 g/2 oz) rice
  flour
1/4 cup (30 g/1 oz) icing
  sugar
120 g (4 oz) butter,
  chopped
1 egg yolk
3 tablespoons iced water
1 egg white, lightly
  beaten

Filling
3 eggs
1 1/2 cups (375 ml/12 fl
  oz.) milk
1/4 cup (60 g/2 oz) caster
  sugar
1 teaspoon vanilla
  essence
1/2 teaspoon ground
  nutmeg

1 Place the flours, icing
sugar and butter in a
bowl. Rub in the butter
with your fingertips until
the mixture is fine and
crumbly. Add the egg yolk
and almost all of the iced
water, and stir with a knife
until the mixture comes
together, adding more
water if necesary. Turn
onto a lightly floured
surface and press together
until smooth. Divide the
dough into 12 equal
portions. Roll out and line
twelve 10 cm (4 inch)
fluted tart tins. Refrigerate
for 20 minutes.
2 Preheat the oven to
moderate 180°C (350°F/
Gas 4). Cover each
pastry-lined tin with a
crumpled sheet of baking
paper and fill with a layer
of baking beads or rice.
Place the tins on a large
baking tray and bake for
10 minutes. Discard the
baking paper and beads or
rice and bake the pastry
for a further 10 minutes,
or until lightly golden and
dry. Allow to cool. Brush
the base and side of each
pastry case with beaten
egg white.
3 To make the filling,
reduce the oven to slow
150°C (300°F/Gas 2).
Combine the eggs and
milk in a mixing bowl,
and whisk to combine.
Add the sugar gradually,
whisking to dissolve
completely. Stir in the
vanilla, strain the mixture
into a jug, then pour into
the pastry cases. Sprinkle
with the nutmeg and bake
for 25 minutes, or until
the filling is just set.
Serve the custard tarts at
room temperature.

NOTE: For blind baking,
if you don't have baking
beads, use raw rice or
dried beans. They can be
kept and used again.

CHOCOLATE BROWNIES

Preparation: 20 minutes
Cooking: 40 minutes
Makes 24

150 g (5 oz) butter,
  chopped
125 g (4 oz) dark
  chocolate, chopped
3 eggs, lightly beaten
1 1/2 cups (375 g/12 oz)
  caster sugar
1 teaspoon vanilla
  essence
1 cup (125 g /4 oz) plain
  flour
1/4 cup (30 g/1 oz) cocoa
  power
icing sugar, to dust

1 Preheat the oven to
moderate 180°C (350°F/
Gas 4). Grease a 20 cm
(8 inch) square tin with
oil or melted butter Line
the base with baking
paper, extending over two
opposite sides (to help
you lift the brownies out).
2 Bring a small pan of
water to a simmer.
Remove from the heat.
Put the butter and
chocolate in a heatproof
bowl, place over the pan
(don't let the base of the
bowl sit in the hot water)
and stir occasionally until
smooth. Remove from the
heat and cool slightly.
3 Use a whisk to beat the
eggs, sugar and vanilla
together in a large bowl.

CUSTARD TARTS (top) and CHOCOLATE BROWNIES.

Add the melted chocolate mixture and whisk together. Stir in the combined sifted flour and cocoa. Do not overbeat.

4 Pour into the tin and bake for 40 minutes, or until slightly risen and just firm. Leave to cool in the tin (the brownie will sink back down on cooling). Lift out and cut into squares. Dust with icing sugar to serve.

STORAGE: Can be stored in an airtight container for two days.

VARIATIONS: For nut brownies, add 1 cup (125 g/4½ oz) of chopped roasted macadamias, walnuts or pecans to the mixture. For white chocolate brownies, use white chocolate melts instead of the dark chocolate. For marshmallow brownies, add 1 cup (45 g/1½ oz) of mini marshmallows to the raw mixture.

To make a brownie ice cream sandwich, cut brownies into small squares and sandwich two squares together with vanilla ice cream. Serve with a hot chocolate fudge sauce as a dessert.

285

CHOCOLATE CARAMEL SLICE.

CHOCOLATE CARAMEL SLICE

Preparation: 15 minutes
Cooking: 20 minutes
Makes 24 triangles

125 g (4 oz) plain sweet
  biscuits, crushed
80 g (2³⁄₄ oz) butter,
  melted
2 tablespoons desiccated
  coconut
400 g (13 oz) can
  sweetened condensed
  milk
125 g (4 oz) butter, extra
¹⁄₃ cup (90 g/3 oz) caster
  sugar
¹⁄₃ cup (115 g/4 oz)
  golden syrup
250 g (8 oz) milk
  chocolate melts
1 tablespoon vegetable
  oil

1 Grease a shallow
30 x 20 cm (12 x 8 inch)
cake tin, line the base and
sides with foil and grease
the foil. Mix together the
biscuits, melted butter and
coconut. Press the mixture
evenly into the tin and
smooth the surface.
2 Combine the condensed
milk, extra butter, sugar
and golden syrup in a
small pan. Stir over low

heat for 15 minutes, or
until the sugar has
dissolved and the caramel
is smooth, thick and
lightly browned. Remove
from the heat and
leave to cool slightly. Pour
the caramel over the
biscuit base and smooth
the surface.
3 Put the milk chocolate
melts and oil in a
heatproof bowl. Half fill a
saucepan with water and
bring it to the boil.
Remove from the heat and
place the bowl of
chocolate over the pan,
making sure the base of
the bowl is not sitting
in the water. Stir
occasionally until the
chocolate has melted and
the mixture is smooth.
Spread the chocolate
mixture over the caramel.
Allow to partially set
before marking into
24 triangles. Refrigerate
until firm.

STORAGE: The slice can
be stored in an airtight
container in a cool place
for up to two days.
VARIATION: Use dark
chocolate melts in place
of milk chocolate.

FRUIT MINCE PIES

Preparation: 30 minutes
Cooking: 30 minutes
Makes 24

2 cups (250 g/8 oz) plain
flour
2/3 cup (85 g/3 oz) icing
sugar
150 g (5 oz) butter
2–3 tablespoons iced
water
icing sugar, to dust

Fruit mince
1/3 cup (40 g/1 1/4 oz)
raisins, chopped
1/3 cup (60 g/2 oz) soft
brown sugar
1/4 cup (30 g/1 oz)
sultanas
1/4 cup (45 g/1 1/2 oz)
mixed peel
1 tablespoon currants
1 tablespoon chopped
almonds
1 small apple, grated
1 teaspoon lemon juice
1/2 teaspoon finely grated
orange rind
1/2 teaspoon finely grated
lemon rind
1/2 teaspoon mixed spice
pinch of nutmeg
25 g (3/4 oz) melted
butter
1 tablespoon brandy

Make decorative pastry tops for Christmas FRUIT MINCE PIES.

1 To make the fruit mince, combine the ingredients in a bowl and then spoon into a sterilized jar. You can use the fruit mince straight away but the flavours develop if kept for a while. You can keep it in a cool dark place for up to 3 months. (You can use shop-bought fruit mince if you are short for time.)

2 Preheat the oven to moderate 180°C (350°F/ Gas 4). Brush two 12-hole shallow patty tins lightly with melted butter. Place the flour, sugar and butter in a bowl and rub in the butter with your fingertips until fine and crumbly. Add almost all the water and mix with a knife until it just comes together.

3 Turn out onto a lightly floured surface and gather into a ball. Roll out two thirds of the pastry and cut out 24 rounds with a biscuit cutter. Fit the rounds into the tins.

4 Divide the fruit mince among the pastry cases. Roll out the remaining pastry and cut out 12 rounds with the same cutter. Using a smaller, fluted cutter, cut a circle from the centre of each. Place the large circles on top of half the pies and press the edges to seal. Place the smaller circles on the remainder. Bake for 25 minutes, or until golden. Leave in the tins for 5 minutes, then lift out with a knife and cool on wire racks. Dust lightly with icing sugar.

287

VANILLA SLICE

Preparation: 40 minutes
Cooking: 15 minutes
Makes 9

2 sheets ready-rolled puff
pastry
1 cup (250 g/8 oz) caster
sugar
3/4 cup (90 g/3 oz)
cornflour
1/2 cup (60 g/2 oz)
custard powder
3 cups (750 ml/24 fl oz)
milk
1 cup (250 ml/8 fl oz)
cream
60 g (2 oz) butter
2 teaspoons vanilla
essence
3 egg yolks

Icing

1 1/2 cups (185 g/6 oz)
icing sugar
1/4 cup (60 g/2 oz)
passionfruit pulp
2 teaspoons lemon juice
15 g (1/2 oz) butter,
softened

1 Preheat the oven to
very hot 240°C (475°F/
Gas 9). Grease two baking
trays with oil. Line the
base and sides of a
shallow 23 cm (9 inch)
square cake tin with foil,
leaving the foil to hang
over two sides. Place the
pastry sheets on the
baking trays. Prick all over
with a fork and bake for
8 minutes, or until golden.
Remove from the oven
and trim each pastry sheet
to a 23 cm (9 inch)
square. Place one sheet in
the tin, top-side-down.
2 Combine the sugar,
cornflour and custard
powder in a pan.
Gradually add the milk
and cream and stir until
smooth. Stir the mixture
constantly over medium
heat for 2 minutes, or
until it boils and thickens.
Add the butter and
vanilla essence, and stir
until smooth.
3 Remove the mixture
from the heat. Whisk in
the egg yolks until
combined. Spread the
custard over the pastry in
the tin and cover with the
remaining pastry, top-
side-down. Allow to cool.
4 To make the icing,
combine the icing sugar,
passionfruit pulp, lemon
juice and butter in a
heatproof bowl. Place the
bowl over a pan of
simmering water and stir
until the icing is smooth
and glossy. Remove from
the heat. Lift the slice out
of the cake tin, using the
foil 'handles' to help you.
Spread the icing over the
top of the slice and leave
it to set before cutting
into squares with a sharp
serrated knife.

Top the VANILLA SLICE with a passionfruit icing.

CHOCOLATE ECLAIRS

Preparation: 50 minutes
Cooking: 25 minutes
Makes 12

60 g (2 oz) butter
1/2 cup (60 g/2 oz) plain
   flour, sifted
2 eggs, lightly beaten
100 g (3 1/2 oz) dark
   chocolate, chopped

Cream filling
300 ml (10 fl oz) chilled
   cream
1 tablespoon icing sugar

CHOCOLATE ECLAIRS are made using choux pastry.

1 Preheat the oven to hot 210°C (415°F/Gas 6–7). Line a tray with baking paper and mark with 10 cm (4 inch) lines, as a piping guide.
2 Put the butter in a pan with 3/4 cup (185 ml/ 6 fl oz) water. Stir over medium heat until the mixture comes to the boil. Immediately remove from the heat and beat in the flour. Return to the heat and beat until the mixture comes together and leaves the side of the pan. Allow to cool slightly and then transfer to a bowl.
3 Beat the mixture to release any more heat. Gradually add the egg, a little at a time, beating well after each addition, until thick and glossy. You may not need to add all

the egg. A wooden spoon should stand up in the mixture—if it is too runny, the egg has been added too quickly. Beat for several minutes more, or until thickened.
4 Spoon into a piping bag fitted with a 1 cm (1/2 inch) plain nozzle. Pipe twelve 10 cm (4 inch) fingers, a little apart, onto the tray, cutting off with a wet knife. Bake for 10 minutes, then reduce the heat to moderate 180°C (350°F/ Gas 4) and bake for 15–20 minutes. Pierce for the steam to escape, and cool on a wire rack.
5 Put the chocolate in a heatproof bowl. Half fill a

saucepan with water and bring it to the boil. Remove from the heat and place the bowl of chocolate over the pan, making sure the base of the bowl isn't sitting in the water. Stir until the chocolate has melted. Cut each eclair in half with a serrated knife and spread chocolate along the top half. Leave on a wire rack until set.
6 To make the filling, put the cream and icing sugar in a bowl and beat until stiff. Spoon or pipe into the bottom half of each eclair and top with a chocolate lid.
Serve immediately.

289

BAKLAVA is a traditional Greek sweet pastry.

BAKLAVA

Preparation: 15 minutes
Cooking: 30 minutes
Serves 8

3 ½ cups (435 g/14 oz)
  walnuts, finely chopped
1 cup (155 g/5 oz)
  almonds, finely
  chopped
½ teaspoon ground
  cinnamon
½ teaspoon ground
  mixed spice
1 tablespoon caster sugar
16 sheets filo pastry
40 g (1 ¼ oz) butter,
  melted
1 tablespoon olive oil

Syrup
1 cup (250 g/8 oz) sugar
3 whole cloves
3 teaspoons lemon juice

1 Preheat the oven to
moderate 180°C (350°F/
Gas 4). Grease a shallow
18 x 28 cm (7 x 11 inch)
tin. Mix together the
walnuts, almonds, spices
and sugar in a bowl.
2 Divide the mixture into
three portions. Place one
sheet of pastry on a work
surface. Brush half the
sheet with the combined
butter and oil, then fold in
half along the width. Trim
the edges of the pastry to
fit the dish. Place in the

base of the dish. Repeat
the process with another
three sheets of pastry.
3 Sprinkle one portion of
the walnut mixture over
the pastry. Repeat the
pastry process with four
more sheets. Sprinkle with
the second portion of
walnut mixture. Continue
with another four sheets
of pastry, the remaining
walnut mixture and the
final four sheets of pastry.
Trim the edges.
4 Brush the top of the
pastry with the remaining
butter and oil mixture.
Score the slice evenly into
four lengthways, but not
cut through to the base.

Bake for 30 minutes or until golden and crisp.

5 Meanwhile, make the syrup. Combine the sugar, cloves, lemon juice and 2/3 cup (170 ml/5½ fl oz) water in a small pan. Stir constantly over low heat until the mixture boils and the sugar has dissolved. Reduce the heat and leave to simmer, without stirring, for 10 minutes. Allow to cool.

6 Pour the cooled syrup over the hot slice. When cold, cut the slice into squares or diamonds.

CRUNCHY MUESLI SLICE

Preparation: 10 minutes
Cooking: 50 minutes
Makes 18 fingers

250 g (8 oz) butter
1 cup (250 g/8 oz) caster sugar
2 tablespoons honey
2¼ cups (225 g/7 oz) rolled oats
¾ cup (65 g/2¼ oz) desiccated coconut
1 cup (30 g/1 oz) cornflakes, lightly crushed
⅓ cup (30 g/1 oz) flaked almonds
1 teaspoon mixed spice
½ cup (95 g/3 oz) finely chopped dried apricots
1 cup (185 g/6 oz) mixed dried fruit

CRUNCHY MUESLI SLICE makes a good lunchbox filler.

1 Preheat the oven to warm 160°C (315°F/ Gas 2–3). Grease a shallow 30 x 20 cm (12 x 8 inch) cake tin, line the base and sides with paper, and grease the paper.

2 Combine the butter, sugar and honey in a small pan. Stir over low heat for 5 minutes, or until the butter has melted and the sugar has dissolved.

3 Place the oats, coconut, cornflakes, almonds, mixed spice and fruit in a large bowl, and stir to combine. Make a well in the centre. Pour the butter and sugar mixture into the

well and stir thoroughly.

4 Press the mixture firmly into the tin. Using a sharp knife, score the slice into 18 fingers. (Do not cut through to the base.) Bake for 45 minutes, or until golden. Leave in the tin for 15 minutes before turning out onto a board to cool. Cut into fingers when cool.

STORAGE: Store in an airtight container for up to three days.
VARIATION: You can use golden syrup instead of honey.

SHORTBREAD

Preparation: 20 minutes
Cooking: 40 minutes
Makes 8 wedges

1 cup (125 g/4 oz) plain
  flour
1/2 cup (90 g/3 oz) rice
  flour
150 g (5 oz) butter,
  chopped
1/4 cup (60 g/2 oz) caster
  sugar, plus 1 teaspoon
  to sprinkle

1 Preheat the oven to
warm 160°C (315°F/
Gas 2–3). Using a bowl as
a guide, draw an 18 cm
(7 inch) circle on a sheet
of baking paper. Sift the
flours into a large mixing
bowl and add the
chopped butter and sugar.
2 Using your fingertips,
rub the butter into the
flour until the mixture
resembles fine
breadcrumbs. Turn out
onto a lightly floured
surface and gather into a
smooth ball.
3 Turn the paper pencil-
side-down and press out
the dough to fit the circle.
Pinch the edges to
decorate. Score into eight
wedges, sprinkle with the
extra caster sugar and
bake for 40 minutes. Cool
on a wire rack and break
into wedges to serve.

STORAGE: Will keep for
up to 4 days in an airtight
container.
HINT: Shortbread will
come out of the oven soft
and will firm up when left
to cool.

LITTLE LEMON TARTS

Preparation: 40 minutes +
  10 minutes refrigeration
Cooking: 15 minutes
Makes about 24

2 cups (250 g/8 oz) plain
  flour
pinch of salt
125 g (4 oz) butter,
  chopped
2 teaspoons caster sugar
1 teaspoon lemon rind
1 egg yolk
2–3 tablespoons iced
  water

Filling
125 g (4 oz) cream
  cheese, softened
1/2 cup (125 g/4 oz)
  caster sugar
2 egg yolks
2 tablespoons lemon
  juice
1/2 cup (160 g/5 1/2 oz)
  sweetened condensed
  milk
candied lemon, to garnish

1 Preheat the oven to
moderate 180°C (350°F/
Gas 4). Brush two 12-hole
patty tins with oil. Sift the

Pinch the edges of the SHORTBREAD to decorate.

You can use the basic recipe for LITTLE LEMON TARTS, to make jam tarts.

flour and salt into a bowl, add the butter and rub in with your fingertips until the mixture resembles fine breadcrumbs. Add the sugar, lemon rind, egg yolk and water, and mix with a knife until the mixture just starts to come together. Turn out onto a lightly floured surface and gather together in a ball. Cover in plastic wrap and refrigerate for 10 minutes.

2 To make the filling, beat the cream cheese, sugar and egg yolks with electric beaters until smooth and thickened. Add the lemon juice and condensed milk and beat until well combined.

3 Roll out the dough between sheets of baking paper to 3 mm (¹/₈ inch) thick. Using a 7 cm (2³/₄ inch) fluted, round cutter, cut rounds from the pastry. Gently press the pastry into the patty tins. Lightly prick each one three times with a fork and bake for 10 minutes, or until the pastry is just starting to turn golden.

4 Spoon 2 teaspoons of the filling into each pastry case. Bake for another 5 minutes, or until the filling has set. Leave to cool slightly before removing from the tins. Garnish with candied lemon strips.

VARIATION: For jam tarts, place 1 tablepoon strawberry, apricot or fruit conserve into the unfilled tart shells and bake for 10–15 minutes, or until the jam has melted. Allow to cool before serving.

BASIC BISCUITS

Preparation: 20 minutes
Cooking: 15 minutes
Makes about 50 biscuits

125 g (4 oz) butter,
  cubed
1/2 cup (125 g/4 oz)
  caster sugar
1 egg
1/4 teaspoon vanilla
  essence
1 cup (125 g/4 oz) plain
  flour
1 cup (125 g/4 oz) self-
  raising flour

1 Preheat the oven to
warm 160°C (315°F/
Gas 2–3). Line two baking
trays with baking paper.

Beat together the butter
and sugar until creamy.
Add the egg and vanilla,
and beat well. Fold in the
sifted flours to form a
soft dough.
2 Turn the dough out
onto a sheet of baking
paper and cover with
another sheet. Roll out to
5 mm (1/4 inch) thick.
Using biscuit cutters, cut
out shapes and place on
the trays.
3 Bake in batches for
10–15 minutes, or until
lightly golden. Cool on a
wire rack. Make up one of
the following fillings and
use to sandwich the
biscuits together. Or
simply spread the biscuits
with one of our icings.

CARAMEL FILLING

Melt 30 g (1 oz) butter,
1/2 cup (95 g/3 oz) soft
brown sugar and
1/2 cup (160 g/5 1/2 oz)
condensed milk in a pan,
then bring to the boil.
Boil for 1 minute, or until
the mixture thickens.
Cool, then spread on the
biscuits. For a variation,
stir in 1 tablespoon
chopped glacé ginger.

LIME BUTTER FILLING

Beat 60 g (2 oz) softened
butter and 1 cup (125 g/
4 oz) icing sugar until
smooth. Add the finely
shredded rind of a lime
and 1–2 teaspoons of lime
juice. Beat until the filling
is spreadable.

CHOCOLATE AND PEANUT FILLING

Beat together 50 g (1³/4 oz) softened butter and 1 cup (125 g/4 oz) sifted icing sugar until well combined. In a separate bowl, mix ¹/3 cup (90 g/3 oz) peanut butter with 100 g (3¹/2 oz) melted chocolate. Beat into the butter mixture, then beat in 1 tablespoon boiling water.

ORANGE CREAM CHEESE FILLING

Beat ³/4 cup (185 g/6 oz) cream cheese with ¹/4 cup (30 g/1 oz) sifted icing sugar. Add the finely grated rind of an orange and beat until creamy.

MARSHMALLOW FILLING

Put the biscuits on a plate with a marshmallow on top of each one. Cook for 10 seconds in the microwave, then sandwich with another biscuit. Alternatively, lay the biscuits on a baking tray with a marshmallow on top of each one and bake in a moderate 180°C (350°F/Gas 4) oven for 1 minute. Sandwich with another biscuit.

PEPPERMINT FILLING

Mix 2 cups (250 g/8 oz) sifted icing sugar with 5–6 teaspoons hot water and a few drops of peppermint essence.

VANILLA ICING

Mix 1¹/4 cups (155 g/5 oz) sifted icing sugar with 1 tablespoon softened butter, ¹/2 teaspoon vanilla essence and 2 tablespoons boiling water.

CHOCOLATE FLECK ICING

Make vanilla icing as above and gently mix in 2 tablespoons grated dark chocolate.

PASSIONFRUIT GLACE ICING

Mix 1¹/4 cups (155 g/5 oz) sifted icing sugar with 2 tablespoons passionfruit pulp in a heatproof bowl. Stir over simmering water until smooth and glossy.

HEDGEHOG SLICE is crunchy with pieces of biscuit.

smooth the surface.

3 Place the chocolate and butter in a small heatproof bowl. Bring a pan of water to a simmer, then remove from the heat and place the bowl over the pan (don't let the base of the bowl sit in the water). Stir until the mixture is melted and smooth.

4 Spread the topping over the slice and make a swirling pattern if you wish. Refrigerate for 1 hour. Use the foil 'handles' to lift the slice from the tin. Cut into squares to serve.

STORAGE: Store in an airtight container in a cool dark place, or in the refrigerator if the weather is warm.

HEDGEHOG SLICE

Preparation: 20 minutes +
1 hour refrigeration
Cooking: 5 minutes
Makes 20

125 g (4 oz) butter
1/2 cup (125 g/4 oz)
caster sugar
125 g (4 oz) plain sweet
biscuits, crushed
1 cup (100 g/3 1/2 oz)
walnuts, chopped
1/2 cup (60 g/2 oz) cocoa
powder
1 egg, lightly beaten
125 g (4 oz) cooking
chocolate, chopped
30 g (1 oz) butter

1 Line the base and sides of a 20 cm (8 inch) square cake tin with foil, leaving the foil to hang over two sides. Combine the butter and sugar in a large heavy-based pan. Stir over medium heat until the butter has melted and the sugar has dissolved. Reduce the heat to low, add the crushed biscuits, walnuts and cocoa, and stir until well combined.

2 Remove the mixture from the heat and cool slightly. Add the egg and stir until thoroughly combined. Press the mixture into the tin, using the back of a spoon to

MATCHSTICKS

Preparation: 40 minutes +
1 hour refrigeration
Cooking: 15 minutes
Makes 12

2 cups (250 g/8 oz) plain
flour
pinch of salt
180 g (6 oz) butter
1 teaspoon lemon juice

Chocolate icing
1/2 cup (60 g/2 oz) icing
sugar, sifted
1 tablespoon cocoa
powder

Vanilla icing
2 cups (250 g/8 oz) icing
sugar, sifted
1/2 teaspoon vanilla
essence

Filling
3/4 cup (250 g/8 oz)
raspberry jam
1 1/4 cups (315 ml/10 fl
oz) cream, whipped

1 Sift the flour and salt
into a large bowl. Add the
butter and, with a knife,
cut in the butter until just
coated with the flour.
Combine 3/4 cup (185 ml/
6 fl oz) cold water with
the lemon juice and add
most of it to the bowl.
Cut in with a knife,
without breaking up the
butter. Add more of the
liquid if necessary.
2 With floured fingers,
gently bring the mixture
together into a rough ball.
Turn out onto a floured
surface and form into a
rectangle. Do not knead.
Roll the dough out to a
45 x 15 cm (18 x 6 inch)
neat rectangle.
3 Fold the dough into
three layers by folding the
bottom third up and then
the top third down. Seal
the edges lightly with a
rolling pin. Give a quarter
turn clockwise: the top
edge will now be to the
right as if it were a book.
Cover and refrigerate for
15 minutes. Repeat
rolling, folding and

turning four more times.
Refrigerate between
rollings if the dough
becomes too soft. Chill
for at least 30 minutes
after the final rolling.
4 Divide the dough in
half and roll each half out
to 30 x 20 cm
(12 x 8 inches), then cut
into twelve 10 x 5 cm
(4 x 2 inch) pieces.
5 Grease two baking trays
and line with baking
paper. Put the pastry on
the trays, cover and chill
for 20 minutes. Preheat
the oven to moderately
hot 200°C (400°F/Gas 6).
Bake for 10 minutes, or
until puffed and golden.
Cool on a wire rack.
6 To make the chocolate
icing, mix the sugar and
cocoa with 1 tablespoon
hot water. Spoon into a

paper icing bag.
7 To make the vanilla
icing, mix the sugar and
vanilla with 3 tablespoons
hot water in a heatproof
bowl. Place the bowl over
a pan of barely simmering
water and stir until the
icing is smooth and
glossy. Spread the icing
over half of the pastry
pieces. Pipe diagonal lines
with the chocolate icing
and drag a skewer along
the icing at intervals to
give a feathered effect.
Leave on a wire rack until
the icing has set.
8 Spread the jam and
cream over the un-iced
halves of the pastry and
then sandwich together
with the iced tops.

NOTE: You can use
ready-rolled puff pastry.

Use a skewer to give MATCHSTICKS feathered icing.

DESSERTS

Desserts are a wonderful starting point for the novice cook. It is difficult to go far wrong once sugar, chocolate and cream are involved... Desserts can range from a simple piece of poached fruit or bowl of home-made sorbet, to fabulous creations of pastry, meringue and summer berries.
If you, or any of your friends and family, have a sweet tooth then this is the chapter for you.

PROFITEROLES

Preparation: 30 minutes
Cooking: 50 minutes
Serves 8–10

Choux pastry
50 g (1 3/4 oz) butter
3/4 cup (90 g/3 oz) plain
  flour, sifted twice
3 eggs, lightly beaten

Filling
1 1/2 cups (375 ml/
  12 fl oz) milk
4 egg yolks
1/3 cup (90 g/3 oz) caster
  sugar
3 tablespoons plain
  flour
1 teaspoon vanilla
  essence

110 g (3 1/2 oz) good-
  quality dark chocolate
2 teaspoons vegetable oil

1 Preheat the oven to hot 210°C (415°F/Gas 6–7). Put the butter in a large heavy-based pan with 3/4 cup (185 ml/6 fl oz) water and stir over medium heat until coming to the boil. Remove from the heat and quickly beat in the flour. Return to the heat and continue beating until the mixture comes together, forms a ball and leaves the side of the pan. Allow to cool slightly.
2 Transfer to a bowl and beat to release any more heat. Gradually add the beaten egg about 3 teaspoons at a time, beating well after each addition, until all the egg has been added and the mixture is thick and glossy—a wooden spoon should stand upright in it. (If it is too runny, the egg

has been added too quickly. Beat for several more minutes, or until thickened.)
3 Spoon heaped teaspoons of the mixture onto two baking trays, leaving room for spreading. Sprinkle the baking trays with water— this creates steam, helping the puffs to rise. Bake for 20–30 minutes, or until browned and hollow sounding, then remove and make a small hole in the base of each one with a skewer. Return to the oven for 5 minutes to dry out. Cool on a wire rack.
4 To make the filling, put the milk in a small pan and bring to the boil. Set aside while quickly whisking the yolks and sugar in a bowl, until combined. Whisk in the

PROFITEROLES are a little fiddly to make, but fabulous for a special occasion.

flour. Pour the hot milk slowly onto the egg mixture, whisking constantly. Wash out the pan, return the milk mixture and bring to the boil, stirring with a wooden spoon until the mixture comes to the boil and thickens. Transfer to a bowl and stir in the vanilla essence. Lay plastic wrap directly over the surface to prevent a skin forming, then refrigerate until cold.

5 Pipe the filling into the profiteroles through the hole in the base, using a piping bag and nozzle. Melt the chocolate and oil gently, stir until smooth and dip the profiterole tops in the chocolate.

299

BAKED CHEESECAKE

Preparation: 30 minutes + refrigeration
Cooking: 55 minutes
Serves 6–8

250 g (8 oz) butternut cookies
1 teaspoon mixed spice
100 g (3½ oz) butter, melted
500 g (8 oz) cream cheese, softened
⅔ cup (160 g/5½ oz) caster sugar
1 teaspoon vanilla essence
1 tablespoon lemon juice
4 eggs

Topping
1 cup (250 g/8 oz) sour cream
½ teaspoon vanilla essence
3 teaspoons lemon juice
1 tablespoon caster sugar
nutmeg, to sprinkle

1 Line the base of a 20 cm (8 inch) round springform tin with foil and brush it with oil. Finely crush the biscuits in a food processor for 30 seconds, or put in a plastic bag and roll with a rolling pin. Transfer to a bowl and add the mixed spice and butter. Stir until the crumbs are all moistened, then spoon the mixture into the tin and press it firmly into the base and side. Refrigerate for 20 minutes, or until firm.
2 Preheat the oven to moderate 180°C (350°F/ Gas 4). Beat the cream cheese until smooth. Add the sugar, vanilla and lemon juice, and beat until smooth. Add the eggs, one at a time, beating well after each addition.
3 Pour the mixture into the tin and bake for 45 minutes, or until just firm to the touch.
4 To make the topping, combine the sour cream, vanilla, lemon juice and sugar in a bowl. Spread over the hot cheesecake, sprinkle with the nutmeg and return to the oven for a further 7 minutes. Cool, then refrigerate until firm.

VARIATION: To make a baked chocolate cheesecake, make the crumb base with butter, plain chocolate biscuits, a pinch of ground cinnamon and ½ teaspoon instant coffee powder. For the filling, mix together 500 g (1 lb) cream cheese, 2 eggs, 125 g (4 oz) sugar, ½ teaspoon vanilla essence, 1 tablespoon cocoa powder, 225 g (7 oz) melted cooking chocolate, 375 g (12 oz) sour cream and 45 g (1½ oz) melted butter. Pour into the crust and

Our BAKED CHEESECAKE has a sour cream topping.

CHEESECAKES made with gelatine do not require cooking. Just leave in the fridge to set.

bake as above. You will not need a separate topping. Chill for 6 hours before serving.

CHEESECAKE

Preparation: 30 minutes + refrigeration
Cooking: 5 minutes
Serves 6–8

250 g (8 oz) plain sweet biscuits
125 g (4 oz) butter, melted
3 teaspoons gelatine
250 g (8 oz) cream cheese

$^1/_3$ cup (80 ml/2 3/4 fl oz) lemon juice
1 teaspoon grated lemon rind
$^1/_2$ cup (125 g/4 oz) caster sugar
1 cup (250 ml/8 fl oz) cream, whipped

1 Lightly grease a 20 cm springform tin with oil or melted butter. Line the base with baking paper. Finely crush the biscuits in a food processor or in a bag with a rolling pin. Mix together with the melted butter. Press into the base and side of the tin and refrigerate for 10 minutes.

2 Sprinkle the gelatine over 2 tablespoons water in a small bowl. Place over a pan or bowl of hot water and leave until spongy. Stir until dissolved. Beat the cream cheese, lemon juice, rind and sugar with electric beaters for 4–5 minutes, or until smooth. Add the cooled gelatine to the bowl and beat well.
3 Using a large metal spoon, fold the whipped cream into the cream cheese mixture. Spoon evenly into the tin, carefully smooth the surface and refrigerate until set.

The furrows in the side of the FRESH FRUIT PAVLOVA stop it crumbling and give a decorative look.

FRESH FRUIT PAVLOVA

Preparation: 15 minutes
Cooking: 40 minutes
Serves 6–8

4 egg whites
1 cup (250 g/8 oz) caster
  sugar
1 1/2 cups (375 ml/
  12 fl oz) cream,
  whipped
1 banana, sliced
125 g (4 oz) raspberries
125 g (4 oz) blueberries

1 Preheat the oven to slow 150°C (300°F/ Gas 2). Line a large baking tray with baking paper and draw a 20 cm (8 inch) circle on the paper. Beat the egg whites with electric beaters in a large dry bowl until soft peaks form — any hint of grease will prevent the egg whites foaming. Gradually add the sugar, beating well after each addition. Beat for 5–10 minutes, or until all the sugar has completely dissolved.

2 Spread the meringue mixture onto the tray inside the circle. Shape the meringue evenly, running the flat side of a flat-bladed knife along the edge and over the top.

3 Run the knife up the edge of the meringue all the way round, making furrows. This strengthens the pavlova, stops the edge crumbling and gives it a decorative finish.

4 Bake for 30 minutes, or until the pavlova is pale and crisp. Reduce the heat to very slow 120°C (250°F/Gas 1/2) and bake for a further 10 minutes. Turn off the oven and leave the pavlova inside to cool, using a wooden spoon to keep the door ajar. Top with the whipped cream and arrange the banana, raspberries and blueberries on top.

STORAGE: Pavlova is best eaten on the day it is made. Serve immediately once the pavlova is topped with the cream and fruit.

GRANDMA'S PAVLOVA

Preparation: 30 minutes
Cooking: 1 hour
Serves 6–8

4 egg whites
pinch of salt
1 cup (250 g/8 oz) sugar
2 teaspoons cornflour
1 teaspoon white vinegar
1 cup (250 ml/8 fl oz)
  cream, whipped
pulp from 3 passionfruit
strawberries, for
  decoration

1 Preheat the oven to very hot 240°C (475°F/ Gas 9) and lightly grease a 32 x 28 cm (13 x 11 inch) baking tray. Line the tray with a very wet piece of brown paper.

2 Place the egg whites and salt in a small, dry mixing bowl. Using electric beaters, beat until stiff peaks form. Add the sugar gradually, beating constantly after each addition. Beat until the mixture is thick and glossy, and all the sugar has dissolved.

3 Using a metal spoon, fold in the cornflour and vinegar. Spoon the mixture into a mound on the tray. Lightly flatten the top of the pavlova and smooth the sides. (This pavlova should have a cake shape and be about 2.5 cm/1 inch high.)

4 Reduce the oven to warm 160°C (315°F/ Gas 2–3). Bake the pavlova for 1 hour, or until it is pale cream and crisp. Remove the pavlova from the oven while it is warm, then carefully turn it upside down onto a plate and peel away the paper. (If the pavlova is cold, the paper will stick. It may crack slightly underneath but this is normal.) Leave the pavlova to cool.

5 Spread the soft centre of the pavlova with whipped cream. Decorate with the passionfruit pulp and some whole strawberries. Cut into wedges to serve.

![Grandma's Pavlova topped with whipped cream, passionfruit pulp and strawberries]

GRANDMA'S PAVLOVA has a more chewy, less brittle meringue.

FRUIT FOOL

Preparation:15 minutes +
  refrigeration
Cooking: Nil
Serves 4

2 red pawpaw or papaya,
  about 1 kg (2 lb)
1–2 tablespoons lime
  juice
3 tablespoons vanilla
  sugar
1 1/4 cups (315 ml/
  10 fl oz) cream

1 Peel and seed the
pawpaw and mash the
flesh until smooth. Do not
do this in a food processor
or it will be too runny.

2 Add the lime juice and
vanilla sugar, to taste—
according to the
sweetness of the fruit.
3 Whisk the cream until
soft peaks form, then fold
through the mashed
pawpaw. Spoon into
serving glasses and chill
until ready to serve.

VARIATIONS: For
rhubarb fool, use 500 g
(1 lb) stewed rhubarb
instead of the pawpaw.
For mango fool, purée
3 large mangoes in a food
processor, process with
1 cup (250 ml/8 fl oz)
custard, then fold in
1 2/3 cups (410 ml/13 fl oz)
whipped cream.

FRUIT FOOL, made using pawpaw and lime juice.

BLACKBERRY JELLY

Preparation: 10 minutes +
  4 hours refrigeration
Cooking: 20 minutes
Serves 6–8

300 g (10 oz) fresh
  blackberries, or thawed
  frozen blackberries
3/4 cup (185 g/6 oz)
  caster sugar
3 tablespoons vodka,
  optional
3 tablespoons gelatine

1 Place the blackberries
(with any juice), caster
sugar, vodka and 1 litre
water in a pan. Stir over
low heat until the sugar
has dissolved. Cover and
bring to the boil, then
reduce the heat and
simmer for 15 minutes.
Uncover and cool for
10 minutes.
2 Place the fruit in a
muslin-lined sieve and
strain into a bowl without
pushing any fruit through.
Put a little of the juice in a
small pan, sprinkle the
gelatine in an even layer
over the surface, leave to
go spongy, then stir over
low heat until dissolved.
Do not boil. Combine
with the remaining juice.
3 Wet a 1.25 litre jelly
mould and pour in the
jelly mixture. Refrigerate
for 4 hours, or until set.

PEACH MELBA

Preparation: 25 minutes
Cooking: 10 minutes
Serves 4

300 g (10 oz) fresh
  raspberries, or thawed
  frozen raspberries
2 tablespoons icing sugar
1 1/2 cups (375 g/12 oz)
  sugar
1 vanilla bean, split
  lengthways
4 firm ripe peaches
vanilla ice cream, to
  serve

1 Put the raspberries and icing sugar in a food processor and purée. Pass through a strainer and discard the seeds. Stir the sugar, vanilla bean and 2 1/2 cups (600 ml/20 fl oz) water in a pan over low heat until the sugar has completely dissolved.
2 Bring the sugar syrup to the boil and add the peaches, ensuring they are covered with the syrup. Simmer for 5 minutes, or until tender, then remove the peaches with a slotted spoon and carefully remove the skin.
3 Put a scoop of ice cream on a plate, add a peach then spoon the raspberry purée over the top.

BLACKBERRY JELLY, with optional vodka for the adults!

PEACH MELBA—named in honour of Dame Nellie Melba.

305

LEMON DELICIOUS

Preparation: 20 minutes
Cooking: 1 hour
Serves 4

60 g (2 oz) butter
3/4 cup (185 g/6 oz)
  caster sugar
3 eggs, separated
1 teaspoon grated lemon
  rind
1/3 cup (40 g/1 1/4 oz)
  self-raising flour, sifted
1/4 cup (60 ml/2 fl oz)
  lemon juice
3/4 cup (185 ml/6 fl oz)
  milk
icing sugar, to dust

1 Preheat the oven to moderate 180°C (350°F/ Gas 4). Brush a 1 litre ovenproof dish with oil. Using electric beaters, beat the butter, sugar, egg yolks and lemon rind in a small bowl until the mixture is light and creamy. Transfer to a larger mixing bowl.
2 Add the flour and stir with a wooden spoon until just combined. Add the lemon juice and milk, and stir in gently.
3 Place the egg whites in a clean, dry bowl. Using electric beaters, beat until firm peaks form. Add to the lemon mixture and gently fold in until just combined, using a metal spoon.
4 Spoon the mixture into the dish. Place the dish in a deep baking tray and pour boiling water into the tray to come a third of the way up the side of the dish. Bake for 1 hour. Sprinkle with the sifted icing sugar. Serve with some of the sauce spooned over the top.

NOTE: It is important to beat egg whites in a clean dry bowl. The slightest hint of grease or moisture will prevent the egg whites foaming. Any yolk in the whites will do likewise.

Sprinkle the LEMON DELICIOUS with icing sugar to serve.

CLAFOUTIS is a classic French batter pudding, and very simple to make.

CHERRY CLAFOUTIS

Preparation: 15 minutes
Cooking: 35 minutes
Serves 6–8

500 g (1 lb) fresh
  cherries, or 800 g
  (1 lb 10 oz) can pitted
  cherries, well drained
1/2 cup (60 g/2 oz) plain
  flour
1/3 cup (90 g/3 oz) sugar
4 eggs, lightly beaten
1 cup (250 ml/8 fl oz)
  milk
25 g (3/4 oz) butter,
  melted
icing sugar, to dust

1 Preheat the oven to moderate 180°C (350°F/ Gas 4). Brush a 23 cm (9 inch) glass or ceramic shallow pie plate with melted butter.
2 Pit the cherries and spread into the dish in a single layer. If using canned cherries, drain them thoroughly in a sieve before spreading in the dish. If they are still wet, they will leak into the batter.
3 Sift the flour into a bowl, add the sugar and make a well in the centre. Gradually add the combined eggs, milk and butter, whisking until smooth and free of lumps.
4 Pour the batter over the cherries and bake for 30–35 minutes. The batter should be risen and golden. Dust with icing sugar. Serve immediately, with cream.

NOTE: A clafoutis (pronounced 'clafootee') is a classic French batter pudding, a speciality of the Limousin region. Clafoutis comes from 'clafir', a dialect verb meaning 'to fill'. It is traditionally made with cherries but you could use blueberries, blackberries, raspberries, or small, well-flavoured strawberries may be used. Use a shallow pie dish or the top will not brown.

RICH CHOCOLATE SELF-SAUCING PUDDING

Preparation: 20 minutes
Cooking: 55 minutes
Serves 6–8

1 1/2 cups (185 g/6 oz)
self-raising flour
1/4 cup (30 g/1 oz) cocoa
powder
3/4 cup (1850 g/6 oz)
caster sugar
90 g (3 oz) butter,
melted
3/4 cup (185 ml/6 fl oz)
milk
2 eggs, lightly beaten

Sauce
1 1/2 cups (375 ml/
12 fl oz) milk
185 g (6 oz) dark
chocolate, chopped

1 Preheat the oven to moderate 180°C (350°F/ Gas 4) and grease a deep 2.25 litre ovenproof dish. Sift the flour and cocoa into a large mixing bowl. Add the sugar and make a well in the centre.
2 Add the butter and combined milk and eggs. Using a wooden spoon, stir until all the ingredients are just combined and the mixture is smooth, but do not overbeat. Pour the mixture into the prepared dish.
3 To make the sauce, put

RICH CHOCOLATE SELF-SAUCING PUDDING.

the milk, chocolate and 1 cup (250 ml/8 fl oz) water in a small pan. Stir over low heat until the chocolate has melted and the mixture is smooth.
4 Pour the sauce gently over the pudding mixture. Bake for 45–50 minutes, or until the pudding is firm to the touch. Serve with cream or ice cream and fresh fruit, if desired.

STORAGE: Self-saucing puddings are best served immediately.

STICKY DATE PUDDING

Preparation: 30 minutes
Cooking: 1 hour 10 minutes
Serves 6–8

2 cups (370 g/12 oz)
chopped pitted dates
1 1/2 teaspoons
bicarbonate of soda
1 teaspoon grated fresh
ginger
90 g (3 oz) butter
1 cup (250 g/8 oz) caster
sugar
3 eggs
1 1/2 cups (185 g/6 oz)
self-raising flour
pinch of ground cloves
1/2 teaspoon mixed spice

Caramel sauce
150 g (5 oz) butter
1 cup (185 g/6 oz) soft
  brown sugar
1/3 cup (115 g/4 oz)
  golden syrup
3/4 cup (185 ml/6 fl oz)
  cream

1 Preheat the oven to moderate 180°C (350°F/ Gas 4). Grease and line the base of a deep 23 cm (9 inch) round cake tin. Put the dates in a pan with 1 3/4 cups (440 ml/ 14 fl oz) water, bring to the boil, then remove from the heat. Add the bicarbonate of soda and ginger, and leave for 5 minutes. Coarsely mash with a potato masher.
2 Cream the butter, sugar and 1 egg. Beat in the remaining eggs one at a time. Fold in the sifted flour and spices, add the date mixture and stir until well combined. Pour into the tin and bake for 1 hour, or until a skewer comes out clean when inserted into the middle of the pudding. Cover with foil if the pudding is overbrowning. Leave to stand for 5 minutes before turning out onto a plate.
3 To make the caramel sauce, put all the ingredients in a pan and stir over low heat until the sugar has dissolved. Simmer for about 3 minutes, or until the

sauce has thickened slightly. Brush some sauce over the top and sides of the pudding until it is well glazed. Serve immediately with the sauce and cream.

VARIATION: For a quick-mix steamed pudding, grease the base and side of a 1 litre pudding basin. Place a round of baking paper in the bottom of the basin. Put the empty basin in a large pan on a trivet or upturned saucer and pour in enough cold water to come halfway up the side of the basin. Remove the basin and put the water on to boil. Sift 150 g (5 oz) self-raising flour into a bowl. Add a

pinch of salt, 120 g (4 oz) softenened butter, 150 g (5 oz) sugar and 3 eggs and beat to combine. For chocolate pudding, add 2 tablespoons cocoa and 90 g (3 oz) choc bits. For treacle pudding, add 2 tablespoons treacle. Pour into the basin. Lay a sheet of foil on a work surface, cover with a sheet of baking paper and make a pleat in the middle. Grease the paper and place over the top of the basin. Tie string around the rim and over the top. Lower the basin into the boiling water and cover tightly. Cook for 1 3/4 hours, topping up the water as necessary.

Serve STICKY DATE PUDDING with cream or crème fraîche.

CREME CARAMEL

Preparation: 25 minutes +
  6 hours refrigeration
Cooking: 35 minutes
Serves 8

1 cup (250 g/8 oz) sugar

Custard
1 litre milk, warmed
1/2 cup (125 g/4 oz)
  sugar
6 eggs
1 1/2 teaspoons vanilla
  essence

1 Preheat the oven to moderate 180°C (350°F/ Gas 4). Grease eight 1/2 cup (125 ml/4 fl oz) ramekins.

2 Put the sugar in a pan with 1/4 cup (60 ml/2 fl oz) water. Stir over low heat until the sugar has dissolved. Bring to the boil, then reduce the heat and simmer until the mixture turns golden brown. To avoid a burnt flavour, remove the pan from the heat just before the caramel reaches the desired colour. It will continue to darken even after cooking has finished. Pour a little hot mixture into each ramekin and swirl to cover the base. Set aside.

3 To make the custard, put the milk and sugar in a pan and stir gently over low heat until the sugar has dissolved. Whisk together the eggs and vanilla for 2 minutes, then stir in the warm milk. Strain the mixture into a jug and pour it into the ramekins.

4 Place the ramekins in a deep baking dish. Pour hot water into the baking dish to come halfway up the sides of the ramekins. Bake for 30 minutes, or until the custard is set and a knife comes out clean when inserted into the centre. Allow to cool, then refrigerate for at least 6 hours. To unmould, run a knife around the edge of each custard and gently upturn onto a serving plate. Shake gently to remove, if necessary. Serve with whipped cream, fresh fruit and wafers, if desired.

STORAGE: Can be kept in the fridge for up to 1 day.
VARIATIONS: The custard for crème caramel can be flavoured with spices such as cardamom, cinnamon and nutmeg, with lemon or orange rind, or with your favourite spirit or liqueur.

Chill CREME CARAMEL for six hours before serving.

CHOCOLATE MOUSSE

Preparation: 20 minutes +
2 hours refrigeration
Cooking: 5 minutes
Serves 4

250 g (8 oz) good-
quality dark chocolate,
chopped
3 eggs
¼ cup (60 g/2 oz) caster
sugar
1 cup (250 ml/8 fl oz)
cream, softly whipped

Use good-quality chocolate for CHOCOLATE MOUSSE.

1 Put the chocolate in a heatproof bowl. Half fill a saucepan with water and bring to a simmer. Remove from the heat and place the bowl over the pan, making sure it is not sitting in the water. Stir occasionally until the chocolate has melted. Set aside to cool.

2 Using electric beaters, beat the eggs and sugar in a small bowl for 5 minutes, or until the mixture is thick, pale and increased in volume.

3 Transfer the mixture to a large bowl. Using a metal spoon, fold in the melted chocolate and then leave the mixture to cool. Fold in the whipped cream until just combined.

4 Spoon into four 250 ml (8 fl oz) ramekins or dessert glasses and refrigerate for 2 hours, or

until set, before serving.

VARIATION: For a rich chocolate mousse without using cream, try this simple variation. It will make enough for six people. Break 175 g (6 oz) dark chocolate into pieces and place it in a heatproof bowl. Bring a small pan of water to a simmer, remove from the heat and place the bowl over the pan (don't let the base of the bowl sit in the water). Stir until the chocolate melts. Separate 5 eggs and put the whites in a large clean glass bowl. Cool the chocolate a little and gently stir in the egg yolks. Whisk the egg whites with a balloon

whisk or electric beaters until they are stiff, add one tablespoon of the egg whites to the chocolate mixture and mix it in well. Add the chocolate mixture to the remaining egg whites and fold the whites into the chocolate, making sure you do not lose too much volume. Divide the mixture among six 150 ml (5 oz) ramekins. Chill in the refrigerator for 4 hours, or until set.

Serve POACHED PEARS with thick cream or mascarpone.

POACHED PEARS

Preparation: 10 minutes
Cooking: 1 hour 10 minutes
Serves 4

4 large beurre bosc or
Josephine pears
1 1/2 cups (375 ml/12 fl
oz) sweet dessert wine
(Sauternes; Muscat)
3/4 cup (185 g/6 oz)
sugar
1 vanilla pod, split
lengthways
1 cinnamon stick

1 Peel the pears, keeping
the stalks attached. Put
1 1/2 cups (375 ml/12 fl oz)
water in a large pan with
the wine, sugar, vanilla
pod and cinnamon. Stir
over medium heat until
the sugar has dissolved.
Bring to the boil and
simmer for 5 minutes.
Stand the pears upright in
the syrup and gently
spoon over a little syrup
to coat them.
2 Cover and simmer
gently for 30–40 minutes,
or until tender. Test if
they are cooked by
piercing with a sharp
knife. Remove from the
pan with a slotted spoon.
3 Remove the vanilla pod
and cinnamon stick. Bring
the syrup to the boil, then
boil rapidly for
15 minutes, or until
reduced by half. Pour over
the pears to serve.

APPLE STRUDEL

Preparation: 20 minutes
Cooking: 25 minutes
Serves 6

30 g (1 oz) butter
4 green cooking apples,
peeled and thinly sliced
2 tablespoons orange
juice
1 tablespoon honey
3 tablespoons sugar
1/2 cup (60 g/2 oz)
sultanas
2 sheets ready-rolled puff
pastry
3 tablespoons ground
almonds
1 egg, lightly beaten
2 tablespoons soft brown
sugar
1 teaspoon ground
cinnamon

1 Preheat the oven to hot
220°C (425°F/Gas 7).
Brush two oven trays with
melted butter. Heat the
butter in a pan and cook
the apples for 2 minutes,
or until lightly golden.
Add the orange juice,
honey, sugar and sultanas
and stir until the sugar
dissolves and the apples
are just tender. Leave to
cool completely.
2 Place a sheet of pastry
on the work surface. Fold
in half and make small
cuts in the folded edge at
2 cm (1 inch) intervals.
Open out and sprinkle
with half the almonds.

APPLE STRUDEL.

BAKED APPLES.

Drain the apples and place half in the centre of the pastry. Brush the edges with egg and fold together, pressing firmly.
3 Place the strudel on the baking tray, seam-side-down. Brush with egg and sprinkle with half the sugar and cinnamon. Repeat with the other sheet and filling. Bake for 20–25 minutes until crisp.

HINT: For quick strudel, spread canned apple along one edge of a sheet of puff pastry. Sprinkle with sugar and sultanas, fold over the pastry to enclose, brush with egg yolk, cut holes in the top and bake for 20 minutes.

BAKED APPLES

Preparation: 20 minutes
Cooking: 40 minutes
Serves 4

4 **Granny Smith apples, peeled and cored**
¹/₄ **cup (55 g/2 oz) raw sugar**
¹/₄ **cup (40 g/1¹/₄ oz) dried figs, chopped**
¹/₄ **cup (45 g/1¹/₂ oz) dried apricots, chopped**
¹/₄ **cup (30 g/1 oz) slivered almonds**
1 **tablespoon apricot jam**
¹/₄ **teaspoon ground cardamom**
¹/₄ **teaspoon ground cinnamon**
30 g **(1 oz) butter**

1 Preheat the oven to moderate 180°C (350°F/ Gas 4). Brush a deep ovenproof dish with melted butter.
2 Gently roll the apples in the sugar. Mix together the figs, apricots, almonds, jam and spices, stuff into the apples and put in the dish. Dot with butter. Bake for 35–40 minutes, or until tender. Serve immediately.

NOTE: This is an excellent quick stand-by dessert for emergencies. You do not even need to peel the apples.

313

ENGLISH TRIFLE

Preparation: 15 minutes +
overnight refrigeration
Cooking: 10 minutes
Serves 6

85 g (3 oz) packet port
wine jelly crystals
2 tablespoons custard
powder
1 tablespoon caster sugar
2 cups (500 ml/16 fl oz)
milk
250 g (8 oz) **Madeira
cake, cut into cubes**
1/3 cup (80 ml/2³/4 fl oz)
sherry
425 g (14 oz) can sliced
peaches in syrup
whipped cream and
toasted flaked almonds

1 Dissolve the jelly in
2 cups (500 ml/16 fl oz)
boiling water. Pour into a
shallow dish and
refrigerate until set. Cut
into bite-sized cubes.
2 Combine the custard
powder and sugar, and
gradually stir in the milk
until smooth. Stir over
medium heat for
5 minutes, or until the
mixture boils and
thickens. Remove from
the heat and cover the
surface with baking paper
to prevent a skin forming.
3 Put the cake cubes in a
1-litre glass bowl. Sprinkle
with the sherry. Drain the
peaches, reserving half the
syrup. Brush the syrup
over the cake. Pour half

the custard over the cake.
Top with the jelly,
peaches and remaining
custard. Top with the
whipped cream and
almonds. Leave in the
fridge overnight.

VARIATION: It is very
easy to vary the base of a
trifle. Instead of the
Madeira cake, try sliced
jam roll, swiss roll or
chocolate cake.
Alternatively, soak
crushed biscuits such as
sponge fingers or
macaroons in sherry or
sweet wine and use
instead of the cake.

Use cubed Madeira cake as the base for your ENGLISH TRIFLE.

LATTICE BERRY PIE

Preparation: 20 minutes +
  20 minutes refrigeration
Cooking: 55 minutes
Serves 6

2 cups (250 g/8 oz) plain
  flour
150 g (5 oz) cold butter,
  cubed
1 egg, lightly beaten
3 tablespoons ground
  almonds
2 tablespoons caster
  sugar
1 teaspoon ground
  cinnamon
1 kg (2 lb) fresh or
  frozen mixed berries
1 egg, lightly beaten,
  extra

You could also use canned peaches or apples in a LATTICE PIE.

1 Place the flour and butter in a bowl and rub in the butter with your fingertips until fine and crumbly. Add the egg and mix with a knife until the dough just comes together, adding a little chilled water if necessary. Turn out onto a lightly floured surface and gather together.

2 Roll out half the dough to line a deep 19 cm (7¹/₂ inch) fluted flan tin. Chill for 20 minutes. Roll out the other portion to a 24 cm (10 inch) circle. Cut into 1.5 cm (⁵/₈ inch) wide strips with a fluted pastry wheel. Lay half the strips 2 cm (1 inch) apart on a sheet of baking paper. Interweave the remaining strips to make a lattice. Slide onto a baking tray, cover with plastic wrap and chill.

3 Preheat the oven to moderate 180°C (350°F/ Gas 3). Line the pastry shell with crumpled baking paper, fill with baking beads or rice and bake for 10 minutes. Remove the paper and beads and bake the pastry for 10 minutes, or until golden. Leave to cool.

4 Mix together the almonds, sugar and cinnamon and sprinkle into the pastry shell. Spread the berries over the top. Brush the edge of the pastry with egg. Using the baking paper to help, invert the lattice over the top of the tart and trim the edge. Press the edge lightly to seal to the cooked pastry. Brush the top with egg and bake for 35 minutes, or until golden.

LEMON MERINGUE PIE

Preparation: 40 minutes
Cooking: 25 minutes
Serves 8

185 g (6 oz) packet
  shortcrust pastry mix

Lemon filling
1 cup (250 g/8 oz) sugar
¹/₂ cup (60 g/2 oz)
  cornflour
2 teaspoons grated lemon
  rind
³/₄ cup (185 ml/6 fl oz)
  lemon juice
60 g (2 oz) butter,
  chopped
3 egg yolks

Meringue
3 egg whites
¹/₂ cup (125 g/4 oz)
  caster sugar

1 Preheat the oven to hot 210°C (415°F/Gas 6–7). Prepare the pastry according to the instructions on the packet (you will probably have to buy a 340 g/11 oz packet of pastry mix and use half of it). Roll the pastry out thinly to cover the base and side of a 23 cm (9 inch) pie plate. Cut a sheet of greaseproof paper large enough to cover the pastry-lined plate. Spread a layer of baking beads or rice over the paper. Bake for 7 minutes, then discard the paper and beads. Bake the pastry for a further 7 minutes, or until lightly golden. Allow to cool.

2 To make the filling, combine the sugar, cornflour and lemon rind in a pan. Blend in the lemon juice and 1¹/₂ cups (375 ml/12 fl oz) water, and stir until smooth. Stir over medium-high heat for 2 minutes, or until the mixture boils and becomes very thick. Add the butter and stir over the heat for 1 minute, or until the butter has melted. Remove from the heat, quickly add the egg yolks and whisk until combined. Place a piece of baking paper over the surface of the filling and leave to cool. Spread evenly into the pastry shell.

3 To make the meringue, put the egg whites in a small dry bowl (any hint of grease in the bowl will prevent the whites foaming). Using electric beaters, beat until soft peaks form. Add the sugar gradually, beating until the mixture is thick and glossy, and the sugar has dissolved. Spread over the filling. Bake for 5 minutes, then cool before serving.

LEMON MERINGUE PIE.

APPLE PIE

Preparation: 35 minutes
Cooking: 1 hour
Serves 6

2 cups (250 g/8 oz) plain
  flour
1/4 cup (30 g/1 oz) icing
  sugar
185 g (6 oz) cold butter,
  cubed
2 egg yolks
milk, for glazing
caster sugar, for
  sprinkling

Filling
4–5 green cooking
  apples, sliced
3/4 cup (160 g/51/2 oz)
  caster sugar
1/2 teaspoon ground
  cinnamon
6 whole cloves
1 tablespoon marmalade
30 g (1 oz) butter

APPLE PIE is delicious hot from the oven, or as cold picnic food.

1 Grease a 23 cm (9 inch) pie dish. Place the flour, icing sugar and butter in a bowl and rub in the butter with your fingertips until fine and crumbly. Add the egg and mix with a knife until the dough just comes together, adding a little chilled water if necessary. Turn out onto a lightly floured surface and gather together into a ball.
2 Divide the dough into two portions, one slightly larger than the other. Roll the larger portion between two sheets of baking paper to fit the pie dish, then trim the edge. Roll the remaining pastry on a sheet of baking paper to fit the top of the dish. Cover both pastries and refrigerate while making the filling.
3 To make the filling, combine the apple, sugar, cinnamon and cloves with 2 tablespoons water in a large pan. Cover and cook over low heat, stirring occasionally, for 20 minutes, or until the apple has just softened. Remove from the heat and pour off any juice. Remove the cloves. Add the marmalade and butter to the pan, mix and cool.

4 Preheat the oven to hot 210°C (415°F/Gas 6–7). Pile the apple into the pastry-lined pie dish. Brush the pie rim with milk or water. Place the pastry lid over the apple and seal the edge with a fork, trimming any excess. Cut shapes from the leftover pastry trimmings and place on top of the pie. Slash a couple of small holes in the pastry to allow steam to escape. Brush the pie with milk and sprinkle with caster sugar. Bake for 10 minutes. Reduce the oven to moderate 180°C (350°F/Gas 4) and bake for 30 minutes, or until golden brown.

317

FARMHOUSE RHUBARB PIE

Preparation: 40 minutes +
refrigeration
Cooking: 50 minutes
Serves 6

1 1/2 cups (185 g/6 oz)
plain flour, sifted
125 g (4 oz) chilled
butter, chopped
2 tablespoons icing sugar
1 egg yolk
1 cup (250 g/8 oz) sugar
6 cups (750 g/1 1/2 lb)
chopped rhubarb
2 cups (220 g/7 oz)
sliced apple
2 teaspoons grated lemon
rind

3 pieces preserved
ginger, sliced
2 teaspoons sugar, extra
sprinkle of cinnamon
icing sugar, to dust

1 Place the flour, butter
and icing sugar in a bowl
and rub in the butter with
your fingertips until fine
and crumbly. Add the egg
yolk and mix with a knife
until the dough just comes
together, adding a little
chilled water if necessary.
2 Turn out onto a lightly
floured surface and gather
together. Wrap in plastic
wrap and refrigerate for
15 minutes if very soft.
Preheat the oven to
moderately hot 190°C

(375°F/Gas 5). Roll the
pastry out to a 35 cm
(14 inch) circle and fit
into a greased 20 cm
(8 inch) pie plate, leaving
the pastry hanging over
the edge. Chill while you
make the filling.
3 Heat the sugar and
1/2 cup (125 ml/4 fl oz)
water in a pan for
5 minutes, or until syrupy.
Add the rhubarb, apple,
lemon rind and ginger,
then cover and simmer for
5 minutes, or until the
rhubarb is cooked but still
holds its shape.
4 Drain off the liquid and
cool the rhubarb. Spoon
into the pastry base and
sprinkle with the extra
sugar and the cinnamon.
Fold the overhanging
pastry roughly over the
fruit and bake for
40 minutes, or until
golden. Dust with icing
sugar to serve. Delicious
with ice cream or custard.

SUMMER BERRY FLAN

Preparation: 35 minutes +
20 minutes refrigeration
Cooking: 35 minutes
Serves 4–6

1 cup (125 g/4 oz) plain
flour
90 g (3 oz) butter
2 tablespoons icing sugar

FARMHOUSE RHUBARB PIE is a simple, freeform pastry pie.

We used strawberries, blueberries and raspberries for our SUMMER BERRY FLAN.

Filling

3 egg yolks
2 tablespoons caster
  sugar
2 tablespoons cornflour
1 cup (250 ml/8 fl oz)
  milk
1 teaspoon vanilla
  essence
250 g (8 oz)
  strawberries, halved
125 g (4 oz) blueberries
125 g (4 oz) raspberries
1–2 tablespoons baby
  apple gel

1 Preheat the oven to moderate 180°C (350°F/ Gas 4). Place the flour, butter and icing sugar in a bowl and rub in the butter with your fingertips until fine and crumbly. Add 1–2 tablespoons chilled water and mix with a knife until the dough just comes together. Turn out onto a lightly floured surface and gather together.

2 Roll the pastry out to fit a 20 cm (8 inch) fluted flan tin. Trim and refrigerate for 20 minutes. Cover with crumpled greaseproof paper. Spread a layer of baking beads or rice evenly over the paper. Bake for 15 minutes, then discard the paper and beads. Bake for another 15 minutes, or until the pastry is lightly golden.

3 To make the filling, put the egg yolks, sugar and cornflour in a bowl, and whisk until pale. Heat the milk in a small pan until it is almost boiling, then remove from the heat. Add to the egg mixture gradually, beating constantly. Strain into a pan. Stir over low heat for 3 minutes, or until it boils and thickens. Add the vanilla, transfer to a bowl and cover the surface with plastic wrap. Cool.

4 Spread the filling into the cooled pastry shell. Top with the strawberries, blueberries and raspberries. Heat the apple gel in a pan of simmering water, or in the microwave, until it liquefies and brush over the fruit to glaze.

319

PECAN PIE

Preparation: 30 minutes +
20 minutes refrigeration
Cooking: 1¼ hours
Serves 6

1½ cups (185 g/6 oz)
plain flour
125 g (4 oz) butter,
chopped
2–3 tablespoons iced
water

Filling
2 cups (200 g/6½ oz)
pecans
3 eggs, lightly beaten
50 g (1¾ oz) butter,
melted and cooled
⅔ cup (125 g/4 oz)
brown sugar
⅔ cup (170 ml/5½ fl
oz) light corn syrup
1 teaspoon vanilla
essence
pinch of salt

Bourbon cream
1 cup (250 ml/8 fl oz)
cream
1 tablespoon icing sugar
2 tablespoons Bourbon

1 Preheat the oven to
moderate 180°C (350°F/
Gas 4). Place the flour and
butter in a bowl and rub
in the butter with your
fingertips until fine and
crumbly. Add the iced
water and mix with a knife
until the dough just comes
together. Turn out onto
a lightly floured surface
and gather together.
2 Roll out the pastry to fit
a 23 cm (9 inch) flan tin.
Trim the edge and
refrigerate for 20 minutes.
Pile the pastry trimmings
together and roll out on a
sheet of baking paper to a
rectangle about 2 mm
(⅛ inch) thick.
Refrigerate until needed.
3 Cut a sheet of
greaseproof paper large
enough to cover the
pastry-lined tin. Crumple
the paper, lay over the
pastry base and spread
with a layer of baking
beads or uncooked rice.
Bake for 15 minutes.
Discard the paper and
baking beads and bake the
pastry base for another
15 minutes, or until
lightly golden. Allow to
cool completely.
4 To make the filling,
spread the pecans over the
pastry base. In a large jug,
whisk together the eggs,
butter, brown sugar, corn
syrup, vanilla and salt
until well combined. Pour
the mixture over the nuts.
5 Using a fluted pastry
wheel or small sharp
knife, cut narrow strips
from half the pastry. Cut
out small stars with a
biscuit cutter from the
remaining pastry. Place
over the filling. Bake for
45 minutes, or until firm.
Cool completely and
serve at room
temperature.

PECAN PIE is a traditional American favourite.

6 To make the bourbon cream, put the cream and icing sugar in a small bowl. Using electric beaters, whip until soft peaks form. Add the Bourbon and fold through with a metal spoon until it is just combined with the cream. Serve with the Pecan pie.

STORAGE: The pie can be kept refrigerated for up to a day.
NOTE: The pecan is native to North America and is much used in the cooking of the American South.

TIRAMISU means 'pick-me-up' in Italian.

TIRAMISU

Preparation: 30 minutes +
    2 hours refrigeration
Cooking: Nil
Serves 6–8

3 cups (750 ml/24 fl oz)
    strong black coffee,
    cooled
3 tablespoons dark rum
2 eggs, separated
1/4 cup (60 g/2 oz) caster
    sugar
250 g (8 oz) mascarpone
1 cup (250 ml/8 fl oz)
    cream, whipped
16 large savoyardi
    (sponge finger) biscuits
2 teaspoons dark cocoa
    powder

1 Put the coffee and rum in a bowl. Using electric beaters, beat the egg yolks and sugar in a small bowl for 3 minutes, or until thick and pale. Add the mascarpone and beat until just combined. Fold in the whipped cream with a metal spoon.
2 Beat the egg whites until soft peaks form. Fold quickly and lightly into the cream mixture with a metal spoon, trying not to lose the volume.
3 Dip half the biscuits, one at a time, into the coffee mixture (don't leave them to soak or they will become soggy and break up). Drain off any excess liquid and arrange the biscuits in the base of a deep serving dish. Spread half the mascarpone cream mixture over the biscuits.
4 Dip the remaining biscuits in the coffee mixture and repeat the layers. Smooth the surface and dust liberally with cocoa powder. Refrigerate for at least 2 hours (and up to a day) to let the flavours develop.

CREPES SUZETTE is a traditional French dessert.

CREPES SUZETTE

Preparation: 30 minutes +
   30 minutes resting
Cooking: 30–40 minutes
Serves 4

1 cup (125 g/4 oz) plain
   flour
1 cup (250 ml/8 fl oz)
   milk
1 egg
30 g (1 oz) butter,
   melted

Orange butter
200 g (6¹/2 oz) softened
   butter
2 tablespoons finely
   grated orange rind
¹/3 cup (90 g/3 oz) sugar
2 tablespoons icing sugar
¹/2 cup (125 ml/4 fl oz)
   orange juice
¹/4 cup (60 ml/2 fl oz)
   Grand Marnier

1 Sift the flour into a
bowl and make a well in
the centre. Mix together
the milk, egg and butter
and pour into the well in
the flour. Whisk together
until the batter is smooth
and free of lumps. Pour
into a jug, cover and leave
for at least 30 minutes.
2 To make the orange
butter, beat the butter
with electric beaters or a
wooden spoon until

creamy. Add the rind,
sugar and icing sugar, and
beat well. Add the
combined orange juice
and Grand Marnier,
¹/2 teaspoon at a time,
beating well after
each addition.
3 Heat a small crepe pan
and lightly grease with
melted butter. Pour in just
enough batter, swirling, to
thinly cover the base of
the pan. Cook for about
20 seconds, or until the
edges just begin to curl.
Turn the crepe over and
lightly brown the other
side. Cook the rest of the
crepes, greasing the pan
when necessary.
4 Place the orange butter
in a large frying pan and
heat until foaming.
Working quickly with
tongs, dip the crepes, one
at a time, into the pan,
then fold into quarters.
Serve with ice cream.

NOTE: For traditional
Crêpes Suzette, dip each
crepe in the orange butter
and fold in the pan, then
push to one side,
continuing until all crepes
are folded in the pan.
Pour over a little liqueur
and flambé with a match.
VARIATION: This is a
basic crepe batter. The
crepes can be used for
other recipes or simply
served with lemon and
icing sugar.

SUMMER PUDDING

Preparation: 30 minutes +
overnight refrigeration
Cooking: 5 minutes
Serves 4–6

200 g (6½ oz)
strawberries, hulled and
quartered or halved
150 g (5 oz)
blackcurrants
150 g (5 oz) redcurrants
150 g (5 oz) raspberries
150 g (5 oz) blackberries
caster sugar, to taste
6–8 slices good-quality
white bread
fresh berries and cream,
to serve

SUMMER PUDDING can also be made as individual puddings.

1 Put all the berries except the strawberries in a large pan with ½ cup (125 ml/4 fl oz) water and heat gently until the berries begin to collapse. Add the strawberries and turn off the heat. Add sugar, to taste (how much you need will depend on how ripe the fruit is and how sweet your tooth). Set aside to cool.
2 Line a 1-litre pudding basin or six 150 ml (5 fl oz) moulds with the bread. For the large basin, cut a large circle out of one slice for the bottom and cut the rest of the bread into fingers. For the small moulds, use 1 slice of bread for each, cutting a circle to fit the bottom and strips to fit the sides. Drain a little of the juice off the fruit mixture. Dip one side of each piece of bread in the juice before fitting it, juice-side-down, into the mould, leaving no gaps. Do not squeeze it or flatten it or it will not absorb the juices as well.
3 Fill the centre of the mould with the fruit and add a little juice— keep any fruit mixture which won't fit, for serving with the pudding. Cover the top with a layer of dipped bread, juice-side-up, and cover with plastic wrap. Place a plate which fits inside the dish onto the plastic wrap, then weigh it down so that it presses on the pudding. Refrigerate overnight. Carefully turn out the pudding and serve with any extra fruit filling, or berries and cream.

323

BAKED RICE CUSTARD

Preparation: 20 minutes
Cooking: 1 hour
Serves 4

¹/₄ cup (55 g/2 oz)
  short-grain rice
2 eggs
¹/₄ cup (60 g/2 oz) caster
  sugar
1 ¹/₂ cups (375 ml/
  12 fl oz) milk
¹/₂ cup (125 ml/4 fl oz)
  cream
1–2 teaspoons grated
  lemon rind
1 teaspoon vanilla
  essence
¹/₄ cup (30 g/1 oz)
  sultanas or currants
¹/₄ teaspoon ground
  nutmeg or cinnamon

1 Preheat the oven to
warm 160°C (315°F/
Gas 2–3). Grease a deep
20 cm (8 inch) round
ovenproof dish
(1.5 litre capacity).
2 Cook the rice in a pan
of boiling water until it is
just tender, then drain.
3 Whisk the eggs, sugar,
milk, cream, rind and
vanilla essence for about
2 minutes. Fold in the
cooked rice and sultanas
or currants. Pour the
mixture into the dish
and sprinkle with nutmeg
or cinnamon.
4 Put the ovenproof dish
in a deep baking tray.

Pour enough water into
the tray to come halfway
up the side of the dish.
Bake for 50 minutes, or
until the custard is set and
a knife comes out clean
when inserted into the
centre. Remove from the
baking tray immediately,
but leave for 5 minutes
before serving. Serve with
cream or stewed fruits.

CLASSIC BAKED EGG CUSTARD

Preparation: 5 minutes
Cooking: 30 minutes
Serves 4–6

3 eggs, lightly beaten
¹/₃ cup (90 g/3 oz) caster
  sugar
2 cups (500 ml/16 fl oz)
  milk
1 teaspoon vanilla
  essence
¹/₄ teaspoon ground
  nutmeg

1 Preheat the oven to
moderate 180°C (350°F/
Gas 4). Grease a deep
1 litre ovenproof dish.
2 Whisk the eggs, sugar,
milk and vanilla essence
for 2 minutes. Strain into
the dish and sprinkle with
the nutmeg.
3 Place the dish in a
baking tray and pour
enough hot water into the
baking tray to come
halfway up the side of the

dish. Bake for 30 minutes,
or until the custard is set
and a knife comes out
clean when inserted into
the centre.

CREAMED RICE

Preparation: 15 minutes
Cooking: 1 hour 10 minutes
Serves 4–6

90 g (3 oz) short-grain
  rice
1 litre milk
¹/₂ cup (125 g/4 oz)
  caster sugar
1 teaspoon vanilla
  essence

1 Rinse the rice in a
colander until the water
runs clear. Drain well.
2 Place the milk in a pan,
add the sugar and vanilla
and heat until it is about
to boil.
3 Add the rice and stir for
1 minute, or until the
mixture returns to the
boil. Reduce the heat and
simmer for 1 hour, or until
the rice is tender.

VARIATION: Add
2 tablespoons of sultanas
or 2 teaspoons grated
orange rind with the rice.

*From the top: CLASSIC
BAKED EGG CUSTARD;
CREAMED RICE; BAKED
RICE CUSTARD*

ICE CREAM

Preparation: 30 minutes +
  chilling and freezing
Cooking: 15 minutes
Serves 4

1 cup (250 ml/8 fl oz)
  milk
1 cup (250 ml/8 fl oz)
  cream
1 vanilla pod, split
  lengthways
6 egg yolks
¹/₂ cup (125 g/4 oz)
  caster sugar

1 Combine the milk and cream in a pan and add the vanilla pod. Bring to the boil, then remove from the heat and set aside for 10 minutes.

2 Using a wire whisk, beat the yolks and sugar together in a bowl for 2–3 minutes, until thick, creamy and pale, then whisk in the warm milk. Scrape the seeds from the vanilla pod into the mixture. Discard the pod.

3 Wash the pan, and pour the mixture into it. Stir over very low heat until thickened. This will take about 5–10 minutes. To test, run a finger across the back of the wooden spoon—if it leaves a clear line, the custard is ready.

4 Pour the custard into a bowl and cool to room temperature, stirring frequently to hasten the cooling process.

5 Pour into a shallow metal container, cover the surface of the custard with plastic wrap or baking paper and freeze for about 2 hours, or until almost frozen. Scoop into a chilled bowl and beat with electric beaters until smooth, then return to the tray and freeze again. Repeat this step twice more before transferring to a storage container. Cover the surface with baking paper or plastic wrap to stop ice crystals forming on the surface, then a lid.

6 To serve, transfer the ice cream to the refrigerator for about 30 minutes to soften slightly. Ice cream will keep, well sealed, in the freezer for up to 1 month.

VARIATIONS: To make strawberry ice cream, chop 250 g (8 oz) strawberries in a food processor just until smooth. Stir into the custard mixture after the

VANILLA ICE CREAM (top) and CHOCOLATE ICE CREAM.

first freezing and beating, then continue the recipe as directed.

To make banana ice cream, thoroughly mash 3 ripe bananas (or for a finer texture, purée in a food processor). Stir into the custard mixture when it has first been frozen and beaten, along with 1 tablespoon lemon juice. Continue as directed. This will serve 6.

To make chocolate ice cream, make the custard using 2 cups (500 ml/ 16 fl oz) milk, 1 cup (250 ml/8 fl oz) cream and a split vanilla pod. Whisk 8 egg yolks with the sugar and then stir in 2 tablespoons sifted cocoa powder. Gently whisk the hot milk into the egg yolk mixture and make the custard as before. Meanwhile, chill a deep 20 cm (8 inch) square cake tin in the freezer. Add 250 g (8 oz) warm melted chocolate to the warm custard and stir constantly until the chocolate has mixed through. Allow to cool, then pour into the chilled cake tin and freeze and beat as for vanilla ice cream.

PASSIONFRUIT AND ORANGE SORBET.

PASSIONFRUIT AND ORANGE SORBET

Preparation: 15 minutes + churning and freezing
Cooking: Nil
Serves 4

3 cups (750 ml/24 fl oz) orange juice
³/4 cup (185 g/6 oz) passionfruit pulp
¹/2 cup (125 g/4 oz) caster sugar
2 egg whites, lightly beaten

1 Combine the orange juice, passionfruit pulp and sugar in a large bowl. Pour into a metal tray and freeze until just firm around the edges. Do not allow to become too firm.
2 Transfer to a bowl or food processor and beat with electric beaters or process. Refreeze. Repeat this step twice more, adding the egg white the final time, with the beaters or motor running. Return to the tray, cover with greaseproof paper and freeze for 3 hours, or until firm.
3 Alternatively, pour the mixture into an ice cream machine and churn for about 30 minutes.

RHUBARB CRUMBLE

Preparation: 15 minutes
Cooking: 40 minutes
Serves 4–6

1 kg (2 lb) rhubarb
²/₃ cup (160 g/5¹/₂ oz)
  sugar
1 cup (125 g/4 oz) plain
  flour
¹/₂ cup (95 g/3 oz) soft
  brown sugar
³/₄ teaspoon ground
  cinnamon
100 g (3¹/₂ oz) butter

1 Preheat the oven to moderately hot 200°C (400°F/Gas 6). Trim the rhubarb, cut into short lengths and put in a pan with the sugar. Stir over low heat until the sugar has dissolved, then cover and simmer for 10 minutes, or until the rhubarb is soft but still chunky. Spoon into a deep, round ovenproof dish.

2 Put the flour, brown sugar and cinnamon in a bowl, add the butter and rub in with just your fingertips until the mixture resembles coarse breadcrumbs.

3 Sprinkle the crumble over the stewed rhubarb and bake for 25 minutes, or until the topping is golden brown.

RHUBARB CRUMBLE (top) and APPLE BETTY.

VARIATION: For an apple crumble, peel and core 8 green cooking apples and cut each one into 8 wedges. Place in a pan with 3 tablespoons water, bring to the boil, then reduce the heat to low and cover. Cook for about 15 minutes, or until the apples are just soft. Remove from the heat, drain and then stir in 2 tablespoons caster sugar. Spoon into a dish and make the crumble topping as above.

APPLE BETTY

Preparation: 15 minutes
Cooking: 45 minutes
Serves 4–6

5 cooking apples, peeled,
  cored and chopped
100 g (3¹/₂ oz) butter
¹/₂ cup (95 g/3 oz) soft
  brown sugar,
  plus 1 tablespoon
grated rind of 1 lemon
¹/₄ teaspoon ground
  cinnamon
pinch of ground
  nutmeg
3 cups (240 g/7¹/₂ oz)
  fresh breadcrumbs

1 Cook the apples with 1 tablespoon of the butter, 1 tablespoon sugar and the rind, cinnamon and nutmeg, for 15 minutes, until the apples are soft enough to beat to a purée.
2 Preheat the oven to moderate 180°C (350°F/ Gas 4). Melt the remaining butter in a frying pan over low heat and add the breadcrumbs and the remaining brown sugar. Toss until all the crumbs are coated and then fry, tossing, until golden brown.
3 Spread one-third of the crumbs in a 1 litre ovenproof dish and layer with half the apple purée. Repeat with layers, then finish with the final portion of crumbs. Bake for 20 minutes, or until crisp and golden brown.

PLUM COBBLER has a scone dough topping.

PLUM COBBLER

Preparation: 15 minutes
Cooking: 45 minutes
Serves 6–8

750 g (1 1/2 lb) fresh blood plums, quartered
1/4 cup (60 g/2 oz) caster sugar

Topping
1 cup (125 g/4 oz) self-raising flour
1/2 cup (60 g/2 oz) plain flour
1/4 cup (60 g/2 oz) caster sugar
125 g (4 oz) butter, chopped
1 egg
1/2 cup (125 ml/4 fl oz) milk
icing sugar, to dust

1 Preheat the oven to moderate 180°C (350°F/ Gas 4). Lightly grease a 2 litre ovenproof dish.
2 Put the plums in a pan with the sugar and 1 tablespoon water. Stir over low heat for 5 minutes, or until the sugar dissolves and the fruit softens slightly. Spread into the ovenproof dish.
3 To make the topping, sift the flours into a bowl, add the sugar and stir to combine. Add the butter. Using your fingertips, rub in the butter until the mixture resembles fine breadcrumbs. Combine the egg and milk, whisk until smooth, then stir into the dough mixture.
4 Place large spoonfuls of the dough on top of the layer of plums. Bake for 30–40 minutes, or until the cobbler topping is golden and cooked through. Dust with icing sugar and serve immediately.

GOLDEN SYRUP DUMPLINGS

Preparation: 15 minutes
Cooking: 30 minutes
Serves 4

1 cup (125 g/4 oz) self-
raising flour
40 g (1 1/4 oz) butter,
chopped
1 egg
1 tablespoon milk

Syrup
1 cup (250 g/8 oz) sugar
40 g (1 1/4 oz) butter
2 tablespoons golden
syrup
1/4 cup (60 ml/2 fl oz)
lemon juice

1 Sift the flour and a pinch of salt into a bowl. Using your fingertips, rub in the butter until the mixture is fine and crumbly, and make a well in the centre. Using a flat-bladed knife, stir the combined egg and milk into the flour mixture to form a soft dough.
2 To make the syrup, put 2 cups (500 ml/16 fl oz) water in a large pan with the sugar, butter, golden syrup and lemon juice. Stir over medium heat until combined and the sugar has dissolved.
3 Bring to the boil, then gently drop dessertspoons of the dough into the syrup. Cover and reduce the heat to a simmer. Cook for 20 minutes, or until a knife inserted into a dumpling comes out clean. Spoon onto serving plates and drizzle with some of the syrup. Serve the dumplings immediately with whipped cream.

HOT PASSIONFRUIT SOUFFLE

Preparation: 15 minutes
Cooking: 25 minutes
Serves 4–6

2 egg yolks
1/2 cup (125 g/4 oz)
passionfruit pulp (about
6 passionfruit)
2 tablespoons lemon
juice
3/4 cup (90 g/3 oz) icing
sugar
6 egg whites
icing sugar, to dust

1 Preheat the oven to hot 210°C (415°F/Gas 6–7). Lightly grease four 1-cup (250 ml/8 fl oz) ramekins or 1 large soufflé dish. Sprinkle the base and side with caster sugar. Place a collar of baking paper around the dishes, secure with string and lightly grease the paper.
2 Combine the egg yolks, passionfruit pulp, lemon

GOLDEN SYRUP DUMPLINGS.

Bake HOT PASSIONFRUIT SOUFFLE with a collar around the dish, then remove before serving.

juice and half the icing sugar in a large bowl and whisk well.

3 Using electric beaters, beat the egg whites in a large bowl until soft peaks form. Gradually add the remaining icing sugar, beating well after each addition.

4 Using a large metal spoon, fold the egg white mixture through the passionfruit mixture in batches. Spoon into the dishes. Using a flat-bladed knife, cut through the mixture in a circular motion 2 cm (1 inch) from the edge. Place the dishes on a large oven tray and bake for 20–25 minutes, or until the soufflés are well risen and cooked through. Cut the collars from the dishes and serve the soufflés immediately, sprinkled with sifted icing sugar.

VARIATION: To make Chilled berry soufflés, prepare six 125 ml (4 fl oz) soufflé dishes by wrapping a double strip of baking paper around the outside of each, extending 2 cm (³/4 inch) above the rim, then tying with string. Brush the collar and dish with oil or butter, sprinkle with sugar, shake to coat evenly, then tip out any excess. Place 3 tablespoons water in a small heatproof bowl. Sprinkle with 3 teaspoons gelatine and leave to go spongy. Bring a large pan with 4 cm (2 inches) water to the boil, remove from the heat and carefully lower the gelatine bowl into the water. Stir until dissolved; cool slightly. Purée 150 g (5 oz) raspberries and push through a sieve. Mash another 150 g (5 oz) and mix both lots together. Fold in the cooled gelatine mixture. Beat 1¹/4 cups (315 ml/ 10 fl oz) cream into soft peaks. In a separate bowl, beat 4 egg whites into stiff peaks, then gradually beat in 2 tablespoons of sugar until dissolved. Fold the cream into the raspberries, followed by the egg white. Spoon into the dishes and chill for several hours, until set. Remove the collars to serve.

CHRISTMAS PUDDING

Preparation: 40 minutes +
2 nights standing
Cooking: 7 hours 20 minutes
Serves 10–12

500 g (1 lb) mixed
sultanas, currants and
raisins
300 g (10 oz) mixed
dried fruit, chopped
50 g (1³/4 oz) mixed peel
¹/2 cup (125 ml/4 fl oz)
brown ale
2 tablespoons rum or
brandy
juice and rind 1 orange
juice and rind 1 lemon
225 g (7 oz) suet, grated
1¹/3 cups (250 g/8 oz)
soft brown sugar
3 eggs, lightly beaten
2¹/2 cups (200 g/6¹/2 oz)
fresh white
breadcrumbs
³/4 cup (90 g/3 oz) self-
raising flour
1 teaspoon mixed spice
¹/4 teaspoon freshly
grated nutmeg
60 g (2 oz) blanched
almonds, chopped

1 Put the dried fruit,
mixed peel, ale, rum,
orange and lemon juice
and rind into a large bowl,
cover and leave overnight.
2 Mix the fruit mixture,
suet, sugar, eggs,
breadcrumbs, flour, spices,
almonds and good pinch
of salt in a large bowl.

Leave for 10 minutes so
the breadcrumbs absorb
any extra liquid and the
mixture thickens.
3 Cut an 80 cm (32 inch)
square from a clean piece
of calico or an old tea
towel and boil it for
20 minutes. Remove,
wring out (wearing rubber
gloves to prevent
scalding) and spread on a
clean work surface. Dust
the calico with a thick,
layer of sifted plain flour,
leaving a border around
the edge. Spread the flour
out with your hands—it is
important that you get an
even covering as the flour
forms a seal to prevent the
pudding absorbing any
water. Place the pudding
mixture in the centre of
the calico and bring the
points of the material
together. (Drape the
calico over a bowl if you
find it easier.) Gather in
all the excess, trying to
make the folds neat and
even (they will leave an
imprint on the finished
pudding). Tie the top as
tightly as possible with a
piece of unwaxed string—
there must be no gap
between the calico to let
water in. Tie a loop into
the end of one of the
pieces of string—this will
act as a handle for getting
the pudding in and out of
the water.
4 Hook a wooden spoon
handle through the loop

of string and lower the
pudding into a large pan
of boiling water with a
trivet at the bottom—the
pan should be large
enough for the pudding to
move around. Cover the
pan and boil for 5 hours.
If the water level drops,
add a little more boiling
water around the edge of
the pudding. The pudding
should not rest on the
base of the pan. Remove
from the water and hang
in a well-ventilated, dry
place where it will not
touch anything else. Make
sure the calico ends all
hang to one side so they
do not drip all over the
pudding. Leave overnight.
5 Untie the cloth and, if
there are still damp
patches, spread it out to
make sure the calico dries
,all over. When ,dry, re-
wrap and tie with a new
piece of unwaxed string
and store hanging in a
cool, dry place for up to
4 months. When you wish
to serve, boil for 2 hours,
hang for 15 minutes, then
remove it from its cloth.

VARIATION: The mixture
can also be put into a
greased pudding basin,
covered with a layer of
greaseproof paper and foil
and steamed in a pan of
water for 8 hours. For
instructions on preparing
the basin and steaming,
see page 309.

CREME BRULÉE

Preparation: 15 minutes +
3 hours refrigeration
Cooking: 15 minutes
Serves 6

1 1/4 cups (315 ml/10 fl
oz) cream
1 1/4 cups (315 ml/10 fl
oz) thick cream
1 vanilla pod
5 egg yolks
2 tablespoons caster
sugar
1/4 cup (60 ml/2 fl oz)
caster sugar, extra

1 Place the cream and
thick cream in a pan and
stir to combine. Split the
vanilla pod lengthways
and add it to the pan.
Bring slowly to the boil
over low heat. Beat the
egg yolks and sugar with a
wire whisk for 1 minute,
or until pale and
thickened slightly.
2 Pour the just-boiled
cream into the yolk
mixture, whisking
continuously, then discard
the vanilla bean. Return to
the pan and place over
low heat. Cook, stirring,
for 5 minutes, or until the
custard thickens—do not
allow it to boil. Pour into
six 3/4-cup (185 ml/6 fl oz)
ramekins. Cool slightly,
then refrigerate for at least
3 hours, or until the
custard has set.
3 Preheat the grill until
very hot. Sprinkle the
extra caster sugar evenly
onto the surface of each
custard, then grill under
high heat for 3 minutes,
or until the sugar on top
has dissolved and
caramelized. Cool
completely before serving.
(Do not put them in the
fridge or the sugar will
soften.)

STORAGE: Crème
brûlées can be kept in the
fridge for up to a day
without the toffee
topping. Serve them
within 30 minutes of
caramelizing the sugar. It
is important that the
brûlées are not
refrigerated after this step.
HINT: Restaurants use an
extremely hot commercial
grill called a salamander,
or a special brûlée iron
(something like a
branding iron), to achieve
a hard toffee topping on
this dessert. It is difficult
to recreate this at home.
However, good results can
be had by melting the
sugar with a small butane
blowtorch, available from
hardware stores. Follow
the manufacturer's
directions for use and be
extremely careful if you
decide to try this.

CREME BRULEE.

Use all sorts of leftover bread to make BREAD AND BUTTER PUDDING.

BREAD AND BUTTER PUDDING

Preparation: 20 minutes +
1 ½ hours soaking
Cooking: 40 minutes
Serves 4

60 g (2 oz) mixed raisins
and sultanas
2 tablespoons orange
juice or brandy
30 g (1 oz) butter
4 slices good-quality
white bread or brioche
loaf
3 eggs
3 tablespoons caster
sugar
3 cups (750 ml/24 fl oz)
milk
3 tablespoons cream
¼ teaspoon vanilla
extract

¼ teaspoon ground
cinnamon
1 tablespoon demerara
sugar

1 Soak the raisins and
sultanas in the orange
juice or brandy for
30 minutes. Butter the
slices of bread or brioche
(remove the crusts or
leave them on, whichever
you prefer) and cut each
piece into 8 triangles.
Arrange the bread in a
1 litre ovenproof dish.
2 Combine the eggs with
the sugar, add the milk,
cream, vanilla and
cinnamon and mix well.
Drain the raisins and
sultanas and add any
liquid to the custard.
3 Scatter the soaked
raisins and sultanas over
the bread and pour the

custard over the top.
Cover with plastic wrap
and refrigerate for 1 hour.
4 Preheat the oven to
moderate 180°C (350°F/
Gas 4). Sprinkle the
pudding with the
demerara sugar and then
bake for 35–40 minutes,
or until the custard has set
and the top of the
pudding is crunchy
and golden.

NOTE: Use good-quality
bread. Ordinary sliced
white will tend to become
soggy when it soaks up
the milk.
VARIATION: You can use
all sorts of bread or cake
leftovers. Try Danish
pastries, croissant and any
fruit loaves or buns.

335

SWEET TREATS

For a children's party or a rainy afternoon when it's fun to be in the kitchen, fudge or rocky road are ideal treats. All our sweet treats are easy to make, with a little parental guidance, and perfect for wrapping up in cellophane and pretty boxes and giving away as Christmas presents.

VANILLA FUDGE

Preparation: 10 minutes + cooling
Cooking: 25 minutes
Makes 12 pieces

2 cups (500 g/1 lb)
  caster sugar
1 cup (250 ml/8 fl oz)
  cream
1 teaspoon vanilla
  essence

1 Lightly grease a 21 x 11 cm (9 x 5 inch) loaf tin with melted butter or oil. Line the base with baking paper, extending over two sides. Place the caster sugar, cream and a pinch of salt in a heavy-based pan. Stir over low heat, without boiling, until all the sugar has dissolved. Increase the heat slightly, until the mixture is just simmering. Cover and cook for 3 minutes.

2 Remove the lid and clean the sugar from the side of the pan with a wet pastry brush. Do not stir the mixture. Continue to boil the fudge for about 10 minutes, or until it reaches 115°C (240°F) on a sugar thermometer. If you don't have a thermometer, drop a little of the mixture into a glass of cold water. It should form a 'soft ball' when squeezed between your thumb and forefinger.

3 Remove from the heat, cool slightly and stir in the vanilla essence. Beat with electric beaters for 1–2 minutes, or until the mixture loses its gloss and begins to thicken. Quickly pour into the tin and smooth the surface. Cover and leave to set. Cut into small squares, or shapes. Shown here dusted with cocoa powder. Refrigerate for up to 1 week.

CHOCOLATE FUDGE

Preparation: 15 minutes + cooling
Cooking: 20 minutes
Makes 12 pieces

2¹/₂ cups (310 g/10 oz)
  pure icing sugar
¹/₂ cup (125 ml/4 fl oz)
  milk
30 g (1 oz) butter
2 tablespoons cocoa
  powder, sifted
1 teaspoon vanilla
  essence

1 Lightly grease a 21 x 11 cm (9 x 5 inch) loaf tin. Line the base with baking paper, extending over two sides. Place the icing sugar, milk, butter and cocoa in a heavy-based pan. Stir over low heat without boiling until the mixture is smooth and the sugar has

Cut VANILLA and CHOCOLATE FUDGE into pieces, or into shapes with a biscuit cutter.

dissolved. Brush the mixture from the sides of the pan with a wet pastry brush.

2 Bring the mixture to the boil. Boil, without stirring, for 8 minutes, or until it reaches 115°C (240°F) on a sugar thermometer. If you don't have a thermometer, drop a little of the mixture into a glass of cold water. It should form a 'soft ball' when squeezed between your thumb and forefinger.

Leave to cool slightly, add the vanilla and beat with electric beaters until the mixture starts to thicken and loses its gloss. Pour into the tin, cover and leave to set. Cut into pieces when set.

337

Instead of RUM BALLS, you can flavour with brandy or whisky.

RUM BALLS

Preparation: 20 minutes
 + 50 minutes refrigeration
Cooking: 5 minutes
Makes about 25

200 g (6¹/2 oz) **dark
 cooking chocolate,
 finely chopped**
¹/4 cup (60 ml/2 fl oz)
 cream
30 g (1 oz) **butter**
50 g (1³/4 oz) **chocolate
 cake crumbs**
2 teaspoons **dark rum**
¹/2 cup (90 g/3 oz)
 chocolate sprinkles

1 Line a baking tray with
foil. Place the chocolate
in a bowl. Combine the
cream and butter in a
small pan and stir over
low heat until the butter
melts and the mixture is
just boiling. Pour the hot
cream mixture over the
chocolate, and stir until
the chocolate melts and
the mixture is smooth.
2 Stir in the cake crumbs
and rum. Refrigerate for
20 minutes, stirring
occasionally, or until just
firm enough to handle.
Roll heaped teaspoons of
the mixture into balls.

3 Spread the chocolate
sprinkles on a sheet of
greaseproof paper.
Carefully roll each rum
ball in the sprinkles,
then place on the
tray. Refrigerate for
30 minutes, or until firm.
Serve in paper cases.

HARD CARAMELS

Preparation: 15 minutes +
 setting
Cooking: 25 minutes
Makes 50

1 cup (250 g/8 oz) **sugar**
90 g (3 oz) **butter**
2 tablespoons **golden
 syrup**
¹/3 cup (80 ml/2³/4 fl oz)
 liquid glucose
¹/2 cup (160 g/5¹/2 oz)
 condensed milk
250 g (8 oz) **dark
 chocolate, chopped**

HARD CARAMELS are perfect for wrapping up as a gift.

1 Grease a 20 cm (8 inch) square cake tin. Line the base and sides with baking paper, and grease the paper. Put the sugar, butter, syrup, glucose and condensed milk in a heavy-based pan. Stir over medium heat without boiling, until the butter has melted and the sugar has dissolved completely. Brush the sugar crystals from the side of the pan with a wet pastry brush.
2 Bring to the boil, then reduce the heat slightly and boil, stirring, for about 10–15 minutes, until the mixture reaches 122°C (250°F) on a sugar thermometer. If you don't have a thermometer, drop a little mixture into a glass of cold water. It should be brittle but sticky between your thumb and finger.
3 Remove from the heat immediately. Pour into the tin and leave to cool. While the caramel is still warm, score squares with an oiled knife. Snap into squares when cold.
4 Line two 32 x 28 cm (13 x 11 inch) baking trays with foil. Put the chocolate in a heatproof bowl. Half fill a pan with water and bring it to the boil. Remove from the heat and place the bowl over the pan, making sure it is not sitting in the water. Stir until melted. Cool slightly, then dip the

Serve WHITE CHRISTMAS during the party season.

caramels one at a time into the chocolate and set on the trays. Store in an airtight container for up to a month.

WHITE CHRISTMAS

Preparation: 10 minutes + 30 minutes setting
Cooking: 5 minutes
Makes 24

1 ¹/₂ cups (45 g/1 ¹/₂ oz) rice bubbles
1 cup (100 g/3 ¹/₂ oz) powdered milk
1 cup (125 g/4 oz) icing sugar
1 cup (90 g/3 oz) desiccated coconut
¹/₃ cup (80 g/2³/₄ oz) chopped red glacé cherries

¹/₃ cup (80 g/2³/₄ oz) chopped green glacé cherries
¹/₃ cup (40 g/1 ¹/₄ oz) sultanas
250 g (8 oz) white vegetable shortening (Copha)

1 Line the base and sides of a shallow 28 x 18 cm (11 x 7 inch) tin with foil.
2 Combine the rice bubbles, powdered milk, sugar, coconut and fruit in a large mixing bowl. Make a well in the centre.
3 Melt the shortening over low heat. Cool slightly, then stir into the dry ingredients.
4 Spoon into the tin and smooth the surface. Chill for 30 minutes, or until set. Cut into pieces to serve. Store in the fridge for up to 10 days.

PEANUT BRITTLE

Preparation: 20 minutes +
cooling
Cooking: 15 minutes
Makes about 500 g (1 lb)

2 cups (500 g/1 lb) sugar
1 cup (185 g/6 oz) soft
brown sugar
1/2 cup (175 g/6 oz)
golden syrup
60 g (2 oz) butter
2 1/2 cups (390 g/13 oz)
roasted, unsalted
peanuts

1 Line the base and sides
of a shallow 30 x 25 cm
(12 x 10 inch) swiss roll
tin with foil or baking
paper. Grease the foil with
melted butter or oil.
2 Combine the sugars,
golden syrup and 1/2 cup
(125 ml/4 fl oz) water in a
large heavy-based pan.
Stir over medium heat

without boiling until the
sugar has completely
dissolved. Brush the sugar
crystals from the side of
the pan with a wet pastry
brush. Add the butter and
stir until melted. Bring to
the boil, reduce the heat
slightly and boil without
stirring for 15–20 minutes.
The mixture must reach
150°C (250°F) on a sugar
thermometer, or a little
dropped in cold water will
be brittle and not sticky.
Remove from the heat.
3 Add the peanuts and
fold in lightly, tilting the
pan to help mix—don't
overmix or it will
crystallize. Pour into the
tin and smooth the surface
with a buttered spatula.
Leave the tin on a wire
rack for the brittle to
cool. Break into pieces
when almost set. Store in
an airtight container for
up to 3 weeks.

Use roasted unsalted nuts to make PEANUT BRITTLE.

TOFFEE APPLES

Preparation: 10 minutes +
setting
Cooking: 20 minutes
Makes 12

12 small red or green
apples, very crisp
4 cups (1 kg/2 lb) sugar
2 tablespoons white
vinegar
red or green food
colouring

1 Line two 32 x 28 cm
(13 x 11 inch) baking
trays with foil. Grease the
foil lightly with oil.
2 Wipe the apples well
with a clean, dry towel.
Push a wooden lolly stick
or thick skewer into the
stem end of each apple.
3 Combine the sugar,
vinegar and 2 cups
(500 ml/16 fl oz) water in
a large, heavy-based pan.
Stir over medium heat,
without boiling, until the
sugar has completely
dissolved. Brush the sugar
crystals from the side of
the pan with a wet pastry
brush. Add the food
colouring. Bring to the
boil and boil without
stirring for 15–20 minutes.
The mixture must reach
138°C (275°F) on a sugar
thermometer. If you
don't have a sugar
thermometer, test by
dropping a little mixture
into cold water. It will be

brittle ('small-crack' stage).
Remove from the heat
immediately.

4 Dip the apples, one at
a time, into the toffee to
coat. Lift out and twist
quickly to coat evenly.
Drain, then place on the
trays. Leave to set at room
temperature. When set,
wrap each toffee apple in
cellophane and tie with
ribbon. Can be kept for
up to two days.

HINT: It is important that
the apples are at room
temperature when they
are dipped into the hot
toffee. If they are too
cold, the toffee will form
bubbles on the surface.

COCONUT ICE

Preparation: 20 minutes +
 1 hour setting
Cooking: Nil
Makes 30 pieces

2 cups (250 g/8 oz) icing
 sugar
¹/₄ teaspoon cream of
 tartar
400 g (13 oz) can
 condensed milk
3¹/₂ cups (315 g/10 oz)
 desiccated coconut
2–3 drops pink food
 colouring

1 Brush a 20 cm (8 inch)
square cake tin with oil or
melted butter. Line the

TOFFEE APPLES (top) and COCONUT ICE.

base with baking paper.
2 Sift the icing sugar and
cream of tartar into a large
bowl. Make a well in the
centre and add the
condensed milk. Stir in
the coconut, half at a
time. Mix with your hands
until well combined.
3 Divide the mixture in
half. Tint one half with
pink food colouring.
Using your hands, knead
the colour through evenly.
4 Press the pink mixture

over the base of the tin,
cover with the white
mixture and press down
firmly to even the surface.
Refrigerate the coconut
ice for 1 hour, or until it is
firm. Remove from the tin
and cut into squares or
bars to serve. Can be
stored in an airtight
container in a cool place
for up to three weeks.

SMALL TOFFEES (left) and TOASTED MARSHMALLOWS.

SMALL TOFFEES

Preparation: 10 minutes + setting
Cooking: 25 minutes
Makes 24

4 cups (1 kg/2 lb) sugar
1 tablespoon vinegar
hundreds and thousands
  or desiccated coconut,
  for decoration

1 Line two deep 12-cup patty tins with paper cases. Combine the sugar and vinegar with 1 cup (250 ml/8 fl oz) water in a large, heavy-based pan.
2 Stir over medium heat without boiling until the sugar has completely dissolved. Brush the sugar crystals from the side of the pan with a wet pastry brush. Bring to the boil, then reduce the heat slightly and boil without stirring for 15–20 minutes. The mixture must reach 150°C (300°F) on a sugar thermometer. If you don't have a sugar thermometer, test by dropping a little mixture into cold water. It will be brittle but not sticky. Remove the pan from the heat immediately.
3 Pour into patty cases and decorate with hundreds and thousands or desiccated coconut. Leave to set at room temperature. Store in an airtight container in a cool dry place for up to a week.

TOASTED MARSHMALLOWS

Preparation: 25 minutes + overnight setting
Cooking: 3 minutes
Makes 36

1 1/2 cups (375 g/12 oz)
  caster sugar
5 teaspoons gelatine
1 teaspoon vanilla
  essence
3/4 cup (65 g/2 oz)
  desiccated coconut

1 Line a 30 x 20 cm (12 x 8 inch) shallow cake tin with foil and brush with melted butter or oil.
2 Using electric beaters, beat the sugar and 1/2 cup (125 ml/4 fl oz) water for 3 minutes.

3 Combine the gelatine with ¹/₂ cup (125 ml/ 4 fl oz) water in a small bowl. Stand the bowl in hot water until the gelatine becomes spongy, then stir until dissolved. Add to the sugar mixture and beat with electric beaters for 10 minutes, or until thick and white. Add the vanilla essence. Pour into the tin and spread out evenly. Leave overnight to set at room temperature.

4 Preheat the oven to moderate 180°C (350°F/ Gas 4). Spread the coconut evenly on a flat baking tray. Bake for about 3 minutes, or until golden (watch the coconut carefully when toasting as it can quickly burn). Pour onto a plate to cool.

5 Turn the marshmallow out of the tin and cut it into cubes. Place the toasted coconut in a plastic bag and add a few cubes of marshmallow at a time. Shake to coat. Store in a single layer in an airtight container in a cool dark place for up to a week. Keep flat.

ROCKY ROAD

Preparation: 20 minutes + refrigeration
Cooking: 5 minutes
Makes 30 pieces

250 g (8 oz) **pink and white marshmallows, halved**
1 cup (160 g/5¹/₂ oz) **unsalted peanuts, roughly chopped**
¹/₂ cup (105 g/3¹/₂ oz) **glacé cherries, halved**
1 cup (60 g/2 oz) **shredded coconut**
350 g (11 oz) **dark chocolate, chopped**

1 Line the base of a shallow 20 cm (8 inch) square cake tin with foil, leaving it to hang over two sides. Mix together the marshmallows, peanuts, cherries and shredded coconut.

2 Put the chocolate in a heatproof bowl. Half fill a pan with water and bring to the boil. Remove from the heat and place the bowl over the pan, making sure it is not sitting in the water. Stir occasionally until the chocolate has melted.

3 Add the chocolate to the marshmallow mixture, and mix. Press evenly into the tin. Refrigerate for several hours, or until set. Lift out and cut into small pieces. Store in an airtight container in the fridge for up to two weeks.

ROCKY ROAD is a favourite for children's parties.

JAMS AND PICKLES

For anyone who has a fruit tree or a vegetable patch, making your own jams, marmalades and pickles is a skill well worth having. Kept in properly sterilized jars, jams and pickles will keep for six months, in a cool dark place. Once opened, they can be stored in the fridge for up to a month.

THREE-FRUIT MARMALADE

Preparation: 30 minutes + overnight soaking
Cooking: 2¼ hours
Fills twelve 250 ml (8 fl oz) jars

1 grapefruit
2 oranges
2 lemons
3 kg (6 lb) sugar

1 Scrub the grapefruit, oranges and lemons under hot running water with a soft bristle brush, to remove the wax coating. Slice the quartered grapefruit and halved oranges and lemons very thinly and place in a large non-metal bowl. Put the pips in a piece of muslin, tied securely with string. Add to the bowl with 2.5 litres water, cover and leave overnight.
2 Put two small plates in the freezer. Transfer the fruit and water to a large pan. Bring slowly to the boil, then reduce the heat and simmer, covered, for 1 hour, or until the fruit is tender. Meanwhile, 'warm' the sugar by spreading in a large baking dish and heating in a very slow 120°C (250°F/Gas ½) oven for 10 minutes, stirring occasionally.
3 Add the warmed sugar to the fruit all at once. Stir over low heat, without boiling, for 5 minutes, or until all the sugar has dissolved. Return to the boil and boil rapidly for 50–60 minutes. When the marmalade reaches 104°C on the sugar thermometer, start testing for setting point: remove from the heat and place a little marmalade on one of the plates. A skin will form on the surface and the marmalade will wrinkle when pushed with your finger when setting point is reached. Leave to cool for 10 minutes, then remove any scum from the surface. Remove the muslin bag.
4 Spoon the cooled marmalade into hot, sterilized jars and seal. Turn upside-down for 2 minutes, then turn back again and leave to cool completely. Label and date for storage.

Jars must always be sterilized before jams are put in them for storage, or bacteria will multiply. To sterilize your jars and lids, rinse with boiling water, then do not dry with a towel (even a clean tea towel may have germs on it) but place in a warm oven for 20 minutes, or until completely dry.

STRAWBERRY JAM

Preparation: 30 minutes
Cooking: 1½ hours
Fills six 250 ml (8 fl oz) jars

5 cups (1.25 kg) sugar
1.5 kg (3 lb) strawberries
½ cup (125 ml/4 fl oz)
   lemon juice

1 'Warm' the sugar by spreading in a large baking dish and heating in a very slow 120°C (250°F/Gas ½) oven for 10 minutes, stirring occasionally. Put two plates in the freezer. Hull the strawberries and put in a large pan with the lemon juice, sugar and ½ cup (125 ml/4 fl oz) water. Warm gently, without boiling, stirring carefully with a wooden spoon. Try not to break up the fruit too much.
2 Increase the heat and, without boiling, continue stirring for 10 minutes, until the sugar has thoroughly dissolved. Increase the heat and boil, without stirring, for 20 minutes. Start testing for setting point: place a little jam on one of the cold plates; a skin will form on the surface and the jam will wrinkle when pushed with your finger. It could take up to 40 minutes to reach setting point. Remove from the heat and leave for 5 minutes before removing any scum that forms on the surface. Pour into hot sterilized jars, seal and label.

LEMON CURD

Preparation: 15 minutes
Cooking: 20 minutes
Fills two 250 ml (8 fl oz) jars

1½ tablespoons finely
   grated lemon rind
¾ cup (185 ml/6 fl oz)
   lemon juice
185 g (6 oz) soft butter,
   chopped
1 cup (250 g/8 oz) caster
   sugar
12 egg yolks

1 Combine the rind, juice, butter and sugar in a heatproof bowl over a pan of simmering water. Stir until the butter has melted and the sugar dissolved.
2 Add the egg yolks to the bowl and stir until the mixture thickens to coat the back of the spoon. This will take about 15–17 minutes and the heat must be low or the mixture will curdle.
3 Strain the curd into a jug, then pour into cooled sterilized jars. Seal immediately. Store in the fridge for up to 3 weeks, unopened. Use within a week of opening.

MIXED BERRY JAM

Preparation: 20 minutes
Cooking: 30 minutes
Fills four 250 ml (8 fl oz) jars

1 kg (2 lb) mixed berries
   (we used strawberries,
   raspberries,
   blackberries,
   blueberries, mulberries
   but any combination of
   fresh berries will do)
⅓ cup (80 ml/2¾ oz)
   lemon juice
1 kg (2 lb) sugar
25 g (¾ oz) jam setting
   mixture

1 Put two small plates in the freezer. Place the berries and lemon juice in a saucepan and gently cook for 10 minutes. Add the sugar and stir over low heat until it dissolves.
2 Boil for 15 minutes and then remove from the heat. Add the jam setting mixture and boil rapidly for a further 5 minutes. Test for setting point: place a little jam on a cold plate; a skin should form on the surface and the jam will wrinkle when pushed with your finger.
3 Pour into hot sterilized jars. Seal and label.

Clockwise from top right:
STRAWBERRY JAM;
MIXED BERRY JAM;
LEMON CURD.

APRICOT AND ALMOND JAM

Preparation: 20 minutes + overnight soaking
Cooking: 1¼ hours
Fills eight 250 ml (8 fl oz) jars

500 g (1 lb) dried apricots
6 cups (1.5 kg/3 lb) sugar
½ cup (45 g/1½ oz) flaked almonds

1 Place the apricots in a large non-metal bowl. Add 2 litres water and leave to soak overnight.
2 Place two small plates in the freezer. Pour the apricots and water into a large pan. Bring slowly to the boil, then reduce the heat and simmer, covered, for 45 minutes, or until the fruit is soft. 'Warm' the sugar by spreading in a large baking dish and heating in a very slow 120°C (250°F/Gas ½) oven for 10 minutes, stirring occasionally.
3 Add the sugar to the fruit. Stir over low heat, without boiling, for 5 minutes, or until all the sugar has dissolved. Return to the boil and boil, uncovered, for 20 minutes, stirring occasionally. When the jam reaches 104°C on the sugar thermometer, start testing for setting point: place ¼ teaspoon jam on one of the plates. A skin will form on the surface and the jam will wrinkle when pushed with your finger when setting point is reached. Allow the jam to cool for 5 minutes, then remove any scum from the surface.
4 Spoon into hot, sterilized jars and seal. Turn upside-down for 2 minutes, then invert and leave to cool.

LIME MARMALADE

Preparation: 40 minutes + overnight soaking
Cooking: 1¼ hours
Fills ten 250 ml (8 fl oz) jars

1 kg (2 lb) limes
2.25 kg (4½ lb) sugar

1 Scrub the limes under hot, running water to remove the wax coating. Cut them in half lengthways, then slice thinly. Place in a large non-metal bowl with 2 litres water. Cover with plastic wrap and leave overnight.
2 Place two small plates in the freezer. Place the fruit and water in a large pan. Bring slowly to the boil, then reduce the heat and simmer, covered, for 45 minutes, or until the fruit is tender. 'Warm' the sugar by spreading in a large baking dish and heating in a very slow 120°C (250°F/Gas ½) oven for 10 minutes, stirring occasionally.
3 Add the sugar to the fruit and stir over low heat, without boiling, for 5 minutes, or until all the sugar has dissolved. Then boil rapidly, without stirring, for 20 minutes. When the marmalade reaches 104°C on the sugar thermometer, start testing for setting point: place ¼ teaspoon marmalade on one of the plates. A skin will form and the marmalade will wrinkle when pushed with your finger when setting point is reached. Cool for 5 minutes, then remove any scum.
4 Spoon the marmalade into hot, sterilized jars. Turn upside down for 2 minutes, then invert and cool. Label and date.

RASPBERRY JAM

Preparation: 20 minutes
Cooking: 35 minutes
Fills seven 250 ml (8 fl oz) jars

1.5 kg (3 lb) raspberries
⅓ cup (80 ml/2¾ oz) lemon juice
6 cups (1.5 kg/3 lb) sugar

Clockwise from top left: LIME MARMALADE; APRICOT AND ALMOND JAM; RASPBERRY JAM.

1 Place the raspberries and lemon juice in a large pan. Gently stir over low heat for 10 minutes, or until the raspberries have softened. 'Warm' the sugar by spreading in a large baking dish and heating in a very slow 120°C (250°F/Gas ½) oven for 10 minutes, stirring occasionally.
2 Add the sugar to the pan and stir, without boiling, for 5 minutes or until the sugar has completely dissolved.
3 Put 2 small plates in the freezer. Bring the jam to the boil and boil for 20 minutes, then start testing for setting point: place ¼ teaspoon jam on a cold plate. A skin will form on the surface and the jam will wrinkle when pushed with your finger when setting point is reached. Cool for 5 minutes, then remove any scum from the surface. Pour into hot sterilized jars and label.

SPICY DRIED FRUIT CHUTNEY

Preparation: 30 minutes
Cooking: 1¹/2 hours
Fills seven 250 ml (8 fl oz) jars

400 g (13 oz) dried
  apricots
200 g (6¹/2 oz) dried
  peaches
200 g (6¹/2 oz) dried
  pears
250 g (8 oz) raisins
200 g (6¹/2 oz) dried
  dates, pitted
250 g (8 oz) onions
250 g (8 oz) green
  apples, peeled and
  cored
4 cloves garlic, finely
  chopped
2 teaspoons salt
1 teaspoon ground cumin
1 teaspoon ground
  coriander
1 teaspoon ground cloves
1 teaspoon ground
  cayenne pepper
3¹/4 cups (600 g/1¹/4 lb)
  soft brown sugar
2¹/2 cups (600 ml/
  20 fl oz) malt vinegar

1 Finely chop the
apricots, peaches, pears,
raisins, dates, onions and
apples. Place in a large
stainless steel or enamel
pan. Add the garlic, salt,
cumin, coriander, cloves,
cayenne pepper, brown
sugar, vinegar and 3 cups
(750 ml/24 fl oz) water.
2 Stir over low heat until
the sugar has dissolved.
Bring to the boil, then
reduce the heat and
simmer over medium heat
for 1¹/2 hours, or until the
mixture has thickened and
the fruit is soft and pulpy.
Don't increase the heat or
the liquid will evaporate
too quickly and the
flavours won't develop.
3 Spoon the chutney into
hot, sterilized jars, and
seal. Turn upside-down for
2 minutes, then invert and
cool. Label and store for
1 month before serving to
let the flavours develop.

TOMATO SAUCE

Preparation: 25 minutes
Cooking: 2 hours
Fills six 250 ml (8 fl oz) jars

2 teaspoons black
  peppercorns
2 teaspoons whole cloves
2 teaspoons allspice
2.5 kg (5 lb) firm ripe
  tomatoes, roughly
  chopped
1 large onion, chopped
50 g (1³/4 oz) tomato
  paste
4 cloves garlic, crushed
2 teaspoons ground
  ginger
1 teaspoon salt
¹/4 teaspoon cayenne
  pepper
600 ml (20 fl oz) white
  wine or cider vinegar
500 g (1 lb) sugar

1 Place the black
peppercorns, cloves and
allspice in a small muslin
bag and tie securely.
2 Place the muslin bag in
a large heavy-based pan
with the chopped
tomatoes, onion, tomato
paste, garlic, ginger, salt,
cayenne pepper and
vinegar. Bring slowly to
the boil, then reduce the
heat and simmer for
45 minutes.
3 Add the sugar and stir
for 5 minutes to dissolve.
Bring to the boil then
reduce the heat and
simmer for 1 hour, or until
thickened and pulpy. Stir
frequently during cooking
and watch the mixture
does not burn.
4 Remove the muslin bag.
Cool a little, then place in
batches into a coarse
sieve. Use a wooden
spoon to press the juice
firmly from the pulp.
Discard the pulp and
return the juice to the
cleaned out pan. Reheat
gently for 10 minutes then
pour into hot sterilized
jars and seal while hot.
Label and store for a
month before using, to let
the flavours develop.

NOTE: Allspice is also
known as pimento.

*TOMATO SAUCE (top) and
SPICY DRIED FRUIT
CHUTNEY.*

RICH MINT JELLY

Preparation: 20 minutes +
   overnight standing
Cooking: 40 minutes
Fills three 250 ml (8 fl oz) jars

1 kg (2 lb) green apples
1/2 cup (125 ml/4 fl oz)
   lemon juice
3 cups (60 g/2 oz) fresh
   mint leaves
sugar
2–3 drops green food
   colouring

1 Wash and cut the apples
into thick slices, without
peeling or coring. Put the
apple, lemon juice,
2 1/2 cups of the mint
leaves and 1 litre water in
a large heavy-based pan,
and bring to the boil.
Reduce the heat and cook
for 10 minutes, or until
the apple is a soft pulp.
Break up any large pieces
with a wooden spoon.
2 Strain through a piece
of muslin into a bowl—do
not press the liquid
through or it will become
cloudy. Leave overnight.
3 Put two plates in the
freezer. Measure the
strained juice and return it
to the pan. Add 1 cup
(250 g/8 oz) of sugar for
each cup of liquid. Stir
over low heat without
boiling until the sugar has
dissolved completely.
Bring to the boil, then
reduce the heat slightly

and simmer on low heat
for 20 minutes, or until a
little mixture on a cold
plate forms a skin and
wrinkles when pushed.
4 Finely chop the
remaining mint and add
with the colouring. Stir
well. Remove from the
heat and leave for
5 minutes. Pour into hot,
sterilized jars and seal.

PICCALILLI

Preparation: 30 minutes +
   overnight soaking
Cooking: 20 minutes
Fills six 250 ml (8 fl oz) jars

400 g (13 oz)
   cauliflower, chopped
1 small cucumber,
   chopped
200 g (6 1/2 oz) green
   beans, chopped
1 onion, chopped
2 carrots, chopped
2 celery sticks, chopped
4 tablespoons salt
1 cup (250 g/8 oz) sugar
1 tablespoon mustard
   powder
2 teaspoons ground
   turmeric
1 teaspoon ground
   ginger
1 fresh red chilli, seeded
   and finely chopped
1 litre white vinegar
200 g (6 1/2 oz) frozen
   broad beans, peeled
1/2 cup (60 g/2 oz) plain
   flour

1 Combine the
cauliflower, cucumber,
beans, onion, carrot,
celery and salt in a large
bowl. Add enough water
to cover the vegetables,
and cover with an
upturned small plate to
keep the vegetables
submerged. Leave to soak
overnight.
2 Drain the vegetables
well and rinse under cold
running water. Drain
again and put in a pan.
Add the sugar, mustard,
turmeric, ginger, chilli and
all but 3/4 cup (185 ml/
6 fl oz) of the vinegar.
Bring to the boil, then
reduce the heat and
simmer for 3 minutes. Stir
in the broad beans.
3 Blend the flour with the
remaining vinegar and stir
it into the piccalilli. Stir
until the mixture boils and
thickens. Stand hot,
sterilized jars on a
wooden board or cloth-
covered surface and spoon
the piccalilli into the jars,
then seal while hot. Turn
the jars upside-down onto
their lids. Leave for
2 minutes, then invert the
jars. Label. Store for a
month before using, to
give the flavours time to
develop fully.

*RICH MINT JELLY (top) and
PICCALILLI.*

DILL PICKLES

Preparation: 15 minutes +
  overnight standing
Cooking: 5 minutes
Fills one 750 ml (24 fl oz) jar

500 g (1 lb) small firm
  Lebanese cucumbers,
  quartered lengthways
salt, to sprinkle
3 cups (750 ml/24 fl oz)
  white vinegar
3 tablespoons caster
  sugar
2 tablespoons yellow
  mustard seeds
2 tablespoons dill seeds
2 tablespoons black
  peppercorns
6 sprigs of fresh dill

1 Place the cucumber in a
colander and sprinkle with
salt. Cover with a dry
cloth and leave overnight.
Rinse under cold water
and drain thoroughly.
2 Put the vinegar, caster
sugar, mustard seeds, dill
seeds and black
peppercorns in a pan.
Bring to the boil, then
reduce the heat and
simmer for 5 minutes.
Pack the cucumbers with
6 sprigs of dill in a warm
sterilized jar. Pour in the
liquid with the seeds.
Press gently to remove
any air bubbles. Seal the
jar, label and store in a
cool dark place for at least
a month before serving,
shaking occasionally.

NOTE: Make sure the
cucumbers are kept
completely covered in the
vinegar solution.

PICKLED BEETROOT

Preparation: 30 minutes
Cooking: 30 minutes
Fills one 750 ml (24 fl oz) jar

8 beetroot
6 sprigs of fresh rosemary
1 onion, thinly sliced
zest of 1 orange
1 cup (250 ml/8 fl oz)
  white vinegar
1 cup (250 ml/8 fl oz)
  malt vinegar
1/2 cup (125 g/4 oz)
  caster sugar

1 Cook the beetroot in a
large pan of boiling water
for 20 minutes, or until
tender. Drain and leave to
cool. Remove the skin
from the beetroot and
discard. (Wear rubber
gloves to do this to
prevent your hands from
being stained.)
2 Cut the beetroot into
thick slices and layer in a
large warm sterilized jar
with the rosemary, onion
and orange zest. Leave
2 cm (3/4 inch) at the top
of the jar empty.
3 Combine the vinegars
with the sugar in a pan.
Stir over low heat until
the sugar dissolves. Bring

to the boil, then reduce
the heat and simmer for
5 minutes. Allow to cool
before pouring over the
beetroot. Seal, label and
store in a cool dark place.

NOTE: To make zest, cut
strips of rind from the
orange with a sharp knife.
Remove the white pith
from the rind and cut the
rind into fine strips.

PICKLED ONIONS

Preparation: 20 minutes
Cooking: 5 minutes
Fills one 1 litre jar

1 kg (2 lb) pickling
  onions
1 litre malt vinegar
2 tablespoons allspice
2 teaspoons sea salt
2 tablespoons black
  peppercorns
6 cloves
3 bay leaves

1 Peel the onions and
rinse well. Pat dry and
pack into sterilized jars.
2 Put the remaining
ingredients in a pan. Bring
to the boil, then reduce
the heat and simmer for
2 minutes. Cool slightly
and pour over the onions.

*From the top: DILL PICKLES;
PICKLED BEETROOT;
PICKLED ONIONS.*

BASIC RECIPES

There are some basic recipes that you will find you use over and over again for a variety of different dishes. A white sauce (béchamel) can be layered and baked in lasagne, served over vegetables, mixed with seafood to make a creamy pie, or flavoured with cheese or herbs. Similarly, a shortcrust pastry will usually be the same whether it's filled with berries, a creamy quiche mixture or meat and sauce.
Many of the following basic recipes will have appeared within this book, but as part and parcel of a whole dish. But, for when you need a quick reference, turn to these pages for your basic pastries, stocks, dressings, savoury and sweet sauces.

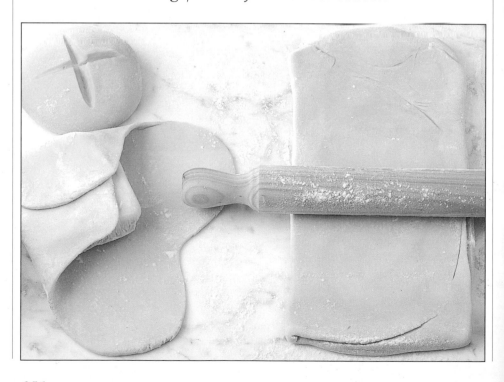

PASTRIES

Whether it is shortcrust, Danish, choux or puff, beautiful pastry with a light buttery touch can raise any dish to sublime heights. Perfect pastry that melts in the mouth is one of the hallmarks of a great cook—follow a few commonsense rules and you'll probably find it all rather easy.

PLAIN SHORTCRUST PASTRY

2 cups (250 g/8 oz) plain flour
125 g (4 oz) cold butter, chopped
1 egg yolk
3–4 tablespoons cold water

1 Sift the flour into a large mixing bowl and add the butter. Rub the butter into the flour with your fingertips until the mixture resembles fine breadcrumbs.
2 Add the combined egg yolk and 3 tablespoons of the water. Cut the liquid in with a knife to form a dough, adding the remaining water if necessary. Turn onto a lightly floured surface and gather together into a smooth ball (do not knead, or you will have tough pastry). Cover with plastic wrap and refrigerate if not immediately required. If the weather is hot, chill for at least 30 minutes, before proceeding with the recipe as directed.

NOTE: Shortcrust pastry can be made very easily in the food processor, but care must be taken not to overwork it. 'Rub' the butter into the flour by processing in short bursts, using the pulse button if you have one, until the mixture is fine and crumbly. Add most of the liquid and, again, process in short bursts until the mixture just comes together in small particles, adding more liquid if necessary.

If you continue to process until the mixture forms a ball, you will find that it is overworked and the pastry will be tough Instead, turn the mixture out onto a lightly floured surface and press together to form a clump, before rolling out as required.

SWEET SHORTCRUST PASTRY

2 cups (250 g/8 oz) plain flour
125 g (4 oz) cold butter, chopped
1/4 cup (60 g/2 oz) caster sugar
2 egg yolks
1 teaspoon vanilla essence
2–3 tablespoons cold water

1 Sift the flour into a large mixing bowl and add the butter. Using your fingertips, rub the butter into the flour until the mixture resembles fine breadcrumbs. Stir in the sugar.
2 Add the combined egg yolks, vanilla essence and 2 tablespoons of the water. Cut with a knife to form a dough, adding the remaining water if necessary. Turn out onto a lightly floured surface and gather into a smooth ball.

DANISH PASTRY

½ cup (125 ml/4 fl oz)
  warm milk
7 g (¼ oz) sachet dried
  yeast
1 teaspoon caster sugar
2 cups (250 g/8 oz) plain
  flour
½ teaspoon salt
¼ cup (60 g/2 oz) caster
  sugar, extra
1 egg, lightly beaten
1 teaspoon vanilla
  essence
250 g (8 oz) cold
  unsalted butter

1 In a small bowl, mix together the milk, yeast and sugar. Cover and leave in a warm place for 5 minutes, or until the mixture is frothy.
2 Sift the flour into a large bowl with the salt and stir in the extra sugar. Make a well in the centre and add the yeast mixture, egg and vanilla essence all at once. Mix to a firm dough. Turn out onto a floured surface and knead for 10 minutes to form a smooth, elastic dough.
3 Place the dough in a lightly greased bowl, cover and set aside in a warm place for 1 hour, or until doubled in size. Meanwhile roll the cold butter between two sheets of baking paper to a 15 x 20 cm (6 x 8 inch) rectangle and then refrigerate until required.

4 Punch down the dough (give it one good punch with your fist) and knead for 1 minute. Roll out to a rectangle 25 x 30 cm (10 x 12 inches). Place the butter in the centre of the dough and fold up the bottom and top of the dough over the butter to join in the centre. Seal the edges with a rolling pin.
5 Give the dough a quarter turn clockwise then roll out to a 20 x 45 cm (8 x 18 inch) rectangle. Fold over the top third of the pastry, then the bottom third and then give another quarter turn clockwise. Cover and refrigerate for 30 minutes. Repeat the rolling, folding and turning four more times. Wrap in plastic wrap and refrigerate for at least 2 hours before using.

CHOUX PASTRY

60 g (2 oz) butter
½ cup (125 ml/4 fl oz)
  water
½ cup (60 g/2 oz) plain
  flour, sifted
2 eggs, lightly beaten

1 Chop the butter and put in a pan with the water. Stir over low heat until melted.
2 Bring to the boil then immediately remove from the heat and add the flour all at once. Beat with a wooden spoon until smooth. Return to the heat and continue to beat for 2 minutes, or until the mixture forms a mass and leaves the side of the pan.
3 Remove from the heat and transfer to the bowl. Cool for 5 minutes. Add the egg, a little at a time, beating well between each addition, until thick and glossy. You may not need to add all the egg.
4 Shape the pastry onto trays and cook as directed in the recipe. If not completely dried out, return to a slow 150°C (300°F/Gas 2) oven for 5–10 minutes.

ROUGH PUFF PASTRY

90 g (3 oz) unsalted
  butter
90 g (3 oz) cooking
  margarine or lard
2 cups (250 g/8 oz) plain
  flour
pinch of salt
¾ cup (185 ml/6 fl oz)
  cold water
1 teaspoon lemon juice

1 Place the butter and margarine together on a large plate. Using two knives, roughly chop the fats together, then cover and chill. When cold and hard, chop the combined fats into small cubes.
2 Sift the flour and salt

into a large bowl. Add the cubes of fat to the flour. Using a knife, cut in the fat until just coated with the flour. Combine the water and lemon juice and add most of it to the bowl. Cut into the flour with a dinner knife, without breaking up the fat. Add more of the liquid if necessary.

3 With floured fingers, bring together into a rough ball. Turn out onto a floured surface. Do not knead. Roll the dough out into a 45 x 15 cm (18 x 6 inch) rectangle, keeping the sides and ends straight.

4 Fold the dough into three layers by folding the bottom third up and then the top third down. Seal the edges lightly with a rolling pin. Give a quarter turn clockwise: the top edge will now be to the right as if it were a book. Cover and refrigerate for 15 minutes. Repeat rolling, folding and turning clockwise four more times. Refrigerate between rollings if the dough becomes too soft. Chill for at least 30 minutes after the final rolling.

5 Roll and shape or cut the pastry as required in the recipe.

PUFF PASTRY

200–250 g (6^1/$_2$–8 oz) **unsalted butter**
2 cups (250 g/8 oz) **plain flour**
^{1}/$_2$ **teaspoon salt**
^{2}/$_3$ **cup (170 ml/ 5^1/$_2$ fl oz) chilled water**

1 We've given a range of fat quantities—if you've never made puff pastry before, you'll find it easier to use the lower amount. Melt 30 g (1 oz) butter in a pan. Sift the flour and salt onto a work surface and make a well in the centre. Add the butter and water. Blend with your fingertips, drawing in the flour. You should end up with a crumb mixture—if it seems a little dry, add extra drops of water before bringing it all together to form a dough.

2 Cut the dough with a pastry scraper, using a downward cutting action, then turn and repeat in the opposite direction. The dough should now come together to form a soft ball. Score a cross in the top to prevent shrinkage, wrap and chill for 15–20 minutes.

3 Soften the remaining butter by pounding it between 2 sheets of baking paper with a rolling pin. Then, still between the sheets of baking paper, roll it into a 10 cm (4 inch) square. The butter must be the same consistency as the dough or the pastry layers will not be even.

4 Put the pastry on a well floured surface. Roll it out to form a cross, leaving the centre slightly thicker than the arms. Place the butter in the centre and fold over each of the arms to make a parcel. Turn the dough so that it looks like a book with the spine to the left. Tap and roll out the dough to form a 15 x 45 cm (6 x 18 inch) rectangle. Square off the corners—otherwise, every time you fold, the edges will become less neat and the layers will be uneven.

5 Fold the dough like a letter, the top third down and the bottom third up, to form another square, brushing off any excess flour. Turn the dough 90° to bring the spine side to your left and press the seam sides down with the rolling pin to seal. Re-roll and fold as before to complete two turns. Wrap the dough and chill again.

6 Re-roll and fold twice more, chill, then repeat to complete six turns. On a hot day, you may need to chill after each turn. The pastry should now be yellow and ready to use— if it looks a little streaky, roll and fold once more. Chill until required.

STOCKS

The secret to great soups and stews is good stock. Home-made stock will give your dishes a richer, more flavoursome base and, although the cooking time is long, the preparation couldn't be easier. Browning meat bones beforehand adds flavour and colour.

BEEF STOCK

2 kg (4 lb) beef bones
2 unpeeled carrots, chopped
2 unpeeled onions, quartered
2 tablespoons tomato paste
2 sticks celery, leaves included, chopped
1 bouquet garni
12 black peppercorns

1 Preheat the oven to hot 210°C (415°F/Gas 6–7). Put the bones in a baking dish and bake for 30 minutes, turning occasionally. Add the carrot and onion and cook for a further 20 minutes. Allow to cool.
2 Put the bones, carrot and onion in a large, heavy-based pan. Drain the excess fat from the baking dish and pour 1 cup (250 ml/8 fl oz) of water into the dish. Stir to dissolve any pan juices; add the liquid to the pan.
3 Add the tomato paste, celery and 10 cups (2.5 litres) water. Bring to the boil, skimming the surface as required and add the bouquet garni and peppercorns. Reduce the heat to low and simmer gently for 4 hours. Skim the froth from the surface regularly.
4 Ladle the stock in batches into a fine sieve sitting over a bowl. Gently press the solids with a ladle to extract all the liquid. Discard the bones and vegetables and set aside to cool. Refrigerate until cold and spoon off any fat that has set on the top. At this stage you can reduce the stock to concentrate its flavour (dilute before using) and store in the refrigerator for up to 2 days or in the freezer for up to 6 months. Makes 1.75 litres (7 cups).

CHICKEN STOCK

2 kg (4 lb) chicken bones
2 unpeeled onions, quartered
2 unpeeled carrots, chopped
2 sticks celery, leaves included, chopped
1 bouquet garni
12 black peppercorns

1 Put the chicken bones, onion, carrot, celery and 14 cups (3.5 litres) of water in a large, heavy-based pan. Bring slowly to the boil. Skim the surface as required and add the bouquet garni and peppercorns. Reduce the heat to low and simmer gently for 3 hours. Skim the froth from the surface regularly.
2 Ladle the stock in batches into a fine sieve sitting over a bowl. Gently press the solids with a ladle to extract all the liquid. Let the stock cool, then refrigerate until cold and spoon off any fat

that has set on the top. At this stage you can reduce the stock to concentrate its flavour (dilute before using) and store in the refrigerator for up to 2 days or in the freezer for up to 6 months. Makes 2.5 litres (10 cups).

FISH STOCK

2 kg (4 lb) chopped fish bones, heads and tails
1 stick celery, leaves included, roughly chopped
1 onion, chopped
1 unpeeled carrot, chopped
1 leek, sliced
1 bouquet garni
12 black peppercorns

1 Place the fish bones, celery, onion, carrot, leek and 8 cups (2 litres) of water in a large, heavy-based pan. Bring slowly to the boil. Skim the surface as required and add the bouquet garni and peppercorns. Reduce the heat to low and simmer very gently for 20 minutes. Skim off any froth regularly.
2 Ladle the stock in batches into a sieve lined with damp muslin sitting over a bowl. To keep a clear fish stock, do not press the solids, but simply allow the stock to strain undisturbed. Allow

to cool, then store in the refrigerator for up to 2 days or in the freezer for up to 6 months. Makes about 7 cups (1.75 litres)

VEGETABLE STOCK

1 tablespoon oil
1 onion, chopped
2 leeks, chopped
4 carrots, chopped
2 parsnips, chopped
4 sticks celery, leaves included, chopped
2 bay leaves
1 bouquet garni
4 unpeeled cloves garlic
8 black peppercorns

1 Heat the oil in a large, heavy-based pan and add the onion, leek, carrot, parsnip and celery. Cover and cook for 5 minutes without colouring. Add 12 cups (3 litres) of water. Bring to the boil. Skim the surface if required and add the bay leaves, bouquet garni, garlic and peppercorns. Reduce the heat to low and simmer for 1 hour. Skim the froth from the surface of the stock regularly.
2 Ladle the stock in batches into a fine sieve sitting over a bowl. Gently press the solids to extract all the liquid.
3 Leave to cool, then refrigerate until cold and spoon off any fat that has

set on the top. At this stage you can reduce the stock to concentrate its flavour (dilute before using) and store in the refrigerator for up to 2 days or in the freezer for up to 6 months. Makes 2 litres (8 cups).

NOTE: Unpeeled garlic adds a subtle flavour and will not cloud the stock.

FREEZING STOCK
Once you are making stock you may as well make a large amount and freeze some for another time. Simply pour the stock into a measuring jug lined with a plastic bag, so you can measure how much you have, and then divide it up and freeze it in convenient portions. Remove the bag from the jug, label, seal securely and freeze. Alternatively, keep simmering the stock until it is reduced, pour into ice cube trays and freeze. You will now have quite concentrated stock 'cubes' that can be diluted to use.

BOUQUET GARNI
To make a bouquet garni, wrap the green part of a leek loosely around a bay leaf, sprig of thyme, some celery leaves and a few stalks of parsley, then tie with string. Leave enough string for easy removal.

DRESSINGS

Dressing, mayonnaises and vinaigrettes are really very simple to make, so there should be no excuse for reaching for the bottled varieties. Learn how to dress your salads in style at home. Home-made mayonnaise is always a vast improvement on the commercial varieties.

MAYONNAISE

2 egg yolks
1 teaspoon Dijon mustard
1 tablespoon lemon juice
3/4 cup (185 ml/6 fl oz)
   olive oil

1 Whisk together the egg yolks, mustard and lemon juice for 30 seconds, or until light and creamy. Add the oil, a teaspoon at a time, whisking continuously. You can add the oil more quickly as the mayonnaise thickens. Season to taste with salt and white pepper. Alternatively, place the egg yolks, mustard and lemon juice in a food processor and mix for 10 seconds. With the motor running, add the oil in a slow, thin stream. Season to taste with salt and white pepper. Makes about 1 cup (250 ml/8 fl oz).

AIOLI (GARLIC MAYONNAISE)

1 cup (250 ml/8 fl oz)
   mayonnaise
3 cloves of garlic, crushed

1 Mix together the mayonnaise and garlic. Season to taste with salt and pepper. Makes about 1 cup (250 ml/8 fl oz).

THOUSAND ISLAND DRESSING

1/2 cup (125 ml/4 fl oz)
   mayonnaise
1 tablespoon tomato paste
1 teaspoon Worcestershire
   sauce
1 teaspoon French mustard
2 teaspoons chilli sauce

1 Mix together the mayonnaise, tomato paste, Worcestershire sauce, mustard and chilli sauce. Season with salt. Makes about 1/2 cup (125 ml/4 fl oz).

GREEN GODDESS DRESSING

1 1/2 cups (375 ml/12 fl oz)
   mayonnaise
4 mashed anchovy fillets
4 finely chopped spring
   onions
1 clove garlic, crushed
1/4 cup (7 g/1/4 oz)
   chopped flat-leaf parsley
1/4 cup (15 g/1/2 oz) finely
   chopped chives
1 teaspoon tarragon
   vinegar

1 Mix together the mayonnaise, anchovies, spring onions, garlic, parsley, chives and vinegar. Delicious with seafood. Makes about 2 cups (500 ml/16 fl oz).

BASIC VINAIGRETTE

1/2 cup (125 ml/4 fl oz)
   extra virgin olive oil
2 tablespoons white wine
   vinegar
1 teaspoon sugar

1 Put the oil, vinegar and sugar in a small jug. Whisk with a small wire whisk or fork until well blended and season with salt and freshly ground black pepper. Makes about 2/3 cups (170 ml/5 1/2 fl oz).

BALSAMIC DRESSING

2 tablespoons balsamic vinegar
1 teaspoon French mustard
1/3 cup (80 ml/2 3/4 fl oz) extra virgin olive oil
1 small clove garlic

1 Whisk the vinegar and mustard in a small jug. Gradually beat in the oil. Season with salt and freshly ground black pepper. Cut the garlic in half, skewer onto a toothpick and leave in the dressing to infuse for at least 1 hour. Makes about 1/2 cup (125 ml/4 fl oz).

ITALIAN DRESSING

3 tablespoons white wine vinegar
3 tablespoons olive oil
1/2 teaspoon sugar
1 tablespoon chopped fresh basil

1 Place the vinegar, olive oil and sugar in a bowl

and whisk to combine. Stir in the basil and leave to stand for 15 minutes before serving. Makes about 1/2 cup (125 ml/4 fl oz).

CREAMY SALAD DRESSING

1 tablespoon white wine vinegar
1 teaspoon Dijon mustard
1 crushed clove garlic
1/4 cup (60 ml/2 fl oz) oil
1/4 cup (60 ml/2 fl oz) cream

1 Whisk together the vinegar, mustard and garlic in a bowl. Slowly add the oil and cream and whisk until combined. Serve immediately. Makes about 2/3 cup (170 ml/5 1/2 fl oz).

THAI STYLE DRESSING

1 tablespoon fish sauce
2 tablespoon sweet chilli sauce
2 tablespoon lime juice
1 clove garlic, crushed
1/4 cup peanut oil
1 tablespoon chopped fresh coriander

1 Whisk together the fish sauce, chilli sauce, lime juice and garlic. Slowly add the oil and whisk to combine. Stir in the coriander. Serve immediately. Makes about 3/4 cup (185 ml/6 fl oz).

TARTARE SAUCE

1 1/2 cups (375 ml/12 fl oz) mayonnaise
1 tablespoon finely chopped onion
1 teaspoon lemon juice
1 tablespoon chopped gherkins
1 teaspoon chopped capers
1/4 teaspoon Dijon mustard
1 tablespoon finely chopped parsley

1 Mix together the mayonnaise, onion, lemon juice, gherkins, capers, mustard and parsley. Season with salt and white pepper. Top with a few capers to serve. Makes about 2 cups (500 ml/16 fl oz).

BLUE CHEESE DRESSING

80 g (2 3/4 oz) blue cheese
1/4 cup (60 g/2 oz) sour cream
1/2 cup (125 g/4 oz) whole egg mayonnaise
1 tablespoon chopped chives
1 teaspoon white wine vinegar

1 Mash the blue cheese with a fork to a chunky paste. Add the sour cream, mayonnaise and white pepper to taste. Stir in chives and vinegar. Makes about 1 1/4 cups (315 ml/10 fl oz).

SAVOURY SAUCES

Sauces are a quick and easy way to brighten up any meal. Hot savoury sauces can be served over meat (both hot and cold), chicken, seafood, vegetables and even eggs. Asparagus with a buttery hollandaise is a wonderfully stylish dish, and here we give you instructions for an even easier version.

CLASSIC WHITE SAUCE

1 cup (250 ml/8 fl oz) milk
slice of onion
1 bay leaf
6 peppercorns
30 g (1 oz) butter
1 tablespoon plain flour

1 Put the milk, onion, bay leaf and peppercorns in a small pan. Bring to the boil, remove from the heat and leave to infuse for 10 minutes. Strain the milk, discarding the flavourings.
2 Melt the butter in a small pan and stir in the flour. Cook, stirring, for 1 minute until the mixture is golden and bubbling. Remove from the heat and gradually add the milk, stirring until completely smooth. Return to the heat and stir until the mixture boils. Continue cooking for 1 minute or until thick, remove from the heat and season with salt and white pepper. Serve with steamed cauliflower and broccoli. Also good with fish or corned beef. Serves 2–4.

MORNAY SAUCE

1 1/3 cups (350 ml/11 fl oz) milk
slice of onion
1 bay leaf
6 peppercorns
30 g (1 oz) butter
1 tablespoon plain flour
1/2 cup (60 g/2 oz) finely grated Cheddar
1/4 teaspoon mustard powder

1 Put the milk, onion, bay leaf and peppercorns in a small pan. Bring to the boil, remove from the heat and leave to infuse for 10 minutes. Strain the milk, discarding the flavourings.
2 Melt the butter in a small pan and add the flour. Cook, stirring, for 1 minute until the mixture is golden and bubbling. Add the infused milk, a little at a time, stirring between each addition until completely smooth. Continue stirring until the mixture boils and thickens. Boil for 1 minute more and then remove from the heat. Add the cheese and mustard and stir until the cheese has melted and the sauce is smooth. Season to taste with salt and pepper. Serve with grilled lobster (lobster mornay). Also good with grilled oysters, steamed or poached fish or vegetables. Mornay sauce is often poured over the top of dishes and then grilled or baked. Serves 4.

HINT: When preparing sauces such as these, if you don't want to serve them immediately, lay plastic wrap directly onto the surface to prevent a skin forming.

GREEN PEPPERCORN SAUCE

4 steaks or chicken breast
    fillets
1 cup (250 ml/8 fl oz)
    beef or chicken stock
1 cup (250 ml/8 fl oz)
    cream
2–3 teaspoons canned
    green peppercorns,
    rinsed and drained
1 tablespoon brandy

1 Pan-fry the steak or chicken in oil or butter. Remove from the pan and keep warm.
2 Add the stock to the juices in the pan. Stir over low heat until boiling. Add the cream and peppercorns. Boil for 8–10 minutes, stirring until slightly thickened. Add the brandy and boil for 1 minute. Serves 4.

SPEEDY HOLLANDAISE

You can make hollandaise in a food processor: blend 4 egg yolks, 2 tablespoons water and 1 tablespoon lemon juice in the processor for 10 seconds. With the motor running, add 175 g (6 oz) cooled, melted butter in a thin stream.
To make hollandaise in the microwave: melt the butter on high for 1 minute.

Beat the yolks, water and lemon juice together and whisk in the butter. Cook for 1 minute 20 seconds on medium, whisking every 20 seconds. Season well. Serve with fish, eggs or vegetables. Serves 4.

VELOUTE SAUCE

30 g (1 oz) butter
3 tablespoons plain flour
1 1/2 cups (375 ml/
    12 fl oz) chicken, fish
    or veal stock
lemon juice, to taste
1 tablespoon cream

1 Melt the butter in a pan, add the flour and cook over medium heat for 2 minutes, or until a thick paste has formed—be careful not to brown the mixture or it will colour your sauce.
2 Whisk in the stock a little at a time to prevent the mixture becoming lumpy. Cook the sauce, whisking continuously, for 3–5 minutes—it should be quite thick and not have a floury taste.
3 Season with salt, pepper and lemon juice, adding a little at a time. Finally, stir in the cream. Serve immediately, as this sauce will quickly thicken if left to stand. If necessary, add a little extra stock to thin it down. Serve with chicken, seafood or veal. Serves 4.

CUMBERLAND SAUCE

2 oranges
1 lemon
225 g (7 oz) redcurrant
    jelly
2 teaspoons Dijon
    mustard
2 tablespoons red wine
    vinegar
1 cup (250 ml/8 fl oz)
    port

1 Remove the orange and lemon rind with a zester. Place the rind in a small pan with 1 cup (250 ml/8 fl oz) water and bring to the boil. Cook for 5 minutes, then drain the rind.
2 Squeeze the juice from the oranges and lemon and place in a pan. Add the jelly, mustard, vinegar, port and reserved rind. Slowly bring to the boil, stirring as the jelly melts. Reduce the heat to simmer gently for 15 minutes. Season to taste and serve at room temperature or cover with plastic wrap and refrigerate for up to a week. Serve with ham, turkey, venison or game meats. Serves 8.

SWEET AND SOUR SAUCE

2 tablespoons dry sherry
1 cup (250 ml/8 fl oz)
  pineapple juice
3 tablespoons white wine
  vinegar
2 teaspoons soy sauce
2 tablespoons soft brown
  sugar
2 tablespoons tomato
  sauce
1 small red capsicum,
  finely diced
1 tablespoon cornflour

1 Mix together the
sherry, pineapple juice,
vinegar, soy sauce, brown
sugar and tomato sauce in
a pan. Cook, stirring
constantly, over low heat
until the sugar has
dissolved. Bring to the
boil and add the
capsicum.
2 Mix the cornflour in
1 tablespoon water. Add
to the pan and cook,
stirring, until the mixture
boils and thickens. Reduce
the heat and simmer for
2 minutes. Serve at once.
Serve with spring rolls,
pan-fried, grilled or deep-
fried fish and pan-fried
pork or lamb. Serves 6–8.

SATAY SAUCE

1 tablespoon oil
1 large onion, finely
  chopped
2 cloves garlic, finely
  chopped
2 red chillies, finely
  chopped
1 teaspoon shrimp paste
250 g (8 oz) peanut
  butter
1 cup (250 ml/8 fl oz)
  coconut milk
2 teaspoons kecap manis
  or thick soy sauce
1 tablespoon tomato
  sauce

1 Heat the oil in a pan
and cook the onion and
garlic for 8 minutes over
low heat, stirring
regularly. Add the chilli
and shrimp paste, cook for
1 minute and remove from
the heat.
2 Add the peanut butter,
return to the heat and stir
in the coconut milk and
1 cup (250 ml/8 fl oz)
water. Bring to the boil
over low heat, stirring so
that it does not stick. Add
the kecap manis and
tomato sauce and simmer
for 1 minute. Cool. Serve
with chicken skewers,
meat or fish skewers, or
vegetables. Serves 8.

BREAD SAUCE

2 cloves
1 onion
1 cup (250 ml/8 fl oz)
  milk
1 bay leaf
50 g (1 3/4 oz) fresh
  breadcrumbs (made
  using about 3 slices of
  day-old bread)
3 tablespoons cream

1 Push the cloves into
the onion and put in a pan
with the milk and bay
leaf. Bring to the boil,
then remove from the
heat, cover and leave for
10 minutes. Remove the
onion and leaf.
2 Add the breadcrumbs
to the pan and season.
Return to the heat, cover
and simmer gently for
10 minutes, stirring
occasionally. Stir in the
cream. Serve warm with
roasted spatchcock,
chicken, turkey, goose or
game meat. Serves 4.

DEMI-GLACE

Beef Stock
1 kg (2 lb) beef bones
1 tablespoon oil
1 onion, chopped
2 carrots, chopped
5 parsley stalks
2 bay leaves
6 peppercorns

Espagnole
2 tablespoons oil
2 carrots, finely chopped
1 onion, finely chopped
1 stalk celery, finely
  chopped
1 tablespoon flour
$1/2$ teaspoon tomato paste
bouquet garni

1 To make the beef stock, preheat the oven to hot 220°C (440°F/Gas 7). Roast the bones for 1 hour, or until browned. Heat the oil in a large pan and brown the vegetables, being careful not to burn them. Add the bones, parsley, bay leaves and peppercorns and cover with cold water. Bring to the boil, reduce the heat and simmer for 3–4 hours, skimming off the fat as it rises to the surface. Add a little more cold water if needed. You should have about $3^1/2$ cups (875 ml/ 28 fl oz) of stock—if you have more, continue reducing; if less, add a little water. Strain and cool. Remove any fat which sets on the surface.

2 To make the espagnole, heat the oil in a pan and brown the vegetables. Add the flour and cook, stirring, until browned. Add $2^1/2$ cups (600 ml/ 20 fl oz) of the beef stock with the tomato paste and bouquet garni and bring to the boil. Reduce the heat, half-cover the pan and simmer, skimming off any fat, for 30 minutes, or until reduced to 1 cup (250 ml/8 fl oz). Sieve and leave to cool.
3 To make the demi-glace, put the espagnole and the remaining cup of stock in a pan and simmer until reduced by half. Strain thoroughly through a fine mesh sieve or muslin. Serve with beef tournedos, but good with any type of beef steak. Serves 8.

NOTE: Don't use ready-made stock—it is far too salty for this recipe.
VARIATION: To make a beef glace, reduce the strained stock to a thick sticky liquid which will set to a jelly when cold. This gives a rich flavour when added to sauces.

BEARNAISE SAUCE

$1/3$ cup (80 ml/$2^1/2$ fl oz)
  white wine vinegar
2 spring onions, roughly
  chopped
2 teaspoons chopped
  fresh tarragon
2 egg yolks
125 g (4 oz) butter,
  cubed

1 Put the white wine vinegar, spring onion and tarragon in a small pan. Bring to the boil, then reduce the heat slightly and simmer until the mixture has reduced by a third. Allow to cool completely and then strain the vinegar into a heatproof bowl.
2 Add the egg yolks to the bowl, then place the bowl over a pan of barely simmering water. Whisk until the mixture is thick and pale. Add the butter, a cube at a time, whisking between each addition until the mixture is thick and smooth. Season to taste with salt and pepper and serve immediately with pan-fried steak, roast beef or lamb, or poached salmon. Serves 4.

SWEET SAUCES

Custard and creme anglaise can be served over sticky and steamed pudding, simple apple pies or pastries, crumbles and cobblers and just about any baked pudding you can think of. Our rich butterscotch and chocolate sauces are ideal for drizzling over ice cream. Berry coulis is wonderful with plain sponges or ice cream. And zabaglione is perfect with fruit, biscuits or on its own, at any time!

EASY VANILLA CUSTARD

1 cup (250 ml/8 fl oz) milk
1/4 cup (60 ml/2 fl oz) cream
3 egg yolks
1/3 cup (90 g/3 oz) caster sugar
2 teaspoons cornflour
1 teaspoon vanilla essence

1 Put the milk and cream in a pan and heat until almost at boiling point. Immediately remove the pan from the heat.
2 Whisk the egg yolks together with the sugar and cornflour in a heatproof bowl. Slowly pour the hot milk and cream over the egg mixture, whisking continuously. Return the mixture to the clean pan and stir over low heat for 5 minutes, or until the custard boils and thicken. Remove from the heat immediately. Whisk in the vanilla essence. Serve with apple pie, or any sweet pie, pastry or pudding you can think of. Serves 6.

CREME ANGLAISE

3 egg yolks
2 tablespoons caster sugar
1 1/2 cups (375 ml/12 fl oz) milk
1/2 teaspoon vanilla essence

1 Whisk the yolks and sugar in a heatproof bowl for 2 minutes, or until light and creamy. Heat the milk in a small pan until almost boiling, then pour onto the mixture, whisking constantly.
2 Return the mixture to the pan and stir over low heat for about 5 minutes, or until slightly thickened, enough to coat the back of a spoon. Do not allow to boil or the custard will curdle. Remove the pan from the heat, stir in the vanilla essence and transfer to a jug. Serve immediately, or lay a piece of plastic wrap directly on the surface of the custard to prevent it forming a skin. Serve with fruit tart. Good with all fruit pastries and warmed cakes, and anything you would serve with ordinary custard. Serves 4.

HINT: Any thick sauces, such as custard, which aren't going to be served immediately, should be kept with a sheet of plastic wrap directly over the surface to prevent a skin forming on top.

BUTTERSCOTCH SAUCE

125 g (4 oz) butter
1/2 cup (90 g/3 oz) soft
  brown sugar
2 tablespoons golden
  syrup
1/2 cup (125 ml/4 fl oz)
  cream
1 teaspoon vanilla
  essence

1 Put the butter and sugar in a pan and stir over low heat until the butter has melted and the sugar has dissolved.
2 Bring to the boil and add the golden syrup and cream. Reduce the heat and simmer for 10 minutes, or until slightly thickened. Remove from the heat and add the vanilla essence. Serve hot or cold with grilled bananas, grilled peaches, nectarines or other fruit, puddings, waffles and crepes. Serves 6.

DARK CHOCOLATE SAUCE

150 g (5 oz) chopped
  dark chocolate
300 ml (10 fl oz) cream
2 tablespoons caster
  sugar

1 Put chocolate in a bowl. Bring the cream to the boil in a pan. Stir in the sugar, then pour over the chocolate.

Leave for 2 minutes, then stir until smooth. Serve warm. Serves 6.

CHOCOLATE FUDGE SAUCE

1 cup (250 ml/8 fl oz)
  cream
30 g (1 oz) butter
1 tablespoon golden syrup
200 g (6 1/2 oz) chopped
  dark chocolate

1 Put the cream, butter, golden syrup and chocolate in a pan. Stir over low heat until melted and smooth. Serve hot or warm. Serves 6.

BERRY COULIS

250 g (8 oz) mixture of
  berries (strawberries,
  raspberries or
  blackberries)
2–4 tablespoons icing
  sugar, or to taste
1 tablespoon lemon juice
1–2 tablespoons
  Cointreau or Grand
  Marnier

1 Hull the berries. Place the fruit in a food processor and add the sugar and lemon juice. Blend until smooth. Stir in the liqueur. Serve with sorbet or fresh or poached fruit, soufflés, ice cream, pies and tarts. Serves 6.

VARIATION: Make mango coulis using 2 mangoes, peeled, seeded and puréed, or frozen mango purée.

ZABAGLIONE

8 egg yolks
1/3 cup (90 g/3 oz) caster
  sugar
1 1/4 cups (315 ml/10 fl oz)
  Marsala

1 Beat the egg yolks and sugar in a heatproof bowl until pale yellow.
2 Put the bowl over a gently simmering pan of water and beat, adding the Marsala gradually— don't let the base of the bowl touch the water. Beat for 5 minutes, or until thick and frothy. To test if it is ready, dip a metal spoon into the zabaglione, hold it up and if the mixture slides down the back it is not yet thickened enough. If you can draw a line through the zabaglione with a spoon and leave a trail, it is ready. Serve immediately or keep refrigerated for up to 1 day. Serve chilled with fresh blueberries and strawberries or just about any poached or grilled fruits (pears, nectarines, peaches) or with sponge fingers (langues de chats). Serves 10–12.

MAKING PASTA

Our basic pasta dough makes enough to serve 6 as a starter or 4 as a main meal. All the ingredients should be at room temperature before you start. Oil makes the dough easier to work with but you don't have to use it. Use plain or unbleached flour to give a well-textured light dough.

BASIC PASTA DOUGH

300 g (10 oz) **plain flour**
3 large (60 g/2 oz) **eggs**
30 ml (1 fl oz) **olive oil**
a pinch of salt

1 To mix the dough by hand, sift and mound the flour on a work surface or in a large bowl and make a well in the centre.
2 Break the eggs into the well and add the oil and salt. Begin to whisk the eggs and oil together with a fork, incorporating the flour as you do so. Gradually blend the flour with the eggs, working from the centre out. Use your free hand to hold the mound in place and stop leakage if any of the egg escapes.
3 Knead the dough on a lightly floured surface with smooth, light strokes, turning it as you fold and press. It should be soft and pliable, but dry to the touch. If sticky, knead in a little flour.
4 It will take at least 6 minutes kneading to achieve a smooth and elastic texture with a slightly glossy appearance. Put the dough in a plastic bag without sealing, or cover with a tea towel or an upturned bowl. Allow to rest for 30 minutes. (The dough can also be mixed in a food processor.)

ROLLING AND CUTTING BY HAND

1 Divide the dough into three or four manageable portions and cover them.
2 Lightly flour a large work surface. Flatten one portion of dough onto the surface and, using a long, floured rolling pin, roll out the dough from the centre to the outer edge.
3 Continue rolling, always from in front of you outward, and rotating the dough often. Keep the work surface dusted with just enough flour to prevent sticking. When you have rolled a well-shaped circle, fold the dough in half and roll it out again. Continue in this way seven or eight times to give a smooth circle of pasta about 5 mm (1/4 inch) thick.
4 Roll the sheet quickly and smoothly to a thickness of 2.5 mm (1/8 inch). Patch any tears with a piece of dough from the edge and a little water to help it stick.
5 As each sheet is done, transfer it to a dry tea towel. If the pasta is to be used to make filled pasta keep the sheets covered, but if it is to be cut into lengths or shapes, leave

them uncovered while the others are being rolled, so that the surface moisture will dry slightly.

6 For lasagne sheets, simply cut the pasta into the sizes required. The best way to cut lengths such as fettucine is to roll each pasta sheet up like a swiss roll, then cut this into uniform widths with a long, sharp knife. For tagliatelle, cut at 8 mm (⁴/₁₀ inch) intervals, 5 mm (¹/₄ inch) for fettucine, or about 3 cm (1¹/₄ inches) for pappardelle. Discard the offcuts. Place the lengths in a single layer on a tea towel to surface dry for no more than 10 minutes. Or hang long pasta strips to surface dry on floured broom handles or long wooden spoons between two chairs. Lengths can also be cut from the flat sheet, using a long, sharp knife or a pastry wheel. You may find it easier to run the wheel beside a ruler for straight cutting. A zig-zag pastry wheel will give an interesting edge to pasta shapes such as lasagnette and farfalle.

Don't leave pasta to dry in a cold place or in a draught or it may become brittle. Pasta is better if it allowed to dry slowly.

ROLLING AND CUTTING WITH A PASTA MACHINE

1 Clamp the machine securely onto the edge of your work surface. Divide the dough into three or four portions and shape each into a rough log. Keeping the unworked portions covered, take one and flatten it by one or two rolls with a rolling pin. Dust lightly with plain flour.

2 With the machine's rollers at their widest setting, crank the dough through two or three times. Fold it in thirds, turn the dough 90 degrees and feed through again. If the dough feels damp or tends to stick, lightly flour the outside surfaces each time it is rolled until it passes through cleanly. Repeat this folding and rolling process eight to ten times, or until the dough is a smooth and elastic sheet with a velvety appearance. From now on the dough is not folded.

3 Reduce the width of the rollers by one setting and pass the dough through. Repeat, setting the rollers one notch closer each time until you have rolled to the desired thickness. Some machines may roll the sheets too thinly on their last setting, tearing

them. A way around this is to stop at the second last setting and roll the dough through several times. It will come out a little thinner each time. This step also applies to machines that don't roll the pasta thinly enough on the last setting.

4 As each sheet is completed, place it on a dry tea towel. Leave uncovered to surface dry for 10 minutes if the sheets are to be cut, but cover them if they are to be used for filled pasta.

5 For lasagne sheets, cut the pasta to the desired size. For narrower lengths, select the appropriate cutters on the machine and crank each pasta sheet through it. Spread them on the tea towel until ready to be cooked, only covering them if they appear to be drying too much. Long pasta such as tagliatelle can be hung to surface dry on floured broom handles or long wooden spoons balanced between chairs.

INDEX

ACKNOWLEDGEMENTS

STYLISTS:

Mary Harris, Rosemary Mellish, Georgina Dolling, Carolyn Fienberg, Donna Hay, Vicki Liley, Kay Francis, Marie-Hélène Clauzon, Amanda Cooper, Lucy Mortensen, Jane Hann, Amanda Talbot. Anna Paola Boyd, Maria Sampsonis, Tatjana Lakajev, Wendy Goggin, Rachel Mackey, Rosemary Penman, Janelle Bloom, Toiva Longhurst, Margot Smithyman, Nadia Kretchmer, Ann Bollard, Jody Vassallo, Kathy Knudsen.

PHOTOGRAPHERS:

Tony Lyon, Luis Martin, Chris Jones, Joe Filshie, Reg Morrison, Andrew Furlong, Andre Martin, Jon Bader, Andrew Elton, Andy Payne, Damien Wood, Phil Haley, Craig Cranko, Sue Stubbs.

HOME ECONOMISTS:

Tracey Port, Kerrie Ray, Christine Sheppard, Anna Beaumont, Michelle Lawton, Beth Mitchell, Justine Poole, Alison Turner, Jo Forrest, Myles Beaufort, Wendy Brodhurst, Jo Glynn, Alex Diblasi, Sharon Glover, Angela Nahas, Beverley Sutherland Smith,

RECIPE DEVELOPMENT:

Tracy Rutherford, Kerrie Mullins, Jody Vassallo, Dimitra Stais, Roslyn Anderson, Anna Beaumont, Amanda Cooper, Michelle Earl, Lulu Grimes, Kathy Knudsen, Barbara Lowery, Jo Richardson, Melanie McDermott, Voula Mantzouridis, Rebecca Clancy, Alex Grant-Mitchell, Tracey Port, Wendy Berecry, Jacki Passmore, Stephanie Souvlis, Liz Nolan, Amanda Biffin, Sally Parker, Coral Kingston, Jean Miles, Denise Munro, Rachel Mackey, Kerrie Carr, Marie McDonald, Jennene Plummer, Kate Carey, Michelle Lawton.

IMPORTANT

Those who might be at risk from the effects of salmonella food poisoning (the elderly, pregnant women, young children and those suffering from immune deficiency diseases) should consult their GP with any concerns about eating raw eggs.

This edition published in the United States and Canada by Whitecap Books.
First published by Murdoch Books® a division of Murdoch Magazines Pty Ltd,
GPO Box 1203, Sydney NSW 1045

CEO & Publisher: Anne Wilson
Associate Publisher: Catie Ziller
General Manager: Mark Smith
International Sales Director: Mark Newman

ISBN 086411 502 4
PRINTED IN SINGAPORE
Printed by Tien Wah Press, Singapore
First printed 1998. Reprinted 1999.

Distributed in Canada by Whitecap Books Ltd (Vancouver),
Tel 604-980-9852 Fax 604-980-8197 or Whitecap Books Ltd (Toronto),
Tel 416-444-3442 Fax 416-444-6630.
Distributed for Whitecap Books in the USA by
Graphic Arts Center Publishing Company,
Portland Oregon. Tel (503) 226-2402 Fax (800) 355-9685